BUCKMINSTER FULLER INC.
ARCHITECTURE IN THE AGE OF RADIO

Mark Wigley

Buckminster Fuller Inc.

Architecture in the Age of RADIO

Lars Müller Publishers

To my father, Richard (1921–2015)

1

1 RBF tuning in and broadcasting out, photograph for *Kansas City Star*, 1978

PREFACE

The subliminal depths of radio are charged with the resonating echoes of tribal horns and antique drums. This is inherent in the very nature of this medium, with its power to turn the psyche and society into a single echo chamber.

Marshall McLuhan, *Understanding Media: The Extensions of Man*, 1964

Buckminster Fuller streamed himself into the field of architecture for fifty-five years with an unprecedented torrent of words alongside an ever-expanding galaxy of models. He blamed architecture for the traumatic loss of his young daughter in 1922 and had rebooted himself in 1927 with the arrival of his second daughter—obsessively devoting himself to the reinvention of architecture from first principles. Once started, he simply couldn't stop. A kind of architectural fever had taken over. The main symptom was "thinking out loud" at 7,000 words an hour, or a little faster if the theme was especially important. Listening to others was clearly optional and easily avoided by turning his hearing aid off when he spoke. He effectively made a single long and remarkably consistent speech from 1927 to 1983 that confused all stereotypes with its intravenous appeal to a vast, global, multi-generational and improbable mix of students, designers, writers, technocrats, counterculturalists, artists, scientists, journalists, politicians, businesspeople, and military. Yet the argument was more radical than any of them could absorb. Its time may be yet to come.

A small news column in a 1949 issue of *Time* magazine cannily dubbed Fuller's research mode "Bucky Inc."—noting that most architects tended to "chuckle indulgently" when hearing his name but predicting that this would stop if the new "geodesic house" experiment worked out. Fuller's reputation was suspended in a lightweight, aluminum-framed dome covered in transparent plastic. The first model of the concept, done six months earlier, was shown in a somewhat hazy and hence evocative photograph of domestic furnishings and equipment floating in a garden wrapped only in reflections. By 1964 it was no longer a mirage and Fuller was being celebrated on the cover of the magazine with famous architects singing his praises and the domes said to have "covered more square feet on the Earth than any other kind of shelter." The quirkiest of figures was now repeatedly being chosen to produce buildings that represented the state-of-the-art on a global stage. Which is not to say that architects had finally started to listen, or even that they could, since his whole point from the beginning had been to dissolve the basic premises of their field. For all the mountains of articles, exhibitions, films, and TV programs about Fuller, the core of his argument—and there was only ever one argument—remained hidden in plain view. A unique combination of fame and obscurity constructed a kind of sealed bubble around Fuller that is still intact today.

This book is an intellectual biography of Buckminster Fuller that uses his thinking to reframe some of the questions of our own day. It is not a matter of celebrating this short yet monumentally oversized figure. Rather, a close reading of Fuller's archive is used to understand what the field of architecture still works so hard to forget. Looking again at his hyperexposed yet deeply personal and congenitally misunderstood project helps us to engage with the urgent questions of today. It is a key reference point from which to rethink the role of buildings in the age of extreme computation, synthetic materials and life forms, networks of networks, ubiquitous data visualization, radical globalization, radical localization, clouds, and the so-called Internet of Things—these all being synonyms in the end. It cuts to the core of the present, which is always the most intriguing yet difficult thing to see.

Only figures on the margins of a field can bring its blind spots to the fore. The field itself is pulled into visibility by those whose status within it is unclear, seeming to be both inside and outside it at the same time, whether it be outsiders visiting the inside, insiders drifting outside, or those simply who venture too deep inside. Fuller was all of these. He magnified the most basic and most precious gift of the architect: to adjust part of the environment in a way that produces a hesitation in everyday life that provokes a moment of reflection and thereby possible thoughts of a better world. But he did so in a way that produced a hesitation in the everyday routines of the discipline of architecture itself. The outsider on the inside of the inside enables architecture to be seen as if for the first time, and thereby be reinvented. After all, architecture never simply sits there in front of us or even in the past. It is at its core a possibility, an always urgent possibility.

Perhaps it's finally time to digest the radical implications of the fact that the architecture of radio was so permanently urgent for Buckminster Fuller and demanded that he combine the most disconnected bathroom on the planet with the most ephemeral plastic skin with the most comprehensive data visualization interface—a trio of extreme technologies to be wirelessly hooked into the most expanded global networks imaginable to fundamentally reinvent shelter and transform our life and thought. The idea here is simply to listen to Fuller, to tune in to the almost hypnotic cadences of a single, continuous, fifty-five-year-long speech and offer a kind of forensic archeology of his discourse by tracking in detail a set of key interlocked ideas and their associated design projects. It is a matter of listening above all to the repetitions in what Fuller said and to the things in what he said that he might not have been aware of saying. To hear, that is, what only a later generation can hear but might only be able to hear from him.

Brain, Body, Building, Radiation

II Dymaxion House, axonometric drawing, 1929

III RBF while constructing his first dome, Black Mountain College, summer 1949

IV Life suspended inside net. Drawing of typical 4D Tower interior for *4D Time Lock*, 1928

V Motion of atomic particles in cloud chamber from RBF lecture files

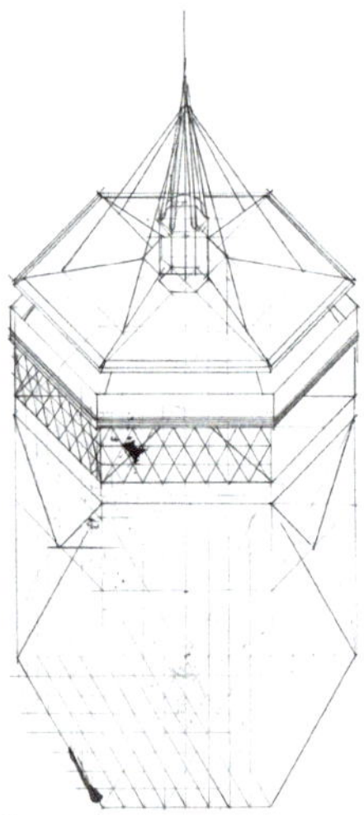

II

III

IV

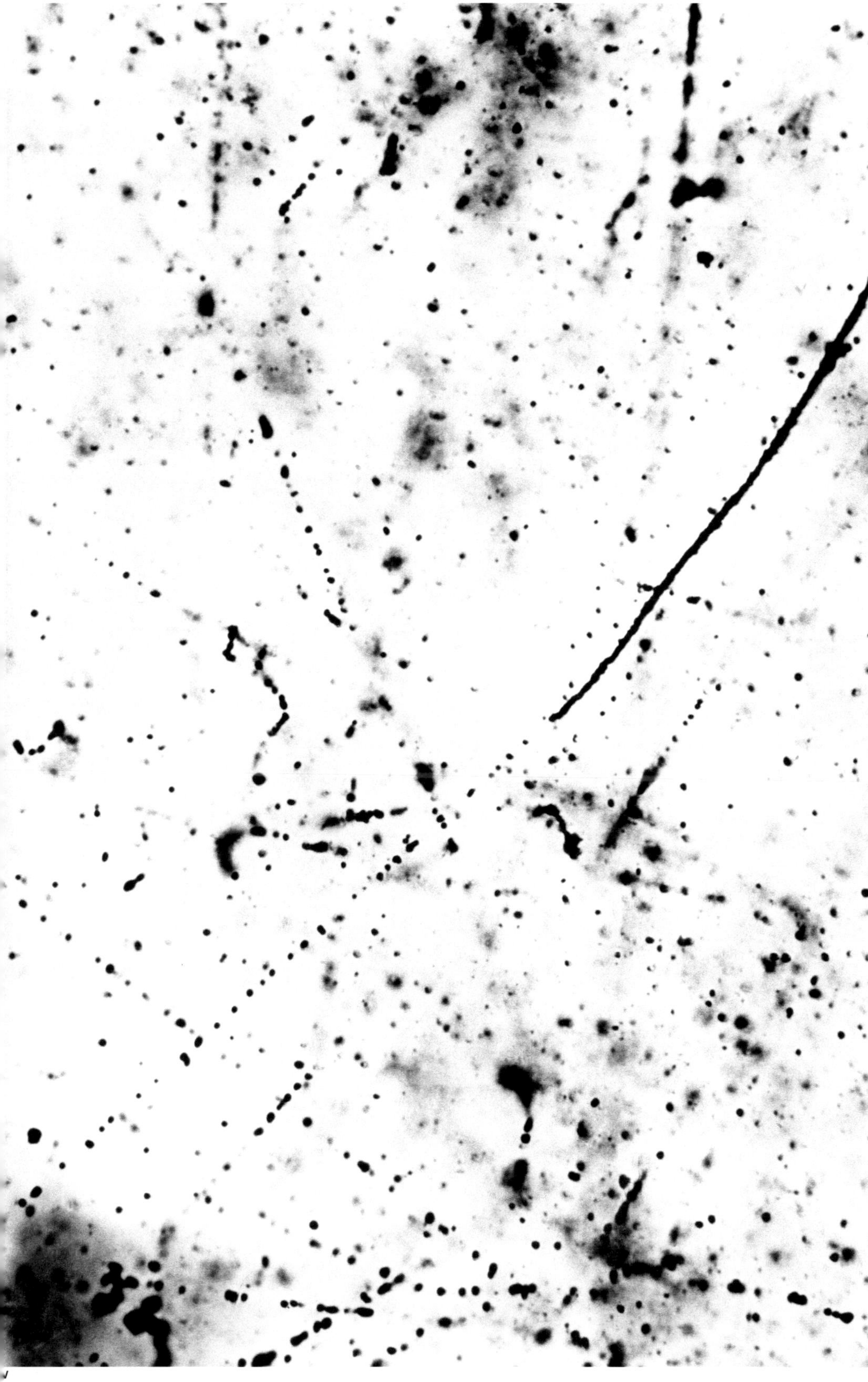

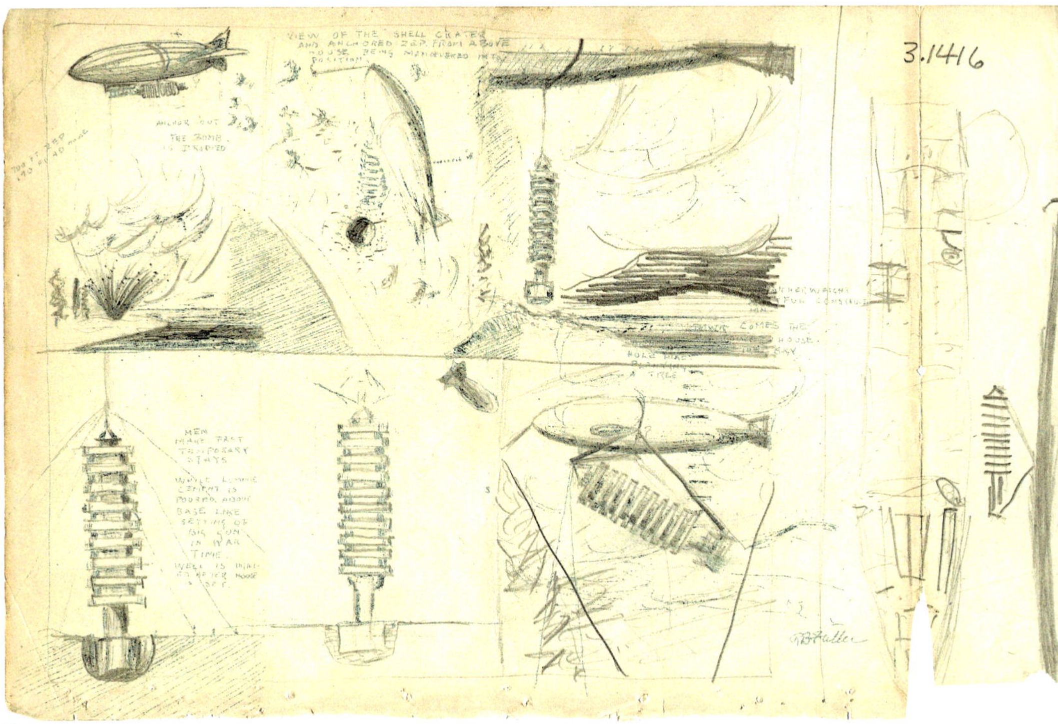

VI

VI Architecture in, of, and on air. RBF early sketch for storyboard of zeppelin delivering 4D Tower, 1928

BROADCASTING SHELTER

Every object, including ourselves, seems to have a radio attached to it. Our environment is busy transmitting and receiving. Each space is flooded by signals. Each event is suspended in overlapping radio waves. We constantly swim in electromagnetic radiation, whether from unthinkably distant galaxies or tiny pulses within our own bodies. An ever-growing array of technologies generates an ever-greater number of radio waves at every scale between our skin and our sun. We are discretely but completely bathed by satellites orbiting far above us, television towers on nearby hills, AM/FM masts on the tallest buildings, cell phone repeaters on neighborhood rooftops and Wi-Fi routers inside buildings, along with the ever-closer range of infrared remote controls and Bluetooth headsets, keyboards and mice in rooms, down to the microtransmissions from ever-thinner smart cards and tags. New galaxies of receivers, sensors, detectors, and scanners continuously decode the flow and contribute to it. Radio breeds more radio. The button on what used to be a key nestled in our palm wirelessly unlocks the car before we get to it and activates a team of radios inside that then engage the layers of signals in the streets to literally drive us through information—with radio about to make the very idea of the driver obsolete. But all the radios at home already make a room without wheels travel even faster and further. Architecture itself has become a high-performance vehicle. It is no longer clear what it is to be in a room, a building, a city, or the countryside. We ultimately live in the invisible world of radiation rather than the visible forms of buildings and cities. Or, more precisely, it is electromagnetic waves that form our buildings and cities. Space itself is defined and redefined by countless hidden vibrations. We tune in to spaces rather than simply occupy them, and usually tune in to many different overlapping spaces at the same time.

The nested spaces of radio we inhabit are infinitely more complex than the spaces of buildings. Our bodies still engage with physical objects, even encountering them as a kind of anchor or resistance against all the unseen flows, but the physical environment is much more intimately sensed and engaged by hidden signals—so closely and continuously that it is not an encounter between visible and invisible worlds but a kind of symbiosis, a vibration between object and radiation. The distinction between them is no longer clear, which is to say that architecture is not so clear anymore.

The defining characteristic of radio is its disinterest in objects. It literally passes right through them. Yet the objects around us are located, marked, connected, exposed, infiltrated, monitored, reorganized, promoted, locked, archived, protected, dissolved, and even destroyed in the space of radio signals. Object and radio have become inseparable as the transmitters and receivers get ever smaller, integrating themselves into the very fabric of the objects that they engage. No simple line can be drawn between things and signals as the miniature radios of billions of RFID tags are being implanted or attached to everything that moves—including people, products, documents, and even ants. Objects simultaneously appear in front of us and within an array of databases. There is an unprecedented blurring of object and information, as if every object lives only to broadcast itself.

It's not just that objects appear to us within an unprecedented density of radio signals and increasingly have radios attached to them. Their very status as objects is determined by radio. The environment in which objects are made and the process of making them are equally awash with transmissions. There is a layered history of signals behind each object. The most solid and seemingly impervious things are now literally the products of radio waves. It is not even clear that we can encounter objects from before the age of radio without bringing the perspective of radio to them. To look at an ancient artifact might be to imagine the world before radio but the very idea of connecting to preradio days is specific to the age of radio. Anyway, an object with its own radio, detected by radio, produced by radio, or simply encountered in the age of radio, is finally not the same object. It is no longer possible to touch a building or a friend without the thought of radio. We treat objects and even ourselves as radios. Everything has become some kind of communication device.

Touch itself has evolved. Stroking the sensitive screens of phones, computers, tablets, remotes, control panels, and appliances gives the sense of palpably grasping and flexing invisible signals with one's body. Many of the micro, local, regional, global, and galactic radio waves are gathered up and rechanneled through the cell phone in our hands in ways that further complicate the experience of the physical environment. A signal from the other side of the planet can be more intimate than a physical embrace. For most people, the cell phone is what wakes them up in the morning; it's the first thing they see, the first thing they touch—with a tenderness normally reserved for a lover or a child—and it is the last thing looked at before sleeping. Consciousness itself is now inseparable from radio, which presumably lurks in the unconscious too, or even has been resident there since the very first shock when radio magically passed through walls and across cities at the turn of the last century.

The invention, construction, management, maintenance, representation, and experience of the built environment is simply unthinkable without radio. Yet radio itself is never treated as a building material or even as an environmental condition. It rarely appears in architectural discourse. Every lecture given by an architect using a wireless microphone and a little wireless remote to change the images—which have increasingly been taken with a cell phone and wirelessly uploaded—occurs in an auditorium that is permanently outfitted with many radios and temporarily is filled with a multitude of portable radios in the phones, tablets, and laptops of the audience. The talk is typically broadcast and rebroadcast to multiple audiences over many channels. Clouds of texts, tweets, and posts circulate before, during, and after the event. Yet the room itself, and the world of buildings and cities being discussed within it, is treated as if it is independent of radio. Architecture is thought of as something to which radio can be added but the addition is of no interest to the field or is an unmentionable threat. Most architects, historians, theorists, critics schools, and magazines act as if there is no architecture of radio, no architecture specific to the age of radio, or as if radio is an undoing of architecture, with radio waves somehow dissolving built form and what it is called on to represent. The very fact that radio passes through buildings is treated as an unspeakable disrespect to the field.

But what does radio mean for the status of objects? In particular, what does it mean for the architectural object, the object that has traditionally been asked to reflect on the status of objects in general? What is the role of the field specifically devoted to the crafting of solids that speak about that which cannot be seen?

Architecture as a discipline was founded around the claim of classical architectural theory that a visible object, a solid building, could literally resonate with the invisible harmonies of the universe and thereby act as a hinge between the material and immaterial worlds. Architecture was seen to be poised between the physical and metaphysical as a unique bridge between substance and idea. Architectural objects, such as a Greek temple, were seen to be unambiguously in the physical world and have certain technical and social responsibilities to that world but, more importantly, to represent ideas beyond that world. They are in the visible but not of the visible. It is not so much that we visit architecture. Architecture visits us from the immaterial world. This transitional status remained in the early twentieth-century arguments for modern architecture, where new kinds of buildings were meant to be embedded in the mechanics of industrialized society but also to transcend and represent the hidden patterns of that new order. Le Corbusier, the most influential propagandist for this architecture, most famously described the house as a "machine for living in," a continuously evolving mechanical tool that nevertheless can connect to higher truths that transcend time and place. This ambition to straddle and blur the line between visible and invisible still organizes the way architecture is represented discussed, taught, and practiced in the twenty-first century. It is even accentuated with so much talk about the logics of the digital, big data, data visualization, and the cloud. Data itself seems have taken on the role of the cosmos. In the most classical of attitudes, each object generated and fabricated by computer is seen as but one of an infinite range of possible imprints from a singular formula. But what does that ever so classical straddling of visible and invisible mean in the age of radio? What is the architectural object called on to do or represent when all objects already take their very definition from countless overlapping radio waves?

An impressive blindness is needed to even temporarily forget about radio. Radio took the already extreme architectural effect of the telephone to a whole new level, completely transforming the spatial order. Any two objects, places, or people could be instantly connected without even the thinnest line of wire. More radically still, any combination of people, places, and objects could be connected. It was no longer about lines of connection, but amorphous and overlapping fields of connectivity. If Le Corbusier could so cannily observe at the opening of his 1923 manifesto *Vers une architecture* that "Architecture is in the Parthenon and in the telephone. How comfortable it might be in our houses!,"[1] the question is how comfortable could architecture be in radio when the very idea of *house* has become an effect of radio. If wires already constituted some kind of embarrassment to architecture—being rarely visible in architectural representations and usually hidden within the buildings themselves—what of the even more radical wireless world?

We live in an age of radio but might not know what that means, and even less have any insight into the role of architecture within it. If architecture as a discipline is still formed around the ability of an object to catch and represent the unseen patterns of the world, acting as a hinge between object and cosmos, material and immaterial, substance and ideas, radio might disturb the discipline by already being such a hinge. Wireless might be even more embarrassing than wired. Architecture in the age of radio might have little to do with radio. Indeed, it might be a form of resistance to it, a new form of disconnection.

After all, architecture has never just been a form of expertise in bridging visible and invisible as advertised. It also crafts a dividing line between seen and unseen. Its function might primarily be a form of hiding, a veil, a defense, or refuge. Even to tune classical architecture into the cosmic waves meant tuning most of the world out, including the material condition of the building itself. A set of buildings could only offer itself as a form of connectivity to the invisible by disconnecting from the lived world. Architecture is not the stage for the performance of everyday life, but the production of a hesitation in everyday life that stimulates thought. It crafts a strategic disconnection more than a connection. Architecture might even be a systematic form of disavowal of radio, and this disavowal has its own history. The question of architecture in the age of radio might well be the question of how and why the field still manages to avoid radio.

RADIO MAN

Buckminster Fuller, who modestly saw his own life as a perfect case study of the evolution of the human species and treated any discussion of the universe as autobiographical, noted that he was born in the same year as the discovery of radio and that the development of his own life matched that of the new wireless medium. It was not by chance that his massive forty-two hours of lectures summarizing "Everything I Know" in January 1975 began with the statement that his birth eighty years earlier had coincided with that of radio. He associates himself with the arrival of a technology that was simply too transformative to be believed: "Absolutely unexpected! My father and mother would say 'Wireless! such nonsense!'"[2] Fuller seemed to understand himself to be a similarly unbelievable technology, a radical instrument that exposes and redeploys hidden patterns. He had evocatively described himself a few years earlier as having arrived on Earth in the disconnected world on "the other side" of radio:

> The year I was born Marconi discovered his wireless, but I was around 8 or 9 when the first SOS occurred on a steamship, and there was any use by society of his wireless, and so I was born the other side of radio and it seemed an obvious part of life and the conditions that I speak about. We were really very isolated human beings.[3]

Fuller came of age alongside and even through wireless, directly participating in the rapid evolution from radical disconnection to equally radical connectivity. His self-appointed role was to imagine the form of shelter appropriate to this irreversible transformation in the way of life and thought. In a lengthy 1955 letter responding to a question from the British artist John McHale about the influences on his work, he highlighted his "electronic experiences" during World War I, starting at the end of 1917 when the small navy ship under his command, the USS *Inca*, was assigned for the latest experiments of Marconi's main rival, Lee de Forest. **figs. 1 and 2** De Forest was the very figure of the new technology at that time. He had made a number of the key inventions and even been the first to heavily promote the use of the word *radio* in 1907 rather than the usual term *wireless*. The twenty-two-year-old Fuller was clearly inspired by both the technology of radio and the ever-restless de Forest. Having been "fired from Harvard for the second time, Fuller was enthralled by this frenetic and permanently controversial inventor/publicist/businessman with a PhD from Yale whose projects had unlimited technical and social ambition, occupied all the mass media of the day, and continuously oscillated between military and domestic, as would his own projects in the decades to come. He proudly recalled his "incidental participation" when de Forest made the first successful voice communication between a ship and an airplane on his small boat. He likewise pointed to his appointment as a "radio officer" the following year such that he found himself participating in

1 Le Corbusier, *Vers une architecture* (1923), translated by John Goodman as *Toward an Architecture* (Los Angeles: Getty, 2007), 95.

2 "The year I was born Marconi invented the wireless, but it did not get into any practical use until I was 12 years of age when the first steamship sends an SOS, it's in distress, by wireless so think of it a great many miles and the world began to know the ship was in distress and ships began to rush to its aid. Absolutely unexpected! My father and mother would say 'Wireless! such nonsense!'" Buckminster Fuller, "Everything I Know" (videotranscript of lecture, Bell Telephone Studios, Philadelphia, PA, January 1975), Session 1, Part 1 (Buckminster Fuller Institute, 1997).

3 Buckminster Fuller, "Buckminster Fuller at Camberwell: A Lecture Given May 19th 1971", Department of Drawings and Archives, Avery Architectural and Fine Arts Library, Columbia University, 2.

1

2

Coming of Age Through Wireless

1 RBF as Commander of the USS *Inca*, 1917

2 Lee de Forest holding his compact radio receiver for test in airplane at Mineola Field, Long Island, New York, August 4, 1916

3 RBF as radio communications officer on USS *George Washington*, 1919

4 RBF and his sister Rosamund in self-made playpen, Bear Island, 1906

5 RBF at Milton Academy

3

4

5

another key radio event when "the human voice was transmitted trans-oceanically for the first time in history."[4] **fig. 3** Fuller had been part of the communications team on the flagship USS *George Washington* when the president of the United States made the record-breaking voice call between his office on the ship in a harbor in France and the Secretary of War sitting in his Washington office.[5] He had become a kind of firsthand witness to the transformative expansion of an inherently expansive medium.

What was crucial in Fuller's recollection of these two events is the sense of a chance intimacy with the history of a technology that when repeated became more like destiny, as if he had been assigned at birth to a lifetime engagement with the evolution of radio. Fuller described a primal encounter with radio, a kind of loss of innocence tied up with the war. It was as if he were focused and strengthened by radio in a way that makes the images of him as a child holding tightly onto his chair, sitting on steps so closely beside and behind his mother, so worried inside his first architectural project for his sister, and walking so coyly in the garden at high school seem more wistful, delicate, even fragile. **figs. 4 and 5** This fragility was still evident in the most revealing press photo late in life, at the height of his influence, with one hand cupped over an ear so he can hear while the other reaches out toward us to make and magnify a point. **fig. 1, page 5** The lure of radio was inseparable from the sense of physical limitations. The primal encounter with radio was the encounter with a new body and even a new brain. The vulnerability of Fuller's extremely poor sight and hearing would somehow be substituted by this new, expansive capacity of invisible waves. A lifetime would be devoted to the ways in which the capacities of the human organism are extended physically and mentally. All subsequent encounters, all the other technologies he engaged, would be understood

4 "The assignments and commissions brought, for instance, incidental participation in the first development of ship-to-plane radio telephony. They also brought subsequent participation in the conversion of radio-telephony from 70-mile-range spark sets to long-distance arc-type equipment. The first instance of the above electronic experiences occurred when a small ship which I commanded was selected for the experimental work of Dr. Lee de Forest. While aboard he established the first successful voice communication ever heard between a ship and an aeroplane. I was later fortunate to be force radio officer for the cruiser and transport force of the United States Atlantic Fleet. [...] On President Wilson's second trip to France, the human voice was transmitted trans-oceanically for the first time in history." Buckminster Fuller to John McHale, 7 January 1955, p. 4, Marquand Rare Books Library, Princeton University. The letter was later published as "Influences on My Work," *Architectural Design* 31 (July 1961): 290–296.

5 After by chance hosting Rear Admiral Albert Gleaves onboard the USS *Inca* during an official inspection of the squadron of such Eagle boats, Fuller received orders to become a temporary Assistant Communication Officer on the USS *Dakota* flagship "for purpose of instruction in communication" (Navy order dated September 11, 1918, Buckminster Fuller Papers, Special Collections, Stanford University (hereafter BFP) Series 2, Box 7). The next month, he was ordered to USS *Great Northern* to continue the temporary assignment for instruction in communication for one trip (Navy order dated October 29, 1918, BFP Series 2, Box 7). Gleaves then retained him in a permanent position on his personal staff as Communication Officer and he went with him to be Special Communications Officer on USS *George Washington* during the presidential voyages to France.

6 Buckminster Fuller, "The Self-Disciplines of Buckminster Fuller," in *Critical Path* (New York: St. Martin's, 1981), 129.

7 "Now for the first time in history a great fleet of ships, sometimes five or ten miles apart, steaming through stormy seas in darkness and without visual knowledge, are in constant communication with each other without overhead wires or submarine cables to restrict conversation, which can be carried on almost as easily as if done between rooms in a great hotel." N. J. Quirk, "Wireless Telephony in the Navy," *Telephony*, January 1908, 30.

8 Fuller inaccurately recalls that the ship was communicating with the Arlington station rather than the one at New Brunswick.

9 "Humanity knew very little when I was young. People did not know much about the rest of the world. [...] The world was local. [...] Utterly unexpected by human society, Marconi invented the wireless the year I was born, and electrons were discovered when I was three years of age, and that first midocean SOS radio saved the ship's passengers when I was 12 years of age. Then in 1919, when I was 24, radio telephony was so perfected by the Bell Laboratory scientists, under US Navy auspices, that on the occasion of President Woodrow Wilson's first post-war peace-treaty trip to Europe in the US Navy transport *George Washington*, a war-converted pre-1914 German luxury liner, ship's radio telephony was transformed from a five-mile-range 'spark set' to a long-range 'arc set' operation and in 1919 the first transatlantic radio conversation by human voice and hearing was transmitted, accomplished between Brest Harbor, France, and Arlington, Va., USA." Buckminster Fuller, "Cutting the Metabilical Cord," *Saturday Review*, September 21, 1974, 12, 56.

10 Fuller, "Everything I Know," Session 3, Part 14 (see note 2).

11 "What happened to me in 1905 happened to our whole culture in the 1920s when radio came in. Kids spontaneously began to notice that the voices on the radio, even if not infallible, really knew a lot more about the world in general than their parents did. The parents didn't know anything beyond their small town, their church, the clubs they belonged to. The radio brought the whole world to the child. 'Papa knows best' has never recovered from that shock. Television was the knockout blow." Robert Anton Wilson, "Interview, R. Buckminster Fuller: The Octagenarian Futurist Philosopher Gives us Eight Years to Tune Up Spaceship Earth," *High Times*, May 1981, 37.

as extensions of that first date with evolution itself. Indeed, technology would finally be understood as a form of radio, an ever-expanding broadcasting of human capacity.

Fuller's retroactive account of his transformative encounters with radio has its own history. By 1981 he had conflated the two wartime experiences into the claim of having "heard the historically first human voice conversation over the radio" in 1917,[6] despite the fact that de Forest had first transmitted a voice across a room at the end of 1906 and enabled conversation between navy ships "as if between the rooms in a great hotel" when his newly formed Radio Telephone Company was hired to develop a wireless fleet for the US Navy in 1907.[7] Fuller was referring to being present at the first successful transatlantic conversation from a ship, a feat that redefined the capacity of the technology and thereby the capacity of society. Just before sailing in April 1919, the president's ship had been outfitted with a new, powerful radio transmitter and a unique net of antenna wires so that it could communicate with the massive, 5,000-foot-long antenna suspended on eight 400-foot-tall masts built by Marconi on the outskirts of New Brunswick, New Jersey. The installation had been appropriated by the government for the bulk of transatlantic radio traffic during the war and substantially upgraded by General Electric in July 1918 to become the most powerful station in the world.[8] The real innovation of the experiment was to have both the station and the ship set up for two-way conversation by radio—enabling the president's office to become mobile. The seemingly unimaginable link at the limits of contemporary technology between a ship in the harbor of Brest on the coast of France and a spidery web of wires above the countryside outside a small town in North America marked for Fuller the truly evolutionary transformation of humanity from fixed local life to global mobility.[9] Nothing could be the same again, no space, or even the human species. In his final essays and lectures, Fuller's own evolution had simply become one with radio itself:

> I don't know how much experience I had of it, but whether I like it or not, I was born in the year that Marconi invented the radio, but it doesn't get into practical use until I was twelve. [...] I was twenty-three the first time we got a human voice over the radio. It happened in the navy, and I was in that operation.[10]

Fuller creatively positioned himself at the very turning point between humanity's unconscious isolated childhood and its conscious radical interconnectivity. His own experience soon "happened to our whole culture" when "radio came in" and "brought the whole world to the child."[11] He often insisted that radio signals do more than stitch the world together: They make the world a world for the first time. The ability of radio to connect people beyond the visible horizon invented the globe itself, a networked planet. The strategic use of radio in World War I marked a radical shift in the evolution of human capacity and mentality, as revealed in the very name of the war. For Fuller, it is the transformative act that constructed a single world. All questions became global questions when the invisible electromagnetic spectrum was consciously occupied and deployed for the first time. War with radio was, as he put it in 1970, "the beginning of the end of geographically isolated humans. [...] The world was integrated by radios, cables, and transport systems of all kinds." No return to the "pre-radio style of life" was possible.[12] Wireless communication globalized every object, action, and reflection.

No building could remain local or static with "radio's world-girdling, national-boundary-eliminating integration," as Fuller celebrated it in 1938.[13] Connectivity is also mobility. Radio turns every building into a ship. In his breathless lifelong narrative on radio, the radicality of initiating wireless communication between ships in war was deepened with the postwar ability to scramble the signals, taking real-time strategic control from individual captains at sea to the telephone in the president's office in the White House.[14] A single static room in one house became intimately connected to a vast network of mobile rooms. Houses themselves, and even whole cities, were about to mobilize. The radio network they occupied was more than global. It extended beyond the planet. It could never have been predicted at the beginning of the nineteenth century that "humans would be able to whisper anywhere around the world apart and at a speed of 700,000,000 miles an hour with their audibility clearly reaching to the planet Venus."[15] Twentieth-century architecture now floated in interplanetary space even when seemingly resting on the ground. Humanity was launched into outer space by radio. Or, in what would eventually become a trademark Fuller argument, it finally woke up to the fact that it had been in outer space all along. Every building became a spaceship. All thought of static solid objects on the ground gave way to a universe of restless and largely invisible waves.

12 Buckminster Fuller, introduction to *A Question of Priorities: New Strategies for Our Urbanized World*, by Edward Higbee (New York: William Morrow, 1970), xxi.
13 Buckminster Fuller, *Nine Chains to the Moon* (Philadelphia: Lippincott, 1938), 282.
14 Buckminster Fuller, "Philosophy, Invention, Experience," in *Systems: Proceedings of the Second Boston Architectural Center Lecture Series 1968* (Boston: The Center, 1970), 13.
15 Ibid., 21.
16 "With World War I, came radio—the development of voice by air—and not just information transmittal by Morse code. By 1922, we have the first amateurs getting out—with Major Armstrong's super-heterodyne regenerator—an amplified voice. Five years later, companies were making these and everyone's home became a voice. Everyone rapidly knew about Lindbergh's flight across the Atlantic. Suddenly, everybody had this in their home, and *it* knew things the local people didn't know. The parents didn't tell the kids anymore, the voice did. [...] My daughter was born in that Lindbergh year, and she was raised on the radio. [...] It was simply this new environmental phenomena [...] new life was coming into the home directly, making the parents and local authorities obsolete. [...] It was only two or three men—Major Armstrong with the radio, de Forest with the tube—who changed all humanity. [...] And with the newer environment, everyone acted differently." Buckminster Fuller, "The Plowboy Interview," *The Mother Earth News* no. 9 (Spring 1971): 7.
17 Ibid., 8.
18 "Where the World's Radios Are," newspaper clipping hand-dated November 1938, BFP Series 8, Box 4, Folder 1.
19 "A typical item still in the laboratory which will have far-reaching effect when making its industrial debut is the radio transmission of power. As indicated by the experiments now being conducted, this will probably be accomplished by focusing of the waves of ray particles by reflection from a deeply concave, metallic gold mirror [...] when success in the experiment has been attained, the wide ramifications of power by radio, dismounting, for instance, all prime movers from transportation. [...] Highly secret are the experiments in this development, but it is known that they are being carried on by the Massachusetts Institute of Technology." Buckminster Fuller, "Ballistics of Civilization," BFP Series 8, Box 3, Folder 11, p. 10. On the wider "Ballistics of Civilization" project, see Jonathan Massey, "Buckminster Fuller's Reflexive Modernism," *Design and Culture* 4, no. 3 (2012): 326–344.
20 "That October (still '17) B was sent to Hampton Roads (after 3 weeks in Boston Harbor) where he was put in command of the Herreshoff-built SS *Inca* which became Lee de Forest's experimental boat. Here he developed ship-to-plane phone, first time successfully. [...] On the *George Washington*'s second trip with Wilson, in Brest Harbor, they talked to Arlington by radio, the first transatlantic voice conversation." Buckminster Fuller, "Family and Career," manuscript attached to letter to Joe Bryant, 1 July 1939, p. 6, BFP Series 2, Box 29.
21 The "Memorandum of Activities: Richard Buckminster Fuller" that was given to *Time* magazine in 1942 when they were doing a portrait on Fuller, and was included at the end of every Dymaxion Index from 1947 on, has the two entries that will be repeated in every subsequent version: "Dr. Lee de Forest came aboard *Inca* for two months and carried out first successful experiments radio conversation plane-to-boat."; "special Communication Duty in USS *George Washington* during President Wilson's trips to France, during which we converted radio voice signals from spark to arc and held first Transatlantic conversation Brest, France, to Arlington, USA." "Memorandum of Activities: Richard Buckminster Fuller," BFP Series 8, Box 5, Folder 1.
22 "Wireless outfit on *Inca* installed for Doctor Lee de Forest who made first tests on her talking from planes and blimps to *Inca*," photograph caption, BFP Series 2, Box 19. "Detailed to *Geo. Washington* as special communication officer. During trips first long distance arc set telephony was tested out and finally made radio contact from *Washington* at Brest Harbor France to Bar Harbor Maine, USA." Ibid.
23 Buckminster Fuller, "Tree-Like Style of Dwelling Is Planned," *Chicago Evening Post Magazine of Art*, December 18, 1928, 5. Fuller's original

Radio was a revolution, an architectural revolution. Fuller insisted that it literally produced a change in the environment itself. It was inevitable that people would start to think and act differently. He marveled that just a couple of radio pioneers whose work was accelerated by the war had "changed all humanity." With the domestication of the radio set in the late twenties, "everyone's home became a voice" bringing news from the other side of the planet, starting with immediately knowing about the success of Charles Lindbergh's transatlantic flight to Paris on May 21, 1927. The full arc of the planet could now be brought into the house. Everything changed. Fuller's daughter Allegra was born in that year and "raised on the radio."[16] Symptomatically, this is also true of his architecture. It too was born in 1927 and brought up on radio. Fuller entered architecture just after the radio set entered the typical house with his extreme design of what would end up being called the Dymaxion House. As with Allegra, radio became his main teacher: "I realized radio was a tool and all electromagnetics was a tool. I became very much impressed with how you can use a tool in changing the environment."[17] In the unpublished 1939 manuscript "Ballistics of Civilization," he drew the first of his countless charts of the evolution of industrialization, with the steeply accelerating curve of increasing technical control over the environment marked by three key events: "auto radio x-ray airplane" in 1895; "airplane and radio adolescence" in 1917; and "wings over the ocean / croon around the world" in 1927. **fig. 6** It is the movement from the discovery of radio in the lab to global broadcasting to all homes that most accelerates mankind's accomplishment of enslaving the inanimate world to its purposes. One version of the manuscript includes a clipping of "Where the World's Radios Are," a November 1938 newspaper report on the total number of radios in each country around the world.[18] Fuller confidently predicted that the next game changer would be the transmission of power by radio.[19] The curve is also that of Fuller's own life. He wrote his first extended autobiographical narrative to brief a journalist that year, a kind of narrative chart of his own industrialization that already includes his two encounters with radio during the war.[20] These encounters then appeared at the beginning of every updated "Memorandum of Activities: Richard Buckminster Fuller" that was sent to lecture venues and the media from that point on and was appended to each edition of the so-called Dymaxion Index monitoring his media coverage from 1947 on.[21] He would retell this narrative with minor variations hundreds of times in lectures, interviews, and essays, elaborating the ever-expanding story with a growing retroactive emphasis on the role of radio at its beginning.

Fuller ultimately saw everything in terms of radio, and his life's work can be understood as an attempt to come to terms with radio. He prepared a private photo album when doing the first version of the Dymaxion House in 1928 in which the captions to photographs of the USS *Inca* and the USS *George Washington* conclude with the two encounters with innovations in radio.[22] A few months later, his first published article on the project appeared in a December 1928 issue of the *Chicago Evening Post Magazine of Art* after one of the editors had attended his presentation in a local restaurant two months before.[23] It was accompanied by the first images of the triangulated and cabled structure of a ten-story tower crowned by the wires of a dramatic, diamond-shaped "radio antennae and radio direction finder" for communication and guiding aircraft—linking all such buildings together into a global net. **fig. 7** The part of the drawing that was not used by the newspaper refers to the building as a "light-full—universal—drudge-proof—dwelling" that can be assembled and delivered in one day.[24] The published image, with its "beam-radio" on top, was likened to a tree planted in the ground and shown among trees in the countryside, but much of Fuller's polemic is devoted to the need to free architecture from a fixed relationship to the land in order to escape the concept of property. It is as if his argument that the universe is made of electromagnetic waves means that the land should be treated more like the waves of the open sea, beyond ownership and governed only by certain internationally shared principles of conduct. The building with a radio becomes a restless ship just as the ship with a radio becomes a building. **fig. 8**

The first press release for the single-floor version of the house contrasted the transformative global capacity of radio to the criminal inadequacy of the housing industry:

> International radio hook-ups to all corners of the Earth, radio photography, etc. become of commercial usage, while millions are made homeless or die as their homes are washed away, or, blown and shaken down around their heads, not the slightest scientific consideration of these events having been considered in their design.[25]

manuscript for the article had the title "Archeology Abandoned in New Recreative Art of Housing Design," BFP Series 2, Box 19. It was developed as the publicity text for the upcoming exhibition of the first model at Marshall Field's department store, BFP Series 2, Box 21.

24 James Ward, *The Artifacts of R. Buckminster Fuller*, vol. 1 (New York: Garland, 1985), 13.

25 Buckminster Fuller, "4D Housing and the Time Dimension: Archeology Abandoned in New Recreative Art of Housing Design," January 1929 press release, BFP Series 2, Box 21, p. 2. This formulation was published in 1932 when Fuller used the press release as the basis for an article: Buckminster Fuller, "Universal Architecture," *T-Square* 2, no. 2 (February 1932): 24.

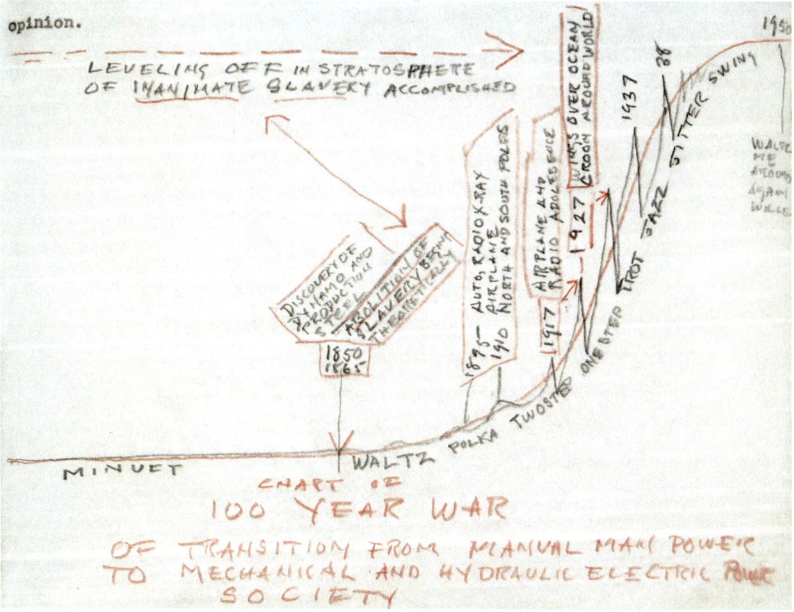

6

6 Chart of technological evolution of society marked by key radio events as accelerants and history of popular dances in "Ballistics of Civilization" manuscript, 1939

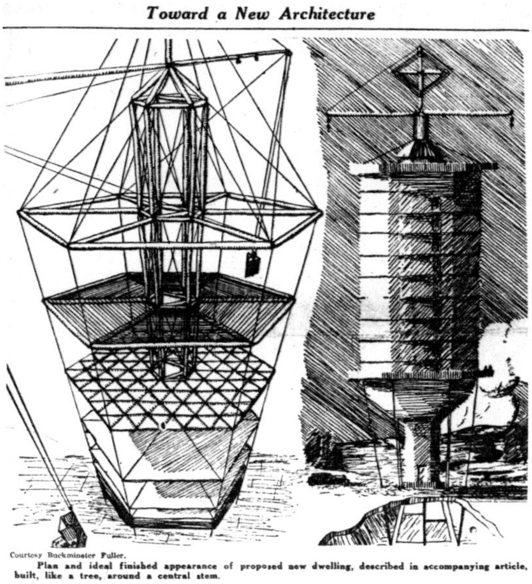

7

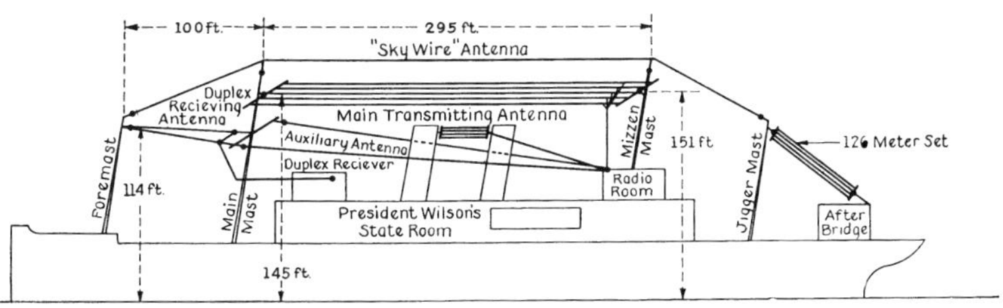

8

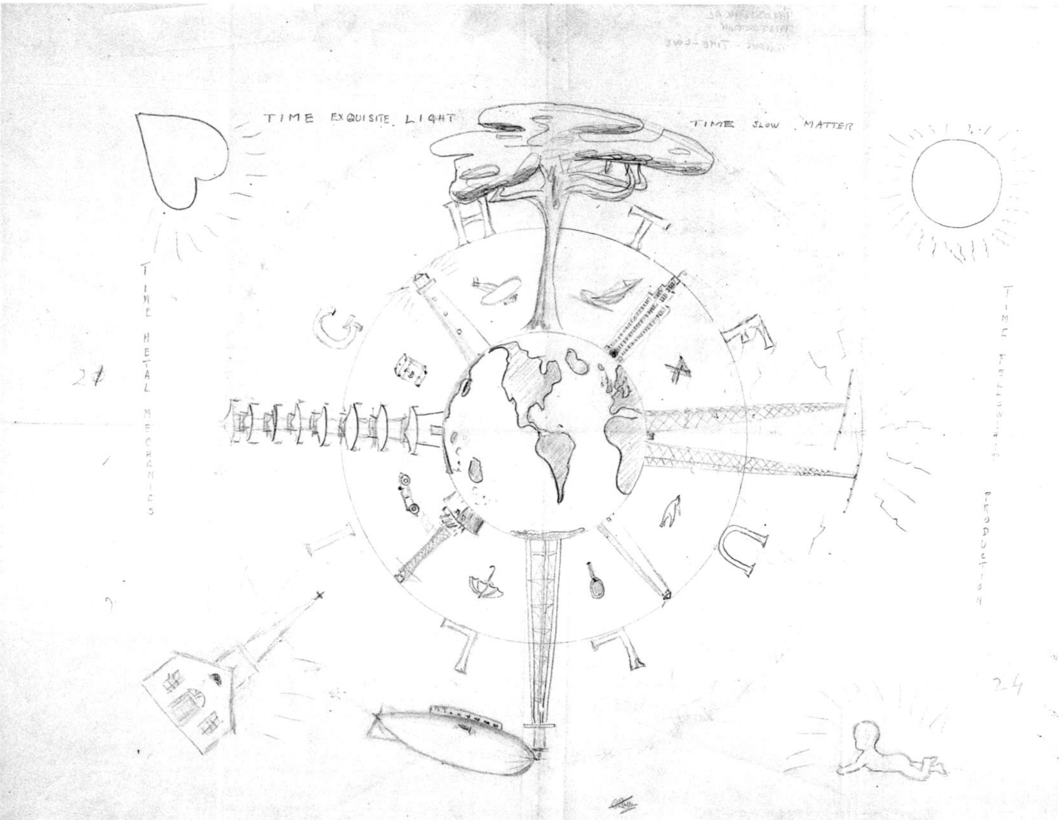

9

Radio Turns Buildings into Ships and Ships into Buildings

7 First publication of Fuller's architecture: 4D Tower in *Chicago Evening Post Magazine of Art,* December 18, 1928

8 Separate receiving and transmitting antennae installed on the USS *George Washington* in 1919, *General Electric Review*, October 1920

9 Manifesto diagram of "Lightful Houses," 1928, with concentric rings of communication defined by radio masts

It is not by chance that the house with which Fuller publicly entered architectural discourse in 1928 featured a built-in radio transceiver in its library through which the occupants would maintain connection with everyone else on the planet in continuous two-way communication for information and education. In mid-1929 he told a group of architects in New York that the room would be well soundproofed and featured "very good radio transmission" without the need for individual microphones so the occupants could simply talk directly to people anywhere in the world. It was not so much a house that had a transceiver within it as a house that was a transceiver. Or, even more radically, it was a transceiver that was a house. At the very least, the destinies of housing and radio were intertwined:

> With the development of this housing, you are going to have a high development of it in radio. [...] When radio first came along, I remember I was very much interested in radio and I saw a lot of it. The first test that Dr. de Forest made, in talking from a battleship to an aeroplane, was made on our boat. So I had a lot to do with radio at that time. Just as the war ceased, the popular value of radio became evident. [...] As soon as the bunk gets out about that, why, radio will begin to get somewhere.[26]

The gathered architects are told that radio will soon develop specialized channels and children can turn the dials to select a subject and hear the very best authorities. A "world floating university" would be established through "radio correspondence" with leading professors from the top institutions around the planet connected to one another and to every house.[27] Houses were to be located within a wireless network rather than a particular physical site.

Radio had become the ultimate architectural site. Fuller even described the central mast from which his house would hang as being "somewhat similar to the radio mast, the dirigible mooring mast, or the battleship mast."[28] As he started to design the building in the first months of 1928, then using the name Lightful House to catch its minimal and radiant quality, he did a crucial manifesto-like pencil diagram showing planet Earth as a small sphere inside a much larger sphere of communication created by radio towers, dirigible moorings, lighthouses, and buildings—with zeppelins, planes, birds, and boats moving freely between them. **fig. 9** The polemical image makes it clear that Fuller's architecture was built in this space of communication. It was in the air rather than on the ground.

The pair of massive radio masts radiating energy in the drawing is shown much bigger than the planet they stand on, and their spherical pattern of radiation is even bigger again, reaching out beyond Earth's atmosphere—as was even more clear in the preliminary sketch for the drawing where the invisible radio waves form an enormous expanding globe engulfing and exceeding the planet. The space defined by the polemically delicate masts

26 Buckminster Fuller, "Dymaxion House Meeting, Architectural League, New York, Tuesday July 9, 1929," in *Your Private Sky: Discourse*, ed. Joachim Krausse and Claude Lichtenstein (Zurich: Lars Müller, 2001), 96. Fuller had earlier marked the communication unit as a rectangle floating in the middle of the downstairs living room on the first plans he submitted for patent in April 1928. All the media equipment is compacted into this factory-assembled unit. Media is not treated as a discrete piece of equipment in the subsequent hexagonal prototypes having a dedicated library space but as an integral service, one of the basic systems of plumbing.

27 Buckminster Fuller, *4D Time Lock* (self-published, 1928), 27. When preparing *4D Time Lock*, Fuller kept a clipping on the new use of radio in Chicago public school classrooms. Harold O. Totten, "Public Schools to Study Radio," *The Chicago Tribune*, undated, BFP Series 2, Box 18.

28 Buckminster Fuller, "Dymaxion House Meeting, Architectural League, New York, Tuesday July 9, 1929," 87.

10 House under and inside radio equipment: 12 Plane 4D Tower for *4D Time Lock*, 1928

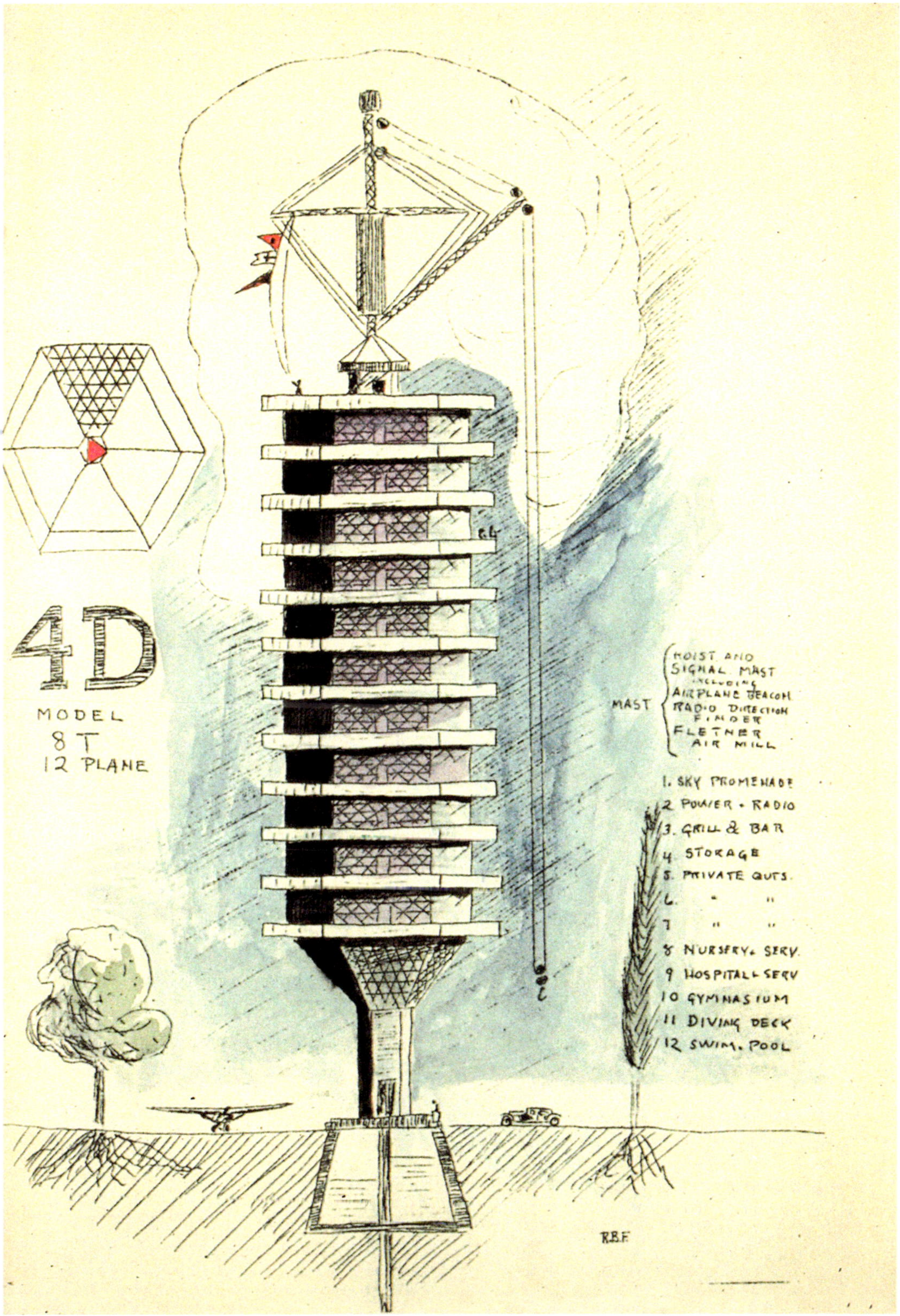

is more substantial than that defined by the seemingly solid planet. The very idea of scale is transformed. Radio masts were the tallest built structures in the world at the time and Fuller symptomatically drew a pagoda-like tower resembling the design of his own housing tower with the same height as the masts appearing on the diametrically opposite side of the planet. His architecture is another mast with its own radiant energy. It occupies the full bandwidth of the planetary system, aspiring to instantaneity and globality. A typical skyscraper is drawn much shorter, within the lower orbit defined by the lighthouse and the radio mast on a ship, so again in the world of signals and communication, but limited in bandwidth and constrained by being fixed in the ground.

Fuller's proposed tower is emphatically mobile. It is dropped in place, any place, by zeppelin but remains, in the words on another of the initial drawings of early 1928, "as free of land statics as a boat."[29] The 4D Plane Tower is a ship with its own radio signal antenna and radio beacon on top embedded in the Power-Radio room occupying the whole top floor. **fig. 10** The large diamond-shaped radio antenna crowning the structure links it to all other buildings and systems of movement. The architecture is on the land but not of the land, connected to the net rather than the ground, a new "one-world town" of portable structures linked by zeppelins, airplanes, and radio waves. It is a wireless house within a networked system of shelter, an instrument of communication like the generic telephone in its network that is Fuller's repeated example of how architecture should be rethought into a networked industry. Shelter becomes that which connects.

Fuller began the promotion of his design in mid-1928 with 200 personally distributed copies of a mimeographed manifesto that contrasted the static and degenerate housing industry to the new networking dynamism of "International telephone, telegraphic photography, and national radio 'hook-ups' from four corners of a continent, to all of a continent."[30] Radio was his ultimate paradigm of a networked future. He even described the physical networking industries of airplane, railway, and automobile as being "like a giant broadcasting system" in need of an upgrade.[31] As part of the promotion of the project, he published his July 16, 1928, letter to his mother insisting that she should sell all her shares in railways to invest in radio and electricity. She needed to know that the inevitable "natural" adoption of his design means that the value of land and any industry associated with it will fall "tremendously" while those associated with the air and airwaves would go up equally dramatically. Her property in the city should also be sold since urban concentrations would soon disperse into a decentralized global network. Yet the isolated island in Maine where he spent much of his childhood must be retained as it would become more

29 Text in Buckminster Fuller 1928 pencil drawing comparing 4D tower to conventional house, BFP Series 25, Box 9, Folder 21A.
30 Fuller, *4D Time Lock*, 2 (see note 27).
31 Ibid., 8.
32 Buckminster Fuller to Caroline Fuller, 16 July 1928, in ibid., 73. The original letter is in BFP Series 2, Box 19.
33 Buckminster Fuller to Caroline Fuller, 11 May 1928, BFP Series 2, Box 19. Anne Fuller maintained the account with investments in radio stocks at the time. See Mrs. R. B. Fuller account with F. M. Zeiler & Co., BFP Series 2, Box 19.
34 "Transportation, distribution, or broadcasting systems, ethereal, or material, are all organized and waiting for the decentralization and standardization of homes. They will develop miraculously." Fuller, *4D Time Lock*, 23 (see note 27).
35 Buckminster Fuller to Wolcott Fuller, 14 July 1928, in ibid., 72. The original letter is in BFP Series 2, Box 19. The General Electric Company that Fuller suggests as a sponsor to his brother, and then recommends to his mother, was at that time one of the biggest in the radio industry.

valuable since it could be easily integrated into the network through the air delivery of one of his houses "with every facility of modern city luxury built in."[32] Airways and radio waves would combine to form a new kind of dispersed planetary city.

Several of Fuller's earlier letters to his mother had made the point even more strongly. He forcefully argued on May 11 that it was urgent for her to abandon railways and invest in airplane companies and radio, saying that it was heartbreaking to him that their value had risen so dramatically since she had ignored his first recommendation but that the acceleration had only just begun. The growth was "just a starter" and she needed to immediately buy RCA, which had already absorbed thousands of smaller radio companies and was about to take off:

> Radio Corp of America while it has had what might seem like a big boom is but in its infancy too. Buy some of that. I will send you sometime soon a very strong paper that I have been writing for many months on this subject and which will astonish you. I know from the secret conferences to date that it is going to make considerable excitement when it is published so I urge you to follow my advice about this as soon as possible. [...] You were always quite a one for prognostications and will be much excited when you receive my paper. This is strictly confidential. It is too early to do any boasting, but it is thought by others as well as myself, and they are of great authority, that I have struck a "goldmine."[33]

Fuller did not mention his house, which is what he had been writing about so intensively for the last months. The transformative paper on radio he was referring to was actually the manuscript on the house. Fuller was just five days away from publicly presenting the idea for the very first time at the AIA annual convention along with the first mimeographed copies of the text, entitled *4D Time Lock*. In a still secret project that he has convinced himself was a game-changer, the house was conceived as both a reflection on and an amplifier of radio. The radical proposition is that autonomous, dispersed shelters interlinked by air and radio would be the very engine of air and radio—with air travel considered a subset of radio.[34] Architecture would be more than in and of radio. It would be the very foundation of an age of radio hinted at during the war and developed rapidly afterward but still awaiting the new form of shelter that would exponentially take it to the next level. Architecture would be the main accelerant of radio.

Fuller unsurprisingly wrote to his brother, Wolcott, in July about the possibility that the same companies that were supporting radio, like General Electric, where Wolcott was working, might want to sponsor his design. He proudly reported that an "electro-physicist, prominent here as one of the independent television engineers, is studying 4D with view to the practical application of his knowledge to the subject."[35] After all, the universe itself is pure radio. *4D Time Lock*, which Fuller finally sent to his mother to let her know what he had been working on for the last six months, insisted that "all matter is of globular, radiating form [...] radiating spheres," although just a small set of its wavelengths is "attuned to our wave length receptivity of consciousness or nervous system of antennae."[36] We only experience a thin slice of the environment but the radio-equipped house can extend the capacities of the body beyond the senses of sight, taste, hearing, and smell to pick up all the signals our organism cannot, and thereby intimately connect the body and brain to the planet and universe. The house would transport its occupants from a fixed position on the ground into the full vibrating bandwidth of the electromagnetic spectrum.

The electromagnetic spectrum had become a matter of intense public debate in 1927, with the US Congress passing the definitive Radio Act which visualized the spectrum as a space that can be occupied like any other, a form of real estate that needs to be regulated—determining that it will be treated as the property of the state that can be leased to broadcasters. Fuller thought of radio as a space beyond ownership, an undoing of the very logic of property. He noted that his one-year-old daughter Allegra already used electric light switches and elevator buttons, babbled into the telephone, and would work a radio set if only he could afford one.[37] He wanted his new kind of house to be leased like a telephone and replaced when a better model came along. He even imagined that it would be advertised on radio and television and ordered for air delivery or subsequent relocation by telephone—a concept he never abandoned.

In this blurring of medium and message, the materials making up the house would be as global as the signals it would send and receive, "just as the common telephone transceiver instrument incorporates essential materials from four different continents of our planet."[38] The visible display of the thinnest of wires for radio at the top of the building as a kind of technological ornament signaled the fact that the heaviness of traditional buildings permanently connected to the ground in one place had given way to an immaterial and omnidirectional connectivity. Fuller's lifelong project was to thin buildings down to minimize the difference between the object and the space of radiation. Solids became open frames with a networked geometry as close as possible to the ephemerality of immaterial networks of communication. Buildings became transceivers suspended within waves, new kinds of ship for an increasingly electronic species.

THE WIRELESS AVANT-GARDE

The clearest precedent for this deep embrace of radio was Vladimir Tatlin's remarkable 1920 design for a monument to the Third International. Its spiraling 400-meter-tall metal geometry was topped by two thin vertical radio masts that are usually overlooked. **fig. 11** Wires stretched horizontally between them at the very peak were to be energized by radio transmitters inside a glass dome perched within the uppermost section of the building's framework. The whole structure is a gigantic radio tower with a series of rotating geometric elements hanging within it. The traditional solidity and stasis of architecture had been inverted. Solids were subordinated to

36 Ibid., 16.
37 Ibid., 138.
38 Fuller, introduction to *A Question of Priorities*, xxiii (see note 12).

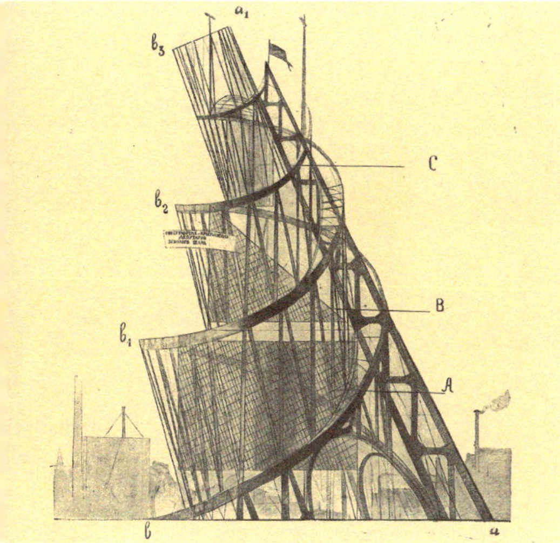

11

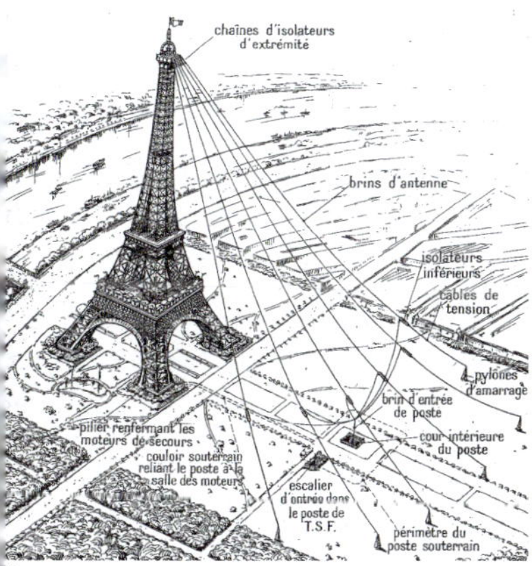

12

13

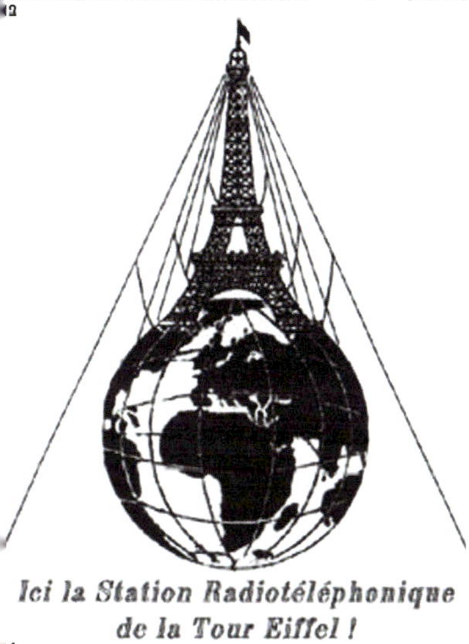

14

15

Planet-Shrinking Masts

11 Vladimir Tatlin, drawing of Monument to the Third International topped by radio station and antenna, in Nikolai Punin, *Pamiatnik III Internatsionala*, 1920

12 Wireless antenna array on Eiffel Tower, 1914

13 Fort Myers Naval Radio Station, Arlington, 1913, contemporary postcard published by W. B. Garrison

14 Logo of first public radio station in France, 1921

15 "Arlington Time," cover of *QST*, November 1916

an open metal frame, made transparent, suspended in the air, and mobilized. As in Fuller's 4D Tower house, people would occupy mobile volumes of double-skinned glass like a thermos that float in an ephemeral lacy frame. Radio is associated with a thinning-down of architecture into an open net. Architecture perforates itself in the name of broadcasting.

Tatlin was of course inspired by the 300-meter-tall Eiffel Tower, which he had visited in 1914. The tower in Paris had an antenna installed in 1903 on Eiffel's own suggestion and funding, in a successful attempt to save his unpopular structure as it was about to be dismantled. It immediately created a local network by communicating with all the military bases in the city, and by 1905 was linking all the bases across the east of France. An underground military radio station was installed in 1909. A set of six huge antenna wires fanned out from the top of tower to the gardens below with the signal wire then disappearing belowground to the control room. **fig. 12** The first successful reception of a human voice from the other side of the Atlantic was accomplished after the beginning of the war when it was able to tune in to an October 1915 signal coming from an equally huge triangular net of wires suspended from the second-tallest structure in the world, the lightweight 600-foot tower that had been erected by the US Navy in 1913 at the apex of a triangle with two 450-foot towers in the fields of Arlington, Virginia, in the hope of establishing a worldwide communication network. **fig. 13** The vast nets of wires and their associated lacy metal frames dwarf the traditional architecture below, at once empowering and infantilizing conventional buildings.

The logo of the Eiffel Tower's first permanent public radio station in 1921, like images of the Arlington towers and Fuller's drawing in 1928 shows the tower much bigger than the planet, subordinating the whole northern hemisphere with its signals. **figs. 14 and 15** A whole series of images showing colossal towers having the scale of the planet had tried to capture the building's unprecedented connectivity to distant parts of the globe—including one from 1913 in which the planet itself appears to be but a balloon moored to the top of the tower by all the lines of wireless connection to every continent. Radio massively increased the effective size of the tallest building in the world. Much taller again, Tatlin's tower was explicitly designed to network a fully socialist planet. It was made for the air and would likewise touch the ground at just a few points, literally straddling the river Helga in Petrograd, the birthplace of the first revolution in 1917.

Tatlin was a sailor who like Fuller had watched as the masts of ships became ever taller and more elaborate frames for radio transmitting and receiving. His design simply aspired to be the biggest radio mast of all. The messages to be sent through the transmitters in its transparent glass hemispherical dome would come from the information office housed in the glass cylinder immediately below that would complete one rotation a day having in turn come up from further below where the executive committee and administration of the party were to be housed in a glass pyramid that rotates once a month, which in turn filters the views of the full congress, which meets in the huge glass cube suspended within the base of the tower that would complete one rotation a year. The surrounding buildings that are dwarfed by the enormous structure would have wires on top of them ready to receive the signals—as can be seen in the original drawing of the project that was pinned on the wall beside the five-meter-tall model that Tatlin built in wood with his students at his studio workshop in Petrograd in November 1920 and became the canonic image of the project when it was published by the critic Nikolai Punin in a small booklet at the same time. **fig. 11** The whole world would ultimately be networked to the tower's communications. The model included the two vertical radio masts on the very top, and even the horizontal broadcast/receiving wire stretched between them. **figs. 19 and 20** Radio could not be left out of the picture. It was the whole point. The "Electrification of Russia" was symptomatically the main theme of the Eighth Soviet Congress in Moscow where the model was reinstalled a month later in the old imperial academy building and briefly inspected by Lenin—with hidden students inside its circular base turning the four geometric solids by hand crank. The combination of vast wired and wireless networks was meant to form a single integrated ecosystem covering the entire landscape—supported on delicate metal frames exemplified by Vladimir Shukhov's lattice structures for electricity and radio towers. Lattices and wires would replace walls. All buildings would soon become part of one hyperextended space of wires and wireless. Monumental ambitions would be sustained by seemingly ephemeral infrastructure. The more delicate the structure, the more territory it would define in a reversal of the conventional logic.

So many of the polemical projects of the twenties in postrevolutionary Russia had radio masts on top of them, with the size and number of wires reflecting the importance of each structure, from the one or two wires on the roof of rural education buildings to the dense geometry of wires woven between the three monster masts on top of the Vesnin brothers' influential Palace of Labor project of 1923 that were to be energized by the central radio station of Moscow inside its tallest volume. **fig. 16** With the Vesnins' design, a set of prismatic solids was again seen to concentrate collective thought and then be radiated out to the world. But the transparent solids that were suspended and spinning within Tatlin's tower now sat heavily and opaquely on the ground with the web-like geometric complexity of his structural frame displaced into the pattern of broadcast wires above. A monumental image of the ephemerality of connectivity is polemically placed on top of a monumental image of solidity.

These two images were effectively placed side by side in the 1927 graduation project of Ivan Leonidov, Aleksander Vesnin's most celebrated student, with the monolith of the huge library of his Lenin Institute paralleled by a net of wires. **fig. 17** The monolith, not accidentally the same height as the Eiffel Tower, is literally suspended in wire like the slender, equally tall radio mast alongside it, with the main broadcasting wire stretched horizontally between their peaks. The whole complex appears in a space defined by wires. Wire for structural support is blurred with wire for communication. More precisely, communication has become structural, both within the building and between the building and the world. In Leonidov's words:

> The research institutes, links with auditoria and reading rooms, are provided with a whole series of devices: telephones, radios, and radio representational and reflecting equipment. By this arrangement the entire academic institute can work together simultaneously on a single project. [...] The connection with the world is through a powerful radio station.[39]

Leonidov rethought the architecture of radio in a range of building types, imagining the transformative role of long-distance transmission of voice and images by radio from central laboratories to a network of a new type of workers' club dispersed across the countryside. Even the distributed volumes within each club would be anchored by an enormous radio mast responsible for life itself: "What are they to listen to on the radio? *Answer*: Life."[40] In several eloquent texts, Leonidov argued that the most slender frame and wires of radio would take over from the traditional function of the monument, developing a series of projects in which colossal radio masts would dwarf any building, with zeppelins, planes, and boats buzzing around them as the only visible signs of the global networking logic of the new world: "Radio and radio-pictures transmitted at a distance, an air- and sea-port become condensers of the movement of world culture."[41] **fig. 18** Architecture without radio was simply unthinkable. The very ability to shelter a new society depended on broadcasting.

Fuller looked at as many publications as he could when he decided to enter the field of architecture in 1927, symptomatically keeping in his chronological files the pages of the Vesnin brothers' 1923 Palace of Labor project published in the magazine *L'architecture vivante* in 1926.[42] The building and its polemical net of broadcasting wires had been featured in international surveys of modern architecture since 1925.[43] Not by chance Jean Badovici's editorial introduction to the *L'architecture vivante* issue on Russian Constructivism that presented the images kept by Fuller ends with the canonic drawing of Tatlin's tower. The project had been the centerpiece of the Soviet display in Paris in 1925 in a simplified three-meter tall model installed by Aleksander Rodchenko alongside the projects by the Vesnin brothers and others. Tatlin's tower was already known in small magazines, having been first published in France by Le Corbusier's *L'Esprit Nouveau* in 1922 (with the unambiguous note: "at the top is the radio station"), in Germany by El Lissitzky and Ilya Ehrenberg's *Veshch/Gegenstand/Objet* in 1922 and Bruno Taut's *Frühlicht* in 1923 and in Switzerland by El Lissitzky and Mart Stam's *ABC* in 1925, along with appearances in seemingly every avant-garde magazine throughout the world. Other Russian projects featuring massive radio installations were also known, like the Vesnin brothers' 1925 design for the Central Telegraph building, competition entries by Vladimir Krinsky, Ilya Golosov, and W. M. Wladimiroff and W. A. Krasilnikoff's 1926 university project linking radio and education featured in Ludwig Hilbersheimer's *Internationale*

39 Ivan Leonidov, "The Lenin Institute of Librarianship," translated from *Sovremennaia Arkitektura*, nos. 4–5 (1927): 119–124, in *Ivan Leonidov: The Complete Works* by Andrei Gozak and Andrei Leonidov (London: Academy Editions, 1988), 44.

40 Ivan Leonidov, "A Club of New Social Type," translated from *Sovremennaia Arkitektura*, no. 3 (1929): 105–111, in ibid., 66.

41 Ivan Leonidov, "Monument to Christopher Columbus in Santo-Domingo," translated from *Sovremennaia Arkitektura*, no. 4 (1929): 148–149, in ibid., 68.

42 BFP Series 2, Box 18.

43 See Walter Gropius, *Internationale Architektur* (Berlin: Florian Kupferber, 1925), 32.

16

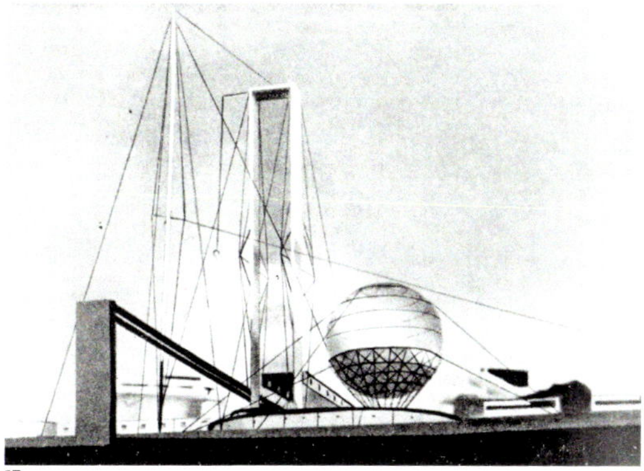
17

The Architecture of Wires

16 Vesnin brothers, Palace of Labor competition entry, 1923, in page from 1926 *L'architecture vivante* in RBF's Chronofile

17 Ivan Leonidov, Lenin Institute Project, 1927

18 Leonidov, Monument to Christopher Columbus, in *Sovremennaia Arkitektura*, 1929

19–20 Model of Tatlin's Monument on exhibit in Petrograd, 1920, with detail of radio antenna on the model

21 Illustration from Le Corbusier, *Vers une architecture*, 1923

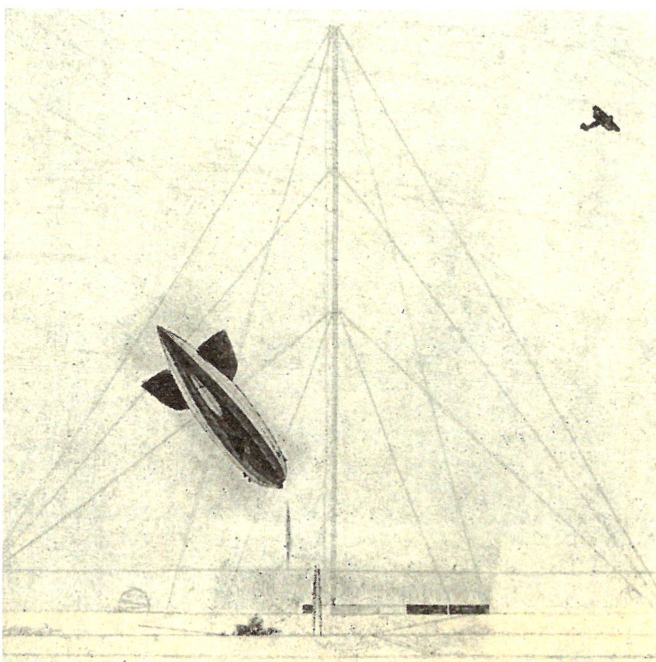
18

19

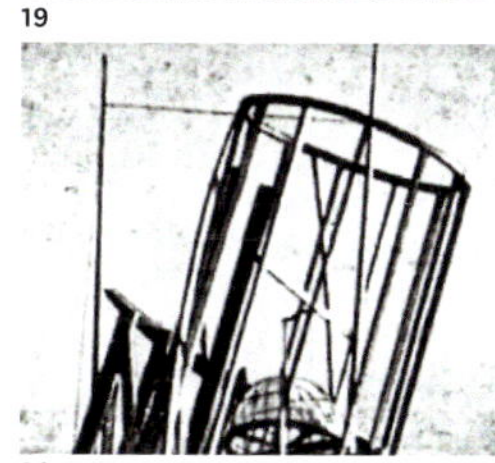
20

21

neue Baukunst survey of 1927.[44] The polemical embrace of radio by the Russian avant-garde could easily be registered by the international field, yet it didn't play a significant role in the development of canonic modern architecture in the following years. While the most influential photographers like Rodchenko and László Moholy-Nagy continued to focus on the lacy geometry of the new radio towers and even on celebrating the domestic act of listening to radio, modern architects typically headed in the opposite direction, reinforcing solidity and stasis while speaking about ephemerality and mobility.

Le Corbusier's 1925 book *Urbanisme*, which was assembled from essays in *L'Esprit nouveau*, used the "comprehensive" horizontal view from the top of the Eiffel Tower as his image of how skyscrapers would oversee the modern world. They can be the "brains" of the city and of the nation because radio, telegraph, and telephone act as an "apparatus for abolishing time and space," through which everything could be concentrated in a single building.[45] The performance of the future city would be defined by its speed of intercommunication. Le Corbusier later told his mass audience that the modern city is dependent on infrastructural systems of "water, electricity, gas, radio,"[46] and he occasionally included radio in the arsenal with which the office building would be empowered to orchestrate the world through information flow: "Electricity meant the limitless speed of information, order-giving and supervision—telegraph, telephone, radio."[47] But each of his towers was fixed in a grid by a rigid transportation network. He was an avid radio listener, tuning in to Radio Paris, the first private radio station launched in the city in the early twenties, every morning at 7:15 when exercising.[48] His 1925 book *L'art décoratif d'aujourd'hui* included an image from an illustrated magazine of a compact radio antenna similar to the large one Fuller would use on the top of his 4D Towers; he had images of the latest domestic radio receiver in his files (the Radiola unit produced by Radio Paris); and he made many radio broadcasts but was in the end more of a telephone architect. He liked to be photographed with a phone or even better on the phone, as if connecting himself to the world he was transforming, and he drew the buried telephone wires alongside the water, gas, and electricity lines that would feed his ideal skyscraper in key diagrams. It was as if he could not visualize the invisible world of radio because he was so addicted to lines. Yet even the visible lines of radio antennas and broadcast wires are erased. His most influential book, and arguably the most influential by any architect in the century, *Vers une*

44 Ludwig Hilbersheimer, *Internationale neue Baukunst* (Stuttgart: Julius Hoffmann, 1927).
45 For Le Corbusier, the skyscraper can act as "City's brains, the brains of the whole nation" through "apparatus for abolishing time and space, telephones, cables and wireless" Le Corbusier, *Urbanisme* (1925), translated as *City of Tomorrow and its Planning* (New York: Payson and Clarke, 1929), 177.
46 Le Corbusier speaking in *Les Bâtisseurs*, 1938 film by Jean Epstein.
47 Le Corbusier, *Manière de penser l'urbanisme* (1946) translated as *Looking at City Planning* (New York: Grossman, 1971), 99. Radio is part of the "inauguration of a complex set of tools for the transmission of ideas and orders," ibid., 54.
48 Nicholas Fox Weber, *Le Corbusier, A Life* (New York: Alfred A Knopf, 2008), 460.
49 Interestingly, Le Corbusier carefully draws two masts and the radio wire stretched between them on his 1929 project for a floating Salvation Army refuge, as if unconsciously aware of the wire that paradoxically allows a boat to be wireless, but he sees buildings as wired for all his polemical attempt to make them appear to be detached from the ground.
50 Brochure for May 1929 exhibition of Dymaxion House at the Harvard Society for Contemporary Art.
51 Buckminster Fuller to Herbert Aberman, 11 May 1931, BFP Series 2, Box 23. Fuller explicitly uses the term *radionic* to undermine static orthogonal geometry with the concept of spherical radiation as he clarified in a 1932 note he added to a 1928 text: "Euclid's fallacial cubistic geometry having been completely abandoned in contempo-physics, for radionic spherical relative growth concept." Fuller, "Universal Architecture," 23 (see note 25).

architecture of 1923, begins its famous embrace of the mobility, self-sufficiency, and modernity of ocean liners with a polemical image juxtaposing a set of the biggest historical monuments of Paris against the silhouette of a contemporary ocean liner. **fig. 21** The image is a play on a popular newspaper image comparing the dimensions of a transatlantic ocean liner to the Eiffel Tower on its side. The accompanying text, originally published in May 1921 in the eighth issue of *L'Esprit nouveau*, compares the modernity of the huge ship to that of the telephone, yet says nothing of the dramatic horizontal line for radio signals in the image that is stretched between the masts at each end of the ship and literally provides the frame in which the immobile historical buildings appear. Throughout the chapter that is cannily entitled "Eyes That Do Not See," we are asked to see the mobile, floating, white horizontal forms of a series of transatlantic liners as the very image of modern architecture but not to see the radio masts and wire for the signals that connect the ships to one another and to cities.[49]

For Fuller, it had to be the other way around. Radio was the defining fact of the age. It was no longer about amplifying the role of a particular building. It was not even a question of adding radio to architecture but rather of finding the architecture within radio. The absence of radio in the thinking of canonic modern architecture would simply confirm that its professed connection to industrialization, technology, and science was just a cover for an essential fear of those very things. Like Leonidov, Fuller imagined a dispersed network of structures with education and collaborative thinking sustained by radio. He even understood industrialization itself as a form of radio broadcast, a radiation outward from the human body that extends its capacities and ultimately envelops the world. Industrialized architecture would inevitably be broadcast. More precisely, it would be a continuous multilateral exchange of transmissions.

The main question for Fuller was not architecture as such, a field he thought was devoted to resisting the way the world was headed, but the more fundamental question of shelter that was inspired by radio. When Fuller turns architecture into a ship floating in electromagnetic waves, it is of course a ship with a radio. A light folded metal surface stiffened by cables like the tensed structure of a yacht acts as a kind of hull that carves out an inhabitable space within the waves, a space that is stable but never still, a shelter for the sailor-citizen but equally a shelter for a radio set that connects sailor and ship to all the other waves. More extreme still, Fuller's architecture both floated within radio and was constructed of radio. Even the shape and substance of the hull can be understood in terms of the geometry of radio itself. What seems to be solid is not so in the end. Radio waves were thought to be the raw material of every element. Fuller's house was "radionic," as he put it in the brochure for the exhibition of the model at the Harvard Society for Contemporary art in 1929.[50] Architecture would directly participate in the endlessly vibrating universe of radiation in which all forms of solidity are just an illusion. Fuller's mission, as he put it in a 1931 letter, is simply to produce "an architecture to embrace a living radionic universe, as opposed to the present static, materialistic compositions."[51] Radio is at once site, material, equipment, program, and goal.

Much of this discourse, and even the way of engaging the technical, professional, media, business, domestic, and military worlds, may well have come from the two months Fuller shared with Lee de Forest onboard his small ship, the USS *Inca*, trying to engineer a wireless conversation with a passing airplane. The first encounter with radio may have been even more decisive than Fuller's memory of it.

After all, it had been de Forest who had done the most to redefine the public image of the invisible world of radio. He was thrilled when he was finally able to transmit voice across his laboratory at the end of 1906 and to mark this dramatic shift from Morse code signals to talking (which had never been a goal for Marconi), he started to use the word *radio*, abbreviating *radiotelegraphic*, which had in turn been derived from *electromagnetic radiation*. The word had appeared in the International Radiotelegraphic Convention signed by the delegates of twenty-seven countries in Berlin just a month earlier in November 1906, but de Forest promptly named his whole enterprise the Radio Telephone Company and its key technology the *radiophone*. The new term took a long time to be picked up. It was not until 1912 that the navy officially adopted it and the first Radio Act regulating communication from ships and land was passed in the wake of the *Titanic* disaster.[52] Radio was still revolutionary and reinventing itself every few months when de Forest was asked to install a compact radio telephone in some blimps and fighter aircraft for the first time and met Fuller onboard the USS *Inca*, the chance rendezvous that Fuller would retroactively treat as a kind of destiny:

> The navy meant, not only getting into the air with airplanes and into the ocean with ships and submarines, but into radio which was really just developing. I was very excited when one of the boats I was commanding was assigned to Dr. Lee de Forest to make the first experiment of talking by voice radio from an airplane to a ship at sea. I felt I was being introduced to a new world.[53]

What was crucial was not just the transformative power of radio as communication between any two spaces, but radiation itself as the construction of a space. A radio broadcast transmitted in all directions and able to be simultaneously tuned in to by countless people in countless places creates a new kind of invisible space that can be occupied. It doesn't just connect and enhance existing territory. It redefines territory itself. De Forest had also been the first to use the word *broadcast* in 1907 and did the first public broadcast by transmitting live music in New York that February to the amazement of local newspapers.[54] The overlapping of the project of radio as private communication—even super private military communication—and of radio as public communication was evident again in early 1908 when de Forest broadcast some phonograph records from the Eiffel

52 On August 13, 1912, "An Act to regulate radio communication" was passed to mandate the use of radio in all vessels and bring transmissions under government control through licenses.

53 Buckminster Fuller, *Buckminster Fuller: An Autobiographical Monologue/Scenario*, ed. Robert Snyder (New York: St Martin's Press, 1980), 30.

54 "Music by Wireless Telephone: Dr. de Forest Sends it from Broadway to the Navy Yard," *New York Tribune*, March 7, 1907, 4.

55 "'Hello Paris!' 'Hello, New York!' Without Wire Next Year is Definite Promise of the Wizard of Aerial Telephony," *The Evening World*, August 21, 1908.

56 Harrold Chapman, "Wireless to Span the Ocean: Marvelous Achievements Expected from this Comparatively New Discovery," *New York Tribune*, November 28, 1909, B8.

57 Ibid.

58 Ibid.

Tower while helping the French military to experiment. He had installed his equipment on the tower for two weeks and later claimed to have set a world record of a conversation with a base in Marseilles 500 miles away and with warships at sea. The French military wanted to use their own less powerful equipment but de Forest negotiated with them that within two years there would be a direct radio link for conversations and music broadcasts between their tower and a set of "eight little copper wires" attached to the top of the 700-foot-tall Metropolitan Life Tower in New York, then under construction as the tallest skyscraper in the world. He promoted the idea the day after signing a contract with Metropolitan Life. Newspapers carefully explained what the French word *antenna* means and enthusiastically visualized the transatlantic link with dotted and zigzag lines to represent the radio signals invisibly crossing the curve of the planet between the two buildings.[55] **figs. 22 and 26**

The streets and surrounding buildings in New York and Paris are symptomatically absent in the drawings. Buildings with antennae were constructed in the air, in the global space of radio, and the thousands of miles between them became but fragments of a second, with de Forest confidently predicting further such links to cities like Havana. The capacity of buildings was dramatically increased. In an uncannily accurate prediction, one newspaper report on the project talked of naval battles, and even the aiming and firing of the guns being directed from an office in Washington, "with every battery and skirmish line in action plainly depicted on screens of white cloth."[56] Military force was presented within a poetics of space conjured up in the ethereal world of invisible waves. The "city of the future" would be transformed when "the ether is turbulent with sound waves" tuned in to by a receiver attached to a "thin wire groping the sky."[57] All the contemporary, unsightly overhead wires for telegraph and telephone, along with underground conduits, would be obsolete. Massive buildings themselves would lose importance as calls would go directly from house to house and land to land. More radically again, in a sentiment that predicts Fuller's core argument, fixed buildings themselves would lose their symbolic weight. Photographs of wireless equipment on the back of an unfortunate military horse and in an automobile accompany the thought that portable radio will be part of the active mobile expansion of the world rather than its consolidation with established heavy urban structures. **fig. 23** The city itself is left behind as the individual with a radio takes the invisibly interconnected collective into the unknown:

> It is asserted that within the near future wireless communication may be established with the most isolated corners of the Earth, that the distinguished hunter may take with him into the African jungle an apparatus which will permit him to give the newspapers prompt accounts of his latest conquest. But this is not yet, though Dr. de Forest has given much evidence on its probability.[58]

Both the science and the science fiction come from de Forest, who had been experimenting with wireless since completing his PhD in 1889 on the reflection of Hertzian waves from the end of wires, and was by far the most articulate about its possible transformative effects. He was dedicated to both the militarization and domestication of the technology, relentlessly installing his equipment in military bases, warships, office buildings, apartments, sheds, yachts, trains, cars, and an airship unsuccessfully attempting to reach the North Pole. He spoke about how just the addition of a flagpole to private houses would enable them to receive opera and how a pocket system for individuals would only need an umbrella as an antenna. He was a pioneer of both the technology and the publicity, even promoting the idea that he had wooed his wife by wireless, having installed the equipment in her bedroom and on the roof of his apartment seventeen blocks away to facilitate their courtship through the winter and finally to make the proposal, a promotion that was just as effective when newspapers recalled the story during the divorce just seven months later.[59] Once again, the story was an excuse to draw the architectural spaces being transformed. The media played a key role in domesticating the new technology with drawings that tried to grasp the arrival of an invisible architecture along with the arrival of a visible architecture of masts, wires, and radio equipment.

Radio increasingly became part of the visual field. The solidity of traditional buildings firmly planted on the ground started to be supplemented by ephemeral metal masts and lacy wires reaching up into the air. Buildings that sprouted major installations, like the de Forest system on the roof of the Waldorf Astoria hotel in New York in 1909, started to look like ships and became marvels featured in magazines.[60] **fig. 28** A new spatial system literally perched on top of an older one—at once magnifying the capacity of buildings and bypassing them in invisibly penetrating all spaces. As cities were occupied by these radio towers on the top of buildings and radio sets started to spread virally through interior spaces, newspapers digested the phenomenon and were joined by an ever-expanding array of specialized magazines. The few early titles like *Modern Electrics* (1908–1913), *Wireless Age* (1913–1925) and *Radio News* (1919–1971), suddenly multiplied in the early twenties with the literal domestication of the technology captured by titles like *Radio in the Home* (1923–1926). The same pattern occurred around the world as the ever more massive installations of the military on the coastlines and countryside that reached high into the sky to transcend the limits of the planet gave way to urban antennas on every skyline and finally to antennas within every house. Buildings no longer simply stood in streets. They were suspended in invisible networks.

Fuller's radical project to relocate architecture into the space of radio was built upon two decades of scientific and popular discourse about the encounter between buildings and radio. His mission was simply to reverse the direction of the conversation. Wouldn't architectural expertise be a form of radio expertise if radio expertise was already a form of

59 "A Wireless Courtship," *San Francisco Chronicle*, March 11, 1906, 5.
60 "Wireless Stations About New York," *Modern Electrics*, September 1919, 253.
61 "The De Forrest System of Wireless Telegraphy," *Scientific American*, August 16, 1902, 102–103.
62 "Tower for Wireless 'Phone: Lee de Forest to Build One on Top of Terminal Building in Park Avenue," *The New York Times*, June 8, 1908, 5. "His Wireless 'Phone Best, He Says. Lee de Forest Declares His Invention Surpasses the Latest French Devices. Carry Voice 500 Miles," *New York Times*, August 1908, 9.
63 See, for example, de Forest's complaint to Marconi about the latter's statement that the ability of de Forest's equipment to allow the president's cruiser *West Virginia* to send a message over 1,100 miles across the sea is "not uncommon" and challenge to a demonstration that his equipment is able to communicate across three to ten times the distance of his rival. "Challenge to Marconi by de Forest Wireless," *The New York Times*, October 31, 1905, 7.
64 "Spanning the Seas with de Forest Wireless," *The New York Times*, July 10, 1904, SM6.
65 Lee de Forest, *Father of Radio: The Autobiography of Lee de Forest* (New York: Wilcox and Follett, 1950), 4.

architectural expertise? De Forest himself could only promote radio by redefining architecture with new structures and new attitudes toward structure. Already by 1902 he had built a visually memorable glass-and-iron room under a 60-foot-tall mast on the roof of a lower Manhattan building as his well-publicized laboratory which communicated with a station at the base of the tallest mast in the country, his 210-foot structure built on Coney Island as both a scientific instrument and a public spectacle. **fig. 24** On the day it was finished, the big mast was already able to communicate with a boat having a 60-foot mast fifty miles away on its way to Havana.[61] De Forest quickly built up a set of 17 interconnecting stations along the Northeast coastline from Washington to Rhode Island, suspending webs of wires at strategic points. His own laboratory kept getting higher to reach ever-greater distances from the heart of the city. Already by 1908 his latest lab was built on top of the Terminal Building on Park Avenue with a 120-foot mast enabling a huge net of suspended wires to reach an effective height of 250 feet.[62] **fig. 25** All the dimensions kept expanding and were closely monitored by the press in a brutal competition of claim and counterclaim that had been dominated by de Forest and Marconi since 1901.[63]

De Forest won an early 1903 competition over his Italian rival to send the most messages the furthest with the most accuracy to get the commission to build huge stations for the US Navy to monitor shipping along on the East Coast, with the nets of wires laced even higher in the air, and he immediately started talking about doing the installations to ring the Great lakes and a set of huge masts in California, Hawaii, Manila, and Hong Kong to communicate across the Pacific. The major victory came the following year when he won the government commission to construct a chain of wireless stations 1,000 miles apart "spanning half the world" by ringing the Pacific Ocean to connect the United States to Asia and interconnect every navy battleship in between. The map of this massive circuit published in the *New York Times* effectively marked a whole new continent, a vast invisible territory defined and guarded by what would later be called a network.[64] **fig. 27** But it was only in 1906 the catalytic year in which de Forest managed to send a message across the Atlantic for the first time, invented the Audion triode tube that would quickly revolutionize the field, and was finally able to send speech rather than Morse code across a room—that he had the sense of having grasped a whole new invisible global territory that was taking over from the visible environment:

> Unwittingly then had I discovered an Invisible Empire of the Air, intangible, yet solid as granite, whose structure shall persist while man inhabits the planet; a global organism, imponderable yet most substantial, both mundane and empyreal; fading not as the years, the centuries fade away—an electronic fabric influencing all our thinking, making our living more noble.[65]

The understanding of objects, space, and people had completely transformed. In a full-page illustrated magazine article in 1907, just as he was introducing the words *radio* and *broadcast*, de Forest poetically described the "trembling [...] wonder" and "weirdness" of using a receiver to tune in to sounds "coming in from nowhere" on waves that are invisible to buildings and people:

Reaching Up to Touch the New Continent of Radio

22 De Forest announces transatlantic radio telephone service, *The Evening World*, August 21, 1908

23 De Forest portable radio-telephone for military use, *Scientific American*, June 19, 1909

24 De Forest Coney Island Station, *Scientific American*, August 16, 1902

25 De Forest wireless tower on Terminal Building in New York, *The Coos Bay Times*, February 13, 1909

THE EVENING WORLD, FRIDAY, AUGUST 21, 1908.

"Hello, Paris!" "Hello, New York!" Without Wire Next Year Is Definite Promise of the Wizard of Aerial Telephony

METROPOLITAN TOWER

LEE DE FOREST.

EIFFEL TOWER

Dr. De Forest Has Already Contracted for Conversation from Metropolitan's High Steeple to the Eiffel Tower's Tall Spire.

"You'll pretty soon be able to murmur to your sweetheart in Paris over the telephone, provided she makes the trip to the top of the Eiffel Tower," says Dr. Lee DeForest, who invented the wireless telephone, "and, furthermore, it won't be very long before you'll be able to hear Caruso singing a new opera role at least six months before the production is made in New York."

Such a prediction, savoring of Bellamy and Verne—nobody even had a thought of Munchausen—fell from the lips of the doctor as he sat, clad in overalls, in his buzzing, zipping wireless telephone laboratory, near the top of the Metropolitan Life Insurance tower, in Madison avenue, yesterday afternoon.

He had just signed a contract with the directors of the Metropolitan Life Insurance Company, which gives him the sole right to use their 700-foot tower in Madison Square—the tallest office building in the world—with the cloud-grazing tip of the Eiffel Tower—the tallest structure in the world.

"In a year," boasts Dr. DeForest, this connection will be completed. Of course, there are numerous experiments to be conducted, and we expect to encounter scores of difficulties, but I am confident that we will establish the connection."

Dr. DeForest is a young man, who looks as if he means what he says, and, furthermore, knows what he is talking about.

"The reason I am so confident," he continued, "is because, when I was in Paris last spring I heard wireless messages from the station at Glace Bay, Nova Scotia, to the Eiffel Tower, and the machine used was of only two horse-power, while we have apparatus of ten times that power, which will make it comparatively easy to connect with the Metropolitan, in New York. The antenna buzzed with the message, and I got my idea then.

"The antenna? That is the wire or network of wire. The word means literally the 'feeler,' and is generally applied to insects, and I think only the French, with their peculiar tact in applying names, would have thought of the application in this particular. Certainly it is most appropriate."

Dr. DeForest not long ago climbed to the top of the Metropolitan tower and adjusted a wire. The connection is to be had just under a circle of arc lights at the very top, under the base of the flagpole.

The aesthetic soul of the architect of the tower, Mr. LeBrun, was shocked.

Sound Waves to Jump Through Space Mile and a Half at a Bound, and Give New York Caruso's Song Rendered in London.

He thought there would be protuberances and wires that would destroy the symmetry of his tower, but not so. There will simply be eight little copper wires extending from the tower to the station, which will be built on the top of the eleven-story part of the Metropolitan Building, on the Fourth avenue side, and these will be absolutely invisible from the street, so there will be no smack in the eye to art.

"My experiments will be comparatively inexpensive," said Dr. DeForest. "I have no towers to build, which ate up so many hundreds of thousands when the wireless idea was new, for the Eiffel and the Metropolitan are already erected. In October, or, at the latest, November, I expect to have wireless telephone communication with the nearby large cities, and before long with Havana.

"When I say," he continued, "that you can hear a new Caruso song an hour or two after he sings it, I mean that if he sings at Covent Garden, London, for instance, the gramophone record is sent to Paris, there adjusted to our apparatus and waved over to our tower in New York.

"The time is not far distant when a passenger in the saloon of an ocean liner will be able to hear the strains of an opera which is being given at the Metropolitan, Manhattan or Covent Garden opera-houses."

22

23

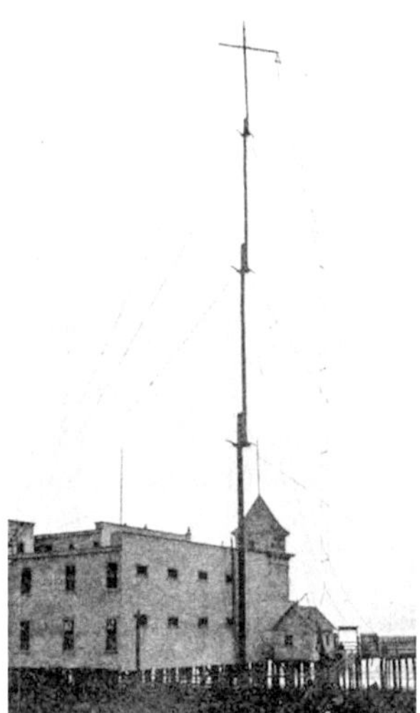

24

25

6

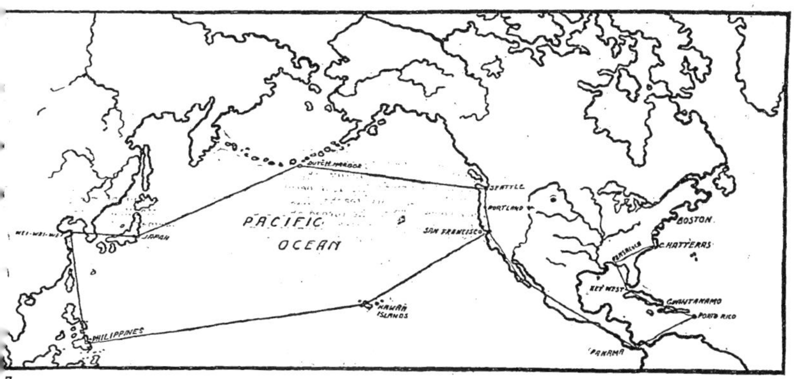

7

26 "Within the near future wireless communication may be established with the most isolated corners of the earth" and all buildings, ships, automobiles, trains, and horses; report on de Forest in *New York Daily Tribune*, November 28, 1909

27 Map of proposed chain of radio stations defining a new massive interior, in "Spanning the Seas with de Forest Wireless," *New York Times*, July 10, 1904

28 De Forest wireless station on roof of Waldorf Astoria, *Modern Electrics*, September 1909

8

> The ether waves which represent the sound vibrations may have passed ove miles of city or wastes of sea, through the walls of hundreds of buildings o over the roofs of the tallest towers. Nothing will retard or obstruct them, an those that stand between are unaware of the silent voices or spirit music tha might be passing them on every side.[66]

The first client for de Forest's new Radio Telephone Company was agai the US Navy with the heavily publicized commission to equip the twen ty-five ships in the so-called White Fleet to be able to talk to one anothe as they circumnavigated the globe for a year starting in December 190 The newspaper advertisements of the 1907 prospectus for the compan already described the goal of likewise talking between buildings withi cities and between international cities. Within a few years, the ambitio was to cover all the land and sea in a single system that would be disinte ested in the line between land and sea, or any line for that matter. Th full-page advertisement of the 1910 prospectus of de Forest's new Nort American Wireless Company featured drawings of the radio masts on th tallest buildings in New York, Chicago, and Cleveland and a map of hi transcontinental wireless network of such stations, continuing the projec of acclimatizing the public to the new confusion of radio and architectur along with the idea of a global net.[67] In the very language which Fulle would later use to describe a new approach to architecture in the late twen ties, the text promises a single "world-wide system" using standardize interchangeable parts to conserve energy and maximize collective expe tise since communication without wires recognizes "no limiting distanc and no national boundaries."

The prospectus predicts that future historians would refer to this as a epochal entry into the Wireless Age but that radio would be the trademar of the company's systems after it had been agreed as the official term at th Berlin conference. Indeed, the crucial move of the conference had bee to call for compulsory intercommunication between all equipment regar less of manufacturer, thereby effectively establishing the idea of a conti uous global system of radio connectivity. De Forest's prospectus furthe confirmed that radio would no longer be confined to stationary object Every large ship would be in communication with every part of the worl within five years. Trains and automobiles would be likewise equipped i a new age of total interconnectivity. As the advertised inventor of th wireless radiotelephone who was already "known from ocean to ocean, de Forest began his signed statement under his ubiquitous portrait at th center of the prospectus by repeating a personal promise of imminen communication between the Metropolitan Life Tower and the Eiffe Tower, and concluded by saying that in a few short years there would b "actual vocal accord" with every other national capital in addition to Pari Yet the Eiffel Tower always remained his best advertisement. The fact tha

66 Lee de Forest, "Listening to Voice and Music by Wireless 'Phone," *New York World*, April 7, 1907, 7.

67 "North American Wireless Corporation," *The Herald-Republican*, May 8, 1910.

68 "Radio telephony, following closely upon the heels of radio telegraphy, is sweeping the country, carrying into the homes of rich and poor alike a modern facility of pleasure and education which is binding the people together in a new and democratic brotherhood," *Radio Enter. the Home* (New York: Radio Corporation of America, 1922), 5.

69 Lee de Forest, *Wireless in the Home* (New York: De Forest Radio and Telegraph, 1922), 2. The patents that de Forest had sold to Westinghouse and others were now inside the RCA government monopoly but he himself was outside it and so was restricted to selling radios to "amateurs," which is to say people at home.

ou could walk under it and see through it, that it is in the air more than t is on the ground, literally permeated by air, reinforced its role in the idea f broadcasting being "on air." It made the dematerialization of the old vorld beneath it palpable, representing the global lacy world of masts and vires taking over from the world of solids.

Even the solidity of the radio equipment itself had to be challenged.)ne of the most transformative consequences of de Forest's Audion tube vas the ability to radically reduce the size of radio sets, setting in motion he relentless miniaturization of electronics. Tens of thousands of portable adios were produced for World War I and the equipment started to be lomesticated in the early twenties after the patents suspended during the var had been sorted out with most of the new vacuum tubes now being nade by the government-formed Radio Corporation of America (RCA) vith its unambiguous motto "World Wide Wireless." Radio would colapse the space between planet and house. After the first licensed radio roadcast stations in the United States started to appear in 1920 and 1921, tarting with one equipped by de Forest, RCA belatedly reacted in 1922 vith a line of domestic receivers that were promoted in a campaign of dvertisements and a heavily illustrated guide entitled *Radio Enters the Iome*.[68] New magazines like *Popular Radio*, *Radio Broadcast*, *Radio Age*, *Radio World*, and *Radio Magazine* were launched the same year with ountless articles on domestic radio and advertisements for "bringing he whole world to your fireside." Similar publications appeared around he world as public broadcasting began in France (1921), England (1922), Germany (1923), and so on. Filled with analysis, history, and practical dvice, they enthusiastically monitored the global expansion of radio in letail while promoting simple domestic equipment like the small Home-)-Phone wireless receiver. They continued the prewar graphic attempt o domesticate radio with repeated drawings of the planet dominated by adio masts, maps of invisible networks, and images of buildings supporting masts and wires but photographs of radios in houses were now increasngly added as the final proof of the transformation. As always, de Forest vas featured and wrote a number of the articles. Brochures like his *Wireless n the Home* of the same year encouraged every house to attach an antenna with drawings of different ways to suspend the wire) and to use models ike his Everyman Radiophone Receiver to take up the hobby of amateur adio or tune in to the broadcasts from the distant masts of the newly stablished public stations: "either for intense competition with others, ear and far or for quiet study and pure enjoyment in the still night ours as you welcome friendly visitors from the whole wide world."[69] The et was so compact that it could leave the house behind. With a carrying andle and only weighing five pounds, it was recommended for hiking nd camping. Images of such portable radio sets on mountainsides, he beach, isolated farmland, jungles, and islands started to proliferate. The increasingly widespread fantasy, which had been relentlessly chaneled and radicalized by de Forest since long before the war, was that the ospitality of the house would finally give way to that of electronics. The adio itself would create the space of domesticity. Domestic intimacy becomes portable and the range of people who can be invited in become infinite. Architecture is expanded then left behind.

Fuller described to friends the pleasure of his second chance encour ter with de Forest when seeing him coming up the gangplank of the US *George Washington* while it was being retrofitted by General Electric wit the most advanced radio for the presidential communications acros the Atlantic. He thoroughly absorbed de Forest's argument about mobi ity through radio and the global dematerialization of solidity, folding i back onto the house itself, turning masts into buildings more than tur ing buildings into masts. He did pencil sketches in early 1929 of perfora ed radio masts rising above and replacing traditional solid spires in th city. **fig. 29** He also had his 4D class, a small group of students and recen graduates, do a number of drawings of a hypothetical scheme of thre 4D Towers alongside a pair of radio masts with wires stretched betwee them for the forthcoming Chicago homeowners' exposition in Ma 1929.[70] The free-floating towers and radio masts rose up over the othe model houses spaced in traditional rows below. The future was literall in the air.

Fuller inevitably included radio masts as models for architecture alon side electricity pylons in an array of photographs of delicate structure that symbolized his central goal of "doing the most with the least" in th November 1932 issue of his new magazine, *Shelter*. **fig. 30** Symptomaticall they are not technical images but popular images that had been clippe from newspapers and magazines. Fuller's files include clippings of th mast of the USS *California* (that featured the extremely efficient doubl curved mesh structure of Vladimir Shukhov's lacy radio tower of 192 in Moscow) from the *NY Herald Tribune* and the 150-meter-tall Berli Radio Tower (inaugurated in 1926 on the occasion of the Great Germa Radio Exhibition) from the *Daily News*.[71] **fig. 31** Fuller had argued in th previous issue that "the subconscious has logicized the fact that th extraordinary mechanical attainment in radio *set* design, and distributio would eventually be revealed in the shelter industry."[72] The house wa already rethought in terms of radio. It was no longer simply a shelterin object with a radio. The very solidity of a physical room had been undon by the possibility of tuning in to radio broadcasts. It is what happened t objects, and even the flow of materials that constituted them, in the ag of radio. A new sense of space, even a new kind of vision, was found i the invisible world. The concept of shelter was revolutionized when eac room could become a window onto the whole world, as Fuller told a jou nalist in 1972:

70 Fuller lectured at the exposition immediately after unsuccessfully presenting the concept to the American Institute of Architects annual convention in 1929, and the first model of the recently renamed Dymaxion House was exhibited at the exposition for two weeks.

71 "Sailors on the Mast of the USS *California*," February 1929. Clipping from *NY Herald Tribune*, BFP Series 2, Box 21.

72 Buckminster Fuller, "Universal Architecture, Essay No. 2," *Shelter* 2, no. 3 (April 1932): 33.

73 Buckminster Fuller, quoted in William Marlin, "Buckminster Fuller Purges Myth and Replaces it with Conscience," *Winnipeg Free Press*, April 3, 1972, 6.

74 Buckminster Fuller to R. M. Ingersol, managing editor of *Fortune* magazine, in *Shelter* 2, no. 5 (November 1932): 124. Fuller contrasts the progressive mandate of *Shelter* to the conservative mandate of *Architectural Forum*, which *Time-Fortune* had taken over, and suggests that the company likewise take over *Shelter* to provide the right balance He even suggests that eventually student tuition fees would be paid to the worldwide broadcasting organization rather than to the universities it would partner with and transform. Ibid., 123.

For instance, in the grand ballroom of the Waldorf, there are over 200,000 programs going on right now. If we could bring in that many receivers of the right kind, we could tune in on this simultaneous but unseen reality. We could better embrace the world. [...] We could have in this one room the ability to comprehend what is happening, to see the trends working in our world.[73]

The comprehensive image of the world that comes in through the walls by radio includes design itself. Fuller built on his 1928 arguments about home education through radio in the November 1932 issue of *Shelter* with impressive foresight in imagining global education through "world-wide broadcast" as the intangible media of radio and television would soon replace the tangible media of books, magazines, and newspapers. He suggested to *Fortune* and *Time* magazines that they should transform themselves into a global broadcasting company with a department of "design-advance" that would transmit ideal scientific designs to hasten evolutionary development. The research of *Shelter* magazine is offered as a model of what could be broadcast in partnership with the research capacity of a network of universities that no longer need to be confined to a single location in the age of electronic communication.[74] Shelter is both medium and message in the age of radio.

Fuller explained to architecture students at Yale in late 1952 that his whole attempt to rethink the house had started in 1927 as an attempt to learn the lessons embedded in his own unusually "accelerated" life and pointedly used his intermittent encounters with radio during World War I as his example. Finding himself in the midst of society's latest experiments being sped up by war, radio had entered "through my pores":

I had a kind of accelerated experience in the navy. [...] I obviously didn't know anything about electronics. I had the kind of experience I had of having de Forest onboard my ship or the fact that I had been appointed force radio officer even though I was not a radio man. It was one of those kind of

29 RBF drawing of "New Spires for Old," early 1929

30 Array of masts as models for shelter systems doing the most with the least, *Shelter*, November 1932

31 "Broadcasting station aerial beacon and night-life restaurant. German efficiency is illustrated in this steel structure in Berlin, where a café has been built part way up the radio tower," *Daily News*, Sept 15, 1928, clipping in RBF's Chronofile

9

30

31

> administrative appointments you get. This thing was going on intermittently with me and I got it through my pores to some extent. The point was that I had been in the midst in that kind of phase when things are really going through something new was being taken on by society, which was radio.[75]

During a three-hour conversation with a newspaper journalist in 1935 Fuller had already associated the thinking behind the Dymaxion House with his first encounter with radio. He said he was not a good radio man but had been assigned to radio and had picked it up at the very moment that it was being intensely developed by the emergency condition of war.[76] The technology had been constrained to spanning limited distances but was about to take off and take the whole world with it.

Fuller's very first manuscript on his house was organized around the idea of radio. The remarkable "Cosmopolitan Homes Corporation: Lightful Products" text of early 1928 literally insisted that the housing industry needed to model itself on the radio industry. Housing was in its infancy as radio was before the urgency of war created the drive toward simplification, mass production, and global distribution of radio units. Fuller warns that the radio industry and the broadcasting stations only succeeded after the war—and will be about to grow "one hundred fold as large a business with the introduction of Lightful Houses"—because the design of the receiving units had been greatly simplified, well promoted, financed for the consumer, and broadly distributed.[77] The house likewise needed to be rethought in every aspect of design, communication, finance, and distribution. Radio would be key. Indeed, the house itself would be part of radio. It's not just that it would have radio installed at its heart and have its outer limits guarded by radio burglar alarms, or even that it would find itself within a network of communication and university education through broadcasts around the world on designated wavelengths.[78] More important, the house would be built within, through, by, and for radio.

75 Buckminster Fuller, audiotape of lecture (Yale University Department of Architecture, October 16, 1952), BFP Series 17, Box 3, Reel 03e. Fuller had earlier clarified that the revolution of "electronics" refers to "radio": "I'd been very fortunate in world war one in being intimate with flying and then the most advanced kind of mechanics that were coming into the world then, and electronics and so forth. We didn't call it electronics then. The name came along quite a few years later. But radio or whatever. And I knew I was participating in things that my mother didn't understand. [...] I realized that the pattern of life was changing very very rapidly." Buckminster Fuller, audiotape of lecture (Yale University Department of Architecture, September 26, 1952), BFP Series 17, Box 1, Reel 2b.

76 "Then Mr. Fuller had to decipher all messages and keep track of every ship in the fleet. He had picked up radio, but it wasn't that he was a good radio man; it was that the admiral thought he had a combination of abilities. Radio wasn't much in those days, but it was the fountainhead of radio as we know it now. But for the war, we should probably never have had radio as it is today, because in peacetime the money could not have been found for the intensive development of it that was a natural concomitant of war necessity. The boundaries of radiotelephony in the early stages were 300 miles, and the hearing was pretty poor too. But all this experience gave Mr. Fuller a background of interest." Janet Mabie, "If Ever Come Dymaxion Days," *The Christian Science Monitor*, September 11, 1935, WM5.

77 "It is just where the radio business was for a number of years before the war. It had worked out its functions and the war (equivalent to our industrial competition, on a small scale, as an economic force toward simplification) developed an industry to commercially provide radio units. BUT the industry and the great broadcasting stations with the thousands of people employed thereby for the wholesale distribution of harmony, amusement and education and news would never have been developed if the receiving set had not been developed and simplified and made commercially popular and had been distributed to the world at reasonable prices, on credit. Radio, as business, has just started its popularity in the stock market, is well founded. It will grow to be one hundred fold as large a business." Buckminster Fuller, "Cosmopolitan Homes Corporation: Lightful Products," BFP Series 8, Box 2, Folder 1, p. 26.

78 "Educational centers of today will no longer have their scholars come to them but broadcast around the world on assigned wave lengths the results of their research, analysis and design." Ibid., 28.

79 "We find that everyone educated today is aware of the waves of the radio etc. completely abstract which we reduce, by stages similar really to reduction by gears of leverage in our material zone, the waves to sounds within our conscious zone. We now by survey of what a human really is, will gather or acquire an ability to judge things in abstract way which we have never done before. [...] Now this man animal has the following nervous or arterial system of antennae buried in his flesh, some of the antennae or wires they might be called carrying two or more messages of divergent wave length, just as our telegraph lines do." Ibid., 46.

80 Buckminster Fuller, "Earth Inc." originally published by the Fuller Research Foundation, 1947, republished in Buckminster Fuller, *Earth Inc.* (New York: Anchor Books, 1973), 7.

81 Buckminster Fuller, "Continuous Man," in Buckminster Fuller, *Ideas and Integrities: A Spontaneous Autobiographical Disclosure* (Englewood Cliffs: Prentice-Hall, 1963), 283.

its occupants would be able to speak from anywhere within it into the radio-telephonic-recording-dictator" to think and set things in motion. The text predicts that the majority of work in the future would involve crystalizing thought into four-dimensional design, talking by radio to machines to control radiation—making and moving things by thinking. The manuscript offers a very elaborate theory that the whole material world is itself nothing but radio, myriad patterns of spherical radiation, countless overlapping wavelengths that are largely unseen but can be brought into consciousness. The discovery and then collective awareness of radio is offered as evidence that all the unseen patterns of the universe can eventually be made conscious and directly engaged with through thought. Just as a radio set converts abstract waves into conscious sounds, the body's own "receiving set," with the nervous system of wires embedded in the flesh acting as antennae for the brain, can tune in to the unseen broadcasts, "the expanding waves of matter" that shape the universe.[79] The house itself can likewise be seen as both a receiver absorbing hidden signals from the world so that its occupant can think, and a transmitter so that those thoughts can directly engage and modify the world. The house would be a radio set housing the radio set that is the human.

Fuller's lifelong attempt to redefine *shelter* by transforming the concept of *house* can be understood as an extended meditation on radio, a meditation that is itself a broadcast phenomenon. The unprecedented density of his performance, in endless lectures, interviews, experiments, essays, books, reports, TV programs, films, poems, LPs, drawings, models, and structures was itself a radio effect, a personal and ever-expanding communication cloud. His relentless strategy was to defamiliarize that which was closest, mobilizing whatever appeared to be most known and stable by challenging, as he put it in 1947, man's sense that "he isn't going anywhere at home."[80] Fuller turned the very images of that which is close—the human body, the house, and the planet—into continuous metabolic flows of energy and information. But he always started his investigations with the house, which no longer sheltered the body and mind against all forms of movement. It became itself a form of movement, a spinning, flexing, interactive object dropped from the air onto a planet moving at a thousand miles an hour and wirelessly connecting its occupants to all the signals from the other minds distributed across Earth, a global network sustaining a "continuous" species: "a world-around interlinked and continuously intercommunicating continuity of consciousness."[81]

WHAT IS A HOUSE?

Buckminster Fuller devoted much of his impossibly energetic life to exploring the question of the house. Yet it was one of his greatest achievements to have never really designed a house as such. Despite all his detailed drawings, models, and prototypes with the label *house*, his remarkable series of experimental designs for domestic spaces from the late twenties to the early fifties launched a systematic assault on the very concept of the house and ultimately on the concept of the architect. Fuller's sustained brilliance was to resist so many of our traditional assumptions, particularly about housing, but to do so from an extremely close range. In fact, he smuggled himself under the very skin of architecture to produce an itch that still aggravates the field today.

The threat was simply to take seriously modern architecture's insistence on the inevitably transformative impact of industrialization. What if the house could actually be a machine for living in? What if it could be manufactured, distributed, and ultimately replaced like any other technology? What if it could be mass-produced in factories alongside the latest aircraft and automobiles and aspire to their lightness, continuous evolution, and speed? Shortly after reading the 1927 translation of Le Corbusier's extended manifesto *Vers une architecture*, Fuller elaborated his own version of the argument and developed the design for his first dwelling machine. In May 1928 he presented the detailed theory and drawings of his renamed 4D House to the annual convention of the American Institute of Architects, who promptly voted to reject any such approach. By taking the call for a modern architecture so seriously, he became unrecognizable within the profession. More precisely, his retooling of the house gave shape to the profession's irrelevance. The stronger his design, the more official disinterest it attracted. Each of the refinements of the details over the next two years made the renamed Dymaxion House less likely to be influential in a field faithfully devoted to the aesthetics of caution.

Nothing about Fuller's design was cautious. Hanging from a tall mast, the hexagonal building was extremely lightweight, portable, energy efficient, self-ventilating, self-temperature-regulating, and self-cleaning. It was a polemically independent building that continuously took care of itself and remained proudly disconnected from any collective infrastructure, sustaining its own power, waste, and communications systems. Every aspect of the space challenged the familiar look, feel, performance, construction, and economics of a house, from its inflated tubular metal structure to the see-through vacuum-sealed outer wall panels of recycled vegetable material, the spongy inflated bladder floor, the pneumatic partitions, the inflatable furniture, the glass tables suspended by neon-lit cables, the molded bathroom unit with atomized spray, the photoelectrically controlled revolving storage units, the pneumatic silver balloon silk doors, and the triangular curtains pulled up from the floor and down from the ceiling. Triangles were everywhere. A triangular-shaped elevator would bring the visitor up from the ground to the floating floor of triangular inflated panels suspended four meters off the ground within a triangular net of cables, looking out at the world through a web of triangular window panels. To inhabit the building is to be suspended above the ground within a dense weave of nested triangles. Even the explanatory text on the most detailed drawings for an early exhibition catalogue is organized in triangles, and inside one of them we are told that the triangle is the basis of "Dymaxion designing" in opposition to the traditional linear approach.[82] **fig. 3**

82 Buckminster Fuller, *4D: Buckminster Fuller's Dymaxion House*, exhibition catalogue (Cambridge: Harvard Society for Contemporary Art, March, 1930).

83 Buckminster Fuller, "Dymaxion House" (lecture to Architectural League, New York, July 9, 1929), in *Your Private Sky: R. Buckminster Fuller, Discourse*, 95 (see note 26).

84 Archibald MacLeish, "After Five Years of Dymaxion History," *Fortune* 6, no. 1 (July 1932): 65–66.

Its inherent stability is used to destabilize the field, enabling the house to be mobilized into something else altogether.

Within the structure's resilient geometric web, all dust, smells, and sounds were to be continuously removed; temperature and humidity, regulated; cooking and laundry, automated; and the whole ceiling would act as a single continuously adjustable diffuse light fitting and heat control. Despite the crisp triangulated geometry, the views in all directions were softened and complicated by the way the plastic outer window panels, ceiling, inner partitions, and bathroom units, like the inflatable furniture, can be variously transparent, translucent, opaque, or colored. Everything was mobile, built in time rather than space, the designer insisted. All the internal equipment units were hung from the central structure and could be repositioned or replaced. The whole structure was itself a mobile unit, rented like a telephone, moved if necessary, or discarded in favor of an upgraded model. For Fuller, the building was always on the move. Since the average wind speed is 12 miles an hour, he described houses as "little ships" continuously moving at that speed, slowing down when it is calm and accelerating rapidly in storms. The idea of the static house was replaced by that of the vehicle, even a kind of spacecraft with its own internal ecology monitored by a wall covered with dials like "the bridge of a ship."[83] The ultralightweight building was meant to be produced in vast quantities by an automotive company and delivered anywhere by a zeppelin, which would simply drop a bomb on the chosen site and plant the structure like a tree in the resulting crater. The inhabitants of the near future would park their slick, teardrop-shaped cars and private airplanes underneath and the dense communication center at the heart of the structure (books, globes, maps, drawing board, typewriter, mimeograph, phonograph, telephone, radio, and television) would reconnect the self-reliant unit to the world it floats so independently from.

Dedicated to multiple forms of efficiency, this high-performance building would be treated as a technical instrument to be continuously refined by a program of scientific research and development as in any other industry. But in radicalizing every aspect of the house, it was no longer even recognizable as a house. When the design was published in *Fortune* magazine in May 1932, the article astutely began with the observation that "the Dymaxion House is, in a certain sense, not a house at all."[84] That which is most familiar, the domestic space of the family, has been defamiliarized through a kind of science fiction presented as a new set of facts with their own irresistible momentum. Fuller's gift was to make the everyday strange simply by bringing it into view. *4D Time Lock*, his self-published manifesto on the 1928 design, begins by pointing out that the traditional house is the most slowly evolving and least studied phenomenon precisely because it is so close to us:

> Just as individuals can criticize themselves with much less facility than others, and only when forced by shocking necessity receive a true picture of themselves, so have the living quarters of the people avoided, to the last, close scrutiny, improvement in design and method of creation, in this marvelous age of industrial progress. It is the subjects farthest removed from personal

contact, and of the least immediate necessity, which have received the most honest and unbiased attention and design, to wit: the aeroplane, automobile, radio, etc.[85]

BROADCASTING SHELTER

Fuller's first formal book, *Nine Chains to the Moon* of 1938, begins by comparing the "utter inefficiency" of the house to the "magical efficiency" of the radio and again argues that the house is the hardest thing to question because we are usually inside it. Only an outsider can interrogate its all-too-familiar condition: "house—a phenomena to which I am, upon first consideration, an outsider. What is a house?"[86] Fuller spent his whole career successfully trying to remain the outsider by directly addressing this deceptively simple question, treating the house as a phenomenon rather than an object, an eccentric cultural and psychological symptom, a source of unnecessary drag that needs to be subjected to a simultaneously technical, anthropological, and philosophical study.

In his sustained assault on all forms of drag, Fuller's response to the question "What is a house?" kept evolving. When exhibiting the design at the Harvard Society for Contemporary Art in May 1929, he started to list the basic functional requirements of a "machine in which to live," echoing the short list in "The Manual of Dwelling" that Le Corbusier offered in *Vers une architecture*.[87] The small exhibition brochure identified what a house must "eliminate" (drudgery, exploitation, selfishness, politics, centralized control), "safeguard against" (flood, electrical storms, fire earthquakes, tornadoes, hurricanes, marauders) and "save time for" (education, amusement, advancement).[88] These should be the real goals of the architect. Yet to take them seriously is already to leave architecture behind Fuller insisted that "this has been in no way a consideration of architecture."[89] To finally think about the house is to embrace scientific experimentation and abandon the fixation on aesthetics of the profession that Fuller repeatedly denounced as but "shelter tailors." Architects are the first piece of equipment to be replaced.

The article on the Dymaxion House in the June 1929 issue of *Architecture* magazine symptomatically ends with the question "What is to become of the architects?" and uneasily suggests that more designers are needed in a fully industrialized building industry rather than less.[90] In place of the usual figure of the architect, Fuller appears in a business suit earnestly demonstrating the movement of the triangular curtains in the model he had been exhibiting around the country. **fig. 35** He was continually photographed in the pose of the salesman to reinforce the basic mission of turning house design into an industrialized mass-market product. He literally became a traveling salesman, a one-man propaganda machine appearing in galleries, museums, architectural societies, arts clubs, schools, conventions, home shows, department stores, hotels, and restaurants. When the model was first displayed at Marshall Field's department store in Chicago in April 1929, Fuller gave a relentless fifty lectures and another sixty when

85 Fuller, *4D Time Lock*, 1 (see note 27).
86 Fuller, *Nine Chains to the Moon*, 10 (see note 13).
87 Le Corbusier, *Vers une architecture* (Paris: Editions Crès, 1923), 96.
88 Brochure for May 1929 exhibition of 4D at Harvard Society for Contemporary Art.
89 Ibid.
90 Henry Saylor, "The Dymaxion House: Conceived by Buckminster Fuller," *Architecture*, June 1929, 335–340.
91 Fuller, "Universal Architecture," 16 (see note 25).

it went to the Harvard Society for Contemporary Art a few weeks later. Images of him talking alongside the model soon appeared in countless newspapers, popular magazines, professional magazines, and newsreels. It was these images that marked the launching of Fuller as a cultural personality who would eventually occupy the cover of *Time* in 1964, having devoted a huge proportion of his efforts to thinking and talking about housing.

Fuller was inseparable from his models throughout his career. The key to all the speeches, texts, exhibitions, and teaching was to animate several models—understood not as representations but as demonstrations of otherwise invisible principles. When first presenting drawings of the Dymaxion House, he recalled his extensive experience presenting "miniature houses" at national "Own Your Own Home" shows in New York and Chicago in the mid-twenties, where he promoted an innovative construction system using fibrous concrete blocks. A group of students helped build the cardboard-based model of his new house design that toured in the first half of 1929 with an electric light glowing inside the central shaft. A much larger aluminum model made by a New York sculptor at the end of that summer and refined over the fall became his key prop and was put on the road. It traveled in a trunk with him to many of the same venues as its predecessor, enabling yet more waves of lectures. Fuller would later estimate that he had given formal lectures to more than 30,000 people during the first three years of such "publicity."[91]

High-quality studio photographs of the aluminum model were taken for popular and professional magazines to demonstrate how such a building would be rapidly assembled and the final daytime and nighttime effect. In what would soon become the most canonic image, the suited designer finally sits beside the carefully lit completed model, seemingly admiring and carefully considering its self-evident advantages, especially the naked woman on the inflatable bed. **fig. 33** Her lack of clothing is meant to communicate the superior temperature control which makes even sheets redundant, but there are actually three naked women in the model. Two are up on the exposed roof terrace, having been together in the bedroom in earlier photographs. More suggestively even, the cardboard model had already featured three naked women in the living room looking up as a man in a suit enters from the elevator. **fig. 34** They float in a seductively liquid space, as shiny as the reflective surfaces they are bathing in. **fig. 36** Newspaper reports were quick to point out the nudity. Fuller's promotional technique was to combine such direct sensual effects in the models with highly abstract and often barely digestible theorization. Straightforward observations and impressively stark statistics would be combined to describe things in completely new ways. The easily grasped object would facilitate the absorption of less easily graspable ideas.

The physical demonstration models and the abstract list of functional requirements evolved in parallel and often appeared side by side. Fuller proudly stood beside the paper model reciting his short list of basic requirements in the earliest newsreel of the Dymaxion House. When he took over *T-Square* magazine in 1932 to further his campaign against the

ELEVATION SHOWING CENTRAL SUPPORTING MAST EXTERIOR COMPRESSION STRUTS & HOUSE SUPPORTED IN TENSION - MAST CONTAINS POWER UNIT AND SERVES AS DISTRIBUTING TUBE FOR AIR LIGHT HEAT ETC. EXTERIOR SHELL OF STRUTURE COMPOSED OF TRANGULAR NON SHATTERABLE VACUUM PLATES
TOP 50 FT. PLAY-DECK SHIELDED BY DURALUMIN HOOD STREAMING WIND OVER TOP & PROTECTING PERSONS - MASTHEAD CONTAINING LENSES FOR UTILIZING LIGHT AND HEAT OF SUN ▵ AREA UNDER HOUSE USED FOR HANGAR & GARAGE CLOSE IN BY METALIC VENETIAN BLINDS WORM-GEAR - ELEVATOR IN MAST
BASE FOR ▵ MAST CONTAINING SEPTIC AND FUEL TANKS
ISOMETRIC SHOWING UTILITY UNITS - GRILL LIBRARY BATH ROOM ETC - THESE UTILITY UNITS ARE MANUFACT. IN TOTO AT FACTORIES AND MERELY HUNG UP IN THE HOUSE IN RADIAL ARRANGEMENT AROUND THE MAST PIPING AND ALL CONDUIT HOOK-UP BEING IN STANDARD MANIFOLD MANNER WITH CONDUIT IN MAST - AS IN COUPLING UP RAILROAD CARS
THE UTILITY UNITS FORM NATURAL PARTITIONS OF THE TOTAL SPACE OF THE PLAN AS OPPOSED TO OUR PRESENT DAY LEGISLATIVE PARTITION WHICH SAYS "YOU SHALL NOT PASS" - EVERY UNIT OF DYMAXION DESIGN IS INDEPENDENTLY RELATED TO THE MASTS THAT IT MAY WITH EASE BE REPLACED BY A MORE DESIRABLE UNIT AS IT DEVELOPS. ALL PRIMARY FURNITURE IS BUILT INTO UTILITIES
BED ROOMS A & B IDENTICAL REVERSED PLANS - EACH CONTAINING OWN ONE PIECE BATH ROOM - WITH AUTOMATIC TEMP. CONTROL ETC. - 6 FOOT TUB-SHOWER ETC. - NO CRACKS FOR BUGS - PNEUMATIC BEDS INFLATABLE TO DESIRED FIRMNESS - NO BED CLOTHES NECESSARY ATMOSPHERE BALANCED FOR HUMAN REQUIREMENTS - SEMI-CIRCULAR HANGING CLOTHES CLOSET - CAPACITY 50 DRESSES. OVOLVING SHELVES BUILT IN TABLE
EQUILATERAL TRIANGLE NOT TO BE REVEALED AS PART OF DESIGN. SHOWN HERE AS IT IS THE BASIS OF
DYMAXION DESIGNING - THE UNIFICATION OF THE DESIGN BEING ANGULAR INSTEAD OF LINEAR
THE UTILITY ROOM - OR CATCH-UP WITH-LIFE-ROOM CONTAINING LAUNDRY UNIT-IN WHICH CLOTHES DEPOSITED DIRTY ARE COMPLETELY CLEANED AND DRIED IN THREE MINUTES - BEING LEFT IN ROUGH - DRY - POCKET - UNTIL DESIRED. ALSO GRILL UTILITY IN WHICH ARE FOUND AUTOMATIC REFRIDGERATION, DISH WASHING MACHINE WHICH WASHES DRIES & RETURNS DISHES TO SHELVES
BED ROOM "B"
BED ROOM "A"
LIBRARY
UTILITY ROOM
LIVING ROOM
LIBRARY - CREATIVE - ABSTRACT "GO-AHEAD - WITH - LIFE - ROOM" AS BALANCE TO MATERIAL UTILITY ROOM - WHERE CHILDREN MAY DEVELOP SELF EDUCATION ON SELECTIVE BASIS - THROUGH BUILT - IN - RADIO - TELEVISION - MAPS - GLOBES OVOLVING BOOK SHELVES DRAWING BOARDS TYP WRITERS ETC THAT THEY MAY GO TOGETHER AS REAL INDIVIDUALS NOT CROWD NONENTITIES
NOTE THAT IN EVERY ACUTE ANGLE TERMINATION OF THE ROOMS A DOOR IS FOUND WHICH IS PNEUMATIC AND IS OPENED AND CLOSED
BY THE WAVE OF THE HAND ACROSS LIGHT BEAM OF PHOTO - ELECTRIC CELL. ALL FLOORS & PARTITIONS ARE SOUND PROOF ▵
THE LIVING ROOM 40 FEET X 20 FEET APPROXIMATELY SHOWING BUILT - IN PNEUMATIC COUCH APPROXIMATELY 15 FEET LONG - HEXAGONAL PNEUMATIC DIVAN BAKELITE FLOOR - TRIANGULARLY SUPPORTED HANGING DINING TABLE IN ANGLE OF WINDOWS FOR MAXIM VISION INDICATOR PANELS ON WALL OF GRILL - GRILL UNIT OPENS INTO L.R.
PLAN - ISOMETRIC - AND - ELEVATION OF A MINIMUM DYMAXION HOME

The Seduction of Triangles

32 Inhabitable three-dimensional web of triangles in page from *4D: Buckminster Fuller's Dymaxion House*, Harvard Society for Contemporary Art Inc. exhibition catalogue, 1930

33 RBF with aluminum Dymaxion House model of late 1929

34 Cardboard Dymaxion House model of early 1929; photograph published in cropped version in *Architectural Forum*, July 1929

35 RBF holding a triangle on cardboard Dymaxion House model in Washington, in *Architecture*, June 1929

36 Close-up of the cardboard Dymaxion House model of early 1929

33

34

35

36

drag of housing, he published the photograph of himself sitting beside the more refined metal model, and the adjacent article expanded his checklist of requirements into "universal conditions of the industrially reproducible shelter."[92] The list had become a program of what should be prevented, what should be maintained, and what should be incubated. The primary defensive goals were now divided into "external destructive forces," which are physical, and "internal destructive forces," which are psychological. In a decisive turn, "nerve-shock proofing," "fatigue proofing," and "repression proofing" became key design objectives. The real aim of the physical structure is mental. The ultimate target, the final requirement listed as "growth," was to free the mind to receive all possible forms of knowledge about the world and to transmit all possible ideas to the world. Having often contrasted the regressive status of the traditional house to the progressive status of radio and telephone, Fuller turned housing itself into a two-way communication system. His list of universal requirements inevitably culminated in the call for a sophisticated communication apparatus at the heart of the building. To shelter is to connect.

Fuller promptly renamed his magazine *Shelter* and devoted every issue to the rethinking of housing. A few years later, he again upgraded the list into "Universal Requirements for a Dwelling Machine" when *Nine Chains to the Moon* returned to the key question "what is this phenomenon, house?"[93] By 1941 the list had been expanded again into the "Universal Requirements for Dwelling Advantage, Teleologic Schedule." The house was no longer a form of protection from the world. On the contrary, it had become a way of taking advantage of the world, a form of leverage. Shelter was not the solid line between body and world but the way of expanding the body outward into the world after bringing the world into the body. The static look of shelter was to give way to the dynamics of real shelter. By 1949 the list was very extensive, having grown from a few sentences in 1929 to many highly detailed pages with layer upon layer of itemized subsets of requirements that included all the steps of research and development, realization, and public relations.[94] The simple checklist had turned into a full program for establishing a "dwelling services industry." The complex and comprehensive list was such a radical rethinking of the concept of house that the word *house* is never used.

Fuller would tweak the list a few more times in the fifties before a final set of minor adjustments to the universal requirements for a "scientific dwelling facility" was made in 1960 for publication in *Architectural Design*, the most influential international magazine of the day.[95] The last correction he made to the page proofs of the issue was the crucial one of adding

92 Buckminster Fuller, "Universal Conditions of the Industrially Reproducible Shelter," *T-Square* 2, no. 2 (February 1932): 37.
93 Buckminster Fuller, *Nine Chains to the Moon*, 33 (see note 13).
94 Buckminster Fuller, "Universal Requirements of a Dwelling Advantage, Teleologic Schedule," 1949, unpublished manuscript in Serge Ivan Chermayeff Papers, Department of Drawings and Archives, Avery Architectural and Fine Arts Library, Columbia University.
95 Buckminster Fuller, "Universal Requirements of a Dwelling Advantage, Teleologic Schedule," *Architectural Design* 30 (March 1960): 3–11.
96 Buckminster Fuller to John McHale, 14 December 1959. John and Magda McHale private archive, Buffalo.
97 Buckminster Fuller, presentation at "Time for Change: Mid-Century Report on Design Progress," conference at the University of Michigan, Ann Arbor, cited in Jeanne Rockwell, "Fuller Describes Unusual Ideas of Future Home," *Ann Arbor News*, April 5, 1949, 10.
98 Fuller, "Influences on My Work," 294 (see note 4).
99 "Not one prospect ever culminated in an order from these shows." Fuller, "Cosmopolitan Homes Corporation: Lightful Products," 4 (see note 77). For the years between the war and the Dymaxion House project and the complex story of the Stockade Building System, see Loretta Lorance, *Becoming Bucky Fuller* (Cambridge, MA: MIT Press, 2009).

his new concept of "continuous man," the single organism made up of all interacting humanity.[96] For Fuller, the real client for design was never an individual. What mattered are the planetary ideas that develop collectively through time and space. Any fixation on an isolated designed object for an individual has to give way to an ever-evolving prosthetic service for a globally networked human consciousness. The house necessarily faded away in this amplification of mankind through "extension, acceleration, and expansion" out beyond the individual body into the universe. The word *house*, and even the image of whatever would replace the house, steadily dissolved into the Standard-of-Living-Package, a core set of portable equipment for sustaining domestic life which could unfold anywhere and was covered by a transparent plastic dome with as little materiality as possible. Fuller's first major presentation of the concept in March 1949 again jettisoned the idea of *house*: "What has been the matter with housing is that we know too much about a house. [...] Why not eliminate the traditional concept of a house and think instead of the essentials of living?"[97] There was finally no significance in visible architecture. The object itself had become irrelevant, giving way to the more elusive geometries of the broadcast network:

> "House," in comprehensive designing, would be as incidental to the world-around network dwelling service as is the telephone transceiver instrument to the overall energy processing in communication systems.[98]

This shift from solid object to collectively engaged mental leverage can be seen in the evolution of labels for Fuller's domestic projects from Fuller House in 1927 to Lightful House, then 4D House in 1928, Dymaxion House in 1929; Dymaxion Shelter in 1932; Dymaxion Deployment Unit in 1940; Dymaxion Dwelling Machine in 1944; the Autonomous Dwelling Facility in 1948; which becomes the Sky Fence House later the same year; and finally the Skybreak House from 1950 to 1956. The weight of the house progressively thinned down over two decades until it disappeared except for a compact mobile package of equipment encased in the lightest possible transparent bubble.

RADIATION CLOUD

At the very beginning of this chain of experimental designs for domestic space, Fuller noted that not a single purchase order had resulted from all his public exhibitions of miniature houses after the war for the otherwise successful Stockade Building System Inc.[99] This would remain the rule. Very little actual building, other than a few incomplete prototypes, resulted from Fuller's subsequent thirty-year publicity campaign for a new kind of autonomous house. The main effect was indirect, which was perhaps the idea all along. The real point of the experimentation, as with the communication center at the heart of each of the designs it promoted, was the radiation of ideas.

In this sense, even the remarkable 1944–1946 Wichita Dymaxion Dwelling Machine that came the closest to actually being mass-produced was first and foremost an incisive commentary, a theoretical reflection on the question of shelter, and therefore on everything. **fig. 39** Fuller's apparent sabotage of the project's realization can be seen as a continuation of his fundamentally philosophical and subversive mission. When lecturing to its team of engineers in 1946, he once again insisted that the question of shelter had never been seriously asked because mankind literally lives inside the frame of measurement that needs to be interrogated. Only when one "gets 'outside' of the whole phenomenon *house*" and takes advantage of the "out-of-house behavior" where technologies are not repressed would the house become visible and self-evidently redundant.[100] To finally see the traditional house is to feel its drag and immediately reject it. Fuller's steady undoing of the house as part of the most optimistic scenario of collective growth is a crucial and captivating story that keeps challenging the architectural field to start thinking.

Fuller repeatedly insisted that "man has been too close to his house to gain perspective" and reached out to the cosmic scale of radiation, the mainly invisible architecture of the electromagnetic spectrum, in order to redefine the object and finally to dissolve buildings into the ultralight transparent domes that act as his final model of housing in an uncanny, unconscious echo of the glass radio transmission dome at the top of Tatlin's 1920 tower. Even then, the domes themselves, arguably his single biggest influence on the built environment as they proliferated virally across the planet, are not important. The whole project had never been about the design of a particular physical shelter but about an attitude, as *Nine Chains to the Moon* had insisted:

> The Dymaxion House was simply an attitude and interpretive principle—a principle of doing the most with the least in consideration of a mobilizing, integrating society necessitous of breaking its exploitable bondage through science.[101]

When shelter is understood as that which gives prosthetic advantage by reducing all forms of physical and mental drag, the traditional work of the designer has to be dissolved. The static object must give way to the dynamic reception, incubation, and broadcast of thought.

Fuller's ultimate goal was that moment in the science fiction narrative with which *Nine Chains to the Moon* ends its extended answer to the question "What is a house?" An "x-ian" creature unexpectedly beamed to Earth in 1937 by a new kind of radio set explains to the astonished radio operator on Earth that the "scientific dwelling machine" on her planet on the other end of the universe was a complete "receiving and sending apparatus" for each individual to record the thinking of all others and to broadcast thoughts that can contribute to their collective evolution.[102] Shelter is

100 Buckminster Fuller, *Designing a New Industry* (Wichita: Fuller Research Institute, 1946), 16.
101 Fuller, *Nine Chains to the Moon*, 348 (see note 13).
102 Ibid., 380.
103 Ibid. The book gives an extended account of the accelerated evolution of radio during the war that produced the new "radio world," the postwar attempt to regressively turn the "world-encircling" radio waves into a new form of monopolized property, and the resistance offered by young amateur radio enthusiasts that both radicalized and domesticated the technology in a way that acted as Fuller's model for a new "scientific dwelling service." Ibid., 292–315.
104 Buckminster Fuller, "Motion Economics," manuscript dated December 1942, BFP Series 8, Box 5, Folder 1, p. 43.
105 "In the electronic communications and other new service "systems," which sell only energy, man's sciences and his practical industries are already tying in directly with the reality of the all-in-motion universe, and that 187,200 miles per second norm become more natural each day to its workers—that is, while at work. Nothing would be more perplexing to a young radio electrician than for "voice" to start flowing in a circuit at rates less than 187,200 miles per second." Ibid., 70.
106 Ibid.
107 "Experience is very slowly reflected, refracted, and incidented energy wave phenomena, diluted to easy scanning proportions subject to rumination analysis and subsequent objective assimilation into the growing body of technology." Ibid., 101.

finally optimized when it becomes the most expansive and unselfish form of radio broadcasting. This story of interplanetary transport through the architecture of radio itself completes the circuit started at the beginning of the book when it argued that the prosthetic extension of the human senses through postwar technology had already "provided an 'actual' sense in the realm of radio in our younger men. In this sense-extension into radiation lies the promise of man's eventually understanding all the secrets of life-in-time."[103] When the species literally feels itself in the invisible space of radio, it finds its shelter and its very thought process there.

"Motion Economics," the unpublished book manuscript that Fuller completed in December 1942 when acting as an economic advisor to the US government during World War II, makes his most extended argument that everything in the universe is in motion at the speed of radio waves since the whole universe is made of radiation. Yet man cannot see motion even if sight is the one human sense that operates at the full speed of radiation: "He cannot see an airplane propeller in motion, or the motion of a climbing vine, or even the motion of a star moving along in brilliant view at thousands of miles a minute, let alone 'see' a radio wave or the all-important heart palpitations of his best girl."[104] The universe is all radio, and we see with radio—but only with the world of electronic communications systems has this speed become palpable. For the first time, science and industry were directly engaged with the "all-in-motion universe." Radio electricians, for example, found 187,200 miles per second completely natural, even if only while at work.[105] This speed needs to be naturalized in all thinking, especially in the economy and in developing democratic processes using radio communication that would make war redundant. Although his imagined audience was political, economic, and military rather than architectural, Fuller associated static architecture with the drawing of unmoving lines that lead to war. His main polemic was that the seemingly shocking speed of radiation actually offers the kind of security falsely promised by solid buildings. He pointed to "war-exploded masonry" as a "devastatingly poignant symbol" of the failure of traditional architecture and the traditional thinking that generated it, which is based on the idea that the world is solid and still. The speed of radiation itself was the real promise of shelter:

> His security of living as guaranteed by 187,200 miles per second as speed of visibility inherent in light radiations contacted through the bedside light switch, or with the doctor, the drug store, the airport, and the marines,—through the telephone wire as focused radiation,—is far greater than the elusive security which the static tradition promised he would find in his masonry walls.[106]

As "world-wide man" acclimatized to this speed through experience—which was itself a radio process of continuous circuits whereby incoming waves were literally absorbed, scanned, refracted, reflected, and fed into and out through technology[107]—any fixed house became but a "nominal 'home'" occupied for a fraction of the time, with all mobile citizens directly and continuously participating in decision making through another "dynamic-circuit-system" of radio, "a direct, electrically-voiced democracy, a

BROADCASTING SHELTER

Democratic Intelligence, articulate at the speed of light."[108] Masonry shelter gave way to the more secure shelter of radio.

It is not by chance that as Fuller stopped designing autonomous single family houses in the mid-fifties, with the last version of the Skybreak House, he had been working with his students at Tulane on the design of a huge fiberglass Sky Eye radio telescope.[109] **fig. 37** Instead of a house with an antenna, the house had become an antenna. Its only goal was to shelter signals coming from across the farthest reaches of the universe. The geodesic dome was now turned upside down and directed toward outer space. It was floated in a circular pool of water so that it could smoothly point in any direction. Once again, architecture was a ship floating on a high speed planetary spaceship and tuning in to signals from other such ships, but these ships were now light-years away. Fuller and his team worked on 300-foot, 600-foot, and 1,000-foot versions of the radio telescope with experts from companies like Marconi, and spoke of the possibility of structures manyfold larger still.[110] As with all the earlier house projects, this was not just shelter understood as the provision of the biggest possible window on the universe, but as the sheltering of life within radiation itself.

While working on the radio telescope project in May 1955, Fuller sent a letter to the military about their call for a "modular shelter for tactical electronic systems." He was responding to the formal request for proposals that would lead to the final contract to build the spherical Radomes for the continental early-warning radar system based on the experimental prototypes that his team had been developing since early 1953. The fiberglass domes were to house the largest and most sophisticated forms of radio being developed by companies like Bendix Radio, whose AN/FPS 20 radar unit became the standard equipment of the defense net, with its curved metal lattice antenna relentlessly spinning within Fuller's dome and a separate rectangular box full of electronics housed beneath. **fig. 41** Fuller's letter

108 Ibid., 110.
109 "Tulane university architecture students have constructed a dome-shaped model of a radio telescope which receives radio waves from outer space." Tulane University News Bureau press release, February 16, 1954, BFP Series 21, Box 1, Folder 9. "Tulane Students Construct Radio Telescope Model," *New Orleans Item*, March 14, 1954, 15.
110 A version of the radio telescope was prepared for Cal Tech and a 300-foot-diameter vision was designed for Australia to support a 250-foot-diameter radio telescope mirror. "The three-quarter sphere structured of these buoyant cigar-shaped struts could float in a control base to a depth comparable to a ping-pong ball in water. [...] Such a structure was highly patentable as it involved the surprise element of a ship bereft of its skin and floated by its naked ribs." Buckminster Fuller, undated letter to potential manufacturers of the fiberglass ribs; 600-foot and 1,000-foot versions were presented by Geodesics, Inc. at the March 25, 1955 meeting of Associated Universities. Buckminster Fuller to Richard M. Emberson, 29 April 1955. Marquand Rare Books Library, Princeton University.
111 Buckminster Fuller to Procurement Office Research and Development Command Rome Air Development Center, Griffiss Air Force Base, 27 May 1955. Marquand Rare Books Library, Princeton University.
112 "I decided long ago that it would be necessary to separate out the mechanics from the structure for a dwelling machine was something like an electronic valve and we had the problem of enclosing and developing a controlled environment within which we would center the unfettered energy valving mechanics. That was the essence of what we were looking for in this present student project—an enclosure with entirely separate packaged mechanics with free interflow deep within the controlled environment" Buckminster Fuller in *Housing Mass Produced: 1952 Housing Conference Held January 14 Massachusetts Institute of Technology*, ed. Phyllis M. Kelly and Richard W. Hamilton (Cambridge, MA: Bemis Foundation, 1952), 27–31, here 30.
113 "We have completely separated the function of enclosure or valving of the convergent energy factors from the interior valving mechanism itself which is like the arrangement of an electronic tube where you have your special machinery that operates best with its own special rhythms and patterns so that by separating the two completely you are able to make very free omni-directional dimesional—this is a new dimension of expansion and control—and not be fettered at all by exterior enclosure which can continually be replaced by a larger shell." Buckminster Fuller, audiotape of lecture (Detroit Museum, April 9, 1952), BFP Series 17, Box 1, Reel 1f. Earlier in the lecture, Fuller countered the idea of the electronic tube as the search for perfect "isolation" with the idea of an enclosure acting as a device to "valve" incoming and outgoing radiation into useful patterns. Ibid., Reel 1c.
114 "Space isolator bears the same relationship to interior mechanisms, events or structures as does the bulb, or tube of an electric light or an electronic 'valve' bear to its vacuum or gas enclosed elements. As with the latter the interior elements are provided with a controlled environment most favorable to their functioning, isolated from the unpredictable variables of external occurrence. As with the bulbs this structure is of such a dimension as to provide the isolating function at ample distance from the interior elements, being structurally in association with the latter only at the base or common origin." Buckminster Fuller to Eleanor Cannon, undated but sent between 23 and 28 September 1949, BFP Series 2, Box 72, Folder 9.
115 K. L. Holm to Buckminster Fuller, 18 March 1931, BFP Series 2, Box 23.

took the final step of literally equating architecture with the technology at the heart of radio. It summarized his experiments since 1927 and directly compared the two primary "energy-valving" goals of all shelter—providing a controlled environment, and providing the means within that environment to do work that impacts the world outside it—to the basic structure of the radio tube, with its spherical glass enclosure isolating a space from the general "frequency environment" of the universe and an apparatus inside the glass for modulating specific frequencies:

> These functions combine complimentarily in the working principles governing design of the thermonic-valves of electronics, i.e., the radio tube—where spherical structures isolate maximum preferred energy behavior environment from the energy frequency environment of comprehensive universe. Within are located apparatus for modulating the frequencies of angularly redirected energy patterns.[111]

Fuller's domes were to be understood as radio tubes with their compact service packages inside transparent spheres to both establish autonomy and facilitate all forms of communication with the world outside. **fig. 40** His architecture aspired to radio in every sense, even to the form of its basic technology. But it is important to note that Fuller was not making this argument because the purpose of the Radome was to house electronics. His lectures on his first house experiments had already used the analogy of the electronic tube. His January 1952 conference presentation of versions of the Skybreak House by MIT students, for example, used the analogy to explain the polemical separation of the compact mechanical Standard-of-Living-Package from the transparent skin of the dome enclosing it: "I decided long ago that it would be necessary to separate out the mechanics from the structure for a dwelling machine was something like an electronic valve and we had the problem of enclosing and developing a controlled environment within which we would center the unfettered energy valving mechanics."[112] A few months later, his public lecture at the Detroit Museum repeated the analogy with "the arrangement of an electronic tube" that offered dwelling a new kind of unfettered omnidirectional freedom.[113] Even more remarkably, Fuller had already described the dome as a "space isolator" like an "electronic valve" when proposing a 60-foot-diameter dome house to his first potential client in October 1949 just a few months after his first prototype dome had been successfully assembled and skinned in plastic at Black Mountain College that summer.[114] The dome and the radio tube were inseparable.

More crucially, the dome was born out of the electronic tube that it echoes. In the middle of March 1931 the editor of *Architectural Record* had invited Fuller to make a lecture on the house of the future a month later at General Electric's headquarters in Schenectady, New York.[115] This was no routine invitation. The company had founded RCA in 1919 and the lecture would take place in the building at the very center of the radio industry which had the two huge radio masts linked by horizontal transmitting and receiving wires on its roof that had acted as the model for the two radio masts in Fuller's first manifesto drawing of Lightful Houses dominating the planet in 1928. **fig. 42** The company thought the talk was a "distinct

37

38

39

40

The Ever-Expanding Architecture of the Radio Tube

37 RBF with model of Sky-Eye radio telescope, *The Tulanian*, April 1954

38 Lee de Forest in his laboratory with Audion tube, *Electrical Experimenter*, November 1915

39 First Wichita House prototype being assembled as an assault on drag, 1945

40 RBF's model for architecture, the Ultraudion radio tube, circa 1910, published by de Forest in *Broadcast Radio*, August 1922

41 Radome in use on DEW line, circa 1956

42 Antenna towers of WGY Schenectady radio station, General Electric Company, 1922

43 RBF and Shoji Sadao, model for 8,000-foot-tall version of Shoriki Tower housing one million in its base, in comparison with Eiffel Tower, 1966

41

42

43

success" and wanted him to return to discuss further the possibilities for applying electrical equipment to his house but also to formalize his ideas about the architectural capacity of tubes: "We hope in the near future to have you prepare an article for us on the application of vacuum tubes to general building problems."[116] The tube would no longer simply be housed by a building. It would accelerate architecture and reshape it in its own image. The 1917 encounter with Lee de Forest, who had invented the triode radio tube, reverberated through all Fuller's work, literally shaping it. De Forest's Audion tube was originally a sphere and an immediate object of fascination in the media. Its shape echoed that of the planet it conquered. Not by chance, it was de Forest's tube (amassed in a large array) that enabled the first voice communication across the 3,800 miles between the Arlington and Eiffel towers toward the end of 1915, having enabled a similar 4,900-mile communication between Arlington and Honolulu a few weeks before.[117] Photographs of de Forest staring intently into his transparent glass globe appeared alongside drawings of the planetary globe with overscaled radio towers talking to each other.[118] **fig. 38** The glass sphere became even more transformative when de Forest finally figured out how to use it for amplifying signals just a year before meeting Fuller.[119]

It is no surprise that Fuller's first text on the Wichita Dymaxion Dwelling Machine in 1946 says that the isolating enclosure of the hemispherical house protects the dynamic internal flows of heat, light, air, sound, and smell as does "an electronic tube protect the free-functioning of its central element."[120] He even compared the way these flows are pulled through the house to the way "radio and radar tensively induce circuits to pull radiation phenomena over almost unlimited distances."[121] The house is a kind of radio tube.

It is not that Fuller sought to imitate the architecture of radio by echoing the design of a tube. Rather, the fundamental concept of shelter was understood to lie already within the organization of the tube. The transparent sphere of the tube shelters the energized filaments that produce the radio signals that provide the real shelter. The sphere is inseparable from the signal. The signal is made possible by the sphere. The invisible architecture is made possible by the visible one. Architecture inevitably has the form of radio equipment, a transparent sphere housing radiant electronics because it is itself radio equipment, a sophisticated transmitter/receiver. The geodesic structure is understood to be part of the electronics that it had dreamed of housing from the beginning and literally housed in the mid-fifties when Fuller's Radomes were selected to shelter the nation's

116 A. L. Kocher to Buckminster Fuller, 1 May 1931, BFP Series 2, Box 23.
117 "By Wireless 'Phone from Arlington to Paris," *The Electrical Experimenter*, December 1915, 393.
118 "Wireless Telephony from Washington to Honolulu," *The Electrical Experimenter*, November 1915, 321.
119 On the precise history of de Forest's tube and the controversies around it, see Sunghook Hong, *Wireless: From Marconi to the Audion* (Cambridge, MA: MIT, 2010).
120 Fuller, *Designing a New Industry*, 35 (see note 100).
121 Ibid., 36.
122 Fuller, "Critical Path Part Four," *Critical Path*, 337 (see note 6). A second version of the tower reduced the height to 8,000 feet.
123 Buckminster Fuller, "How Little I Know," *Saturday Review*, November 12, 1966, 70.
124 "If I go to 1975 just to the right, anything can happen. You are really witnessing an acceleration as we have never seen before in the tune of 800 years which is really to say that within 5 years we may send you around the world by radio. Something as completely surprising as that. Each one of these events has been equally surprising I assure you." Buckminster Fuller, lecture (Town Hall, New York, March 12, 1971), BFP Series 17, Subseries 5, Box 138, Videotape 7c.
125 "A Candid Conversation with the Visionary Architect/Inventor/Philosopher R. Buckminster Fuller," *Playboy*, February 1972, 66.

early-warning radar equipment, with hundreds of his bubbles dotted across the uninhabited northern limits of the continent and then around the world. The original concept of architecture as a networked communication infrastructure of autonomous structures dispersed across the landscape and suspended within radio signals was unambiguously realized.

Even the original sense of inspiration in the ephemeral architecture of radio masts returned with a vengeance. Fuller and Shoji Sadao completed the design and engineering report for a colossal 12,250-foot-tall metal tower in 1966 with housing inside the pyramidal base of the structure at a time when, according to Fuller, the tallest building in the world was a 2,000-foot TV transmission tower.[122] After radio and then television had entered the domestic space of the house, it was just a matter of time before the house literally entered the infrastructure of broadcasting. The Eiffel Tower that had inspired Tatlin to design an even taller radio mast in 1920 is now completely dwarfed by the new mast, being barely visible when polemically included in Fuller and Sadao's drawings and model of the final reduced version of an 8,000-foot tower. **fig. 43** Having just imagined a series of geodesic spheres as space stations heading toward other planets, Fuller designed a tower scaled beyond Earth.

THE HUMAN BEAM

It was not by chance that in the same year as the massive tower project Fuller's essay "How Little I Know" returned to the possibility of beaming people by radio that he had first raised in 1938, even suggesting that the human species must have arrived on the planet that way two million years before, fully formed:

> It seems more likely (In view of the continuous rediscovery of Man as a fully organized being back to ever more remote periods) that the inanimate structural pattern integrity which we call human being was a frequency modulation code message beamed at Earth from a remote location. Man as prime organizing "principle" construct was radiated here from the stars—not as primal cell, but as a fully articulated high-order being.[123]

The human body is described as a complex package of electromagnetic waves with a particular pattern that can be transmitted. The material making up the pattern continually changes but the pattern persists. Fuller pointed to the chart of the successive discovery of all the 92 chemical elements in a 1971 lecture in New York and suggested that "sending people around the world by radio" within the next five years would be no more surprising than any of the other discoveries in the last hundred years of accelerated evolution.[124] It would anyway be a return to the fundamental human condition rather than a technological transformation. In an interview with *Playboy* a year later, Fuller happily returned to the thought that "man probably came to this planet as whole man, a creature very much like we see today. He might have been sent by electromagnetic waves, as is perfectly possible, since man is an aggregate of electromagnetic waves."[125] Fuller had long been fond of telling his audience that the only parts of his body that had returned to the same room to give another lecture after a few years were his glasses and his name, which were more part of him than anything else, even if he was not born with either of them.[126] His own body was always the star exhibit, from the first lectures to the last interviews:

> Everything is a verb, a wave function. I am a wave. You only see me because of interference, because light is bouncing off me. [...] I am not the tons of food water, and air that have gone into supporting this patterned integrity for eight five years; I am the patterned integrity itself.[127]

This pattern that is continually reconstituted by new cells is itself as invis ible and weightless as a telephone message, as "How Little I Know" put it in 1966, and only makes itself known as a series of radiating displacements of the environment.[128] It is a message and therefore can be re-sent. Indeed it has to be forwarded. Man is "essential" to the universe and is therefore probably on countless planets, as Fuller would argue a year later.[129] When converting "How Little I Know" into a poem in 1976 he added a few lines at the end that go further still in imagining that the human species had not only been sent across the galaxies by radio but was itself a synthesis of all intergalactic radiation.[130] Humanity is finally understood as a condensa tion of radio itself.

Whatever we see, no matter how solid, can be broadcast in a universe where everything is a combination of wavelengths. More precisely, what we see is always a broadcast. Solidity itself is an illusion. Already in *Earth Inc.* of 1947, Fuller had noted that the isolation and manipulation of indi vidual chemical elements that allowed the density of orbiting atoms in steel to appear superficially solid had also given birth to radio.[131] Nothing is sealed or static. Everything is in motion with different frequencies, and even the ultimate weightless condition of life itself is sustained by energy radioed to us from the sun.[132] In the foreword to *Out of This World*, a

126 "I think I probably spoke last in Chicago more than seven years ago, and there is none of me left except my glasses and part of my bone structure. All of the rest has gone. So there is really a new part of the process here; my name is much more permanent, and my glasses. And my glasses weren't built in with me when I was born. So it is interesting that even my hair which I cut off isn't as much a part of me as my glasses which I keep with me. And they were not actually born with me." Buckminster Fuller, lecture (Institute of Design, Chicago, February 1948), BFP Series 8, Box 8, Folder 3, p. 12.

127 Robert Anton Wilson, "Interview, R. Buckminster Fuller," 78 (see note 11).

128 "Inaugurating a new individual life which, like a telephone message, weighs nothing in itself but makes itself 'known' by a complex pattern of orderly local physical environment displacements, which—as the circular wave emanating in any liquid such as water, milk or kerosene, from the impact of an object dropped into the liquid—grows or expands regeneratively." Buckminster Fuller, "How Little I Know," 29 (see note 123).

129 "Man is essential to the universe, and we observe in the universe design that the essential functions are provided in an enormous abundance—particularly in the biological. [...] If man is essential in the universe, there are probably a great many planets in the universe on which there are men," Buckminster Fuller, "An Address, given at the 2nd Annual Meeting of the Industrial Designers Society," *Journal of Environmental Design* 2, no. 2 (1967): 18.

130 "Possibly as the synergetic totality / Of all the gravitation / And radiation effects / Of all the stars / In our galaxy / And from all the adjacent galaxies." Buckminster Fuller, "How Little I Know," *And it Came to Pass* (New York: Macmillan, 1976), 56. Fuller had long argued that the complexity of the human organism was rivalled only by the universe itself and that therefore it must have a very special purpose.

131 Fuller, "Earth Inc.," 6 (see note 80).

132 Ibid., 12.

133 Buckminster Fuller, foreword to *Out of This World: American Space Photography*, by Paul Dickson (New York: Dell, 1977), xi.

134 "Even though human beings fool themselves into believing so, they do not build structures with materials. We must now recognize that man assembles *visible module structures* with *sub-visible module electro-magnetic fields and atomic events*. Physics has failed to discover solids, or continuous surfaces, or straight lines, or any reducible to energy." Buckminster Fuller, "Architecture as Ultra Invisible Reality," in *Structure and Technology in the World of the Future*, ed. Arthur Bronwell (New York: John Wiley, 1970), 157.

135 Buckminster Fuller, "R. Buckminster Fuller Talks about Transparency," *House Beautiful*, September 1968, 92.

136 Ibid., 209.

137 Ibid., 94.

138 Fuller continues: "Several hundred thousand different wide-band radio sets can at any time be tuned in anywhere around our biosphere to as many different communications. Going right through our heads now, these programs could be tuned in by the right crystals and circuits. [...] Such arrays could operate even within our brains. [...] For humans to have within their cerebral mechanism the proper atomic radio transceivers to carry on telepathic communication is no more incredible than the transistors which were invented only two decades ago." Buckminster Fuller, introduction to *Expanded Cinema*, by Gene Youngblood (Toronto: Clarke, Irwin and Co., 1970), 26. See also Buckminster Fuller, "Man's Total Communication System," *Evergreen*, October 1970, 39.

139 Buckminster Fuller, "This is the New Invisible World," *TV Guide*, February 6, 1971, 12.

140 Fuller, "Critical Path Part Four," *Critical Path*, 341 (see note 6).

collection of photographs of the American space program, Fuller again insisted that we don't move as objects through space. Rather, we "tune" in or out to particular wavelengths. There are no impervious self-contained objects: "Physics finds that the universe has no solid *things* surrounded by and interspersed with space."[133] Fuller relentlessly undermined the illusion of solidity which traditional architecture is called on to reinforce.[134]

The unsuspecting readers of the September 1968 issue of *House Beautiful* were told that their visible "skin-packaged" body is not their real "weightless" person. All objects and people are streams of energy. In the same way that the atoms in transparent materials have "ample room" to let light waves through, "surprising our scientifically unfounded and only superficially engendered concept of *solidness*,"[135] opaque materials are porous enough to let invisible radio waves through: "at any and all times anywhere around our planet we can now tune in each of many thousands of different wideband radio sets into as many different live programs."[136] Everything is porous to invisible flows and is itself a form of flow. Architecture is always perforated and takes its real structure from hidden patterns. It was just a matter of time before "electric-field controls will make invisible walls" and telepathy would prove to be "ultra, ultra, ultra-high frequency, electromagnetic, brain-wave propagated and transceived images."[137] Building would become brain and brain become building.

Fuller's introduction to Gene Youngblood's pivotal 1970 book *Expanded Cinema* describes the idea of telepathy through miniature radios implanted in the brain as "good science fiction." The traditional concept of solidity is once again dismissed as concentrating on seemingly static surfaces that are but a minute fraction of the universe and are anyway neither static nor solid:

> Society fails to realize that several hundred thousand radio or TV communications are at all times invisibly present everywhere around our planet. They permeate every room in every building—passing right through walls and human tissue. This is to say that the stone walls and human tissue are invisible and nonexistent to the electromagnetic wave reality. We only deceived ourselves into reflexing that walls are solid.[138]

Humans, buildings, planet, and universe were redefined as communication systems. Radio passing through walls was evidence that people could, too. The ultimate ephemerality of the body was inseparable from the ultimate ephemerality of buildings. Telepathy was simply the thought that the brain was already a broadcast system generating its own electromagnetic waves. People don't communicate. People are communication. As Fuller put in in 1971: "Now, the touchable me is not the real me. What I really *am* is my communication, which is absolutely weightless. That's a program going over the set, but it isn't the set."[139] The human brain was later described as a radio transmitter producing electromagnetic waves, "exquisitely ephemeral but exquisitely real," that could even be picked up by orbiting satellites to allow real-time democracy by monitoring the unconscious reactions of everybody on the planet to important questions requiring collective decisions.[140] The idea updated the 1942 concept of voting by wireless in "Motion Economics," which speculated that key questions would be broadcast globally by wireless and telephone and responded to by world citizens in real time using the same technologies. Thirty years later, even the technical infrastructure of radio networks would not be needed as the brain's own transmissions would suffice. Fuller wrote an article in the *New York Times* listing this concept as one of his 10 proposed solutions for improving the world in 1972.[141] Thought itself is treated as an environmental layer of radio broadcasts.

Having already embraced the idea of telepathy in his very first manuscript of May 1928, when "Cosmopolitan Homes Corporation: Lightful Products" reassured the reader that of course we can inaudibly broadcast into one another's minds,[142] Fuller increasingly entertained the idea during his last lectures and texts, as, for example, during the remarkable attempt to summarize all his thinking in the epic series on "Everything I Know" in January 1975. Once again, the perpetually animated performance artist who never hesitated to hop excitedly around or roll on the floor used his own body and the room he was in as the model of the universe and once again the illusion of a singular static solid human body was associated with the fluidity of radio:

> In going through any room we might be in, if you could introduce a couple of million radio sets, wide-band radio sets, each one could be tuned in on a different, there are over two million programs in this room right now, if you have the right machine turned on. There is right here in this room, coming from the satellites, the sensor satellites going around this Earth, is, in this room a program which will tell you where every beef cattle on our Earth is right now. How many there are. That's the new reality. [...] I am now going to point out to you that, in my lifetime, at very close to 80, I've quite a long time and when I was 70 I had already processed over 1,000 tons of food, air and water, which I brought temporarily together to form my hair and my skin, and it got rubbed off and so forth. I've actually processed that many tons. I weighed into the scene of humanity at 7 pounds. I got to be 70 pounds, I got to be 170, I got up to 207. Then I took off 70 pounds and I said, "who's that, cause here I am?" Obviously that was not me. So what of that physical ever was me? [...] We are just pattern integrities, and pattern integrities are conceptual. They can be very high frequency, but we have all kind of high-frequency phenomena. Therefore I see no reason why I couldn't send you from here to there in the Universe by radio, by simply scanning your frequency.[143]

Despite the remarkable fact that most of the thousands of newspaper and magazine articles on Fuller begin with a detailed description of his

141 "World democracy is to be incorruptibly accommodated by continual electronic referendum, being progressively fed by subconsciously telepathic ultra-ultra-high frequency wave propagation, signaling subconsciously reflexed feedback attitudes toward specific propositions coping with evolutionary problems as educationally manifest." Buckminster Fuller, "10 Proposed Solutions for Improving World," *The New York Times*, June 29, 1972, 41.

142 "Of course we can talk inaudibly for great or short distances according to the intensity of our broadcasting into other people's minds, just fourth dimension, there is nothing to the space to be spanned but time." Fuller, "Cosmopolitan Homes Corporation: Lightful Products," 60 (see note 77).

143 Fuller, "Everything I Know," Session 3, Part 6 (see note 2). "We have rockets now; next they may send you around by radio." Buckminster Fuller lecture, quoted in Michael Kernan, "Buckminster Fuller, The Magnetic Presence," *The Washington Post*, February 11, 1976, C2.

144 "By 1985 we should be able to transmit humans around the globe by radio scanning or an equivalently unexpected means." Fuller, "Critical Path Part Two," *Critical Path*, 245 (see note 6).

145 "The mention of the word 'architecture' reminds me, that as soon as we have adjusted people to our 4D purposes, we will drop the use of 'architecture' in conjunction with 4D designing." Buckminster Fuller to Paul Nelson, 10 August 1928, quoted in Fuller, *4D Time Lock*, 85 (see note 27).

idiosyncratic body and the agitated way it moves across the floor and around the world, and despite the fact that he was so often photographed like a dancer in movement, and despite the fact that he was the designer whose body was most associated with his models and structures in countless staged juxtapositions, and despite the fact that his head even appeared as one of his buildings on the cover of *Time*, and despite the fact that he himself based all his lectures and texts on his experience of his own body—especially on the experience of its limitations with very poor sight and hearing—his whole point in the end was that the body is just a transitional symptom of radio. **fig. 44**

The complete diffusion of brain, body, and building into each other as a radio message, which one of Fuller's last books predicts will happen within just a few years,[144] was already implied in his very first texts. Relocating architecture to the electromagnetic spectrum inevitably meant the loss of what the discipline of architecture most protects. Fuller's first self-published text that documents his presentation of the 4D House to the American Institute of Architects annual convention in May 1928 speaks of the need to abandon the very word *architecture* in such projects.[145] The unfavorable reaction cannot have been such a surprise. He wanted his designs to be transitional structures that try to bond with the logic of radio communication to ease the passage into the invisible.

44

44 RBF at work on the floor in London with DNA-RNA group, 1955

Architecture was being asked to undo itself, as becomes clear in the 1970 text on "Architecture as Ultra Invisible Reality" that calls for an "utterly invisible aesthetics":

> Architecture, for example, will be an unobtrusive part of a vastly larger preoccupation of world society with life in universe. When successful, tomorrow's architecture will be approximately invisible—not just figuratively speaking, but literally as well. What will count with world-man is how well the architecture serves humanity while sublimating itself spontaneously. Architecture may be accomplished tomorrow with electrical fields and other utterly invisible environment controls.[146]

Fuller worked toward this new sense of unseen architecture by steadily removing all vestiges of traditional building. The field was stripped to the bones and then even the bones got thinned and then rejected. The few remaining elements were tormented, reworked, and literally weighed before being readmitted. The building aspired to be as ephemeral as possible. A relentless project of dematerialization took the Dymaxion House from a lightweight vehicle in the twenties to being all window in the forties to being a cloud in the sixties on the edge of the ultimate ambition of being all signal. Yet the invisible architecture Fuller sought was to be found rather than invented. It might already be fully operational, as he told a journalist:

> I think that concepts of architecture have gone through and are as yet to go through great transformation. What humans a century hence will identify retrospectively as what they consider to be the architecture of the late twentieth century may not as yet have been so recognized in 1972.[147]

What Fuller was designing is ultimately a change of perspective, a paradigm shift. Architecture must literally disappear. Yet architecture is the only discipline able to see what comes next. He used a 1932 issue of *Architectural Forum* to insist that "the architect's future is now" through anonymous collaborative scientific investigation of shelter in collaboration with the media, yet carefully placed the words *architect* and *architecture* in quotation marks.[148] Two years later, highly refined studio photographs of the Dymaxion House models were shown in an issue of the art journal *Trend* but Fuller argued that only after many years would it possible to understand what really was the architecture being built in this age. Architecture can only be seen in the rearview mirror: "It is impossible to consciously create architecture. To profess architecture is, then presumptuous and fallacious, though a professor of architecture might unselfconsciously create what in time would be discernible as architecture."[149] It was not designed as such. It was an unconscious effect of collaborative intelligence that only later became recognizable. Architecture is always a retroactive judgment

146 Fuller, "Architecture as Ultra Invisible Reality," 153 (see note 134). "The little grey boxes of electronic circuitry disclose functioning containing therein as the latter perform a host of invisible talks conducted at invisible speeds. [...] The functions of today are almost exclusively invisible. To follow the functioning realistically, tomorrow's architecture must also become invisible." Ibid., 154.

147 Buckminster Fuller, response to journalist at Delos Symposion, in *Synergetics Dictionary: The Mind of Buckminster Fuller*, ed. E. J. Applewhite (New York: Garland, 1986), vol. 10, entry 8872.

148 Buckminster Fuller, "The Architect's Future Is Now," *Architectural Forum*, August 1932, 92.

149 Buckminster Fuller, "Industrially Reproducible Architecture," *Trend: An Illustrated Bi-Monthly of the Arts*, May–June, 1934, 118.

150 Ibid., 121.

151 Fuller, "Philosophy, Invention, Experience," 27 (see note 14).

and remains "continually something of the past." Yet the reference point is clear, the emergent invisible "web" of immaterial global networks, from airline trajectories to wireless:

> Possibly the architecture of today will in time be evident as the air routes, as the great network of transportation, a web which is knitting closely together all the peoples on the small globe 'World.' [...] The world is now so closely knit in the matter of communication by publishing or wireless that if we assay to a proper contemplation of the architecture now in the making it is necessary to take into consideration all the structural expressions upon the surface of the globe, the complete survival mechanism as articulated in the industrial intercoursing. [...] The surfaces most evident to the eye are the least important in the contemplation.[150]

Fuller went on to say that the key is the brain, the evolutionary rather than revolutionary intellect of the "non-self-styled architect" that can do the most with the least in a relentless process of refinement through selection. The architecture for the age of radio could not be self-consciously designed as such but if designers abandoned the hangovers of their worst habits, particularly their addiction to the visible surfaces of singular objects, they could go from being the loyal assistants of an unsustainable and unjust use of global resources to acting as incubators of a transformative paradigm shift that might retroactively be seen as architecture. Such a paradigm shift actually requires the figure of the architect. When lecturing to a group of architects in Boston in 1968, Fuller again criticized everything about current professional practice but noted that species become extinct through overspecialization and that architects constitute the "last species of comprehensivists."[151] The multidimensional synthesis at the heart of the field is the most invaluable asset, not just for thinking about the future of buildings but for thinking about the universe. Paradoxically, it is precisely when going beyond buildings that the figure of the architect becomes essential. It is the brain of the architect that becomes the ultimate architecture of the radio age.

For more than half a century, Fuller kept repeating this one destabilizing idea, continuously reworking the basic argument in an unprecedented

45

45 RBF in all-day conversation with Werner Erhard, Masonic Center, San Francisco, January 15, 1977

46

46 RBF lecturing, suspended between models and map

number of venues. It was to an extraordinary degree a single coherent project. Fuller never strayed far from his very first manuscript, the remarkable "Cosmopolitan Homes Corporation: Lightful Products." In fact, he kept going deeper and deeper into it. The project to transform everything by rethinking the idea of shelter in the name of radio worked by restlessly circling a set of key points already written into the first text. It is a project best understood by listening to the countless repetitions, tuning in to the almost hypnotic chanting of mantras in a steady rhythm to hear the nuances that produced a sense of momentum. It was a breathless performance. **figs. 45 and 46** Fuller always had just arrived and was just about to leave—wearing three watches, one for his home time zone on the East Coast of the United States, one for the zone he was in, and one for the time zone he was about to be in.[152] No place or medium was off limits.

> I find myself being asked to meet weekly with and to "think out loud" before an average of three audiences of 2,000, and totaling 6,000 persons, and the numbers are swiftly increasing. In addition to these direct face-to-face audiences, I am averaging six local radio and television broadcasts a week, and twelve transcontinental TV programs in some country around the world.[153]

Fuller was proud of talking at 7,000 words per hour and would even speed up for important occasions. Lectures went for hours into days. Sentences went from paragraphs into pages. One sentence even became a whole book. Never were so many words used to advocate using the least resources. But the real mission of the chain of hard-core yet always incomplete domestic experiments at the heart of this unique propaganda campaign was simply to try to give shape to expansive integrative thinking as the most vital form of radiation. The last pages of the last chapter of Fuller's last book manuscript (posthumously published as *Cosmography*) inevitably returned to the arrival of radio into the average house in 1927 as "a *number-one* anthropological evolution event." It permanently transformed human interrelations through the "radio-amplified authority" of disembodied voices that liberated global thinking and embedded thought itself in the unrestrained spread of electromagnetic radiation traveling on and on through the universe without limit at 700 million miles per hour.[154] The unparalleled gift of Fuller's continuous streams of reflection was likewise to continually and radically change the scale at which we think, and his signal was remarkably consistent from beginning to end. It was ultimately a single broadcast, transmitted over countless channels and still live today. The signal is about architecture and aims to dissolve architecture, yet equally it empowers the collective brain of a future species of architect in, for, and through the age of radio.

152 Richard Cheverton, "'Bucky' Fuller: Visions of Stars and Immortality," *Chicago Tribune*, October 20, 1976, A5.
153 Buckminster Fuller, "Interview with Michael Ben-Eli," *Architectural Design* 42 (December 1972): 750.
154 Buckminster Fuller, *Cosmography: A Posthumous Scenario for the Future of Humanity* (New York: Macmillan, 1992), 255.

47 RBF heading into video recording session of “Everything I Know,” Bell Television Studios, Philadelphia, January 1975

VII

VII World citizen floating in her radically autonomous space capsule, cardboard model of Dymaxion House, early 1929

PIPELESS DREAMS

Our buildings, like ourselves, are filled with pipes. Water, gas, electrici and information flow inside walls, floors, and ceilings, crisscrossing basements and running across rooftops. A complex, interconnected net of tubes supports each space, from the largest waste pipes to the finest wires. Yet these tubes are rarely allowed to enter the space. They are asked to bring things in or take things away but are meant to remain outside. A pipe can enter a room if concealed. It can even assume a theatrically baroque intensity of pattern, like the intricately twisted condenser coils behind a fridge. But any visible tube, even a steam pipe gently folded into a radiator, is destined to be carefully veiled in its own architectural enclosure or replaced as an embarrassin vestige of a more primitive time. Suspended ceilings and elevated floors smoothly evict much of the ever-denser spaghetti of ductwork by simply reducing the perceived dimension of the room. Pipes must always be close to us yet unseen and unheard. A huge effort is made so that the sound of movement within them cannot enter. No evidence of flow is allowed. No rustle, gurgle, whoosh, hum, shudder, click, or thud. An appliance literally filled with pipes and pumps, like a dishwasher, tries to blend into the architecture, hide every vibration, and make no sound, as if magically taking waste outside. The end of a pipe can momentarily appear above a sink, but only if veiled with chrome and design in a fitting meant to reinforce the room not the plumbing. It becomes a work of architecture in its own right, a little building, while the pipe itself must remain behind or below.

The newer smaller, more flexible pipes are not so welcome either. Another huge effort is devoted to hiding all the electrical cords that feed our ever-expanding array of equipment and devices. Even the thinnest wire connecting the mouse to the computer is no longer acceptable. The computer itself wants to disappear into a portable screen, attached more to our body than our buildings. Millions of shor white wires are purchased to support the wireless dream. And most of the signals end up flowing through the ever-higher-capacity fiber-optic cables that keep being laid under the oceans. No satellite can compete with these submerged three-inch-diameter tubes with just a half-inch core filled with some tiny tubes for the flow of lig Our increasingly wireless world is increasingly wired. In a seemingly desperate feedback loop, we demand more and more tubes with more and more capacity occupying more and more of our environment yet with less and less visibility. Every kind of pipe gets upgraded, carries more, reaches further, and embarrasses more. As with those in our own bodies, pipes in buildings are sites of intense and complicated psychological investments.

One of the paradoxical symptoms of the ever-expanding empire of the pipe is the call to hide pipes. Frank Lloyd Wright's 1954 book *The Natural House*, for example, notes that he had entered the field of architecture in 1887 just when pipes had permanently taken up residence inside buildings, transforming their very capacity to support life: "Bowels, circulation, and nerves were new in buildings. But they had come to stay and a building could not longer remain a mere shell in which life was somehow to make shift as it might."[1] Wright became a pioneer in electrical fittings and an innovator with ventilation and heating systems but equally an expert in veiling those systems. The surfaces of most of his rooms are discretely perforated. Openings for light, air, heat, and electricity are woven into the lining as an integral part of the decorative system since it would be so unnatural to expose the pipes that support the natural house: "Wiring for lights, as piping for plumbing and heating, should not show all over the house unless by special design—any more than you would have organs of your body on the outside of your skin. Lighting fixtures should (as should all others) be absorbed *in* the structure, so that their office is *of* the structure."[2] To confront the inside of your building would be to confront the inside of your body. The architect must offer a reassuring veil over the pulsing liquid complexity of the metabolism of both building and body.

Architecture itself might be largely defined by this psychosexual ecology. After all, the basic definition of *interior* is now less to do with walls, doors, and windows and more with the countless valves that regulate the flows in all the tubes and the array of orifices through which material is allowed to enter and leave our spaces. The ever-multiplying vents, sockets, diffusers, switches, and control panels have become exercises in the detailing of discretion. The traditional function of architectural molding to preserve the sense of a secure interior and coherent identity by hiding the inevitable cracks between floor, wall, and ceiling is now concentrated on all the little openings where pipe meets room. Extreme attention is devoted to making the countless perforations in the lining of our spaces seem to be part of the lining rather than threatening openings. Seemingly simple, smooth, continuous surfaces are desired. Simplicity itself is a goal. No building form is as complex as the systems that service it or the activities it services. Architecture is an act of simplification or of veiling complexity. It is dedicated to the skin more than it can ever acknowledge. Perhaps nothing can be as thin as architecture, the art of suspending perforated surfaces within a myriad of flows to paradoxically represent seamless solidity.

The place where the oldest form of pipe surfaces, and where the pipes inside the body are most directly connected to the pipes inside the building, is where the psychosexual drama of the pipe is greatest. To sit on a toilet is literally to sit on a pipe. The pipe has widened itself to become a piece of furniture but remains unambiguously a pipe. The body literally occupies the pipe. More precisely, it is suspended within the pipe, hovering in a gap opened up in an otherwise continuous circuit of water flow, suspended in a space defined by valves. The same is true of the bath, the shower, and the sink, where pipes widen to receive the body and valves regulate the flow to sustain a space that can be entered. The fear of overflow always remains, so the whole room has a drain. The room itself is just an enlarged pipe. Or rather, it is the intersection of enlarged pipes, since yet another orifice in the ceiling discretely pulls moisture and smells into its tubes. It is not so much a room serviced by pipes as the widening of pipes to form a room. To enter the bathroom is literally to enter the otherwise hidden cavities of the building itself, the inside of the inside. Not by chance does the room have the only internal door that always can be locked. The flush more emphatically defines the attempt to draw a line between inside and outside than any front door.

Yet the same suspension of the body in a space that is defined by valves, filters, diffusers, pumps, sensors, and switches occurs whenever air is simply brought in through one vent and drawn out through another. Any room is part of a pipe or the intersection of a number of pipes. Space has become an effect of an intricate choreography of valves. For all the nervous desire to repress pipes, such that each visible pipe is treated as a unique dramatic event, architecture is ever more piped. The increased interest in energy efficiency and passive technologies has only heightened the awareness of the continuous flows in all spaces. The trauma or exhilaration, or exhilarating trauma, of being inside a pipe that people feel in a tunnel, elevator, airplane, or even a hallway, now lurks in seemingly static spaces. Whole new forms of pipe are being added as buildings rest on buried forests of geothermal pipes, recover energy from exhaust air with heat pipes, heat water on their rooftops, heat floors with embedded tubes, cool skyscrapers with vast ice-making plants, and so on. And the patterns of flow have become ever more complicated with the design of convection systems, the recirculation of gray water, and sending gains from solar energy back into the grid. More and more meters read all the flows. The different systems of tubes now monitor one another, with all the overlapping layers of pipe increasingly treated as a single interactive ecological system that includes the occupants.

Pipes take an ever-greater proportion of the space and cost of a building. The architect's dependence on pipe expertise has gone from that of the plumber to an army of specialists, engineers, and consultants. Integrated software platforms have become essential to accommodate the ever-greater variety, density, complexity, sophistication, and interconnectedness of pipes. A drawing of all the pipes in a building is more complex than a drawing of a city. Architects are sometimes trusted with cities but almost never with pipes. The design, fabrication, assembly, monitoring, and maintenance of this intense dance of pipes has become its own art form, with the architect still focused on keeping it all secret.

Pipeless architecture is now unthinkable yet remains the default organizing fantasy of the discipline. Pipes are installed in the unconscious of architecture. They are as hidden in architectural education as they are in buildings. No student will be asked about the pipes in their final project. Knowledge about the usually hidden world of structure is seen as a vital part of any architect's identity, and plays at least a bit part in most conversations, but the world of pipes is a zone of silence, a source of embarrassment at best. The silence is getting louder as the number of pipes increases. The architect is fully aware of all the pipes in trying to veil them, but doesn't even present this veiling as an art form. The veiling is itself veiled. There is a kind of disciplinary hygiene with the world of pipes discussed as little as what happens in the bathroom.

Yet the ever-expanding repressed world of pipes always has its leaks, blockages, and occasional overflows. The building and the discipline periodically gets covered in what it wants to exclude. No repression is ever complete. Pipes sometimes burst into architectural discourse, with designers appearing to eagerly embrace them. They can become features of buildings, even the basic principle. But just as those visible pipes are treated as an event—one set of pipes being theatrically hyperexposed while most of the pipes in the building remain hidden—that building, or even a series of such buildings, becomes an isolated theatrical event in the discipline while most buildings continue to disavow their pipes. In the paradoxical complexity of desire, the very allure of a few exposed pipes—the palpable sense of an illicit encounter—reinforces the default need to bury them. An exposed

1 The hidden intestinal world of tubes. BIM model of piping systems in a building by DPR Construction, 2011

air-conditioning duct will never entice a sewer pipe to the surface. On the contrary. And even the exposed pipe is usually in a new dress. It may be wearing very little—a veneer of bright color, more precisely aligned rivets, designer gaskets—but this sexy outfit that claims the pipe for architecture remains a veil. The same pipe becomes something different when it disappears back inside the building and back to the care of other experts. The dirty secret remains.

The real crime of the pipes is their own fluidity. The tubes that are crucial in sustaining and even making possible the spatial logic installed by the architect relentlessly violate that logic. They exceed the law they maintain. They are a kind of excess, a restless promiscuity that must be veiled, a nest of snakes slithering around in the crevices, entering and leaving the building unobserved, and connecting the building to those around it through ever-larger pipes that reach into the distance, gathering ever more built and social fabric together, subordinating the architect's statement. The world of pipes doesn't only fill the building with secret flows. It turns the whole building into just an elegant fitting, a valve attached to a vast infrastructural net, a designer valve that tries not look to like a valve for fear of pointing to the buried world. If you put your finger inside a faucet, its cool inner surface reaches all the way to a lake in the mountains. Likewise the surface of the sink below reaches all the way to a river or ocean. But equally the surface reaches every other faucet, sink, tub and appliance in the region. All the hidden pipes are interconnected to one another to form a single massive interior space crossing the landscape that infantilizes any building it services. Buildings are constructed on that vast web of pipes rather than a piece of land, and the land itself is increasingly an artifact sustained by pipes, with one set of buried tubes watering the soil when dry and another set catching the runoff when wet. Every garden is plumbed and wired. Hidden sensors increasingly define and maintain the effect of property. The interior defined by the plastic casing of even the smallest wire feeding a room ultimately stretches across the whole continent as the vast web of the electrical grid with individual territory defined by meters rather than walls. The nervousness about pipes is at once personal, social, and political. The pipes that define individual identity also define ever-larger scales of shared identity. The valves that isolate also connect. The very status of private and public is increasingly a question of plumbing. It is the hidden tubes that increasingly draw the key lines. For all our dreams of pipeless space, we are literally organized by the pipes we would rather not talk about.

1 Frank Lloyd Wright, *The Natural House* (New York: Horizon Press, 1954), 15.
2 Ibid., 155.
3 Buckminster Fuller, "Universal Conditions of the Industrially Reproducible Shelter," *T-Square* 2, no. 2 (February 1932): 38.
4 Buckminster Fuller, "Cosmopolitan Homes Corporation: Lightful Products," BFP Series 8, Box 2, Folder 1, p. 4.
5 Buckminster Fuller, *4D Time Lock* (self-published, 1928), 5.
6 Ibid.

No figure more fully captures this psychosexual and political enigma of pipes than Buckminster Fuller. He saw a genuinely modern architecture as nothing but an optimized set of mechanical services. He wanted everything exposed, even including "repression proofing" and "no secrets" in his 1932 list of the basic requirements of shelter, and he literally thought of buildings as valves. Yet he took every opportunity to condemn the world of the plumber, hated the idea of pipes connecting buildings to one another, dreamed of a world beyond pipes, and was hyperobsessed with the cleanliness of toilets. His whole project was about the elimination of waste. Even the relentless attempt "to do the most with the least" was itself understood as a form of mental hygiene. In Fuller's list, the basic requirement of unselfconscious mechanical routines of "refusing" in shelters symptomatically includes mental "elimination by empirical dynamics" alongside "intestinal," "pore cleansing," and "atmospheric control."[3] Cleaning the body, the building, the air, and the mind were inseparable.

Fuller's designs were always organized around a concentrated core of flow management, with the bathroom at the very center. Starting in the early months of 1928, all the versions of what would a year later be called the Dymaxion House have the plumbing compacted into a central shaft for the circulation of light, heat, cooling, water, waste, electricity, ventilation, and people. **fig. 2** The aluminum mast from which the whole structure would hang is a "distributing tube" embedded in a buried cylindrical foundation containing the house's independent sewage, water, oil, and gas tanks. The building must be "absolutely self-supporting" in every sense. It would arrive on the site by air and remain detached from all the fixed lines of roads, sewers, water pipes, and electrical cables. The whole world of the pipe needs to be mastered by the architect, treated as the very heart of architecture, and then left behind. "Cosmopolitan Homes Corporation: Lightful Products," the early 1928 draft of Fuller's first book on the design, denounces "plumbers, putting in the pipes, who would insist on the design being changed to their rules" and imagines the possibility of new concepts like "self-turning-on plumbing."[4] Plumbing has to be reduced, perfected, self-organizing, isolated, and transcended. The whole house literally would hang from a pipe but stage an escape from the world of pipes. *4D Time Lock*, the final version of the book that was self-published later the same year, already specifies that the direct connections of "steam pipes, electrical wires, etc." in the new house would be "supplemented" by "indirect central broadcasting systems" establishing invisible connections by radio and television.[5] The ambition of the building was to be suspended in omnidirectional flows unrestrained by plumbing lines. These unrestricted flows wouldn't just supplement the structure. They were the very point of the structure, the future of the structure, the future of architecture, even of technology itself. The general trajectory of human capacity is "from track to trackless, wire to wireless,"[6] and Fuller would later add "from pipe to pipeless" to the mantra. Plumbing is the first task in a building and the first thing to be left behind.

In *Nine Chains to the Moon: An Adventure in the Story of Thought* of 1938, Fuller's first formal book, the short list of things that cause abnormal human behavior and sustain the modern professions of psychology and psychc analysis begins with "bad plumbing of house or self-mechanism."[7] Pipes ir people, buildings, and cities are the sites of all forms of blockage. Improvec plumbing and attention to "intestinal habits" is the necessary beginnin of truly scientific dwelling.[8] But pipes themselves are always problematic All the usual electrical, water, sewage, and communication systems tha restrict physical, economic, and political mobility have to go.[9]

It is not by chance that the book begins by contrasting the frustratin congestion in the "arterial hook-ups" within and between houses with th "magical" ability of radio to jump instantly to anyplace in the world. Fulle had long been using the mobility, connectivity, and globality of radic as the model for a new shelter industry disconnected from any "arteria system" that ties architecture to the land and the regressive concept o property. Radio starts when pipes stop. The whole planet or, more precise ly, the atmosphere of the planet, becomes the only architectural site. Th bond with the land gives way to a bond with ideas. Traditional plumbin systems block the brain and restrain it from acting in the world, as Fulle told a group of architects in New York in July 1929:

> Now, it is very clear that as long as any two of us have to share the same ston ach, literally having a pipe between our stomachs, so far as our being reall individual, proceeding in the realization of truths as our intelligence present them, we would be licked in putting them into effect.[10]

The evolution of intelligence itself requires the disconnected stomach The picture of "humans linked together by group stomachs and nervou systems as Siamese Millionuplets attempting to develop self or commu nity in relation to the dictates or their intelligence and faith" was intolera ble to Fuller, as he insisted in 1932.[11] Pipes are seen to repress both th individual and the social. They have to be abandoned as the accomplice of both the capitalist ideal of individualism and the communist idea of sharing. The desired Dymaxion alternative is a philosophy of "sel sustaining mobile single-cell production" through separate and indeper dent mechanical equipment.[12]

The real problem with pipes for Fuller is that they are lines, fixed cor duits going from A to B, a constraining of movement to one path. In reverse the problem with all fixed lines is that they function as pipes. A highwa or rail line, for example, is actually a pipe—a repressive tube imprisonin those traveling within it. Fuller's main project was to go from lines to th directionless four-dimensional space of mobility invisibly defined by radic

7 Buckminster Fuller, *Nine Chains to the Moon* (Philadelphia: Lippincott, 1938), 7.
8 Ibid., 324.
9 "They are designed to be dependent primarily on arterial hook-ups with politically or privately monopolized power, light, water, sewage, and communication lines, and are therefore limited to placement within the environs of urban developments, and therefore subject to super-imposition of high realty costs and town assessments [...] constituting, in most states, permanent improvements of the underlying land property." Ibid., 328.
10 Buckminster Fuller, "Dymaxion House Meeting, Architectural League, New York, Tuesday July 9, 1929," in *Your Private Sky: Discourse*, ed. Joachim Krausse and Claude Lichtenstein (Zurich: Lars Müller, 2001), 86.
11 Buckminster Fuller, "Universal Architecture: Essay No. 2," *Shelter* 2, no. 3 (April 1932): 32.
12 Ibid.
13 Buckminster Fuller, "Life of R. Buckminster Fuller for the Harvard '17 Class Reunion," June 1942, BFP Series 8, Box 5, Folder 2, p. 7.
14 "It is a defensible theory that man's security lies not in getting his 'roots into the ground' as the economic moralist of recent years would have it, but contrariwise in his potential mobility to agilely dodge blows and quickly to place himself in [an] environmental position to secure livelihood where his services are needed. This is not gypsy-like mobility for mobility's sake but potential mobility for security's sake as practiced by our pioneer forefathers." Ibid., 13.
15 Ibid.
16 "The 1917 World War forced governments to underwrite just such compound inventions—notably the airplane and the radio which would otherwise still remain but rich sportsmen's toys." Buckminster Fuller, "The Ballistics of Civilization," manuscript dated March 13,

Under the shadow of World War II and literally in blackout conditions, Fuller tried to persuade his classmates at the twenty-fifth reunion of the Harvard class of '17 in 1942 that they were the lucky generation, using radio as his prime example. Despite the loss of so many of the class in World War I, they were fortunate to be the first to engage the "entirely new kind of world" produced by that war. Before the conflict, the radio telegraph had "buzzed communication" across the Atlantic for the first time and "the wireless and trackless had potentially opened up limitless new dimensions of man's practical universe."[13] Yet it took the war to activate that potential, eventually leading to the arrival of the once "preposterous" dream but now everyday reality of popular radio with its ubiquitous "voice in the air." A completely wireless world had become possible but would only be fully realized when the static world of lines was finally abandoned. Reversing the conventional idea that fixed lines in the ground produce security, Fuller argued that real security actually comes from the physical and mental mobility that transcends any line. The traditional concept of roots in the ground" becomes vulnerability rather than strength. Nomadic movement becomes the safest and most social mode.[14] The ability to position oneself wherever opportunity lies would make for a more secure, efficient, cosmopolitan, and productive planet. The transformation from the world of lines—exemplified by the prewar technology of sending a message from A to B through a cable, as in literally sending a "cable"—to the postwar world of omnidirectional communication and radical mobility—exemplified by radio—was the key to mankind's security. Leaving lines behind and embracing the radical connectivity of radio was the only way to avoid another war like the one they were already in.

> If concerning the validity of this theory of security through potential mobility, it is then interesting to note what the statistics of man's mobility increase, as mind and body have been since 1913. We know concerning his message communicating ability increase, for instance, that when we of '17 were eight years old he completed the cable circuit of the world and a message could be relayed about the globe in 12 minutes. But this was from spot to spot, on the cable line only, connecting but a minor fraction of people, requiring thousands of tons of cable, enormous energy expenditure, and the maintenance work of thousands of men. Today the radio amateur with his 1 k.w. trans-ceiver set which, even with motor generator, need not weigh over 200 lbs., can at most times talk to any other amateur anywhere on Earth.[15]

It is as if war had finally perfected a technology that could defeat the logic of fixed lines that cause war. Fuller called on his class to use all their various skills to help turn this potential into a reality, as if completing their assigned task as the radio generation. They were able to shape themselves against war precisely because they had been shaped by war. Having been "explosively hurled forth into World War 1," they "might well be termed The Ballistic Class" with a special capacity to impact things over the horizon.

Fuller was constantly mapping the "ballistic" trajectory of technology into the near future, with radio and aviation as his key reference points for the accelerating emergence of the "trackless wireless" world.[16] He argued in a key conference presentation in 1949 that the house itself would soon be "like a shot [...] impelled violently forward" in an evolutionary leap that would defy expectations because technology itself cannot be channeled down any line.[17] Every channel, even that of a historical trend, is a restraint that will eventually burst. Fuller had just radicalized his house to the extreme—editing it down into just a thin, transparent plastic membrane stretched across a geodesic dome supported by a compact service package—an ephemeral image that was no longer recognizable as a house. He told the audience that overall global expansion of the technological capacity of humans up to that point was impressive but had only occurred in a "veined or linear manner [...] dependent upon piped, wired, tracked paths. Dynamically speaking, his linear paths are all pipes—his car or his train is a section of pipe surrounding him, which section moves progressively to enclose him."[18] The body, the social organism, and thought itself had been continuously piped. Again, future evolution of human capacity needs to be "omnidirectional by wireless, trackless, and pipeless" systems.[19] The pipeless house would be both the consequence of leaving pipes behind and the platform for an even more radical leap beyond pipes.

Fuller never stopped repeating the point that the infrastructural plumbing lines of transport and communication around the globe had enabled a huge expansion in man's "ecological sweep out" since the mid-nineteenth century but that these pipes would burst as "the velocity of integration and increased energy flow leads to an arterial cloggage and explosive high pressure," as he put it in 1950.[20] **fig. 3** They must be transcended by systems that support movement in any direction, at any time, with any acceleration. Lines marked on the surface of the planet must give way to the unmarked volume of its atmosphere "allowing man to choose when and how and where he wishes to move." Fuller's lifelong model was the ship with its autonomous support systems—literally immersed in the ever-shifting flows of air, water, and information. The hyperexpanded world of plumbing had to be compacted into the smallest possible self-sustaining units to free buildings and their occupants to navigate within the flows itself. The revolution would start with the bathroom.

The very first version of the Dymaxion House had a compact bathroom unit with tub, toilet, and sink forming a single fitting at the core of the plan, acting as an interface between the central mast and the spaces "radiating" out from it. This "one-piece unit" includes the wall and floor

1939, BFP Series 8, Box 3, Folder 11, p. 6. "Advanced arts such as radio and aviation finally traffic across the Artic. [...] The newer world—a world of abstracting industry and play, trackless wireless, silver-screened electrically broadcast personalities." Ibid. (first draft), 17.

17 Buckminster Fuller, "Preview of Building" (lecture at *Time for Change* conference, University of Michigan, Ann Arbor, April 1, 1949), BFP Series 8, Box 21, Folder 3, p. 4.

18 Ibid., 7.

19 Ibid.

20 Buckminster Fuller, "Man on Earth," foreword to *Transport—Next Half Century, 1951–2000*, by Ladislav Sutnar (New York: Canterbury Printing Company, 1950); captions to illustration republished in *The Dymaxion World of Buckminster Fuller*, by Robert Marks (New York: Reinhold Publishing, 1960), 162.

21 Buckminster Fuller, "The 4D Letters Patent," reprinted in *4D Time Lock*, 60 (see note 5).

22 Buckminster Fuller, audiotape of lecture (Yale University Department of Architecture, October 16, 1952), BFP Series 17, Box 3, Reel 3d.

23 Buckminster Fuller, quoted in Miriam Alburn, "'U' May Help Build Giant Model of Earth," *Minneapolis Sunday Tribune*, November 6, 1955, 4.

24 Horowitz's "Proposed Autonomous Core Package" was presented at the January 1951 conference at MIT, where other Fuller students presented variations of the Skybreak House. *Housing: A National Security Resource* (Cambridge: Bemis Foundation, 1951). The proposal was covered by several newspapers. See, for example, Robert C. Cowen, "Self-Sufficient House Shapes Up in Architect's Drawings: 'Core' Makes Its Own Heat, Power, Water," *The Christian Science Monitor*, May 23, 1951. The article describing how such a system creates independence from power, gas, and sewage lines appears alongside an article discussing Fuller's project for a mobile autonomous house: "His present structure is a clear expression of his view that there should be complete separation between the shell and the utilities and mechanical equipment. The prototype which has been completed by the Fuller Research Foundation in Canada is a dome, composed of aluminum tubing and aircraft cable covered by translucent plastic, which weighs only .07 pound a cubic foot." Richard Hamilton, "New Avenue Seen for U.S. Home Builder," *The Christian Science Monitor*, May 23, 1951.

and would be "sent out from the factory ready to be set in place, and when set in place ready for use except for connecting up piping," as Fuller's abandoned April 1928 patent application put it.[21] It would be "hung on the mast" at a single point rather than fixed to it, remaining "independent" of both the mast and the adjacent bedroom spaces that it locked into through friction. **fig. 4** Fuller drew a separate plan and elevation of the unit to emphasize its polemical independence. **fig. 6** An additional focused section drawing shows that it is not a room containing a set of sanitary fittings but a set of cleaning tools molded out of a single curved surface that forms the ceiling, wall, and floor before being literally suspended within the central shaft with light, air, water, gas, and waste circulating through it. **fig. 5** The single surface would act as a sophisticated valve, being perforated with controllable orifices, from those in the translucent ceiling admitting more or less light to those of the bath, toilet, and sink, to those in the floor removing excess water. Far from a private space of disconnection from the world, the suspended unit is the very epicenter of connection, locating the body within flow in order to release the mind into flow. The autonomous bathroom is the launch pad for throwing architecture into radiation, and thereby into a whole new status as a prosthetic technology incubating a radical transformation of thought and action. The bathroom becomes the ultimate weapon.

Fuller repeatedly pointed out, as during a 1952 lecture to architecture students at Yale, that the lag between invention and social application—"turning a concept into experiment and into a usable device and getting it accepted by society"—was the shortest in the electronics world of radio, which got into circuits after only three years, and the longest in the world of architecture which took a "horrible" forty-two years.[22] The internalized flows of the bathroom would be the key to collapsing this difference. In a sense, the liquid circuits of the bathroom had to be positioned at the heart of the electronic circuits as their crucial accelerant. Not only would architecture embed itself within radio but radio would be amplified by it. From 1927 on Fuller had said that the wireless global networking industries of radio and aviation were waiting for industrialized housing in order to finally realize their full potential. The future of communication, and therefore all human life, depended on the bathroom.

Fuller regarded the average house as just "a decorated nozzle on the end of a sewer,"[23] and was enthusiastic about systems, like those developed by his student Harold Horowitz, that would allow his lightweight plastic-covered domes to break free of all shared infrastructural networks.[24] Horowitz had led the original student team devoted to the "recirculation of waste" in houses in Fuller's first class at the Institute of Design in Chicago in 1948–1949 and continued the project as a graduate student at MIT in 1951, working on a unit that would dissolve all waste and generate all water, heat, and power. **fig. 7** The dense internal convolutions of a self-sustaining plumbing system that could literally feed itself, with every output folded back around into an input, would act as the very engine of mobility that would release architecture into the omnidirectional waves. The thinness, ephemerality, and even invisibility of the transparent membrane

PIPELESS DREAMS

The Inhabitable Pipe at the Epicenter of an Expanding Universe

2 "Houses that Hang from a Pole!" in *Modern Mechanix and Inventions*, September 1932

3 "History of man's ecological sweep out," *World Design Science Decade, Phase 1, Document 1*, 1963

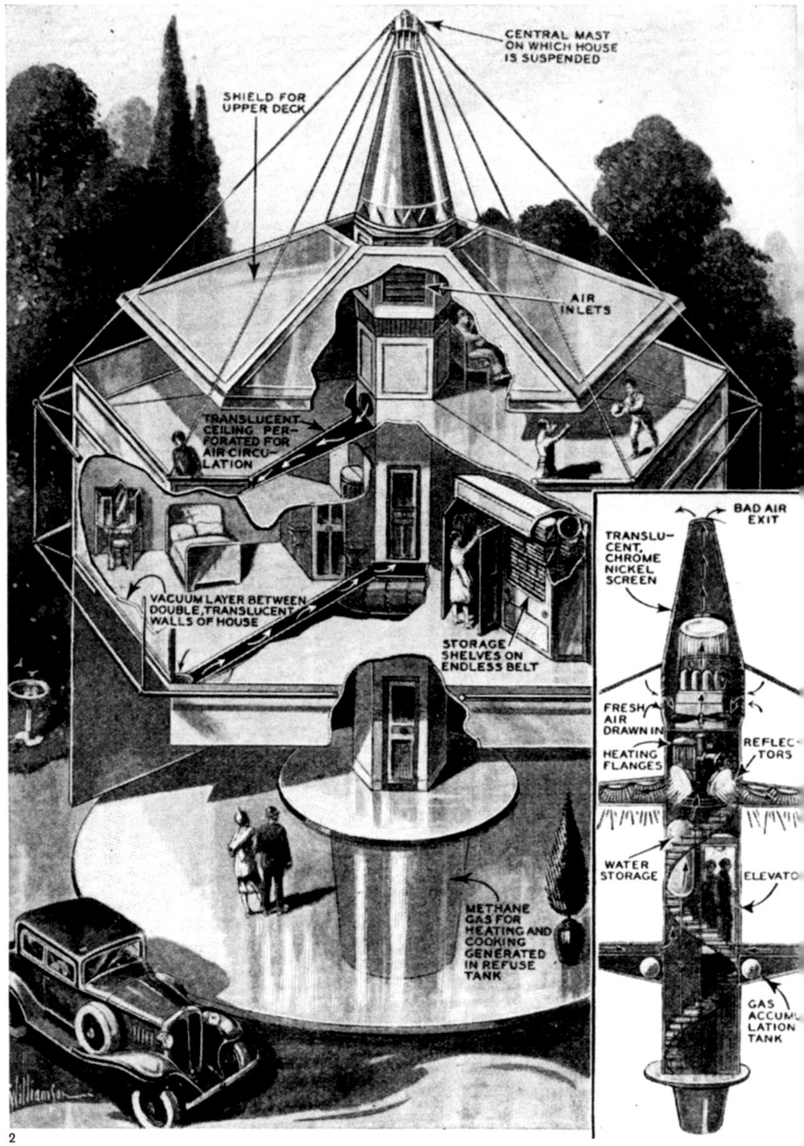

2

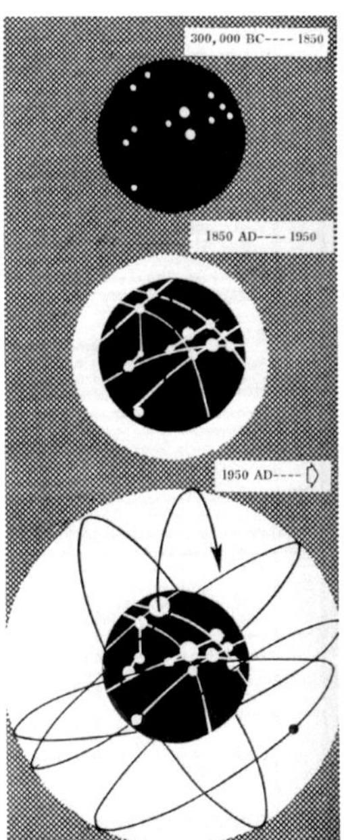

3

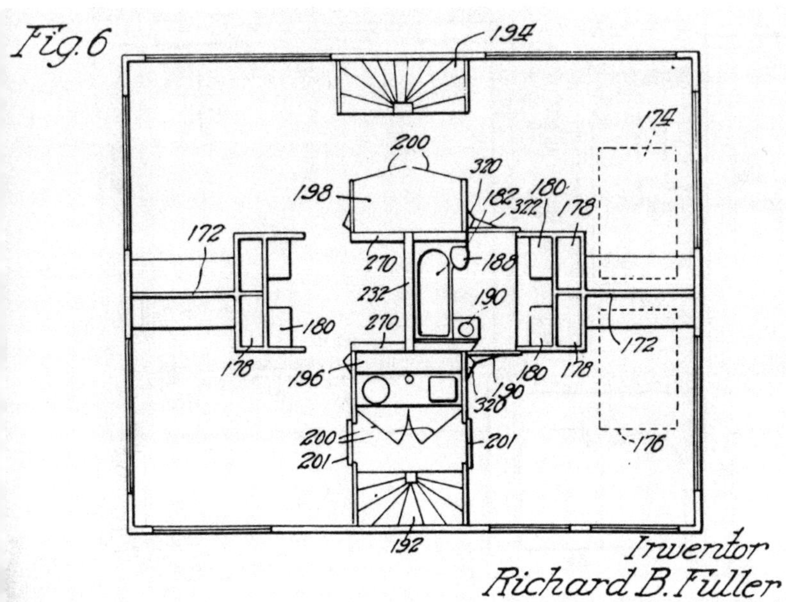

4

4 Plan of the second floor of the 4D House for abandoned patent application of April 1, 1928, published in *4D Time Lock*, 1928

5–6 Plan, elevation, and section of "Unitary one-piece bathroom" of the 4D House for abandoned patent application of April 1928, published in *4D Time Lock*, 1928

7 "Independence," Autonomous Core Package by Harold Horowitz in *The Christian Science Monitor*, May 23, 1951

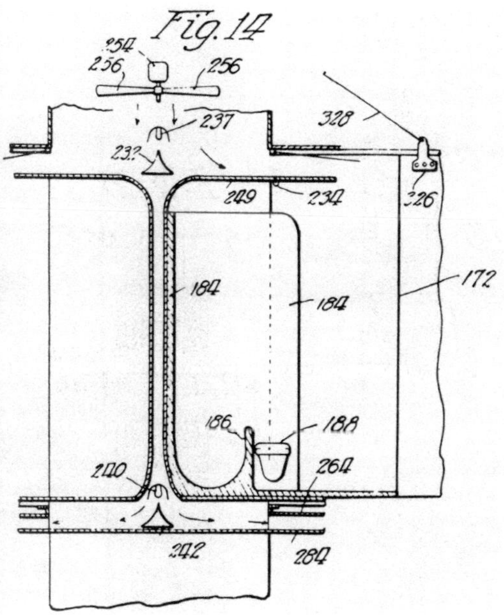

5

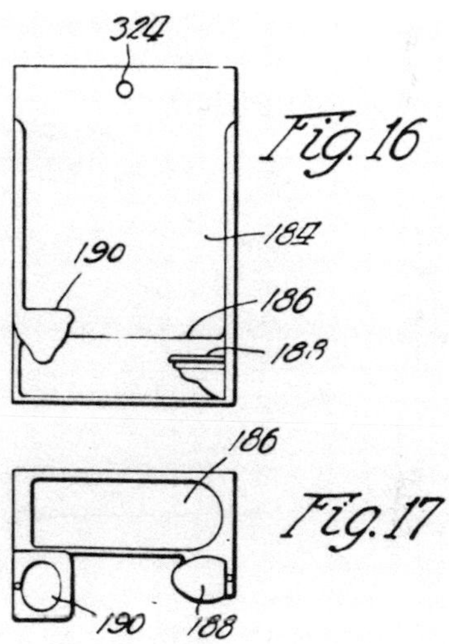

6

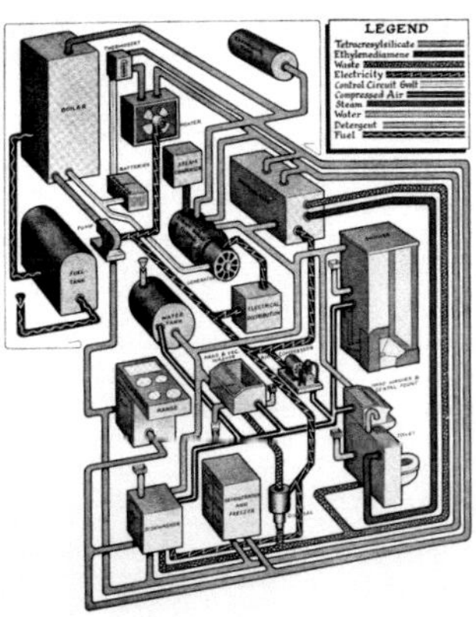

7

defining Fuller's architecture is directly related to the compactness and internal convolutions of the plumbing package. The ambition to ride the radio waves necessarily began by cutting all the plumbing lines and folding them in on themselves in ever-tighter circuits. The more closely a designer attends to the valves of the body, the more the building is able to valve the invisible universe.

Fuller gave a provocative lecture on "Environmental Valving" at the University of Illinois, Urbana, in November 1951. Instead of predictably saying that houses are valves regulating environmental flows, he radicalized the argument by saying that any environmental valve is by definition a house.[25] The very act of modulating radiation creates a shelter. Fuller insisted that all stereotypes about houses have to be defused by undermining the traditional understanding of a building, especially the seemingly straightforward but mistaken sense that it has a solid or impervious form. There is not even such a thing as a continuous surface. Everything we see and touch is full of holes. The unseen structure of any object is a constellation of actions with the same kind of patterns as those found in outer space or the inner space of atoms. Since there are no materials in buildings, only combinations of frequencies, architecture is nothing but the modulation of frequencies. Once again, the model was radio, or more precisely the invention of FM radio with its clearer signals: "I'm under the impression that, as architects, we are coming to a period of frequency modulation in our world of architecture."[26] In reverse, all frequency modulation produces architecture. The question of the valve is simultaneously about the expanded universe of invisible waves of radiation and the internal chemistries of the completely porous human body with its dense networks of tubes and rhythmic frequencies. Architecture, like the body, is a set of valves suspended within the continuous spectrum of waves from the infinitely small scale of atoms to the infinitely large scale of the cosmos. More precisely, architecture is an organic extension of the body's valves. Fuller retold the story of the way that houses had steadily "insinuated" ever more pipes while pretending that these conduits didn't exist. But "finally, our veins began to show" and the necessity for so many pipes was

25 "You may say, 'What is this environment valving!' Well, an environment valve is a house. We get so used to what we think of as a house, that if I started talking about a house or about a building, we'd have to think about the building right away. But if I started off talking about environment valving, you might tend to look at the whole transaction in a different way." Buckminster Fuller, "Environmental Valving" (audio-transcript of lecture, University of Illinois, Urbana, November 14, 1951), BFP Series 18, Box 107, Folder 10, Reel 1, p. 4.
26 Ibid., Reel 2, p. 11.
27 Ibid., Reel 3, p. 8.
28 Buckminster Fuller, "Preview of Building," in *Ideas and Integrities* (New York: Prentice-Hall, 1963), 213. This line was added to the original text of 1949.
29 Fuller, "Preview of Building," 4 (see note 17).
30 "To be able to send a man to the Moon, you first have to be able to give him his own private little Earth, and he's been living on an enormous Earth with great energy-exchanging patterns he knows very little about. [...] Our processes are so secret that nobody really knows anything about plumbing. [...] Everything fundamental about our sewage system was invented in India by 2500 BC. No one has made significant improvements since that time. No architect ever looks back of the purple tiles, no scientist ever studies plumbing. [...] For the first time in history we are employing scientists to work on a little house. It hasn't been thought of, architecturally, as a house, but it's the most important house that's ever been worked on." Buckminster Fuller, "The Designers and the Politicians," in *Ideas and Integrities*, 307 (see note 28).
31 Ibid., 308.
32 Buckminster Fuller, "World Design Initiative," October 10, 1963, speech to UIA congress, in *World Design Science Decade 1965–1975, Phase I, Document 2: The Design Initiative*, ed. John McHale (Carbondale: Southern Illinois University, 1965) 1–104, here, 12.
33 Ibid.
34 "The Bauhaus international school used standard plumbing fixtures and only ventured so far as to persuade the manufacturers to modify the surface of the valve handles and spigots and the color, size and arrangement of the tiles. The international Bauhaus never went back of the wall surface to look at the plumbing, never dared to venture into 'printed' circuits of manifoldly stamped plumbings. They never inquired into the overall problem of sanitary functions themselves. They settled on the real estater's sewers like hens on glass eggs." Buckminster Fuller to John McHale, 7 January 1955, later published as "Influences on My Work," *Architectural Design* 31 (July 1961): 290–296, here 295.

called into question and architects could do the crucial work to "modulate" the empire of plumbing to produce compact patterns of energy flow.[27] Taking care of the body's circuits is the critical first step in connecting with the universe. The architecture of radio begins with the toilet.

CLOSED-CIRCUIT ARCHITECTURE

The space program reaching out beyond Earth's atmosphere became the inevitable model of pipeless mobility. The spaceship profoundly disconnects its occupants. The liquids, solids, and gases within the human body can no longer circulate in an extended infrastructural network. A compact "closed sanitary human metabolic circuitry" had to be developed, a set of tight loops between body and shelter that would enable both to move in unprecedented ways.[28] In 1949 Fuller had predicted that the "atomic space-ship" may dominate the headlines in the decades to come but that the main "evolutionary change" would meantime happen with the traditional house on Earth.[29] He reversed the argument in 1962 and described the spaceship needed to reach the Moon as "a little house [...] the most important house that's ever been worked on."[30] To keep the hypermobile astronaut alive, the everyday plumbing of bodies and buildings could no longer remain secret. Plumbing had to evolve for the first time in thousands of years. New systems, like the "little black box" taking care of all sanitation in space, would quickly become the model for all houses on Earth.[31] Every house would become a spaceship, an "autonomous dwelling device" finally able to be repositioned anywhere, anytime.

In his presentation to the gathered global profession at the October 1963 UIA congress in Mexico City, Fuller once again denounced the disinterest of architects in plumbing and enthused about the task of building the "little house" in space where "there is no sewer system [...] no water supply lines, no electric wires, no supermarkets."[32] **fig. 1** In a summary indictment of the discipline, architects were not part of the space program. Yet the compact self-supporting systems needed in space capsules would soon transform all terrestrial architecture: "We will no longer have to have water pipes and sewer systems, mankind will suddenly start mass reproducing the space-house prototype's pipeless, wireless, trackless ability to deploy man around the Earth's surface as well as in space."[33] The basic mentality of the architect had to shift with the "super functionalism of the space dwelling machine." The profession's default obsession with visual appearance and refusal to look behind the bathroom tiles had to be replaced by a dedication to the hidden and even invisible world, since much of technical performance since World War I had been beyond the senses in the chemical and electromagnetic spheres. All the politics and economics of the traditional building industry had been invested in the plumbing that architects suppress. The fact that architects cared only about the color of bathroom tiles and never looked behind them had been Fuller's main evidence in 1955 that modern architects were not modern and simply "settled on the real estater's sewers like hens on glass eggs."[34] Disinterest in pipes only fed the empire of pipes and inevitably infantilized the architect. Pipeless architecture presupposed a different economy and a whole new species of architect as design-scientist that, as Fuller insisted in 1964, would be better able than a NASA scientist to design the "three-foot diameter, closed-circuit" ecological patterns of an autonomous dwelling without any inputs and outputs of external plumbing, whether on Earth or in outer space.[35] NASA was simply an architectural program awaiting the arrival of the architects.

Fuller started routinely reminding all his audiences that Earth itself was a spaceship, a point he had been making since 1961.[36] Architects had unwittingly been part of the space program all along. Architecture is always something to launch. Or, more precisely, everything is built in outer space. New forms of autonomous ship would emerge to replace the vast net of pipes concentrated into cities, such that New York "is so knit together with underground wires, tubes, cables, and pipes—that in effect Manhattan Island could be lifted in one piece and stood upon end, its roadways and tunnels acting as its supporting columns."[37] Independent packages of plumbing would release architecture from such massive collective webs of pipes, the "metabolic guts" of urbanism that fix it to one place and one set of real estate monopolies.[38] Nomadic fluidity would dissolve anything that is fixed. The always temporary idea of home would expand as the city and the planet become but stops in a continuous voyage: "all concepts of urbanization will become obsolete. Only the Earth and the solar system will be his temporary home. [...] Urbanization is only temporary as the cities become the launching pads for each human's blastoff into world-shuttling citizenship."[39] The space dwelling turns out to be the only commission.

Fuller made a series of connections with NASA, joining some of their research groups and giving papers like "Air-O-Space" at a 1964 joint symposium with NASA at Carbondale.[40] In 1963 he had not hesitated to propose his own "Moon-House" to NASA, a lightweight magnesium geodesic sphere that could be transported as a compact bundle inside a cylinder on a spaceship. Upon landing on the lunar surface, the astronauts would push a button and the bundle would explode open into a full sphere that would be covered with a skin of radiation-insulating material, tied down

35 "Between Russia and the United States, $6 billion has been appropriated to develop the little scientific house in which man will dwell in space or upon the Moon. But we note that though architects profess to be master solvers of space problems, thus far they have not been called into any part of the U.S. space program. [...] Architects can be trained quickly enough and in such a way as to be much more effective in the space program than are those scientists and businessmen who are now handling the program. The architectural scientists will be especially effective in defining the ecological problem and its solution. [...] The problem is to reduce the dimensions of the ecological pattern from a vast tree-air-earth-worm-bird-bee-rain-wind relay system to a three-foot-diameter closed-circuit by which man is able to sustain health for twelve months without sewer disposal or further input supply besides sun radiation." Buckminster Fuller, "The Prospect for Mankind," *Saturday Review*, September 19, 1964, 26.

36 "Biological life is entirely automated. For at least 2,000,000 years, men have been reproducing and multiplying on a little automated space ship called Earth in an automated universe in which the entire process is so successfully predesigned that men did not even know that they were automated, regenerative passengers on a space ship and were so naïve as to think they had invented their own success as they lived egocentrically on a seemingly static Earth." Buckminster Fuller, "Prospects for Humanity," *Saturday Review*, August 29, 1964, 180.

37 Buckminster Fuller, "New York as a Focus of Energy," in *The New York Guidebook*, ed. John A. Kouwenhoven (New York: Dell Publishing, 1964), 32.

38 In contrast to the "ships of sea and sky," the products of the hugely antiquated "so-called building 'industry' [...] don't have to float or fly. They are utterly dependent on sewers, waterlines, electric lines, highway maintenance. They are utterly controlled by the prime landowners, their building codes and readily imposable legal restrictions—all based on the real estates' ownership of the highways-sewers-waterlines—the metabolic 'guts' of all USA towns and cities." Buckminster Fuller, "Legally Piggily," in *Critical Path* (New York: St. Martins, 1981), 90. Fuller's introduction to the book uses the Apollo space program as its reference point, arguing that the architectural profession had to stop trying to "fit our late twentieth century astronautical man-on-Moon visiting capability" into old infrastructural networks and "rehouse the alternately convergent and divergent shuttling phases of four billion uprooting, around-the-world-integrating sometimes transient, sometimes resident, sometimes in cities, sometimes in the country humans—before 2000 AD." Introduction to *Critical Path*, xxv.

39 Buckminster Fuller, "Design Strategy—Statement to a Leading Figure in the World Building Industry—1966," in *World Design Science Decade 1965–1975, Phase 2, Document 5: Comprehensive Design Strategy*, ed. John McHale (Carbondale: Southern Illinois University, 1967), 49.

40 Buckminster Fuller, "Air-O-Space," NASA Research Conference, University of Southern Illinois, Carbondale, November 19, 1964, BFP Series 17, Box 27, Reel 69.

8

9

10

11

13

Launching the Exploding Package

8–10 Flying Seedpod being unfurled by students, Washington University, St. Louis, May 1955

11 RBF and unfurled Flying Seedpod, Washington University, St. Louis, May 1955

12 Flying Seedpod package with skin, Washington University, St. Louis, May 1955

13 RBF with exploding Tensegrity Sphere proposal for space station, Philadelphia, April 18, 1979

12

with cables, and have a "little-black-box of 'housekeeping' equipment' inside it to sustain living and working.[41] Fuller claimed to have been thinking about such a house on the Moon since 1932, understanding the radical mobility and autonomy of the lunar house as an inevitable extension of the logic of his air-deliverable 4D House of 1928. Crossing the line between the atmosphere of the planet and outer space was seen as an inevitable step. Fuller's first explicit proposal for spherical structures for outer space and the Moon came in 1958, based on the Flying Seedpod experiments three years earlier with students at Washington University, where nitrogen within a geodesic frame enabled a compact package to explode out into a 36-foot-diameter Tensegrity Dome that could even have its skin already attached.[42] In the first test, Fuller ran around taking photographs as the students carried the bundle to the center of an empty yard, charged it with nitrogen, then sprung it open like a huge spider that popped itself into the shape of a dome in 30 seconds. **figs. 8–11** The second test was to be bigger, with a double skin of plastic.[43] **fig. 12** That test didn't take place, but the idea of a self-erecting bubble remained a key goal. Fuller was giving lectures on "Architecture for the Space Age" in early 1959 and would make a succession of proposals for unfolding spherical space stations, lunar buildings, and colonies on Mars to NASA and the media throughout the sixties and seventies, excitedly holding up the latest models as if hoping to climb inside them and take off. **fig. 13**

Yet the main flow was in the other direction. NASA acted as the architectural model. The cross section of a space capsule with all the dense intestinal circuits of life-support plumbing systems packed in behind the astronaut and the even denser miniaturized circuits of information packed in front as shown in NASA reports studied and published in architecture magazines by Fuller's colleagues,[44] became the new image of the primitive hut—the most basic condition of architecture rather than its most advanced technological form. **fig. 14** The June 1966 cover of *Arena*, the journal of the Architectural Association in London, made the point by putting drawings of the cone-shaped "first sort of huts" from classical architectural theory alongside NASA images of similarly shaped spacecraft orbiting the planet.[45] **fig. 15** The first hut on the ground sits side by side with the latest hut floating in outer space. The mission of the capsule's high-tech closed metabolic system was to domesticate space, producing the effect of house anywhere, anytime. It was not simply that a new, more advanced house would become possible on Earth. Rather the basic idea of house was intensified. The disconnection from pipes would restore the most fundamental sense of shelter.[46]

41 Lorena D. Joan, "Special to the St. Louis Post-Dispatch EVERDAY magazine," manuscript dated April 16, 1963, BFP Series 2, Box 122, Folder 1. Published as "'Moon House' Designed For US Astronauts," *St Louis Post-Dispatch* June 24, 1963. An April newspaper report describes Fuller as being on the way to present the concept to NASA engineers. Brooks Atkinson, "Moon-House Dreams? Why They're Easy," *Chicago Daily Tribune*, April 3, 1963, A2.

42 Buckminster Fuller to David B. Hill, *Engineering News Record*, 2 January 1959, BFP Series 18, Box 144, Folder 1.

43 The first skinless version of the Seedpod "that folds and unfolds like an umbrella" was successfully tested at Washington University as one-third of a 36-foot-diameter sphere. The second version was to be a "a similar but larger dome having a double 'skin' of plastic." Robert E. Hannon, "An Experiment in Quick Construction: Washington U. Students Erect Skeleton Under the Direction of Its Inventor," *St. Louis Dispatch*, January 15, 1956.

44 See, for example, John McHale, "Outer Space," *Architectural Design* 37 (February 1967): 67–77.

45 *Arena: The Architectural Association Journal*, June 1966. The image of the primitive hut was taken from "Sir W. Chambers' 1791 *Treatise on the Decorative Part of Civil Architecture*, showing his prototypical hut and the origin of the Corinthian Order."

46 The "most forward development in man's ecological capacity" is the space capsule's "little 300-pound black box" that is "entirely removed from sewer and other service mains" and dramatically reduces the typical metabolic systems used on Earth from a fixed complex one

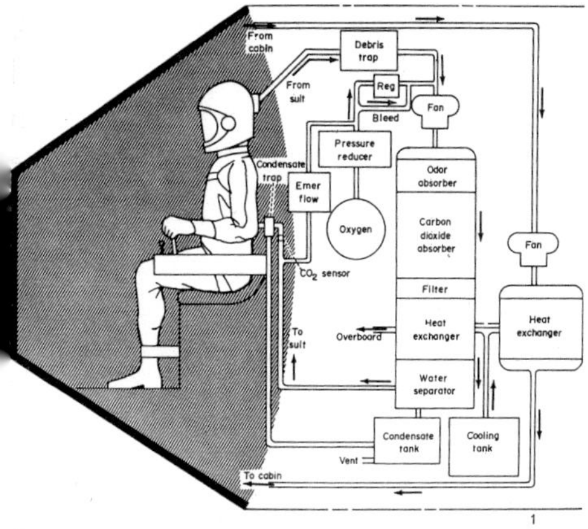

4

5

16

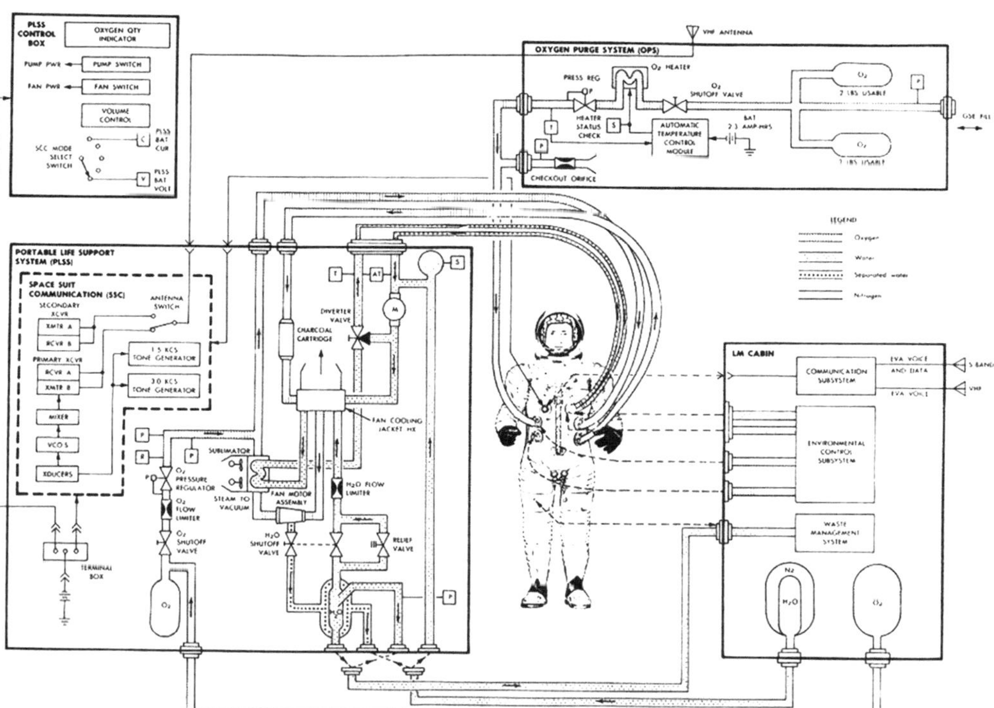

7

Wearing the New Space of Portable Plumbing

14 NASA section of space capsule, *Architectural Design*, February 1967

15 Cover of *Arena: The Architectural Association Journal*, June 1966

16 X-ray of A7L space suit and Portable Life Support System used on all Apollo missions

17 NASA diagram of water, oxygen, electricity, and communication flow in Portable Life Support System for the A7L space suit with interfaces to the astronaut and the Lunar Module cabin, 1968

"The answer to the housing problem lies on the way to the Moon," Fuller told the *Washington Post* in 1966, noting again that terrestrial houses had become increasingly engorged with pipes and wires. These intrusions constituted 18 percent of a typical house after World War I, neared 50 percent after World War II, and had already reached 60 percent by the mid-sixties.[47] The very idea of *house* had been taken over by all the different kinds of pipes and equipment connected to extended nets of collective systems. The black box of the space program offered the way to compact all the internal pipes and disconnect the house.

Soon even the black box was too big. The much more compact portable life-support systems for the space suit worn outside the capsule became the model. All the technical responsibilities of architecture could now be carried out by a backpack. The nest of plumbing inside a small plastic box echoes and completes the internal plumbing of the body in a series of circuits. **figs. 16 and 17** There is finally no building in the way, just the liquid-filled skin of the space suit itself with its one window and six sockets for the umbilical connections to the rectangular support pack. After the successful use of such a system for space walks during the Apollo missions in 1969, Fuller argued that the "little portable electrochemical system about the size and weight of one large air-travel suitcase" could be mass-produced for all the astronauts on Earth.[48] He again condemned the previous five thousand years of disinterest in plumbing and insisted that the horizontal "tubular" system of pipes, highways, and wires on earth cannot be stretched to accommodate even half of humanity. His *Operating Manual for Spaceship Earth* of the same year inevitably speaks of technology "going from wire to wireless, from track to trackless, from pipe to pipeless, from visible structural muscle to the invisible chemical element strengths of metallic alloys and electromagnetics."[49] Pipes buried in heavy buildings would give way to portable life-support packs in the lightest possible domes that in turn would give way to an invisible architecture.

THE FULLER BOWL

Fuller saw himself as having been engaged in his own space program since 1927, developing an ever more compact package of services for an ever-lighter shell. Architecture could only be liberated from pipes by

mile in diameter to a portable "accessory" servicing a four-foot-diameter capsule that would enable man to "deploy almost invisibly" to any site. Fuller argued that the massive use of shared resources by the space program, as the latest form of weaponry, would inevitably and rapidly return to "revolutionize" life on the "home front." Buckminster Fuller, "Report on the 'Geosocial Revolution'," *Saturday Review*, September 16, 1967, 32. "The black box will constitute the first direct application of science to making man a physical and economic success anywhere in the universe—which, of course, includes on Earth." Buckminster Fuller, "City of the Future," *Playboy*, January 1968, 169.

47 Wolf von Eckhardt, "That Bucky Fuller Sure Is a High Flyer: Cityscape Shoots Moon," *Washington Post*, October 2, 1966, 3.

48 Buckminster Fuller, "Vertical Is to Live, Horizontal Is to Die," *The American Scholar* 39, no. 1 (Winter 1969/70): 27–47, here, 46. The essay contrasts the dangerous and limiting constraint of the "one-dimensional tubes of the high speed, exclusively linear, land travel" with the open three-dimensional multidirectional movements in the always vertical condition of ocean, air, and outer space. Ibid., 29. Architecture's release from the "piped-in" world would begin with the astronaut's ever-shrinking black box: "Both the power to operate semiautonomous sanitation automation and the equipment involved will be mass-produced from the experience gained in the Moon and outer space programs and equipment prototyping. The little black boxes that contain all the life-regenerating systems will dispense forever with the Earthians' wasteful piped-in water supply and sewer systems." Buckminster Fuller, "Planetary Planning: The Historical Philosophic Background," lecture of November 13, 1969, in *The American Scholar* 40, no. 2 (1971): 299.

49 Buckminster Fuller, *Operating Manual for Spaceship Earth* (Carbondale: Southern Illinois University, 1969), 34.

50 Buckminster Fuller, "Tree-Like Style of Dwelling Is Planned," *Chicago Evening Post Magazine of Art*, December 18, 1928, 5.

51 Fuller, "Cosmopolitan Homes Corporation: Lightful Products," 55 (see note 4).

52 Fuller, *4D Time Lock*, 60 (see note 5).

53 The plan drawing published in June 1929, for example, shows the final layout of the bathrooms while the elevation drawing still shows an intermediate stage between the first version and the one in the final model. "The Dymaxion House Conceived by R. Buckminster Fuller," *Architecture*, June 1929, 336. Work on the new model started in February 1929 with the purchase of flat aluminum sheets and Fuller sent the plan

taking responsibility for them. Symptomatically, the very first image published of the 4D Tower in a December 1928 issue of the *Chicago Evening Post Magazine of Art* shows a bathroom unit being hoisted up into the otherwise empty frame of the building, about to be attached to the central tube of the mast in order to communicate with the water, sewage, and gas tank shown in the adjacent cutaway drawing of the completed structure. The bathroom always came first. **fig. 7, page 25** It was the first occupant. Its self-contained circuits enabled the tower to be "free as a ship of utilities, sewers and other political hangnails; so light in weight as to be delivered by zeppelin," in the concluding words of the article, Fuller's very first published essay.[50] The bathroom was a completely sealed unit flying in the air, about to land inside a tower which had itself arrived by air. It was a floating bathroom for a floating architecture, a bathroom without which architecture could not fly. It was the compact bathroom that would allow architecture to remain disconnected from the ground. It would keep architecture in orbit around the planet. It was a capsule without windows that allowed the rest of the building to be all window. Sealed off from the world, it would contain all the bodily smells, sounds, and flows to liberate all the nonbodily flows. Communicating only with the inside of the body and the inside of the storage tanks, it would allow the building to communicate with everything else. It was the bathroom unit that enabled Fuller's architecture to immerse itself in the world of radiation. The architecture of radio literally begins in the bathroom.

The dense physical enclosure of the bathroom is paradoxically the first step to take on the path toward the immaterial universe. Fuller's first manuscript on his house in early 1928 protests the fact that society was still in the dark ages since the majority of houses were "still without bathroom or toilets and sewage disposal" and proposes the production of "utility units, such as bathrooms all in one piece with standard manifold connections" with complete "independence" from town sewage and water lines.[51] A few months later, the patent application for the 4D House already details the "unitary one-piece bathroom" at the heart of the plan that integrated tub, toilet, sink and "special flooring unit" and is connected to the pipes in the core and thereby down to the septic, gas, and water tanks that form the base of the core from which the whole house would hang.[52] By the time of the 1929 version of the house, two such compact units combining bath, shower, toilet, and sink were nestled into the triangular geometry at the center of the plan, back-to-back and easily able to be entered from any part of the space through a series of spinning doors operating like valves that would sense the arrival of the body and open without being touched. A lot of the early study drawings had concentrated on different variations of the intersection between the bathrooms and the central mast to choreograph a core made of the flows of people, water, air, light, and electricity.

Before the rest of the house was finalized, the two bathroom units ended up occupying seven triangles of the floor grid, each in an extremely compact layout with only space for one person to stand or sit at the intersection of bath, toilet, and sink.[53] As published in June 1929, the sink had become round to match the curves of the tub and the toilet had picked up the same curves then became more streamlined as it protruded. The unit was not a set of sanitary fittings in a room but a single sanitary fitting that could be entered and occupied, freeing up the rest of the house. It was at the core of the house and of Fuller's narrative about the house. He repeatedly condemned the fact that the majority of houses still lacked a bathroom, calling for a whole new industry.[54] The new bathroom unit was meant to address both the hyperlocal needs of the individual body and the planetary-scaled flows of materials, technologies, logistics, and organizational strategies. If the principles embedded in the Dymaxion House are in this sense "radionic," as the brochure to the May 1929 exhibition of the model at the Harvard Society for Contemporary Art put it, it is because it had been designed "from the inside out."[55] And the inside of the inside is the bathroom units that were to be "manufactured in toto at factories and hung up in the house in radial arrangement around the mast piping" and like the other units, "may with ease be replaced by a more desirable unit as it develops."[56] The space of maximum intimacy, the only space of privacy in Fuller's house, is a creature of extended global flows of ideas and techniques. The inside of the inside is inseparable from the infinite world of radiation that it seems so profoundly isolated from. More surprising still the world of radiation is seen to be dependent on it, even accelerated by it.

The bathroom is a technical instrument, a highly efficient mechanism to be continually upgraded by scientists, but equally it is a sensual space to cocoon the human body when cleaning all the occupant's inner and outer surfaces in preparation for engagement with the expanded universe of radio. The bathroom becomes the very figure of disconnection and reconnection. It's not just the body that emerges from the smallest space in the house but the logic of cleaning. The question of hygiene was highlighted in every lecture, interview, and article about the house. The building itself

and elevation of the evolving model to Henry Saylor, the editor of *Architecture* magazine in May. Buckminster Fuller to Henry Saylor, 9 May 1929, BFP Series 2, Box 21. But the design continued to evolve until the model was first exhibited at the Architectural League in New York on February 7, 1930.

54 "And inasmuch as the majority of these houses have still no bathrooms, there is indeed involved a problem of industrial best-for-all design." Buckminster Fuller, "House for Mass Production," *Architectural Forum*, July 1929, 103.

55 Brochure for May 1929 exhibition of 4D at the Harvard Society for Contemporary Art. This section of text was reprinted (with some changes by Fuller to the final sentences) within the illustrated catalogue for the March 1930 exhibition at the same venue. Buckminster Fuller, *4D: Buckminster Fuller's Dymaxion House*, exhibition catalogue (Cambridge: Harvard Society for Contemporary Art, 1930).

56 Fuller, *4D: Buckminster Fuller's Dymaxion House* (see note 55).

57 "Dymaxion House has Ultra Design," *The Evening Star* (Washington), March 26, 1929.

58 "Hangs His House from a Mast Instead of Resting It on Ground," *The Boston Globe*, May 20, 1929, 13. The treatment of the house as a sanitary mechanism culminated in an essay called "A Conception of a Futuristic House," in the August 1933 issue of *The Sanitary Age*, which compared the "waterless bathroom" of the house without tub or shower to images of conventional sanitary fittings.

59 "I don't care where I put a bathroom, it will always find its contact in one of the triangular areas here." Fuller, "Dymaxion House Meeting, Architectural League, New York," 92 (see note 10).

60 "Now, I had a very interesting experience with this, because at the time of the Dymaxion House, 1927–1928, coming to New York in 1929, there was a man, quite a rich man in New York, and he got quite interested in my Dymaxion House, and he asked me to come give a lecture on it at his house, and Frank Vanderlip, and he invited a lot of people like Clarence Wooley, [who] was the president of American Radiator Standards Sanitary who he thought would be interested in my house, and old Owen D. Young [who] was president of General Electric, he was a very influential man, and he brought all these influential people to see this house. These people were full of really considerable consternation. [...] At any rate, Clarence Wooley, head of Standard Sanitary became very excited when Frank Vanderlip had me show this thing to him, so he wanted to have something done about those bathrooms and my kitchen and things like that. And so I did, then, do work for the Standard Sanitary, used to be called the Pierce Foundation was their research department up in Buffalo. And there I developed what I had also had in the earliest patterns of this thing." Buckminster Fuller, "Everything I Know" (video-transcript of lecture, Bell Telephone Studios, Philadelphia, PA, January 1975), Session 10, Part 15 (Buckminster Fuller Institute, 1997). The Standard Sanitary Manufacturing Company had run an architect's competition in 1930 for a bathroom design, which attracted fifty entries and was published as *The Bathroom: A New Interior* (Pittsburgh: Standard Sanitary Manufacturing Company, 1931). The winning design by an architect from the office of McKim, Mead and White, the premier neoclassical firm in the country, exemplified what Fuller was trying to undermine.

61 Fuller, "World Design Initiative," 10 (see note 32).

62 "There was only one man in the United States designing all the toilet bowls of all the different companies, and I found there was nobody who really knew why a toilet bowl was the way it was except this one man. And he had inherited his art from some English craftsman, and he was in a little top room of a building in Toledo, Ohio. Standard Sanitary and Kohler and all of them were getting their information from him." Fuller, "Everything I Know," Session 6, Part 1 (see note 60).

was seen to expand the rituals of cleaning, such that the body coming out from the bathroom could remain naked in the interest of further cleaning of its pores: "Inhabitants [...] could sleep without bed coverings if they desired as a health measure to enable the air to reach the pores of the body for it is equipped with air purifiers designed to eliminate dust."[57] The house itself had been turned into a form of sanitary clothing. "Before any of the air can come into the house it is purified, making the house a veritable gas mask" that has a symbiotic relationship with the bathroom that is no longer a collection of fixtures—it is a 'sculptural unit,' made in one piece."[58] Fuller highlighted the unit's polemical independence from the house that faithfully extended its cleansing logic, noting in a 1929 presentation in New York, for example, that the unit could have occupied any location in the triangulated grid of the floor plan.[59] It is not so much that the bathroom arrives in the plan as the plan evolves out of the bathroom.

Indeed, the house could not develop further without rethinking the bathroom and its liquids, solids, and smells. After relentlessly promoting the first versions of the Dymaxion House, Fuller stopped working on the project altogether and in 1931 held a research position with the American Standard Sanitary Manufacturing Company, whose president had attended a private lecture about the house in 1929 with other business leaders and was attracted to its bathroom units.[60] Fuller looked at the overall state of the plumbing industry alongside the requested design of an industrialized bathroom unit. It turned out that if architects had been infantilized by plumbers because they were so obsessed with the shell and never bothered to look at the pipes behind the wall surface, no one had really been looking. Plumbing had simply not been a subject of scientific investigation:

> Many scientists live in houses—they look at the plumbing, often find that the plumbing isn't working, twiddle the knob and send for the plumber. You know as architects that you do not design the plumbing that you buy. You design the superficial use and arrangement of fixtures which are designed by non-architects, and manufactured by commerce for you. You are free only to choose the coloring of the bathroom tiles and the coloring of the fixtures. But what goes on back of the bathroom tile is not part of the architectural design. Even if you studied "plumbing" and detailed the plumbing pipe layouts, your design would not be followed or even looked at. The layout would be determined by the plumber's scientifically illiterate craft code and frequent whimsy. The fact is that the plumbing system, and the sewer system, have not been importantly changed for 4500 years.[61]

The only significant development was apparently the water seal that stopped odors entering houses 100 years earlier, a key step in producing the illusion of disconnection from one's body and those of the neighbors. Fuller determined that there was only one man in the United States who had the knowledge of how to design toilet bowls, not only for American Standard Sanitary, which had the overwhelming monopoly on the market, but also all the other manufacturers.[62] He set out to design his own high-performance toilet. Fuller's drawings quickly evolved from traditional fittings of toilet and sink with partially exposed pipes toward fittings which were seemingly molded out of the wall panels that contained all the

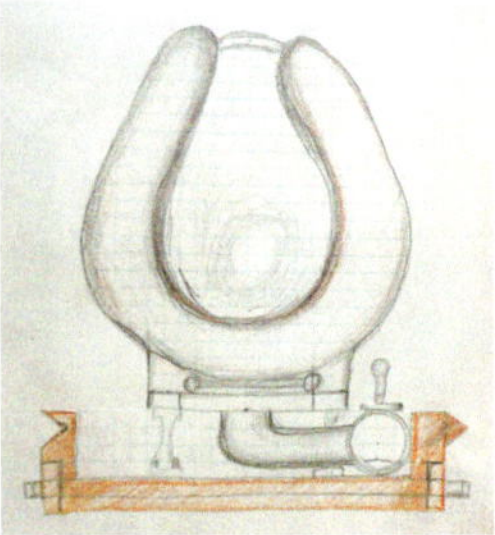

18

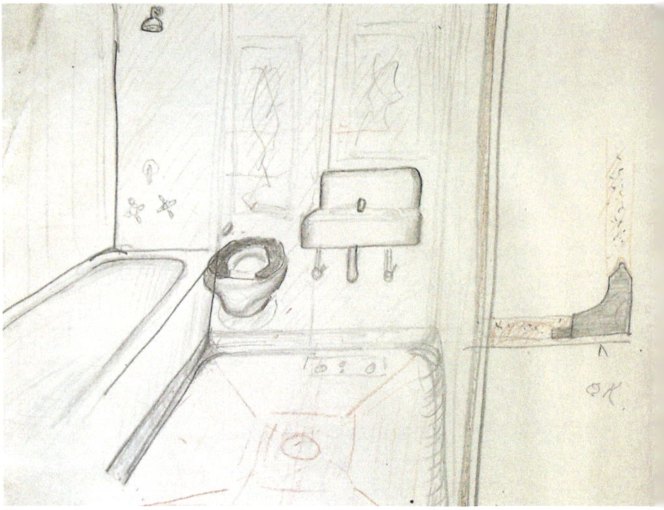

19

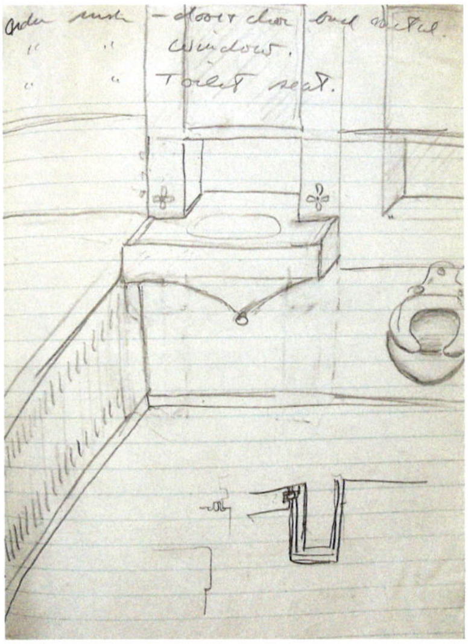

20

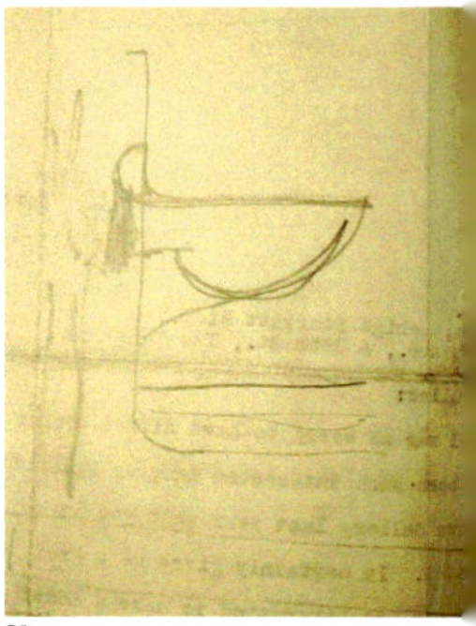

21

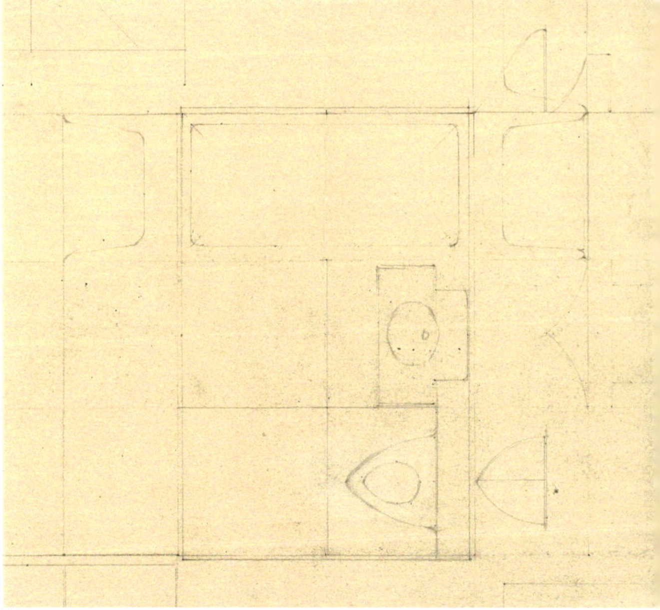

22

The Search for a Frictionless Bathroom

18 Robert Davison drawing of wall-mounted toilet bowl sent to RBF, May 14, 1931

19–20 RBF drawings of bathroom for American Standard Sanitary Manufacturing Company, May 1931

21 RBF drawing of toilet bowl with pivoting, self-supporting lid, May 1931

22 RBF plan and sectional elevation drawing of bathroom, dated May 21, 1931

23 RBF drawing of handle for flow control in shower and bath, May 1931

24 RBF perspective drawing of revised bathroom, dated May 21, 1931

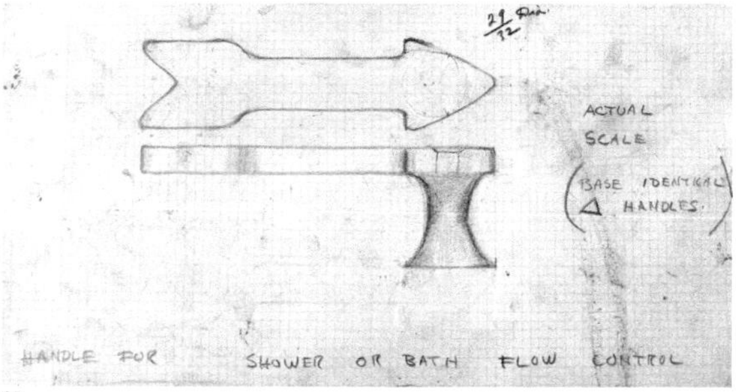
ACTUAL
SCALE
BASE IDENTICAL
HANDLES.
HANDLE FOR SHOWER OR BATH FLOW CONTROL

23

24

plumbing. The ambition was for the toilet and sink to become smooth extrusions of the wall surface itself but the deeper ambition was for the wall surface to become a smooth extrusion of the toilet itself. If the bathroom is the heart of architecture, the heart of the heart is the toilet. Architecture would unfurl itself from the bowl. The inner surface of the compact autonomous pipe splayed outward in ever more ephemeral layers like petals from a stem.

Fuller had accepted the job that was formally offered to him on April 11 by Robert L. Davison, the head of housing research for the newly formed John Pierce Foundation set up by American Standard Sanitary to explore the possibilities of the industrialized house. He began work just over a week later in a Buffalo workshop of the company, exploring how the plumbing and wall structure could be fully integrated. Within a week he was already building the model of a bathroom that reworked Davison's existing plan of back-to-back bathroom and kitchen units that shared the same plumbing, even if he confided to his diary about Davison that he had "found his ideas most limited" since the very first day.[63] Davison's more conventional layout was a step backward in comparison with the original bathroom unit for the Dymaxion House that was devoid of right angles and more compact in having toilet and sink opposite each other.[64] There was an unspoken tension between the two men, exacerbated by Fuller's also having to develop a wall panel concept of Davison's that he thought unworkable. Yet Fuller was excited by the work and happily obsessed on every detail from the sanitary processes to the surfaces, lighting, draining, plumbing, and structural system.

Davison would visit Buffalo periodically and express enthusiasm with the progress, but Fuller always stretched the concept further beyond him. On May 14, for example, Davison sent some hand drawings of sinks and toilets that embedded much of their plumbing in the wall, thinking of this as a major advance. **fig. 18** Fuller promptly incorporated them in his own sketches. **fig. 19** But a week later he was detailing his own more radical designs for the sink, toilet bowl, and tub. His first move was to flip the sink and toilet and blend the sink into the wall to hide the normally exposed plumbing within its curves and have the water come out of the sink itself rather than a visible faucet—with the flow going away from the user toward the wall to limit splashing. **fig. 20** He then blended the toilet into the wall. **fig. 21** The final step was to blend the walls into the ceiling and floor, completing a high-performance envelope with an aluminum ceiling above to distribute light and a cork-lined rubber pan forming the floor below as a drain. There was even a specific concept for a color scheme. Every element

63 Buckminster Fuller, diary entry for April 20, 1931, BFP Series 2, Box 24.

64 On April 6, 1931, two weeks before Fuller started working for the Pierce Foundation, they already had blueprints for a 5'1" × 7'9" bathroom attached back-to-back with a kitchen unit, but with the toilet next to the tub rather than the sink as in Fuller's version. That layout is still seen in blueprints of April 29 and in Fuller's early drawings but was reversed in early May.

65 "Today was an interesting and progressive day with the work. I designed several new features for the bathroom. There will be a tremendous improvement. When I take the equipment to New York for the conference you must come and see it. I am designing this work to do away with much of the weight and complication of present porcelain equipment and all cracks by not copying the old fixtures and methods of assembly. [...] It is excellent experience for me as well and serves to clarify many of the 4D problems. Keep these designs confidential which I will sketch on the next page. [...] Hope you like these drawings. They are not very adequate, but at least let you know what I am doing. [...] The section drawing is in another envelope and colored as I did not like to fold it. This is of course not my one piece bathroom but my adaption of Davison's knockdown one with improvements as far as I dare so with him." Buckminster Fuller to Evelyn Schwartz, 21 May 1931, BFP Series 2, Box 24.

was absorbed into a single system and a single image. Fuller tried to make the fixed grid of enameled metal panels communicate the more radical concept of a space defined by a single folded surface.

A sharp sense of breakthrough came on May 21 with a set of precise pencil drawings capturing the new organization of the bathroom and all of the inner surfaces and knobs in plan, elevation, and perspective. **figs. 22–24** The most care in Fuller's drawings was devoted to the shading of the surface of his new toilet bowl design as a compact smooth extrusion of the wall surface (radicalizing the already pointed shape of the toilet in his 1929 bathroom drawings). Fuller wrote late that evening to Evelyn Schwartz in New York, the woman half his age with whom he was having an intense affair, describing his new bathroom and the way it was focusing his whole 4D effort: "I am designing this work to do away with much of the weight and complication of present porcelain equipment and all cracks by not copying the old fixtures and methods of assembly. [...] It is excellent experience for me as well and serves to clarify many of the 4D problems."[65] The overly restrictive assignment from Davison was acting as a kind of training ground for the more important personal project. Asking that she keep it confidential, Fuller did some pencil drawings for her on his hotel stationery that highlighted all the features, materials, and color scheme of his design, insisting that "this is of course not my one piece bathroom but my adaption of Davison's knockdown one with improvements as far as I dare so with him." **figs. 25 and 27** He was obliged to make a compromise design blending a set of fittings into the wall surfaces of a more traditional arrangement but maintained his private dream of a single-piece sanitary fitting operating as a room as the very core of the 4D world.

The drawings in Fuller's letter are covered with eager notes detailing all the advances but also communicating the philosophical, technical, and aesthetic agenda, the driving impulses or compulsions of the overall 4D mission that would produce a more radical bathroom if released. The section drawing showing how his toilet starts to submerge itself into the wall highlights both its smooth aesthetic—"form of bowl sculptural similar bow of ship with clean sharp line down front"—and its technical performance—"friction roller ball back in wall to hold seat at whatever angle it is elevated to like victrola cover." Smoothness is the key throughout the room, even a smoothness of light, heat, and touch. A radiator for warming the tub to body temperature, for example, is discretely built into the sides of the tub and there are no bolts, hinges, or cracks allowed to be visible or touchable on any surface. A day later, Fuller carefully prepared a watercolor chart of the different colors for each surface of the bathroom. **fig. 26** This continued the thinking of the Dymaxion House, which had all its surfaces and fixtures defined by different colors, and the original 4D Tower of 1928, which had been conceived as a space defined by smooth "4D color progression" from the darkness of black at the center through yellows, greens, reds, and blues through to white at the perimeter. Fuller's obsessive attempt to develop frictionless mechanical tools is finally all about the production of an ethereal atmosphere. The color chart is not an optional final layer of decoration but an integral part of the relentless assault on

PIPELESS DREAMS

Love Letters

25, 27 RBF letter to Evelyn Schwartz dated May 21, 1931

26 “Proposed bathroom coloring — Buckminster Fuller — 5/22/31” RBF watercolor folded into Chronofile

28–30 RBF letter to Evelyn Schwartz dated June 9, 1931

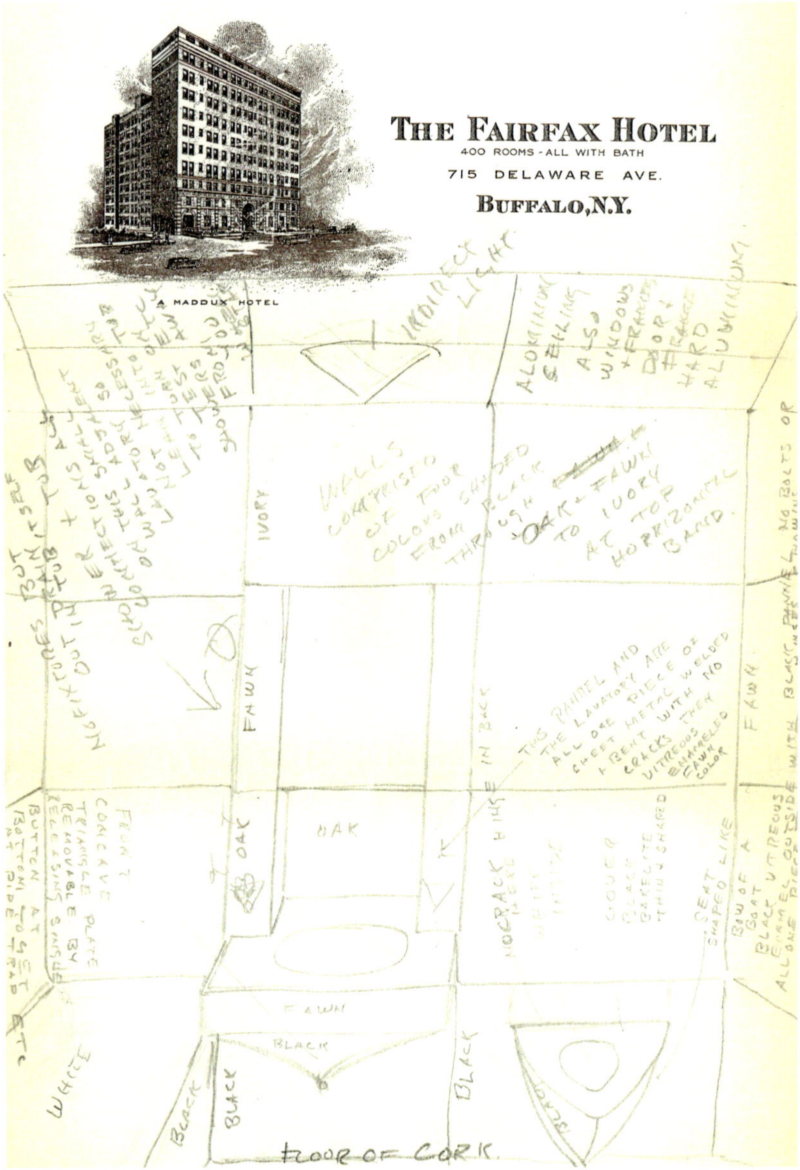

25

26

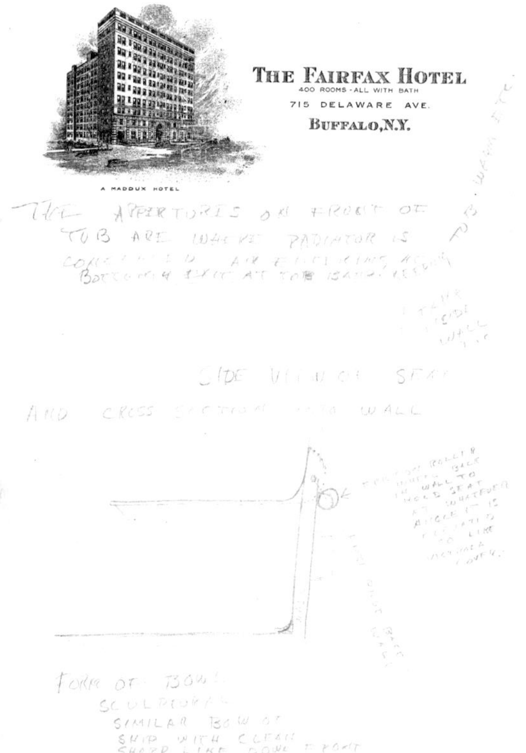
THE FAIRFAX HOTEL
400 ROOMS - ALL WITH BATH
715 DELAWARE AVE.
BUFFALO,N.Y.
A MADDUX HOTEL

27

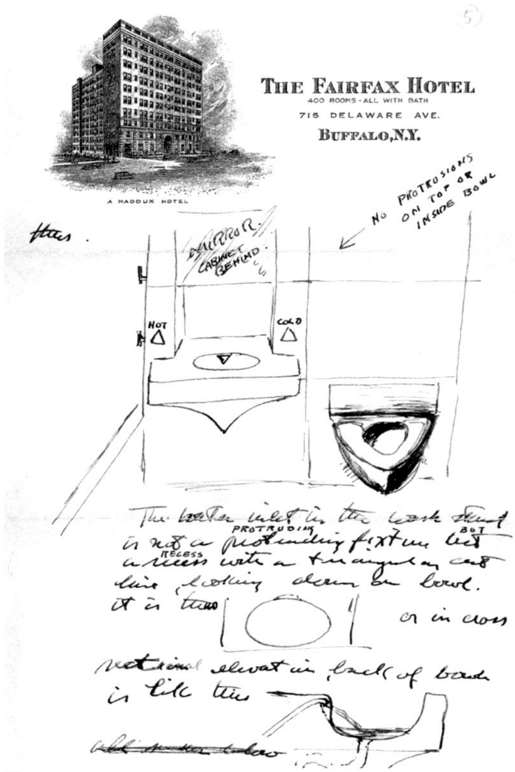
THE FAIRFAX HOTEL
400 ROOMS - ALL WITH BATH
715 DELAWARE AVE.
BUFFALO,N.Y.
A MADDUX HOTEL
NO PROTRUSIONS ON TOP OR INSIDE BOWL
MIRROR CABINET BEHIND
HOT
COLD

28

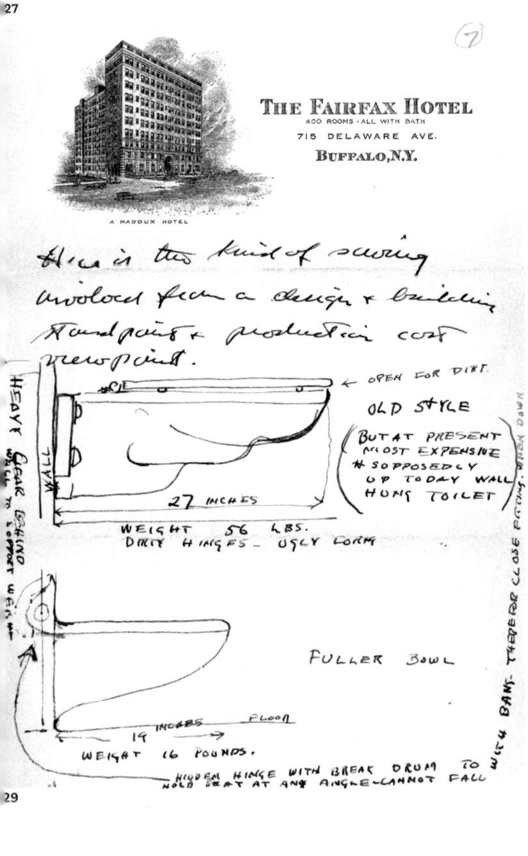
THE FAIRFAX HOTEL
400 ROOMS - ALL WITH BATH
715 DELAWARE AVE.
BUFFALO,N.Y.
A MADDUX HOTEL
OPEN FOR DIRT.
OLD STYLE
BUT AT PRESENT MOST EXPENSIVE
27 INCHES
WEIGHT 56 LBS.
FULLER BOWL
FLOOR
19 INCHES
WEIGHT 16 POUNDS.

29

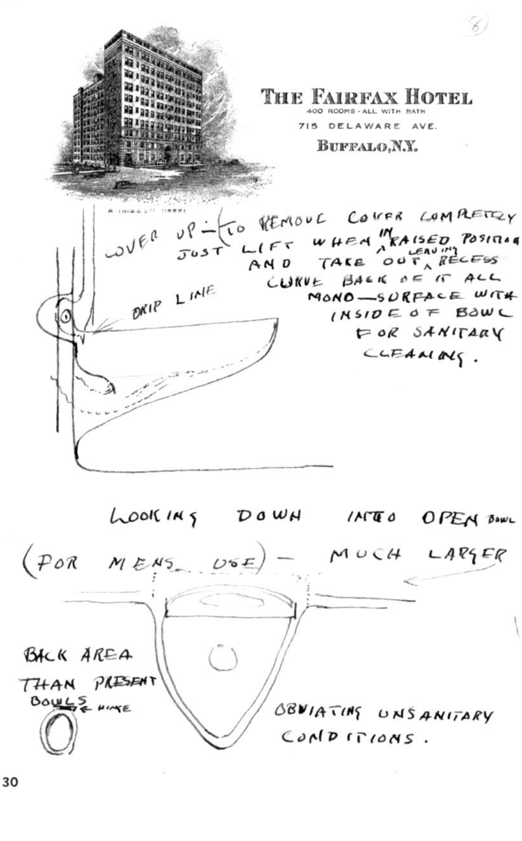
THE FAIRFAX HOTEL
400 ROOMS - ALL WITH BATH
715 DELAWARE AVE.
BUFFALO,N.Y.
DRIP LINE
LOOKING DOWN INTO OPEN BOWL
(FOR MENS USE) - MUCH LARGER
BACK AREA
THAN PRESENT
BOWLS
OBVIATING UNSANITARY CONDITIONS.

30

friction. That evening, Fuller reported to Evelyn that "having designed my own special lavatory and toilet," he had now started to work on the tub design to likewise make it "much more sanitary, better looking, convenient." No element could be left out. He expressed particular pride in the absence of faucets and having found a way to conceal the toilet paper holder in the side of the toilet itself along with the trip handle for the seat.[66] He was engaged in a relentless attempt to blend everything into the vertical wall surfaces and then to blend those surfaces into the horizontal surfaces for lighting, ventilation, and drainage to produce as great a sense of a single enveloping high-performance surface as possible.

A few weeks later, Fuller wrote to Evelyn that sometimes his days on the project were "a pain in the neck and I almost lose interest and at others I feel so elated." That particular day had been one of the painful ones and, as if to reassure himself, he devoted an eleven-page letter to detailing all the accumulated refinements of his bathroom in his obsessive attempt to rid it of all fittings, visible hinges, bolts, and "unsightly cracks or pipes or bulbous-bulging forms apparently meant to fit into the entrails of an elephant."[67] He sketched his redesigned triangular control knobs that wouldn't slip with a wet hand and the single control in the form of an arrow to control the temperature in the shower/tub. He even drew a section through the most up-to-date toilet on the market, pointing out its "dirty hinges—ugly form," bulk, weight, expense, and unacceptable "gap for dirt" under the seat in comparison to the section drawn below it of the new "Fuller Bowl" showing how compact, gapless, smooth, clean, and light it was. **figs. 28–30** A drawing of the whole ensemble celebrates the single buffed metal wall panel accommodating the toilet, sink, and medicine cabinet without any protrusions or seams and everything covered with shiny black enamel to be "as sanitary as a soup plate" and "the same is true of the seat" which is dull black enamel. There are also "no protrusions above or inside the bowl" whose interior was to be covered with white enamel. Even more remarkably, there is a second more detailed section of the Fuller Bowl to show that when the seat is raised, its underside forms a "mono-surface with inside of bowl for sanitary cleaning" and a man's eye view of the bowl from above shows how it gets wider as it meets the wall "obviating unsanitary conditions." Fuller concluded the love letter by saying "it is time someone with taste tackled so intimate and universal a problem, which hitherto seems to have been designed by a vulgar plumbing boss [...] to racket the situation for selfish producers—that's all I can see." He reported that "my one piece bathroom design is also getting better and better" without showing any drawings of it.

Off to one side, hidden even from his most intimate confident, Fuller had been sketching a more compact bathroom unit with the toilet and sink opposite each other as in the original bathroom unit of the Dymaxion House. **fig. 31** This private design was thought of as a single pipe with a set

66 Buckminster Fuller to Evelyn Schwartz, 22 May 1931, BFP Series 2, Box 24.

67 Buckminster Fuller to Evelyn Schwartz, 9 June 1931, BFP Series 2, Box 24. "Sometimes affairs generally give me a pain in the neck and I almost lose interest and at others I feel so elated. Today was more adding the first line, but I am sure all will develop into something good. Have actually done some good to bathroom fixture design anyway." Ibid.

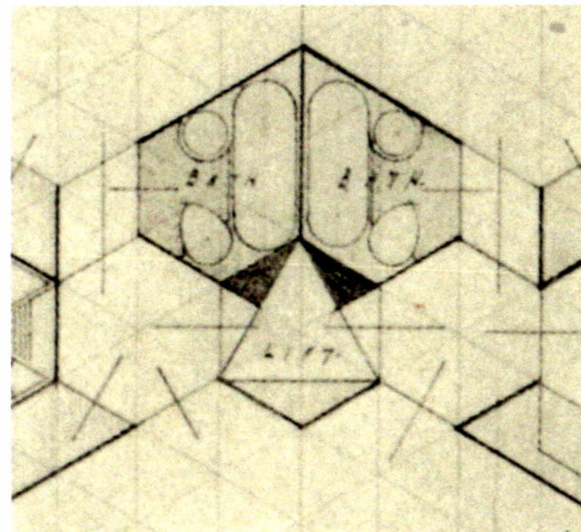

31

32

The Secret Project to Turn the Bathroom into a Mini Dymaxion House

31 Twin bathroom units at the heart of the Dymaxion House, *Architecture*, June 1929

32–34 RBF sketches of private, more compact 4D Bathroom project, with condensed plumbing, wire structure and plexiglass lighting system, 1931

33

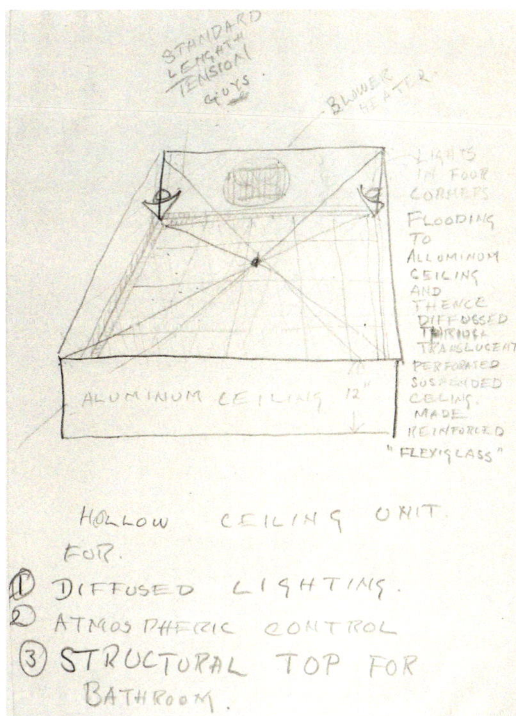

34

of three openings and was structured by criss-crossing wires as in the early house. It was defined more by the ceiling and floor systems than by the wall panels. **figs. 32–34** Some of its features had migrated into the official project. The ceiling system, for example, picked up a perforated plane of plexiglass suspended below the aluminum to distribute the light instead of the earlier light fixture as part of the overall attempt to steadily erase the very idea of fittings. Yet the 4D Bathroom project being quietly incubated in parallel with the Pierce Foundation assignment remained secret, a pattern throughout Fuller's career in which paranoia about intellectual property and the motives of others was inseparable from a deep sense of personal pleasure in the idea of highly secret embryonic growth. The most hyperexposed and talkative architect of all was addicted to the idea of the big secret and what could be more tantalizing than a secret bathroom, a secret project for the most secretive space for secretions?

The final 5 × 7-foot bathroom package containing all the plumbing, wiring, and lighting that would be attached back-to-back against an equally compact kitchen unit was ready to show to the leadership of American Sanitary by July but was blocked, according to Fuller, by the plumbers as a threat to their livelihood, with American Sanitary promptly acquiescing to the demand from the union whose members were the main purchasers of its products. Fuller resigned on July 31 and published a protest article with the canny title "Concealed Plumbing" at the end of 1932 in his new magazine *Shelter*.[68] It reprinted the recent article by the Master Plumbers Association describing his "freakish and revolutionary" house without sewage or water connections as "the most menacing challenge" to their industry but Fuller argued that this "selfish prejudice" was not their fault. It was just the most obvious symptom of the more subtle resistance to transforming the standard of dwellings by the vested interests of capitalism, a protectionism that had quietly but successfully managed to withdraw the support to the Dymaxion House once shown by universities, museums, publications, and associations. Resistance to the autonomous bathroom was but the visible tip of the general resistance to the Dymaxion approach of trying to do the most with the least. Yet it is not by chance that plumbing was the most visible point of resistance to the "economic

68 Buckminster Fuller "Concealed Plumbing," *Shelter* 2, no. 5 (November 1932): 118.

69 Ibid.

70 "Today I lunched with Dunning who told me that you were anxious to have your bathroom design published at an early date. Can we have the drawings and specifications for publication in the Record?" K. L. Holm to Buckminster Fuller, 9 July 1931, BFP Series 2, Box 23.

71 Robert Davison to Buckminster Fuller, 24 July 1931, BFP Series 2, Box 23.

72 "New Housing Designs and Construction Systems," *Architectural Record* 75, no. 1 (January 1934): 36. Davison had presented the bathroom on behalf of American Standard Sanitary at a low-cost housing conference in October 1933.

73 The bathroom that had been published by the magazine "is a meagerly changed version of that very same bathroom, in mechanical and structural identity, which I produced for Pierce Foundation in 1930 in the Buffalo shop. [...] The whole principle of the association of that bathroom and kitchen by a unit manifold of plumbing [...] is clearly demonstrated in the Dymaxion House patent claims filed in 1927." Buckminster Fuller to Howard Myers, *Architectural Forum*, 28 October 1943, BFP Series 8, Box 6, Folder 6, p. 4. In a follow-up letter several weeks later, Fuller devotes a number of pages to Davison's attempts to appropriate the bathroom. "Davison would visit the Buffalo shop in which I had chosen to carry out the work. On his return to New York he would prepare drawings and have them blueprinted and write me a letter instructing me to carry out the work that I had already completed, thus documenting himself as the originator of my work. Finally when the bathroom was completed, he brought it on to New York to show it to Mr. Wooley and the other American Radiator executives. We assembled it in a warehouse room on 11th Avenue. Shortly before the American Radiator executives arrived to inspect the bathroom, Davison, blustering and blushing, asked if I would mind not being present during the inspection. I said that if he would admit that he was representing himself to Mr. Wooley as 'that Dymaxion man who was originating this work' and therefore my presence would show him up, I would agree to withdraw and, of course, immediately terminate my services with the Pierce Foundation. He admitted it was true and I withdrew." Buckminster Fuller to Howard Myers, 3 December 1943, BFP Series 8, Box 6, Folder 6. Fuller argues that after he left the Foundation, Davison maneuvered to get access to Fuller's research files on the Dymaxion House to benefit from them.

74 Prospectus by E. Morrison Nichols for "A Completely Manufactured Bathroom," BFP Series 2, Box 17.

evolution" implied in the Dymaxion House. The transformation of society that such a house would incubate might even start with the person esponsible for the pipes: "so that a plumber, having at last no plumbing-o-plumb, might revert to the uncompromised estate of his birth when he reathed, even though but for a moment, as a human being and not as a ecessity-bred drain cleaner or pipe-twister."[69] Servitude to capitalism is iterally servitude to pipes. The story was clearly far from over for Fuller. Houses were optional but not bathrooms.

Nothing could have been more personal for Fuller. In fact, the real attle at American Sanitary had not been with the plumbers. Fuller and Davison had both been convinced that the prototype bathroom was a big tep forward in the industrialization of housing but their working relationhip rapidly broke apart in late July 1931. Fuller had been in dialogue with Richard Neutra about working together on the more radical concept of the ne-piece bathroom that he was incubating on the side and in early July *Architectural Record* had heard that Fuller wanted to publish a new bathoom and asked him for the drawings.[70] Davison, who had himself been he technical editor at *Architectural Record* before heading research for he Pierce Foundation, accused Fuller of independently presenting their hared work for the Foundation to other interests, provoking Fuller to draft an angry denial reminding him that he had been working on the idea ince 1927.[71] He later argued that Davison's only role had been to turn his drawings into engineering drawings and present them to the directors of American Sanitary as Davison's own work. Years later, he was still angry. Davison published the Pierce Foundation bathroom unit with more conentional fixtures in the January 1934 *Architectural Record* on behalf of American Standard Sanitary,[72] and when *Architectural Forum* proposed a eries of retrospective articles on the Foundation in 1943, Fuller sent the ditors a detailed confidential account of Davison's misrepresentations nd successful attempts to access his files to appropriate the work, reminding the magazine that he had been exploring all dimensions of the industrialized house, including especially the bathroom, since the original Dymaxion House, as was evident already in his first patent drawings.[73] Much of the thinking of the compact bathroom and the idea of autonomous plumbing was already in the first versions of the house in 1928, both n the patent drawings and in the revised model that had led to his appointment at American Sanitary in 1931. But it's equally true that when Fuller was designing that house he already had on file a late 1927 prospectus for "A Completely Manufactured Bathroom" occupying just 44 × 52 inches. Its concept to base a unit around a tub with an internal seat and a sink that olded up into the wall had been proposed by a Chicago builder who had een looking to fund the project.[74] In a sense, the idea of a compact, scientifically advanced, industrialized bathroom precedes that of the industrialized house, to such an extent that again Fuller's house might properly be thought of as an extension of the bathroom.

CLEANING THE ARCHITECT

It was as if Fuller could only return to the house through the bathroom. From 1936 to 1938 he again devoted himself to developing a Dymaxion Bathroom while working as an economic and technological trend consultant to the Phelps Dodge company, obsessing about every detail, and later celebrating his total absorption in the project: "Now, I really did spend two years doing nothing but really getting things the way they could be really right on this."[75] In a sense, he treated the bathroom as a miniature house, developing more drawings than he ever had for the Dymaxion House and working with one-to-one prototypes in the factory. He collaborated closely with fitters and metalworkers to produce a 5 × 5-foot self-contained unit that finally removed the distinction between room and pipe, architecture and fitting. It started by simply compacting the 5 × 7-foot version of 1931 by putting the toilet opposite the sink and passing the plumbing through the side of the tub—keeping many of the 1931 ideas about floor, ceiling, lighting, heating, ventilation, and enamel surfaces. Fuller had done a series of drawings (later backdated to 1929 to 1930, when he had not even begun work for American Sanitary) in which each element became progressively more curved until the whole bathroom was a single smoothly folded figure. **figs. 35–37** The step of the tub at the center of the design is polemically rendered as a double curved inflection of the continuous surface. Discrete functional elements gave way to functional inflections. Everything evolved into smoothness except the original "Fuller Bowl" of 1931, which now acted as the model for everything else. The curves of the space come out of the toilet. The first built version of mid 1936 had less curvature but included the Fuller toilet bowl and was photographed by *Harper's Bazaar* at the end of the year for their February 1937 issue, with Fuller carefully editing the caption to the single gleaming image to say that it would be available for order the following month and could be installed in any room near plumbing pipes.[76]

More impressively, F. S. Lincoln, the same photographer Fuller had used for the early publications of his 4D Housing Tower and Dymaxion Car, did a set of photographs of the relentlessly smooth bathroom unit for in-depth coverage in the January 1937 issue of *Architectural Record*.[77] Demonstrating just how personal the bathroom was, Fuller himself even appeared in one of the photographs. **fig. 38** In what might be the very first publication of a naked architect, he is seen standing in the tub intently cleaning his foot in a remarkable celebration of personal hygiene that his

75 Fuller, "Everything I Know," Session 10, Part 14 (see note 60).
76 "Dymaxion Bathroom," *Harper's Bazaar*, February 1937, 104.
77 "Integrated Bathroom: Phelps Dodge Bathroom Designed for Mass-Production," *Architectural Record*, January 1937, 40–41.
78 Christopher Morley, "The Bowling Green," *Saturday Review*, January 23, 1937, 13; *Architect's Journal*, February 11, 1937, 282; *House Beautiful*, March 1, 1937, 124.
79 "We should be having a packaging toilet. We package our foods inbound, so we might as well package it coming outbound, [...] so these very valuable chemistries can go off where they are supposed to. [...] When Nature takes a terrific amount of trouble to separate things, as for instance our liquids and the solids coming out of us, it is preposterous to put them back together again, so it is quite easy then to develop your apparatus in ways that the liquids and the solids do not get mixed up, but it has been [...] we have engineering, we have all kinds of hydraulics, we know exactly what the frictions are in pipes, and so forth, but and then we have sewage disposal, big sewage disposal plants that just cities will buy, but nobody going into direct research to see what this really means. At your own home, really at the site. And it is something that really could be engaged in very, very readily, and there is just no nonsense about it." Fuller, "Everything I Know," Session 11, Part 2 (see note 60). Fuller already had the idea of preserving human waste for methane production in the 1928 version of his house and made the concept central to his 1932 proposal of a shelter for the USSR. With "no pipes to freeze," a tractor connected "by flexible tube to tubing in mast" would convert the solid waste into gas to power the shelter. Buckminster Fuller, "Scientific Shelter for USSR," *Shelter* 2, no. 5 (November 1932): 94–95.

friend and drinking partner Christopher Morley immediately published without comment in the January issue of his own magazine, *Saturday Review*, with the permission of *Architectural Record*, as did *The Architect's Journal* in London the following month and *House Beautiful* in March.[78] In this widely circulated image, Fuller no longer sits outside an architectural model looking at a naked woman inside. He has himself become the naked model seen inside the full-sized artifact. Architect and bathroom have become one—so much so that the fact that it is Fuller inside is never stated in any of the magazines and the remarkable gesture of cleaning himself for the camera is never subsequently referred to. Nudity itself goes unnoticed—as if Fuller is able to go about his personal rituals of hygiene as privately on the pages of mass-circulation magazines as within the Dymaxion House itself, or any house that had been enhanced by this new piece of sanitary equipment.

The accompanying drawings in *Architectural Record* already show the revised design of November 1936 which had fully absorbed the Fuller Bowl into the curved skin of the capsule. **fig. 39** Even the toilet lid that Fuller had been obsessively detailing for five years was treated as part of the surface. **fig. 40** The 1931 fantasy of the single folded surface had finally been realized. The toilet, bath/shower, sink, soap holders, shelves, step, floor, ceiling, sidewalls, mirror, lighting, heating, ventilation, and entry were all part of a continuous double-curved surface of molded sheet metal or preferably plastic—with all the pipes nestled within the curves. The horizontal and vertical section drawings show how the pipes wrap and define the rounded spaces for the body, placing it within the very heart of the flow, turning the sophisticated valve of liquid, light, and heat into a cocoon. **fig. 41** An unpublished isometric blueprint captures the complete confusion of surface, space, and pipe awaiting the human body. Minimal fluids were needed and recycling was maximized. Nothing coming out of the body would leave the house. Even the solid waste was automatically shrink-wrapped for later use.[79] Simple hookups for connection to air, water, waste air, waste water, sewage, and electricity enabled it to be installed in any house and de-installed equally easily. It was a polemically autonomous unit and appeared so since its outer, more boxy, curves were designed to be seen. The portable room could break down into pieces slender enough to pass through any conventional door. **fig. 42** Fuller imagined that people would want to take their bathroom with them, as a kind of prized possession or even as an intimate extension or container of their body. The bathroom would be at once the most intimate space and the most mobile.

It was like a portable personal cave with its internal curves closely molded to the curves of the body and internally heated to be the same temperature. It was in every sense a frictionless space with a single naked person smoothly nestled inside it. It was a uterine haven from straight lines, a sanctuary of pure fluidity and mobility—a place to renovate mobility itself. Its polemically closed circuits allowed Fuller's house to be a polemically open circuit. But crucially it didn't need that house, or any house. It would usually land in houses but was most at home in the space of movement: "The ranges of uses for the unit is broad: Pullman, planes,

PIPELESS DREAMS

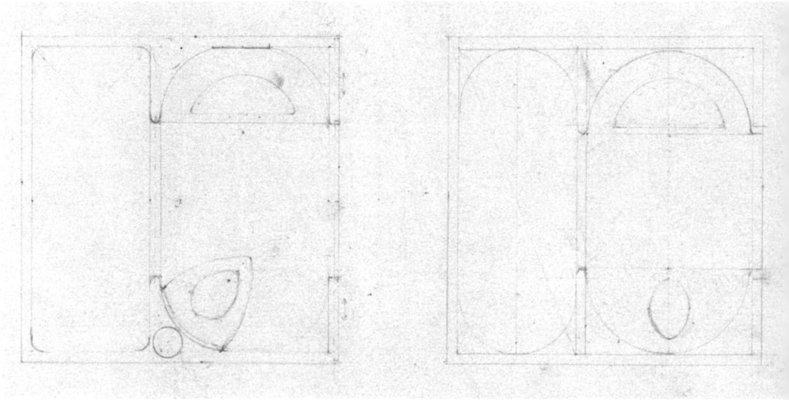

35

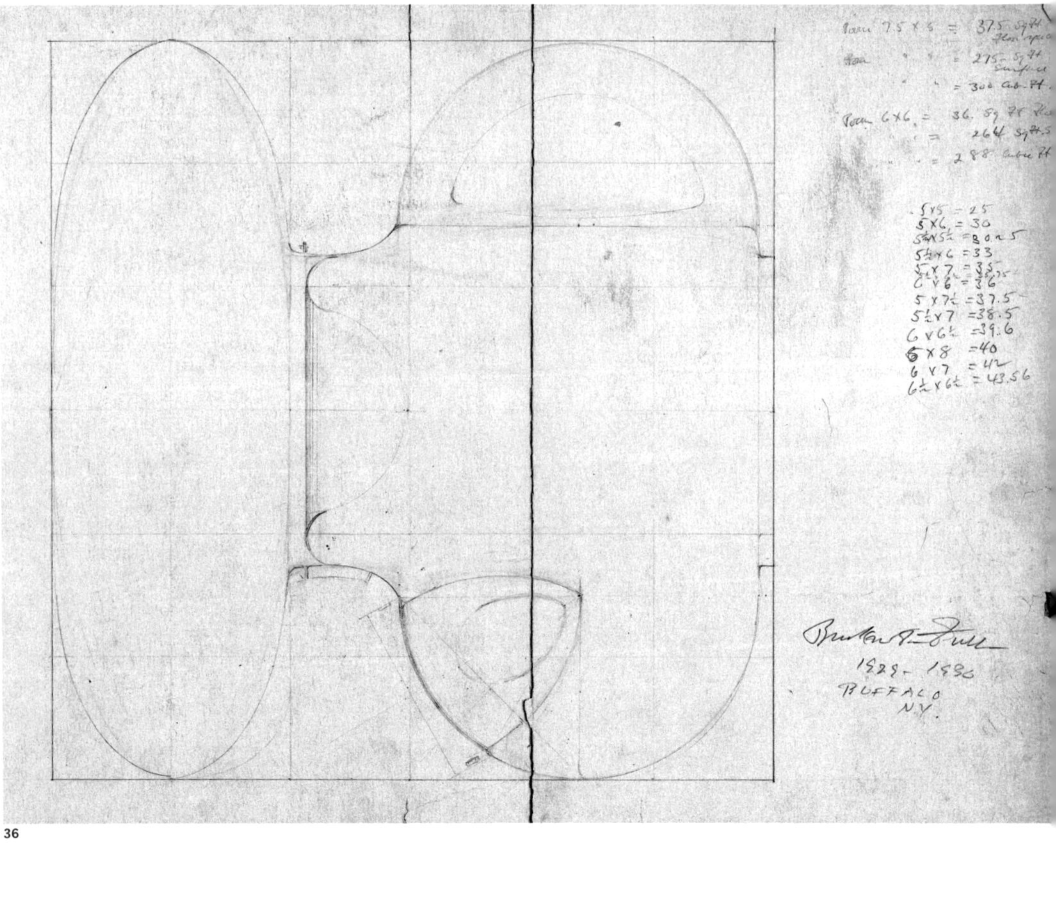

36

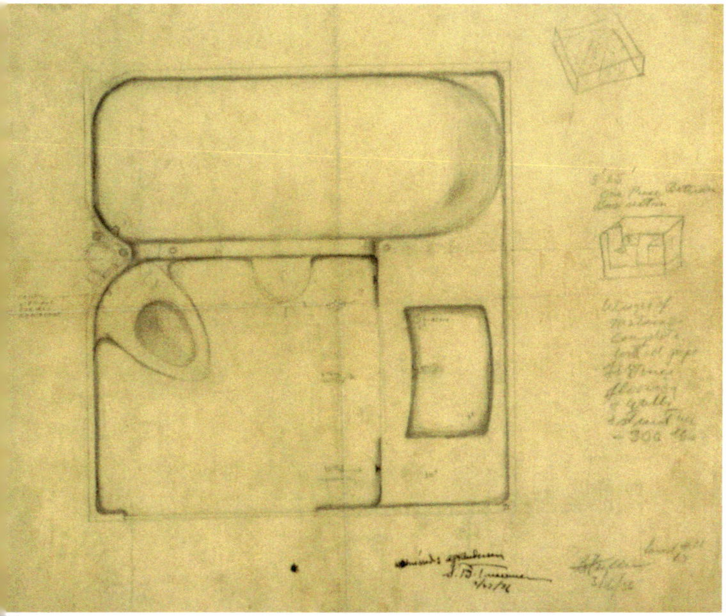

37

8

Smoothing the Architecture and the Architect

35–37 RBF's evolving drawings of Dymaxion Bathroom Unit, 1936

38 F. S. Lincoln December 1936 photograph of RBF in prototype of the first version of Dymaxion Bathroom Unit for Phelps Dodge Corporation, *Architectural Record*, January 1937

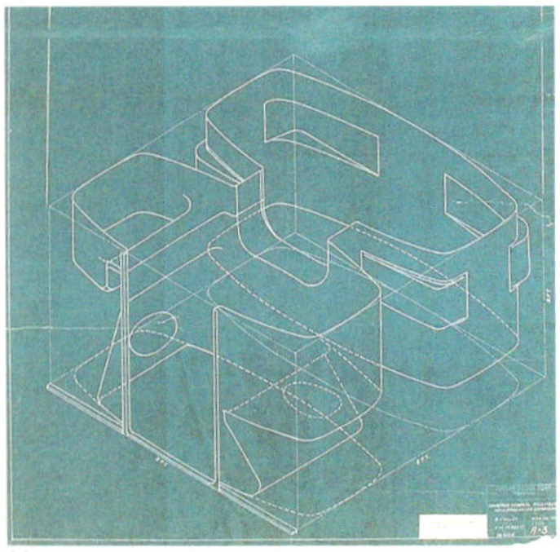
39

40

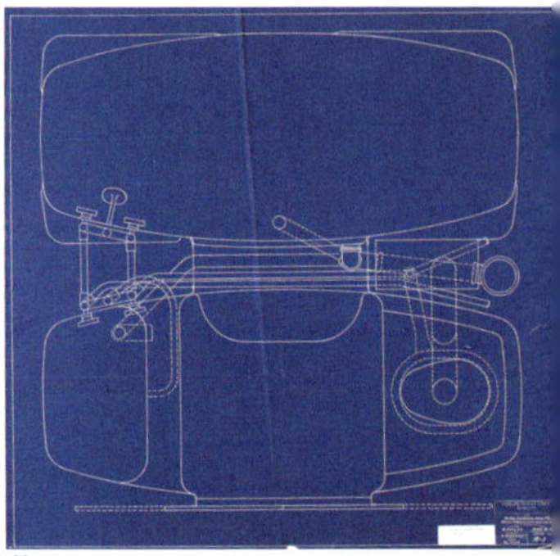
41

Implanting an Inner Space Capsule

39 Blueprint axonometric of second version of Dymaxion Bathroom Unit, 1937, showing new form first published in *Architectural Record*, January 1937

40 RBF demonstrates toilet lid of Dymaxion Bathroom Unit prototype, 1937

41 Blueprint plan of second version of Dymaxion Bathroom Unit, 1937, with new organization first published in *Architectural Record*, January 1937

42 Axonometric of Dymaxion Bathroom Unit installation, January 8, 1937

43 RBF delivering Dymaxion Bathroom Unit to Knothole house of Christopher Morley, 1938

44 Undated rendering of final production version of Dymaxion Bathroom Unit in translucent plastic

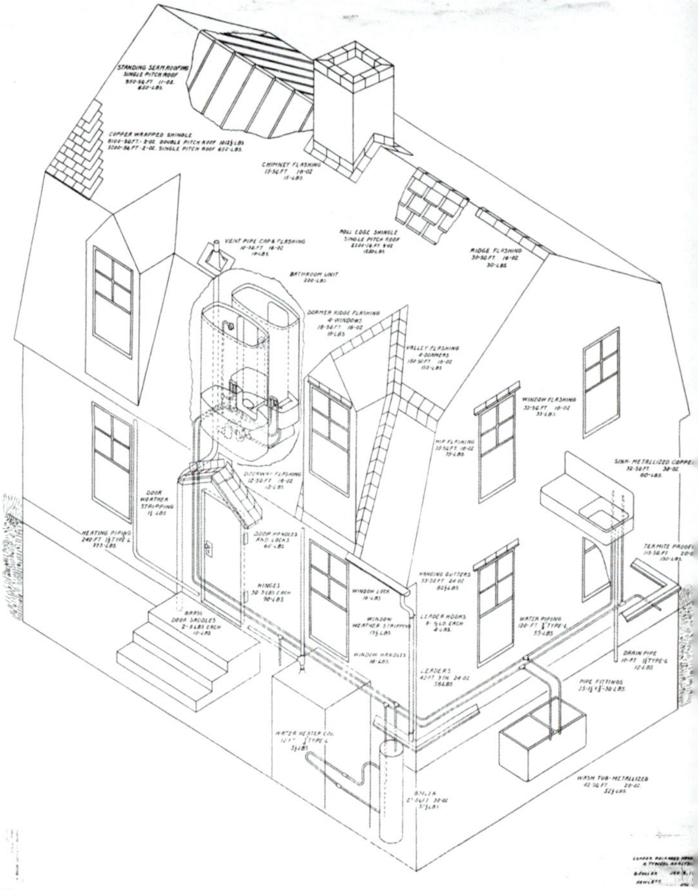
42

43

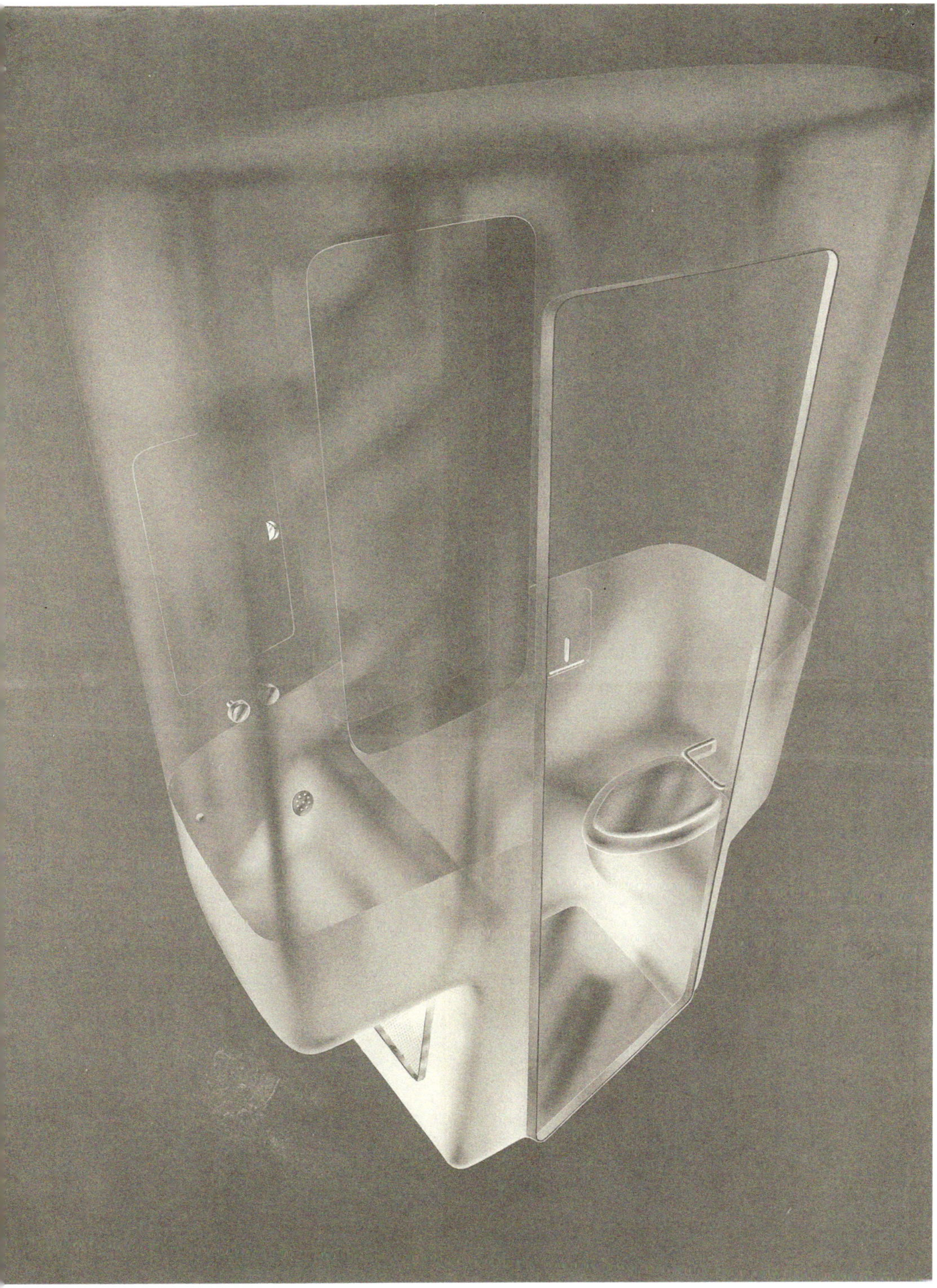

4

trailers, trains, but mainly small homes."[80] The mobility of the bathroon never went away. On the contrary, it pulled the house itself toward move ment. Its own independence was what allowed the house to be indepen dent. More precisely, it was the beginning of a house, the possibility o a genuinely scientific housing instrument.

The agreement to fabricate the new design was made in May 1937.[8 A small test run was imagined. One of the finished bathroom units wa mounted on the back of a pickup truck so Fuller could promote its virtue wherever he went, and he received a lot of coverage in the popular an professional media, which seemed to revive interest in the Dymaxion House with a flurry of new articles. The hopeful slogan was "a bathroon for every bedroom" and there was some success in the fall of 1937 when tw were installed in an apartment in New York and Richard Neutra installe two of the "sensationally new" bathrooms at the heart of the Windshiel House, the clients of which had seen one of the very first prototypes in the fall of 1936.[82] Six units had been made by December of 1937 and thre more were under way to fill firm orders, including one that was driven t Washington by Fuller to be tested by the Bureau of Standards in the hop of getting it to be made part of the government housing program. A fev of Fuller's closest friends like the writer Christopher Morley ordered som to be installed in 1938. **fig. 43** The idea was to keep handcrafting the proto types on demand until going into mass production.[83] Fuller was goin to form a company called "TELEFACTURE Incorporated" to develop i further and guide the manufacture and distribution.[84] He exhibited th bathroom in the courtyard of his close friend Isamu Noguchi in April 193 where the *New York Times* reported that it might serve as a "snare to lure u ultimately into Fuller's Dymaxion House itself "by feeding our America passion for extravagant *cleanliness*."[85] People waited under umbrellas in th rain to admire its functionality, with the artists being particularly enthusia tic. The bathroom had become the ultimate artwork: "convex forms, flow ing logically into one another, helped explain certain aspects of contempo rary sculpture that has seemed, up to this time, obscure. One felt onesel

80 "The Newest Prefabricated Bathroom Is Also Nearest," *The Ladle* (April 1937).
81 W. H. Osborn to Buckminster Fuller, 25 May 1936, BFP Series 2, Box 37.
82 Dietirich Neuman, ed., *Richard Neutra's Windshield House* (New Haven: Yale University Press, 2001), 48. In early 1938 Neutra asked Fuller if he could install one of the units in a demonstration "Health Room" within a residence "which should become a somewhat sensational demonstration of what preventative medical science has to suggest to a contemporary human being." Richard Neutra to Buckminster Fuller, 31 May 1938, BFP Series 2, Box 38.
83 Buckminster Fuller, "Research and Development Program—Prefabricated Bathrooms," report to W. H. Osborn dated December 1937, BFP Series 2, Box 38.
84 "'TELEFACTURE, Incorporated' is the name tentatively adopted for the corporation to be formed for development and exploitation of the prefabricated bathroom unit invented by Buckminster Fuller and perfected by him while in the employ of Phelps Dodge Corporation. This coined word, suggested by Mr. Fuller, reflects the chief activity of the proposed Corporation—development of ideas through design into working units suitable for industrial production. [...] Chiefly this will be a patent-holding, research and development Corporation. It will not engage in manufacture—beyond that of an experimental nature—of units it may control or develop." Memorandum, organization and activities of Telefacture, Inc., May 20, 1938, BFP Series 2, Box 530, Folder 6.
85 Ruth Green Harris, "Art in Our Daily Lives: Aesthetic Considerations That Reach Out into Housing, Utilities and Other Fields," *New York Times* May 1, 1938.
86 Ibid. In reverse, the same article described mistaking Noguchi's new Radio Nurse design for Zenith as "a piece of abstract sculpture." Just as a utilitarian bathroom turned out to be a sculpture, a sculpture turne out to be a utilitarian object. Noguchi "sees no reason why there should not be radios, designed from the inside out, like a good portrait or a good bathroom or a good city."
87 *Art in Our Time* (New York: Museum of Modern Art, 1939), 334.The bathroom appeared in the Design Department section of the exhibition and the Dymaxion House within the Houses and Housing section that was produced as an independent traveling exhibition in collaboration with the United States Housing Authority. It was described as an experimental house not "designed to be built" but containing "elements which will influence housing of the future." "Facts Concerning the Houses and Housing Section of *Art in Our Time* Exhibition at the Museum of Modern Art," MoMA press release, May 10, 1939. Newspaper coverage of the exhibited bathroom included: "Fabricate Complete One-Piece Bathroom,"*Barrons*, October 2, 1939, 5.
88 "The Mechanical Wing," *The Architectural Forum*, October 1940, 92.
89 Buckminster Fuller to Virginia Thorndike, J. Walter Thompson Co., 17 July 1944, BFP Series 2, Box 72, Folder 12, p. 3.
90 Ibid., 4.

inside a piece of metal sculpture designed in relation to you and me."[86] The unit was even exhibited along with the Dymaxion House at MoMA in June 1939 as part of *Art in Our Time*," the tenth anniversary exhibition of the museum on the occasion of the opening of its new building.[87]

The bathroom unit was celebrated as the most advanced machine for cleaning every opening in the human body but never gained momentum—perhaps for that very reason. Even if was completely sealed, the capsule form and hint of its internal folds through the curved entry hole made public what everyone worked so hard to hide, as even revealed in the everyday use of the word *bathroom* in the United States to avoid speaking directly about what goes on inside the space.

The roving publicity campaign itself seemingly turned into another project in 1940 with The Mechanical Wing, a compact trailer containing all the mechanical services of a house, with a Dymaxion Bathroom attached to a kitchen, laundry, and energy unit—using the same logic of internally recirculating all liquids, solids, and gases.[88] Two of the original bathrooms naturally formed the polemical centerpiece of the 1946 version of the Dymaxion House developed in Wichita and were installed in the one completed prototype home but remained a piece of propaganda, a weapon in Fuller's campaign to rethink the capacity and responsibility of architecture.

Working with the Board of Economic Warfare in 1943 and 1944, Fuller had argued for the conversion of the military aircraft industry into the dwelling industry, repeating the arguments he had made since 1927 for a mobile house whose design would be continuously "reprocessed" by a new globally networked industry. Once again, the argument centered on the bathroom. Pipes and wires had been steadily taking over houses. The arrival of permanent plumbing had transformed sanitation and cleaning but the pipes and wires were treated as intruders into the already outmoded yet powerful fantasy of the permanent house and therefore had to be hidden inside walls or moldings. The cost of this "insinuation" of tubes concealing all the "connecting network of pipes, conduits, and wires" was so high that plumbing was only available for the rich.[89] The whole economics of the house inevitably changed when the middle class desired the same level of sanitation and hygiene. All the investment now went into the plumbing rather than the shell. Mechanical services went from being just 3 percent of the budget at the beginning of the century to being 55 percent of the budget just before the war. Yet the concept of pipes as an unwelcome intrusion into the old image of the permanent house remained and "though less than a century old the picture of what constitutes a bathroom is as fixed as what constitutes a castle or an angel." Once again, Fuller was arguing for an advanced mechanical core at the center of the dwelling where "man and his needs are primary" and the overall shell was to be supported by that core—completing the inversion of the house from a permanent fixed shell invaded by external pipes to internal pipes supporting a dynamic, evolving mobile shell. A newly efficient plumbing system had the ability to launch not only a new economics of housing but "whole new economic concepts" about private and common wealth.[90] It is as if the bathroom becomes the engine of the whole economy. Improvements in sanitation and cleaning translate into massive shifts in cultural, technological, and financial capacity.

In late 1943 Fuller wrote to Alfred Bossom, the head of the British Building Mission in North America, about how they might collaborate when Bossom returned to England after the war. The letter addressed all aspects of the industrialization of housing but soon focused on the bathroom. The first step in producing scientific dwelling is to state the objectives; and the first objective was sanitation:

> For instance, we may state that for sanitary reasons, it is important to maintain external and internal bodily cleanliness. Consistent with scientific attitude, let us also employ the best known technical means of solution to this problem. This will free us of the customary limitations imposed only by persistent opinion. In so doing, we quickly discover that the present level of combined pneumatic and radiation techniques can provide far more effective external skin cleansing than hitherto provided by soap and water baths.[91]

These new techniques should be applied to body, clothes, dishes, and the house itself. The permanent war is hygiene and it demands the latest weapons. Fuller went on to say that reducing the amount of water used for cleaning meant that nothing needed to be piped into the house and nothing needed to be piped out, as waste removal would be done through "supercharged oxidation combined with electrical induction techniques served by subsequent vacuum removal." Dehydration would be applied to waste just as it was already applied to food. Input and output would be treated the same. Sanitation would be available to the masses at a higher standard than was currently available to the privileged. It was the huge drain on vital material resources involved in the tonnage of "inflow and outflow plumbing and its attached apparatus" that had brought the building industry to a dead stop during the war, not the war itself. Furthermore the war had accelerated the technical capacity needed for housing. The interiors of large planes, tanks, and submarines served as laboratories for new techniques for "atmospheric conditioning" under conditions considerably more demanding than those of the average house. Fuller concluded the letter by saying that the "accomplishment of advanced sanitary and atmospheric controls minus the in-and-out-flow conduits" is much more than a replacement of outmoded technologies. The "divorce" from dependency on arterial systems would transform every element of the dwelling in a chain reaction of efficiencies, starting with the all-important ability of the dwelling to be mobile:

> This initiates housing's synchronization with the general twentieth century life from track to trackless and wire to wireless. This enables practical consideration of that most precious of libertarian conditions, – privacy, – while at the same time taking advantage of low-rent ground. Individual power plants and radio communication provide the final means of insuring geographical freedom.[92]

Once again, the bathroom was the center of the revolution, enabling architecture to finally synchronize itself with the wider world of radio. It is the

91 Buckminster Fuller to Alfred C. Bossom, Director, British Building Mission in North America, 11 November 1943, BFP Series 8, Box 6, Folder 6, p. 5.
92 Ibid., 7.

45

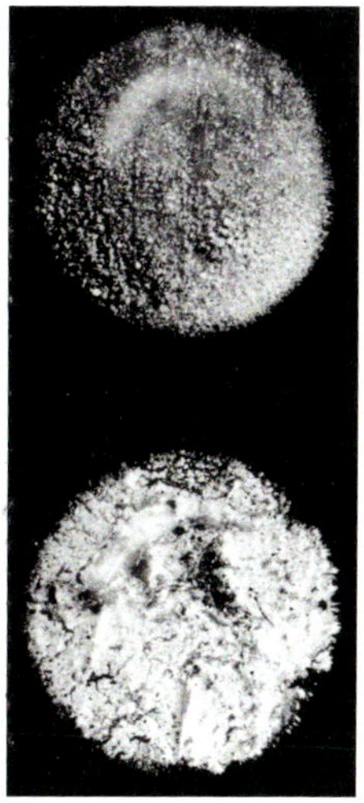

46

Hygiene Overdrive

45 Model of Wichita Dwelling Machine, *Fortune* magazine, April 1946

46 Dirt interspersed with skin pores of students at the Institute of Design, Chicago, 1948

47 Bedroom of RBF's Dome Home, Carbondale, 1960

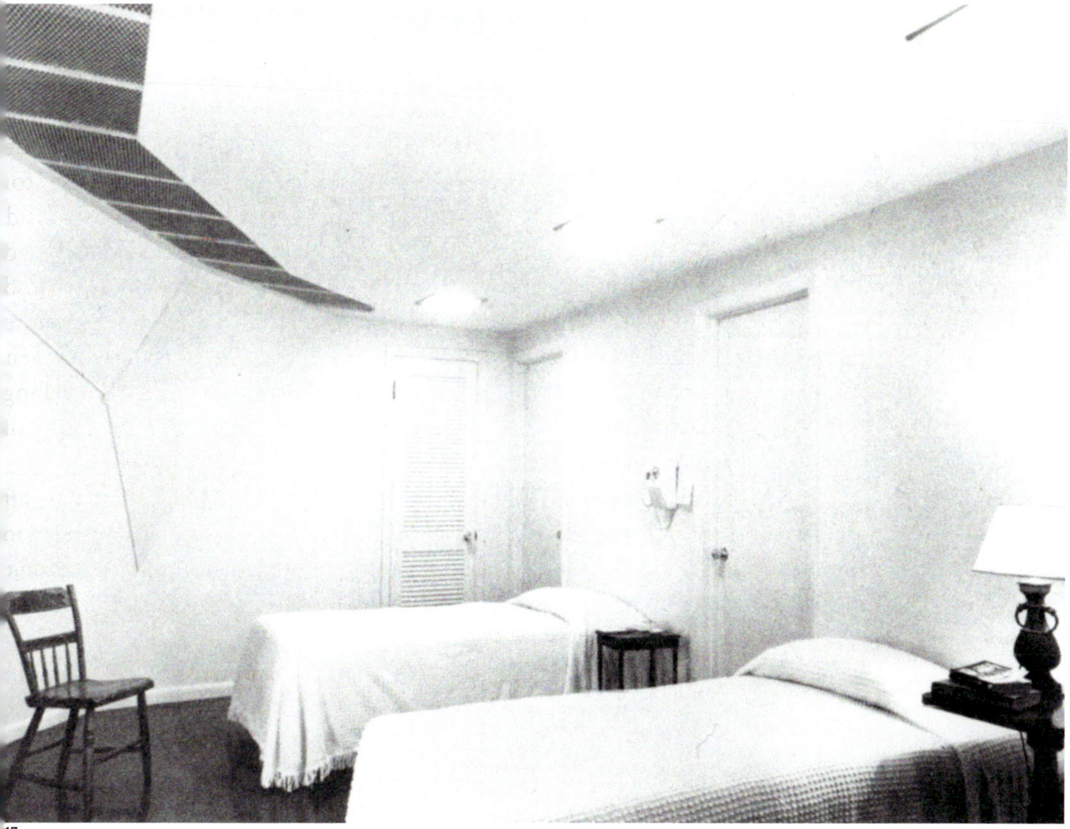

47

very engine of both scientific and personal development. Innovations in hygiene have exponential effects. Not by chance, Fuller wrote a month later to the Honeywell company (inventors of the electronic autopilot in 1942) to condemn the "suspect" world of plumbing and insist that cleansing and heating the human body could be done with radiation and lightweight portable pneumatic equipment that needed to become as scientific as the design of contemporary electronic communication apparatus, going beyond the visible surfaces to locate exponential increases in capacity. The design of "radio receiver circuits," including the broadcast station miles away, was the model for both cleaning and housing in general.[93]

Fuller's letter to Bossom had symptomatically ended by pointing to his own research into "pneumatic skin cleansing." His bathroom unit, for example, was meant to feature a fog gun that would "scavenge" into every pore of the skin to remove dirt. Such a device had already been fantasized in the first versions of the Dymaxion House. Two decades later, Fuller and his architecture students at Chicago and Yale tested the concept by studying all the different kinds of dirt in cities, making close-up microscope images of the dirt embedded in their own pores. **fig. 46** Fuller noted how the dirt fused with the skin of the architecture students into coral-like structures, and he experimented with how to get into the pores with high pressure fog to dissolve it, inspired by the steam cleaning of buildings.[94] The bathroom's own curvaceous body inevitably had to act as a model of cleanliness. Fuller kept pointing out that there were no crevices or even corners in its continuous surface where germs could gather. He was particularly obsessed with the cleanliness of bathrooms, having assistants and students fanatically cleanse every surface of the ones he used and even installing separate toilets in his own Dome Home in 1960 to avoid using the same one as his wife, even if only there a few weeks a year. A bathroom was installed directly behind each bed at the center of the plan. **fig. 47**

93 "The whole principle of plumbing is suspect, with its archeological insinuation of water and sewage lines below grade. Though hidden, these entrails are true parts of 'the house.' Chances are excellent that cleansing, sanitation, relaxation, massage, and general tone-up can be better accomplished by radiation and pneumatic apparatus weighing portable pounds instead of dead weight tons. It is soon evident upon search along these lines, that the design evolution must go below the surface. It must employ as scientific a degree of approach to cleansing and heating the human being as is employed in the design of present electronic communication apparatus. Stages of efficiency must be reached that are not directly visible, and where the effective magnitude increase thousands fold. [...] I don't mean to be an impractical perfectionist or obscure about that. I simply mean that the same attitude obtaining in the devisement of preferred radio receiver set circuits—to which the broadcasting station is an integral part though X miles away—must obtain in the successful design of the total composite dwelling machine service." Buckminster Fuller to W. J. McGoldrick, in charge of Aeronautical Engineering, Minneapolis-Honeywell Regulator Company, 10 December 1943, BFP Series 8, Box 6, Folder 6, p. 3.

94 Fuller describes the experiments of 1948 and 1950: "And I found that it could get into the pores, being really finer molecules than the water molecules, so you get into the pores and if I atomized some water and went in with it there could be a scavenging out of the pores and bring, just really float the dirt away. So we went in for such experiments and you've seen human beings cleaning buildings, a great operation going, and it looks like they're using steam up there it isn't. It's highly very high compressed air with water atomized in it. And it is cleaning that building just beautifully, doing just what I said. [...] We got into experiments of that kind at the Institute of Design in Chicago, and we went in for all kinds of study of the different kinds of dirt that occurred around Chicago [...] we were able to make very beautiful enlarged photographs of the pores of what your skin looks like with dirt on it. And you take a picture of your hand, just the dirty first, and it looks like one thing, but it is completely different when you see it enormously enlarged. There will be literally little hunks lodged out here on the mountain top and so forth, and you can really see how this thing could really work, so we got into studies, then, of all the types of dirt that were known in the total Chicago area, that you might get into there. There are many types you can really classify those. And, incidentally, a team of the students at the Institute of Design in Chicago went out and interviewed dermatologists in Chicago. In the first place we went to some of the local hospitals, we got names of what were considered the best dermatologists in Chicago, and they called on them, and every one of them said the worst thing you could have for your skin is soap. So that was worth paying some attention to, we felt, and so if you could get a way of cleaning our skin without use of the soap, it could be very, very excellent, and we found we could." Fuller, "Everything I Know," Session 11, Part 2 (see note 60).

95 House plan in pencil, BFP Series 2, Box 18.

96 "Fuller's House," *Fortune*, April 1946, 171.

97 The only exception is the special bathroom unit that Fuller designed for the Dymaxion Dwelling Unit, a cylinder in which the bath, toilet, and sink are suspended over a septic tank, and tubes feed people, liquids, and electricity into compact circular house.

98 Buckminster Fuller, *Designing a New Industry* (Wichita: Fuller Research Institute, 1946), 9.

99 Buckminster Fuller, transcript of lecture (San Quentin State Prison, January 31, 1959), BFP Series 8, Box 15, Folder 11, p. 14.

Despite Fuller's relentless mission to do the most with the least, there were always "his and hers" bathrooms at the heart of his houses, starting with the first version in 1928. Drawings of rectangular "Fuller Houses" of March 1928 (preceding even the "4D" label that preceded "Dymaxion") have two bathrooms at the center of the plan.[95] Not by chance, the very first published image in December 1928 showed two bathroom units being hoisted aboard the tower. The whole story begins with a pair of bathrooms. Within the logic of massive industrial production of identical units, each bathroom unit is understood to have a particular user. The model of the Wichita House published in *Fortune* took the logic of his and hers so far as to color the interior of the two molded plastic bathroom units pink and blue.[96] **fig. 45** The different versions of the model house developed with students at the Institute of Design in Chicago for the original Necklace Dome in 1948 had two bathrooms. Even the Standard-of-Living-Package of 1948/49 to be assembled on the back of a truck for people escaping cities that would be destroyed within seven days had two bathrooms. The minimum condition for survival is two bathrooms. The Dymaxion Bathrooms might clean the most with the least but having less of them was never an option.[97] The drive toward efficiency would begin with a polemical multiplication of cleaning. The threat of microbes was the very driver of the house and the hyperexpanded networks it would float within.

BATHROOM BRAIN

The house itself was always a potential threat. Fuller was already saying in 1928 that his "more sanitary" house would, like its occupants, clean itself automatically. A special system of compressed air and vacuum would filter the air every six minutes and evacuate all the dust, odors, and germs from the top of the central mast as "bad air." All surfaces were seen as potential sites of contamination to be countered by design. Doorknobs, for example, had to be removed because they transfer germs so efficiently. These were not matters of detail. Fuller's whole project for a new kind of house was launched as a form of "preventive pathology" against the diseases bred" by housing. He attributed the death of his first daughter, which had initiated the original Fuller Houses project, to the fact that:

> Nobody seemed to know where the housing traditions and the diseases they bred came from and why they were going on. I could not seem to maintain the health conditions as I wanted them in the kind of rentals I could afford and I blamed it very much on housing. [...] If we were to really attempt preventive pathology, we would question how these things started, and it seemed to me in 1927, we would learn to measure and to adopt the enormous amount of data being set down by technologists everywhere [...] and equally in its end use, prevent much of the present inroads of physical and mental and moral diseases into good health and well-being and general happiness.[98]

During a typically autobiographical four-hour lecture inside the San Quentin State Prison in early 1959, Fuller described the apartment in which he did the original 4D manuscript and house design as "the most sanitary hole I could find because we did have this baby."[99] **fig. 49** He had done detailed drawings of the new apartment in July 1928, with plans including all the bathroom fittings and perspective renderings including Anne and Allegra, along with panoramic photographs from the window showing the view of the yacht harbor.[100] For Fuller, this domestic space was the center of everything. His pencil drawing of Anne at her writing desk in the living room points out the location of all the other rooms in the house and is entitled *Bird's eye view of the Fuller Industries plant administration and living quarters*.[101] The space in which to imagine the factory-built house was itself an imaginary factory that blurred professional and domestic. There were even detailed charts correlating Allegra's physical and intellectual development with the physical and intellectual development of Fuller's work.[102] The initiation and evolution of the 4D project is interwoven with the progress of liquid and solid feeding, refusing water constipation, weight, height, sleep, sitting up, walking, talking, etc. It is not by chance that Fuller did *Diapers*, a watercolor of his naked wife bent over the bathroom tub washing the diapers, voyeuristically framed by the doorway but presented in scientific rather than sensual terms with more care taken in the rendering of the sanitary fittings than in the human form.[103] **fig. 48** The arrival of a new child, a more "sanitary" space, cleaning and a new project to revolutionize housing were inseparable.

Fuller used the three hours a day that his wife spent washing diapers like a billion other women worldwide, as his image of the sheer stupidity of the conventional house in a May 1929 talk alongside his model of the Dymaxion House at the City Club Forum in Chicago.[104] Ten hours a day also had to be spent vigilantly "keeping the baby from killing herself" given all the threats posed by the unscientific condition of even the most modern "mechanized" apartment. Housing is the very epicenter of danger Fuller pointed out that two million people die in houses each year that fail to protect them from external threats of floods, tornadoes, and earthquakes and countless more die from threats posed by the house itself including the "multi-millions who die from dirt in cracks in housing annually."[105] Dirt was the ultimate domestic danger. Fuller pointed out that the majority of individual houses still lacked bathrooms and that people moved to cities "for some measure of sanitation" but even the latest apartment they could find would be 5,000 years behind in the age of "flights to Europe in 36 hours and universal radio hookup."[106] Fuller once again used radio to shame architecture, as he had in the press release for the very first exhibition of his house which culminated in a celebration of its pair of bathroom units and multiple forms of automated hygiene of all surfaces atmosphere, body, clothes, and dishes with "air brushes for cleaning" to provide just the final more personal touch.[107]

In the San Quentin lecture thirty years later, Fuller directly related his sense that that architecture was responsible for his first daughter's death

100 BFP Series 2, Box 19.
101 Ibid.
102 Ibid.
103 *Diapers*, watercolor dated 1928, ibid.
104 "She spends 3 hours a day on the baby's diapers, not pleasant to mention, but she is only one of a billion women doing this, three billion hours wasted daily on this item alone, wasted because it can be licked mechanically in an industrial best-for-all housing design." Buckminster Fuller, Excerpts from address on "Mass Production of Houses in Factories" (illustrated by model) at the City Club Forum luncheon Tuesday, May 28, 1929, BFP Series 2, Box 21, p. 4.
105 Ibid., 2.
106 Ibid., 4.
107 Buckminster Fuller, "4D Housing and the Time Dimension: Archeology Abandoned in New Recreative Art of Housing Design," January 1929 press release, BFP Series 2, Box 21, p. 2.

48

49

50

51

The Liquid Architect

48 *Diapers*, RBF painting of Anne Fuller doing washing, Chicago, 1928

49 Allegra, RBF, and Anne, Lincoln Park, Chicago, 1928

50 RBF, and demonstration plastic bathroom unit for Wichita House prototype, 1946

51 RBF lecture, *Architectural Forum*, January–February 1972

52 RBF swimming

52

with his awareness after being in the navy of the new technologies that had been accelerated by the war but had not yet been applied to housing, particularly radio: "We didn't call it electronics in those days—you might call it radio or whatever it is."[108] His acute fear of invisible microbes and equally acute desire for architecture to dematerialize into the invisible world were linked. For him, all hygiene is ultimately mental. The bathroom itself is even the crucial instrument for thought, as argued in a 1964 lecture on the use of electronic media in education:

> A bathroom isn't just a piece of machinery. It is intimate to the fundamental routine of cleanliness, morality, and clean thinking. The ability to cope with filth-bred fungi bacteria and their ravaging, through sanitary waste disposal and ready-to-hand soap and running water, has many subconsciously important relationships to the scheduled inaugurations of the progressive cerebral capabilities of the new life.[109]

The bathroom is part of the brain, contributing to the unique growth of the individual mind. In this sense, a bathroom is never shared. It is linked to what Fuller described as the most basic need for "autonomy" in the young evolving brain. It is not by chance that he associated the inability to incubate or tolerate "original thought" in the constraining grid of desks in the typical childhood classroom with the "horrid smells" he experienced in the shared bathrooms on his first day at school.[110] The autonomous mind would be sheltered by an autonomous bathroom. Private bathrooms are more important for education than schools. Providing bathrooms and sanitary waste disposal to the homes in a slum in Caracas, for example, "would up the IQ capabilities fifty percent in a short space of time,"[111] and television would efficiently provide "the pipelines for great teachers to reach the eager brains."[112] Once again, the demand to go from pipe to pipeless tied toilet to thought.

In a 1942 essay that yet again called for architecture's disconnection from the empire of buried pipes,[113] Fuller noted that the words *sane* and *sanitary* share the same roots: "the degree of probability of preservation of inherent sanity in the individual is proportional to the degree of maintenance of inherent sanitation in the environment."[114] But the transformation of essential sanitary functions into puritanical thinking was emphatically rejected. The eight hours a day of rituals for cleaning house, dishes,

108 "Just before she was four years old she caught pneumonia and died. During those years with a new life whom we loved very much, we were very frustrated with the incapabilities that existed, such as the kind of room we could rent, the kind of apartment we could have, etc. The physical environment seemed terrible. By this time I had had a whole lot of experience in flying and new technology. We didn't call it electronics in those days—you might call it radio or whatever it is—but I had had excellent experience in the NAVY. I had been sent to the Naval Academy and I knew how to make big ships work. I knew a whole lot about mechanics. The fact that the housing we were in was very poor made me feel many times that these conditions which we were operating under were in many ways responsible for this child's sickness. The fact is, I was right because spinal meningitis, infantile paralysis and influenza have actually been brought under control in the years since." Buckminster Fuller, lecture, San Quentin Prison, 8 (see note 99).

109 Buckminster Fuller, "The Music of the New Life: Thoughts on Creativity, Sensorial Reality, and Comprehensiveness," December 10, 1964, keynote lecture in Washington, *Music Educators Journal* 52, no. 5 (April–May 1966): 134.

110 Ibid., 137.

111 Ibid., 134.

112 Ibid., 128.

113 The essay rejects housing plans that "still start with sewer, water and light arteries laboriously buried in the ground, a three-thousand-year-old invention, immediately immobilizing all subsequent design." Buckminster Fuller, "I figure," unpublished manuscript of November 1942, in *Ideas and Integrities*, 91 (see note 28). The essay calls for a "derooting" of shelter by "freeing his dwelling from its parasitic subsistence on the back of an industrial jungle host of sewer, water, gas and garbage systems." Ibid., 93.

114 Ibid., 116.

115 Ibid., 114.

116 Ibid., 117.

117 Buckminster Fuller, "World Game," in *Critical Path*, 212 (see note 38). "Nothing has been really bringing about more contamination for human beings than the splashing of toilets and wet plumbing. And this is very valuable chemistry [...] it isn't waste at all!" Buckminster Fuller, Design Science Institute press conference, New York, June 28, 1972. Cited in E. J. Applewhite, *Synergetics Dictionary: The Mind of Buckminster Fuller* (New York: Garland, 1986).

food, linen, clothes, and "self-cleaning, internal and external"—a major investment that was "devoted to yesterday's dirt, lest that dirt become today's filth and tomorrow's disease"—needed to be divorced from any ideas of purification.[115] The purity of humanity was a given. Cleanliness was no longer to be valued as the inspiration of "moral sanitation" through necessary hardship, self-limitation, or self-discipline. Hygiene is a fundamental survival function to be scientifically revolutionized by a whole new set of technologies, procedures, and cycles. The goal was what Fuller called "'quickness' in sanitation—that is, in degree of spontaneity equivalent to unconscious and therefore natural act, making possible free action in every direction."[116] He organized his own day around obsessive efficient cleansing cycles, monitoring and noting every detail. With prunes at the heart of his Dymaxion Diet, he was hyperdedicated to cleaning his every pipe and pore. After all, his desire to disconnect from the collective pipes in the ground was also about the fear of contagion by others. The project of the Dymaxion Bathroom was to "eliminate all wet plumbing, which has been responsible for breeding most of all the infectious bacteria heretofore entering human abodes, while also eliminating the infectious splashback feature of water-filled bowls and their water-flushed toilets."[117] Fuller was far from reluctant to share his fluids with others but wanted no fluids in return. The pipeless world is ultimately a form of hygiene. **fig. 52**

This cleaning is not about suppressing the body's chemistries. On the contrary, it is a kind of embrace of normally hidden solids, liquids, and gases. The hyperextension of the mind is seen to be liberated by exposing all the fluid circuits of the body and keeping them close—literally. Rather than interrupt the flow of thought during his endless extemporaneous lectures about the pipeless future, Fuller used to urinate inside the leg of his trousers until he borrowed equipment from NASA to urinate in full flight. His daughter Allegra recalls the seemingly philosophical look that would accompany his use of this storage system as audiences waited for the stream of words to resume. **fig. 51** It was finally the most portable of bathrooms for the brain—minimum distance between toilet and thought.

This is much more than the modern architect's generic association of the aesthetics of cleanliness with health and the clarification or even purification of thought, as exemplified by Le Corbusier's polemics in the twenties on the cleansing power of the white surface. With Fuller, it was a full-blown fixation with its own array of compulsive habits and displaced intellectual and aesthetic effects. These effects again go far beyond the illicit pleasure that Le Corbusier took in exposing all the pipes holding up the sink in his own apartment and bringing sinks and bidets out of the bathroom, or his intense devotion to the bathroom itself as the only room in a free plan. Le Corbusier eventually did his own sanitary fittings, including a rethinking of the toilet, and he was unique in drawing the infrastructural lines that would feed his towers. In discussing the goal of "hygienic living conditions" in *La ville radieuse* of 1933, for example, he reprinted his 1930 drawings of the water, gas, electricity, and sewage lines coming up into a seven-story urban building to be shared by its occupants and argues that the same thing could happen with a skyscraper of fifty floors. But the purpose of the diagram of his idealized tower showing the buried water gas, electricity, and telephone lines heading into its base was actually to show how the building would disconnect the occupant from those lines, turning the human body into a huge eyeball freely focusing on the horizon.[118] The sanitary aesthetic is exactly that, a sanitizing of bodily experience into pure vision. Alongside the diagram, Le Corbusier spoke of "the upkeep of the human machine" including "cleaning, draining the toxic substances" as a precondition for the visual sense of harmony; but sanitation itself would be the core experience with Fuller. It is not left behind to engage with the infinite horizon. It is the very possibility of engagement with the world beyond vision.

Fuller condenses the pipes but never leaves them. **fig. 50** On the contrary, he pulls the pipes out of the ground and bundles them up inside each living space as the very structure of that space. His mania actually unleashed the whole world of pipes. In one more twist in the contradictory psychodrama of pipes, the pipeless architect became the patron saint of piped architecture.

LIQUIDITY CRISIS

In the late sixties and early seventies, an armada of pipes was launched by a generation explicitly inspired by Fuller's transformation of mechanical services from embarrassing secret to central fetish. The countercultural experiments of the so-called radicals were filled with tubes, often being all tube. Groups like Archigram, Haus-Rucker-Co, and Coop Himmelb(l)au expanded space suits into flexing rooms and compacted houses into mobile space capsules, with all the pulsating veins showing. Everyone became an astronaut enveloped by thin skins plugged into compact pumps and information systems—at home anywhere on, above, or beyond the planet. Tubes rather than land were exposed as the real site of architecture

David Greene's sophisticated Living Pod of 1966 most fully confused house and spaceship by explicitly following Fuller's program for the autonomous mobile house, even including two intricate "wash capsules" into the sides of its digestive form for "total automatic body cleaning equipment."[119] **fig. 54** All the pumps, tanks, valves, filters, and life-support tubes were now draped around the outside of the molded capsule and plugged into various sockets where needed. Coop Himmelb(l)au's Villa Rosa of 1968 was a mobile pneumatic and information pumping station that generated inflatable spaces that were maintained by a spaghetti of feeder tubes—starting with a room and its bed coming out of a space helmet–shaped suitcase and expanding to the size of a multistory building **fig. 53** Architecture took the form of an intricate plumbing system theatrically on display inside a transparent bubble that wanted to lift off the

118 Le Corbusier, *La ville radieuse* (1933), translated as *The Radiant City* (New York: The Orion Press, 1964), 36. The section republishes Le Corbusier's report to the 1930 meeting of CIAM in Brussels.

119 David Greene, "Living Pod," *Architectural Design* 36, no. 11 (November 1966): 573. Greene echoes Fuller in noting that these technologies will ultimately undo the very idea of the house. "A basic assumption about housing has always been that the human being needs a house, an assumption that needs to be reassessed in terms of the possibility of increasing personal mobility and technological advance. [...] It is likely that under the impact of the second machine age the need for a house (in the form of permanent static container) as part of man's psychological make-up will disappear." Ibid.

120 Reyner Banham, "A Home Is Not a House," *Art in America* 53, no. 2 (April 1965): 70–79.

121 Klein's collaborator Werner Ruhnau recalls the influence of Buckminster Fuller on the Air Architecture projects. Werner Ruhnau, "Interview," in *Air Architecture: Yves Klein*, ed. Peter Noever and Francois Perrin (Los Angeles: MAK, 2004), 106.

ground—a dream of flying plumbing. Even the architects wore space helmets attached to umbilical tubes. Haus-Rucker-Co likewise wore their own helmets in 1967 and expanded helmets into rooms and portrayed themselves attached to their projects by umbilical cords in outer space. **fig. 55** They also started to integrate the tubes and wiring into the surface of their transparent bubbles. The plumbing was literally brought to the surface to envelop the inhabitant. But it was Michael Webb's Suitaloon of 1966 that went one step further in taking the idea of the space suit as a portable house to the extreme, building all the life-support and communications systems into the lining of the transparent suit itself, turning the intricate folded pattern of intestines into the only visible sign of shelter. **fig. 58** In reverse, many of his colleagues made intestinal cities. In Warren Chalk's Underwater City of 1964 there is only a three-dimensional network of pipes; and the basic structure of Peter Cook's Plug-in City of the same year is a network of service "tubes" into which expendable spaces can temporarily be plugged. A wide range of designers explored a kind of intravenous or umbilical architecture with pods, buildings, clusters, cities and planetary networks taking the form of plumbing. To live was to be inside pipes. The decidedly noncountercultural designs of the so-called High Tech architects were soon likewise launched as a celebration of pipes but pipes to look at rather than inhabit. The façade might be covered with pipes in a polemical reversal of their usual disavowal, most famously in the 1971 design by Piano and Rogers for the Pompidou Center, but they don't form the structure or envelope itself. The radical gesture of living in tubes quickly gave way to the more traditional concept of spaces served by tubes.

This domestication of the pipe through hypercontrolled exposure was already evident in Reyner Banham's 1965 essay "A Home Is Not a House."[120] The text promotes Fuller's concept of a mobile ephemeral plastic dome serviced by a compact living package but symptomatically the images of this "un-house" drawn by the Beaux-Arts trained architect François Dallegret lovingly turn the "intestinal complexity" of the cluster of pipes for air-conditioning, fumes, waste, water, power, radio, telephone, and music into a precise composition, a sculptural flower of plumbing. **figs. 56 and 59** It is a reversal of the 1961 project for an "Air Conditioned City" by Yves Klein and Claude Parent, where Fuller's ideal of a Garden of Eden environment for naked bodies is sustained by an independent but vast hidden world of buried plumbing that barely exposes itself aboveground.[121] **fig. 57** With the "un-house," the naked bodies of Dallegret and Banham (or, more precisely Banham's head photo-collaged onto Dallegret's lean body since the less-than-svelte Banham was too embarrassed to become the first English historian to show his body) sit alongside their electronic plumbing, lovingly admiring it as the most natural of plants. Pipeless architecture would now be emphatically, visibly, and elegantly piped, even in the most minimal of architectures. An architecture of radical transparency would expose no disorderly fluids. The pipes themselves would testify to aesthetic and technical control. At the other end of the scale, Louis Kahn's medical research laboratories building of the same year in Philadelphia put all the elevators, exhaust and intake vents, cables, and pipes in monumental shafts on the outside of the building,

PIPELESS DREAMS

53

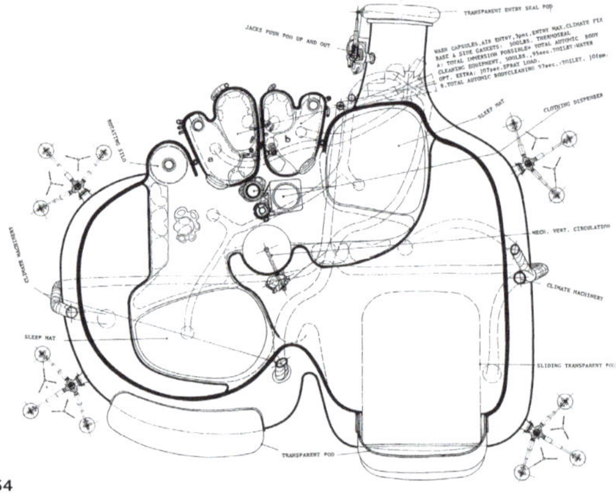

54

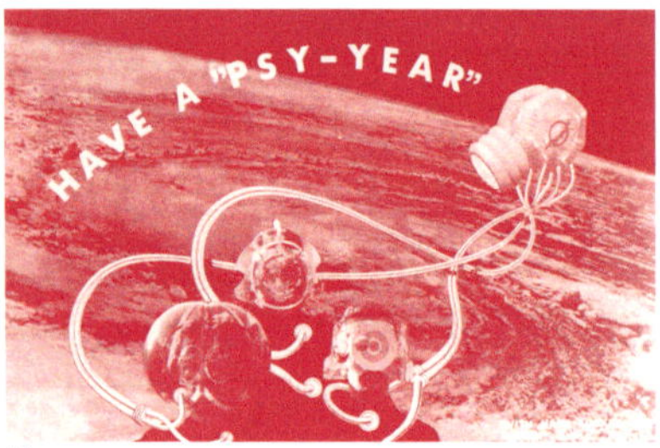

55

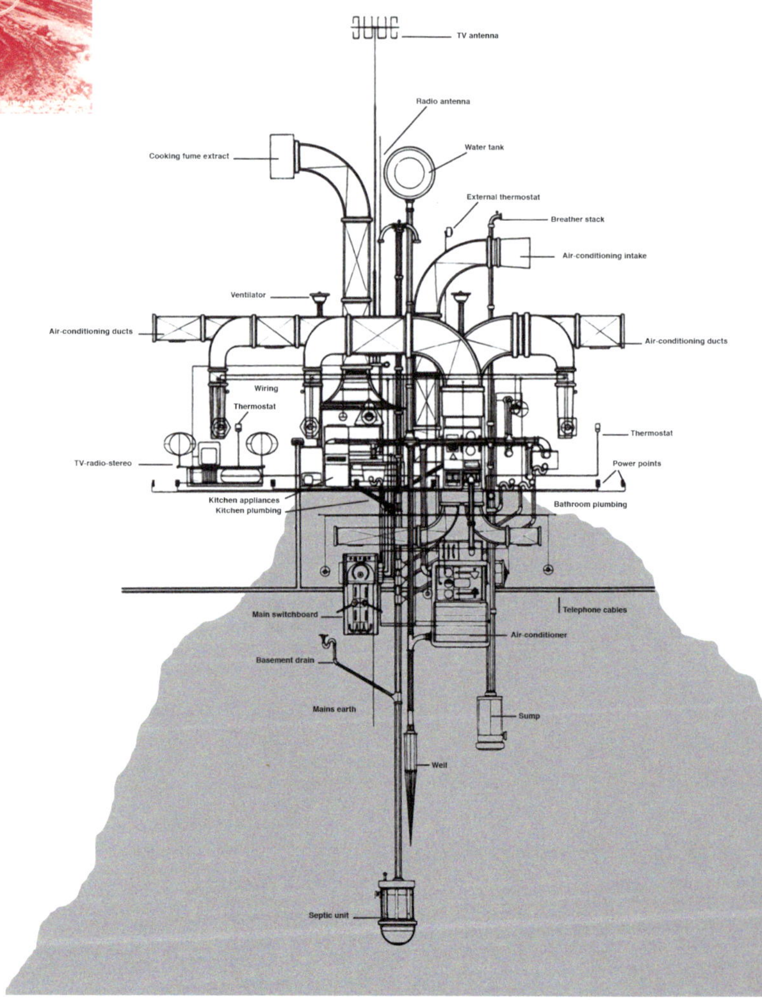

56

The Plumbing Avant-Garde

53 Coop Himmelb(l)au, Pneumatic living unit: Prototype. Project Villa Rosa, 1968

54 David Greene, Living Pod, plan at upper level, 1966

55 Haus-Rucker-Co, Environment Transformer helmets and Yellow-Heart Space Capsule for Two, "Have a Psy-Year" end-of-year card, 1968

56 François Dallegret, Anatomy of a Dwelling, from "A Home Is Not a House," by Reyner Banham, *Art in America,* April 1965

57 Yves Klein with the collaboration of Claude Parent, Underground Area of a Climate-controlled City ("Climate Control of Space"), ca. 1959. Ink and pencil on tracing paper, 73 × 48 cm

58 Michael Webb, Cushicle, Dave inside fully inflated Suitaloon, 1966

59 François Dallegret, The Environment-Bubble: Transparent Plastic Bubble Dome Inflated by Air-Conditioning Output, from "A Home Is Not a House," by Reyner Banham, *Art in America*, April 1965

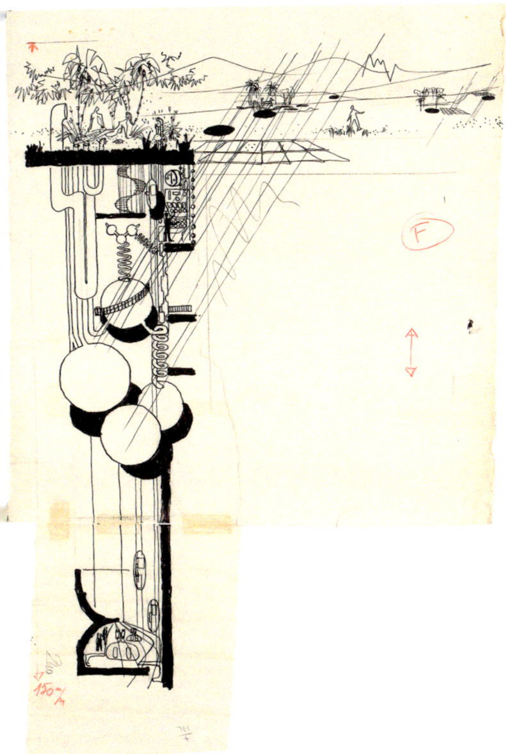

57

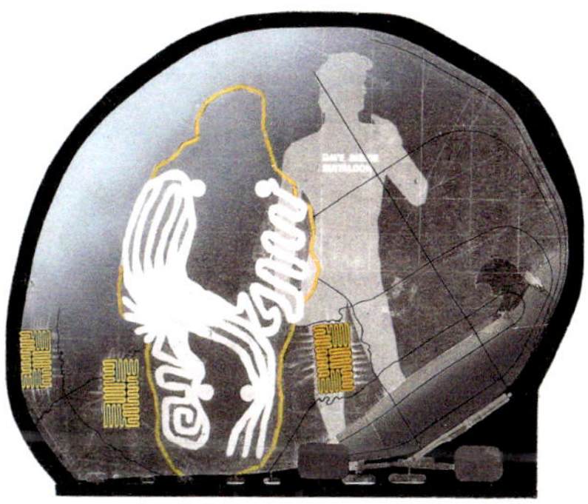

58

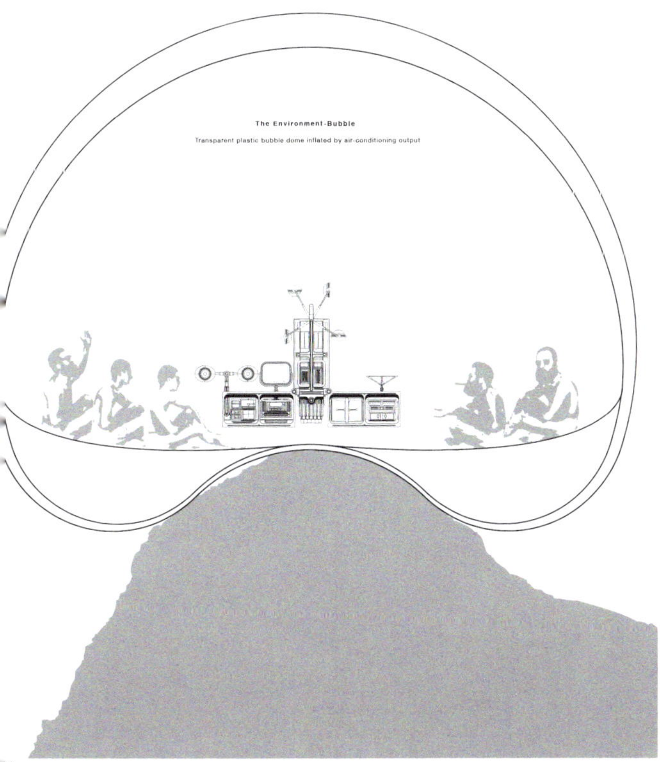

59

with the labs themselves sheathed in glass. It would seem that the pipe was no longer forbidden, no longer the space of unmentionable flows, noises chemicals, and waste. But Kahn—in a brilliant comment that Banham himself would only later note in his key book on environmental services—had already made it clear that the opposite was the case:

> I do not like ducts; I do not like pipes. I hate them very thoroughly, but because I hate them so thoroughly, I feel they have to be given their place If I just hated them and took no care, I think they would invade the building and completely destroy it.[122]

More than half a century later, the psychodrama of the pipe remains fully intact in all its contradictory force. The dream of pipeless architecture can pretend that pipes don't exist or turn them into architecture. Either way architecture is threatened by the systems of flow that make it possible Architects might have a certain pride that their buildings can leak, that pushing the envelope sometimes lets a little of the outside in, but the permanent leaking from the hidden inside of the inside is unmentionable. The architect is increasingly enveloped by pipes and sensitive to the complex flows within even the simplest structure, but the allure of the pipeless dream gets only stronger as the pipes keep breeding. Flows of air, people, goods materials, energy, information, images, techniques, and capital are all basic to the definition of space, and can become part of the architect's vocabulary, but liquidity remains fundamentally troubling to the discipline and its core sense of what a building is. The whole point of architecture is to suspend the sense of liquidity. The subject is almost too sensitive, too important to talk about. It is as if every building is already understood to carry the architect's permanent unspoken and wishful label: "this is not a pipe."

Fuller knew no such fear. The two single-piece molded bathrooms "without any cracks" at the heart of the original clothing-optional Dymaxion House had all the channeling for the conduits "within the walls themselves which would be made of translucent plastic material that "the light comes through."[123] The plastic could be "a beautiful green one, or pink, or whatever color you want" but both the body and the nest of pipes that wrap and service it would always be on blurry display. Even the bathroom is broadcasting. The image of the body is the first transmission, the first prosthetic extension. In a late 1936 image Fuller confidently presents his naked rear end to us, nestled within the curves of the metal bathroom that was designed to be of translucent plastic. **fig. 60** He is happily cocooned in the heart of the heart of his world, motionless for once inside the very circuits of flow the compact closed circuits of plumbing that are the necessary precondition for radical connectivity through the open circuits of radio. His intimate capsule seemingly floats in the blackness of outer space. He posed under studio lights for the gifted photographer F. S. Lincoln during the *Architectural Record* shoot in this remarkable unpublished image in which cleanliness sensuality, architectural performance, and the performance of the architect are one—a polemically personal manifesto to the infinite hospitality of the self-feeding pipe that renders his colleagues forever modest.

122 Louis Kahn, in *World Architecture One*, by John Donat (London: Studio Books, 1964), 35.

123 Fuller, "Dymaxion House Meeting, Architectural League, New York," 96 (see note 10).

60 F.S. Lincoln, unpublished photograph of RBF in prototype of first version of Dymaxion Bathroom Unit for Phelps Dodge Corporation, December 1936

VIII

VIII RBF photographing plastic-covered resin-impregnated Tulane University Cardboard Dome at demonstration to Air Force, 1954

THE PLASTIC LINE

We live in plastic. So much of what is around us is quietly plastic, from the thin layer of vinyl paint on the walls and polyurethane on the floors to all the fittings, pipes, wiring, fastenings, gaskets, furniture, panels, and packaging. There is plastic on and inside most of the objects we see, from the skins of our books to the cases of our equipment to the body of the latest aircraft. We even see our world through the plastic lens of eyeglasses or contacts and the films sandwiched between the layers of glass in windows. We are ourselves increasingly plastic, with a wide range of polymers against our skin and integrated into our bodies, from the fabrics of our clothes to the ever-expanding array of hearing aids, teeth, joints, arteries, and organs. We are almost always looking at, through, and from plastic and yet rarely see it. It is as if plastic is so ubiquitous, so integral to our environment, that it is not perceived.

Plastics are a crucial dimension of our material world. They are everywhere, all the time, vital to almost any construction, device, or event. They handle countless basic physical responsibilities but also the most extreme demands for high performance. Plastic has an unprecedented range. As a synthetic polymer—a formula that can be endlessly reconfigured—it has a massive bandwidth that allows it to infiltrate, support, protect, or transform almost any situation. Plastic is never a simple material. It is not so much a set of properties as a capacity to transform. Its ability to adopt any shape and level of performance is itself transformative. Our world is not just filled by plastic. It has become a plastic world. Even those who want to leave our industrialized environment behind, going as far from cities as possible to bond with nature, are usually wrapped in high-performance plastic fabrics, sleeping in a plastic tent tied down with plastic ropes, eating food in plastic bags, drinking from plastic containers, looking at nature through their plastic sunglasses, and carrying plastic-encased electronics in a plastic backpack. You can escape from cities but not from plastic.

Yet plastic remains largely invisible. We act as if our cities and buildings have no plastic. This blind spot is remarkable in architectural discourse, where vast quantities of polymers are specified to be used but rarely seen. The field simply doesn't want to see all the plastic that is such a major part of the substance and effect of buildings. The usual commitment to be faithful to the inner properties of materials falls away in the face of plastic. The very word "material" is reverently invoked by architects to capture a sense of authenticity, of truth to the intrinsic qualities of building elements, but plastic is not treated as a material. It is as if the plasticity of plastic, its ability to take any form, perform any role, and imitate any other material, renders it immaterial—lacking its own properties.

This blindness is no accident. Plastic is a deep, even traumatic challenge to the field. The first generation of building materials were found: stone, wood, animal skin, mud, dung, and ice. Architecture was a matter of cutting, stacking, stretching, weaving, pressing, pounding, smoothing, drying, and tying. The next materials were made, or, more precisely, cooked: concrete, metal, and glass. New physical properties were engineered with a lot of heat in factories and building sites. Finally, with plastic, it is all chemistry. Born in test tubes, plastic is the quintessential twentieth-century material. If modern architecture is associated with the freedom and efficiency offered by concrete, metal, and glass, then it is not so modern after all. It remains cooked and cut. A more modern architecture would be incubated in laboratories rather than in furnaces, quarries, and mills. With plastic, architecture becomes a laboratory experiment. Perhaps this is already being realized. The high-performance plastics in boats, airplanes, cars, shoes, and skis are increasingly found in buildings. The range of possible performance of plastic is now so great that it can be argued that buildings are produced within that range. Architecture now lies within plastic rather than plastic within architecture. Plastic has become a fundamental material that changes the roles of all other materials. Concrete, metal, and glass arrive to any building site with a long history and a responsibility to represent ancient values of stability and security. But they are now asked to behave in new ways, taken into the laboratory to greatly expand their capacity. Architecture has become a branch of chemistry. Even stone and wood, the natural materials celebrated by architectural tradition, have been transformed by plastic. To preserve and protect old structures and values, plastics are deployed in specialized gaskets, fibers, impregnations, and films. Even plastic itself now has to be preserved using other plastics. Plastic has history. For the first time, it is not just the material of the future. It is fully embedded in our present and past. It's time to acknowledge, archive, and analyze it.

Think of the last 100 years of discourse devoted to the transformative properties of glass. Modern architecture is simply unthinkable without it. Glass is seen to liberate buildings and the people who use them. Nothing similar happens with plastic, despite the fact that it so often outperforms glass—being lighter, stronger, more resilient, and able to take any shape or degree of transparency, color, or texture. Glass is only able to perform today because of all the hidden films of plastic within it and the plastic gaskets and seals around it. Plastic is suspended inside glass and glass is suspended inside plastic. If the ability of glass to dissolve walls made the dream of modern architecture possible, plastic is the most modern of materials whose history coincides with that of modern architecture yet remains some kind of unacceptable presence within the field. It is as if it is still too modern today.

But what if plastic is never simply added to, coating, simulating, filling, insulating, or reinforcing architecture, but is architecture itself? What if this unmentionable material has long been carrying out the most fundamental of architectural responsibilities? After all, the main role played by plastic is to draw a line, defining a space by making a division between inside and outside, the most basic gesture of the architect. Think of the plastic coating on every wire that defines a space for the electricity, the plastic chamber that defines a space for the ink in a pen, the plumbing that defines the space for water, the layer of paint that defines an interior by keeping the weather out, the casing of an appliance, the seal on a joint, and so on. The role of plastic is always to draw and hold the line.

BUBBLETOPIA

In the mid-sixties, architects explored the possibility that a building might be nothing more than the drawing of such a plastic line. Magazines were filled with curvaceous bubbles, capsules, and pods. Synthetic chemistry took over the role of providing the primitive hut, the basic shelter supporting human life. The solidity of traditional building gave way to the thinnest film defining the line between inside and outside. Buildings became all window. The "environment bubble" of François Dallegret's Un-House of 1965 is emblematic. A portable, transparent, double-skinned plastic dome inflated and serviced by a compact equipment package replaces the traditional house and all the social values associated with it. Likewise Michael Webb's inflatable Cushicle of 1966, Haus-Rucker-Co's Balloon for Two of 1967, Hans Hollein's cylindrical Mobile Office of 1969, Ant Farm's 50 × 50 Pillow of 1969, and so on. A new generation of experimental architects were no longer photographed earnestly at their drawing boards or on lecture podiums but look out at us from inside their plastic bubbles, capsules, pods suits, helmets, and glasses—a new kind of portrait of the architect, softly distorted by plastic. **figs. 1 and 2** No special argument is made in favor of the material. Plastic is simply presented in its transformative transgression of the solidity of traditional architecture. The quivering plastic skin takes the modern architect's dream of lightness, movement, and transparency to its extreme. Buildings finally become modern in becoming portable, packable, flexible, instant, inexpensive, animate responsive, expandable, and expendable.

This plastic wave was not only an experimental critique of traditional buildings by young radicals unlikely to build outside happenings, galleries and the pages of magazines. The critique even became the official representation of national cultural and technological pride. In Expo 67 in Montreal, the countless plastic objects displayed at previous world's fairs gave way to plastic buildings. The United States was represented by the largest plastic building in history, Buckminster Fuller and Shoji Sadao's 250-foot diameter sphere. **fig. 4** Nineteen hundred plexiglass domes suspended within a steel net were linked together to form a single membrane between inside and outside, a huge plastic ball held together by a geodesic frame The interior space was a vast, twenty-story-high void with exhibits on a few floating platforms linked together by the longest escalators ever built. The curves of the transparent acrylic only lightly distorted the view of the fair, city, and sky from the inside—dramatically realizing the dream of being all-window, with visitors and exhibits seemingly hovering over the landscape. From the outside, the sunlight bounced off all the plastic faces to produce the effect of a huge translucent ball with mysterious shapes lurking within, a shimmering solid with an elevated monorail literally piercing right through it. This image of a glowing ball vibrating with inner activity continued at night as the interior lights reflected off the inner faces and the moonlight off the outer faces.

The effect of the shiny plastic sphere echoed that of the plexiglass wraparound visor of the fiberglass helmet on the aluminized nylon space suit displayed on the highest platform inside the sphere, along with the capsules, satellites, lunar excursion vehicles, and parachutes of the forthcoming Apollo mission to the Moon. **figs. 5 and 8** The astronaut's spherical helmet and the geodesic bubble both demonstrated the extreme redefinition of enclosure made possible by the most advanced technological research programs. A plastic sphere is offered for the species that now wraps itself in plastic to survive in outer space. The building itself was thought of as a spacecraft, not so much built in Montreal as momentarily touching down. Not by chance does a canonic image show it at night with its glowing

1 Hans Hollein inside his Mobile Office, 1969

2 Coop Himmelb(l)au inside their Restless Sphere, Basel, 1971

1

2

THE PLASTIC LINE

3

4

5

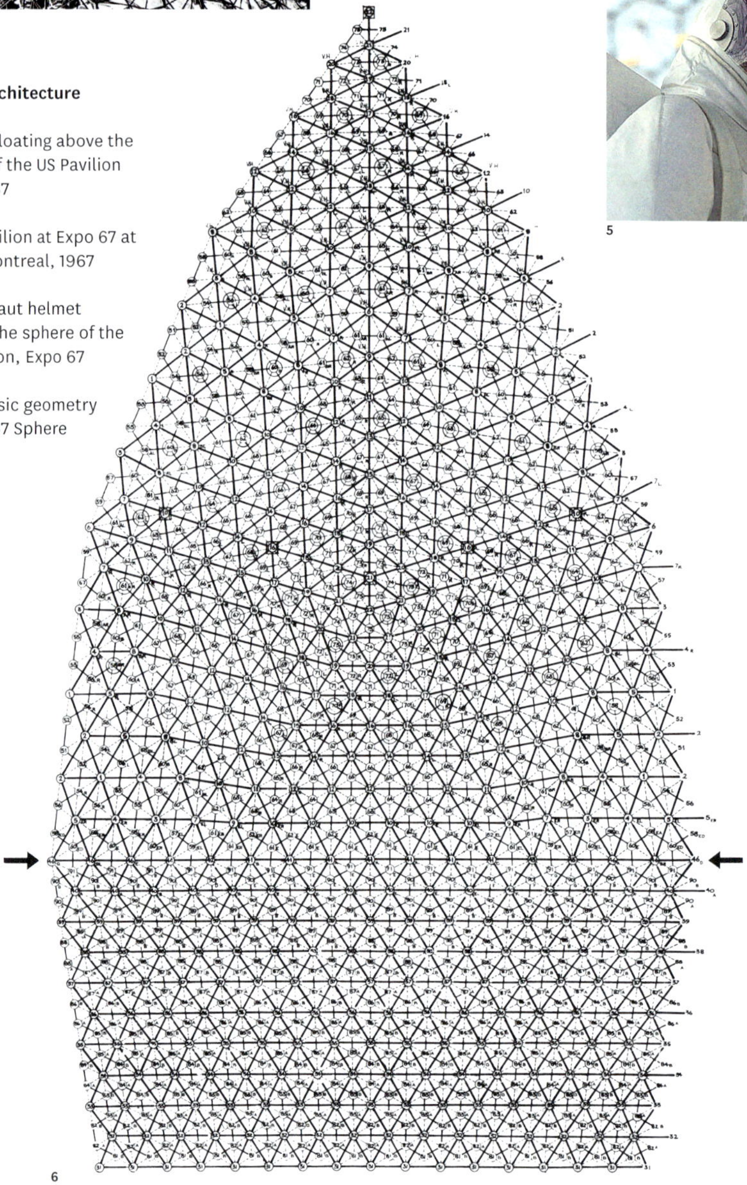
6

Lunar Architecture

3 Moon floating above the sphere of the US Pavilion at Expo 67

4 US Pavilion at Expo 67 at night, Montreal, 1967

5 Astronaut helmet reflects the sphere of the US Pavilion, Expo 67

6 Geodesic geometry of Expo 67 Sphere

7

Assembling the Plastic Spaceship

7 Geodesic web of Expo 67 Sphere under construction, 1966

8 NASA Surveyor Lunar Lander on exhibit in Expo 67 Sphere

9–12 1900 plexiglass domes for skin arriving on site and being installed, 1967

8

9

10

11

12

surface seemingly echoing the Moon seen floating above it. **fig. 3** Plastic was the launchpad to the future.

The 141,000 square feet of continuous plastic skin is referred to but ultimately overlooked in the extensive coverage of the sphere in architectural journals around the world. The reports are captivated by the geodesic geometry of the steelwork, dwelling on the network of interlocked triangles on the outside and hexagons on the inside rather than the acrylic membrane suspended between the two. **figs. 6 and 7** *Architectural Design*, for example, described the "clear spanning lacey filigree of metal, which will appear weightlessly poised against a background of cloud and sky."[1] Repeating an ancient bias, structure is privileged over surface, even if the only purpose of the structure is to hold up the surface, to hold the thin line between inside and outside in place, the "skybreak," as Fuller called it. The dimension of the hexagons was actually determined by the largest sheet of plexiglass (10 × 12 feet) that was available at the time to mold each dome. **figs. 9–13** Plastic drove the whole design. A few of the reports note that the plexiglass was tinted green-bronze to reduce glare, but all the reports act as if they are not affected by the material. There is a usually a reference to the "transparent acrylic skin" at the beginning of each text and a few images in which the surface disappears in providing a clear window out from the inside. Yet there are always some other images from the outside that catch the reflections off the shiny plastic that render the interior mysterious and leave the sphere ambiguously poised between transparent, translucent, and opaque. These include closer views in which the surface of the curving array of hexagon-based plastic domes appears dark and shiny, yet with the pattern of the geometry of the web from the far side of the sphere seemingly imprinted onto it. **fig. 14** Each hexagon seems to be filled with many smaller hexagons in a kind of multiplication of the pattern that seems to thicken the plastic surface. Views from a distance likewise show a kind of eccentric, mottled pattern inside the regular geometry of the surface. These more complex daytime and nighttime images tell a very different story than the accompanying analytical and technical text.

Progressive Architecture is the only professional journal that finally succumbed to the sensuous effect of the plastic, but only after the main anonymous report had done the usual technical account of the geometry of the metal space frame. A second essay of personal impressions of the fair by a writer happily loses sight of the metal:

> The first impression of the United States Pavilion depends on the light and the time of day. It might appear as thousands of reflective facets in direct sunlight, as a ghostly bubble on grey days, as a rosy diaphanous bloom at sunset, or as a glowing crystalline container of forms and colors after nightfall. Anyway it is a beautiful object.[2]

Similar descriptions dominated the coverage in newspapers and popular magazines, but this ever-changing effect was repressed in architectural publications—a major feat in the face of the largest plastic building in

1 "US Pavilion," *Architectural Design* 37 (July 1967): 333–337.
2 James T. Burns, "How It Is," *Progressive Architecture* 48 (June 1967): 158.

13

The Magic Skin Arrives, Deepens and Burns

13 "Human Spiders Spin a Web," *National Geographic*, May 1967

14 Expo 67 sphere, *Japan Architect*, August 1967

15–16 Expo 67 sphere on fire, May 20, 1976

14

15

16

history and the sensation of the fair. Fuller's real architectural contribution is understood to be the geometric frame and even the passing references to the plastic skin quickly fade away as the building is quickly added to the list of major works of twentieth-century architecture. The surface was only momentarily acknowledged again when one of the acrylic domes caught fire during renovation work on the afternoon of May 20, 1976 dramatically engulfing all the others in a twenty-minute blaze that raced around the sphere in a fiery wave of molten skin that stripped the building down to a blackened frame. **figs. 15 and 16** Plastic only became visible in its threat to the steel geodesic structure, which would symptomatically be restored twenty years later without the skin.

When architects think of Fuller they don't think of plastic. The indelible image is the spidery geodesic web. Yet geodesics were always inseparable from plastic. The first paragraph of Fuller's 1954 patent for the geodesic dome symptomatically ends with "covering or lining this frame with a skin of plastic material."[3] The plastic covering is not an optional extra but the very reason for the lightweight structure. It is not by chance that the first geodesic dome that Fuller constructed was encased within a skin of plastic. He did the project with students, as he would for decades with all the subsequent domes. His class at the Institute of Design in Chicago in early 1949—his very first appointment as a teacher—finished constructing a collapsible and packable 14-foot-diameter Necklace Dome in aluminum struts internally tensioned with aircraft cable. In July a group of the students folded up the structure and took it to Fuller's summer session at Black Mountain College in the countryside of North Carolina along with a double-skinned plastic membrane to cover it. The assignment there was to test the plastic that would provide shelter and thermal insulation—with tire valves in each section of plastic enabling the skin to be inflated. The idea was to prototype the concept of what would soon be called the Skybreak House, in which a plastic dome produces a new kind of domestic space without walls. Living inside a dome would be barely distinguishable from living outside. A detailed plastic-covered model of such a radical assault on the traditional concept of the house had been built in Chicago by three of the students, complete with all furniture, appliances, panels, artwork, and molded bathroom, with trees on both the inside and outside of the dome to show that it did not interrupt nature. It was brought to Black Mountain, where Fuller had it repeatedly photographed among the vegetation around the school to communicate the "Garden of Eden" effect of the most minimal enclosure. He insisted that the latest technologies would so reduce the footprint of architecture that people would be returned to a direct experience of the pretechnological world. Architecture would no longer be an agent of disconnection. To live in a dome would be to connect oneself to the world. Architecture is to finally be revolutionized by the lightest possible plastic membrane.

3 Buckminster Fuller, "Geodesic Dome (1954) U.S. Patent 2,682,235," in *Inventions: The Patented Works of R. Buckminster Fuller* (New York: St. Martin's Press, 1983), 130.

4 One of the rare exceptions, an image of Fuller and a group of students holding up the plastic dome with the three women on the platform to "show off strength, lightness of 50-pound, aircraft cable dome," appears in a survey article, "What do You Know About the Geodesic Dome?," by Ken Olsen and Al Miller, *Better Homes and Gardens*, June 1957, 194. The image was used by Fuller in lectures.

As the summer session began, the Necklace frame was quickly unfolded. **fig. 18** Its cables were steadily tightened and, with the help of a temporary mast, the dome formed itself over the course of just a few hours in the grass just below the windows of Fuller's second-floor studio room. Three students proudly held the rigid frame up above them on their fingertips to demonstrate its lightness before it was fixed about three feet off the ground on a ring of posts. **fig. 17** Fuller and eight of the students swung on it like children for the camera to demonstrate its surprising strength. Soon there were fourteen students enthusiastically hanging in the air. **fig. 19** The plastic skin was then unfolded and a small wooden platform was hung from the frame on wire cables at a height that would place a standing person's head at the center of the enclosed space. But Fuller immediately lay on his back across the platform to gaze up through the double skin of transparent polyethylene as it was being inflated. **fig. 20** The air pump was still connected when he sat on a chair on the platform, earnestly studying the sky through this "pneumatic" film sealed in inflated hexagons and pentagons. **fig. 22** His fingers unconsciously arched to shape a dome in his lap as he looked upward in a newly tender way with the delicate geodesic net swirling around him. The dome idea had only really arrived in this crucial moment when the new skin offered a different way to see and think. It hovered like a shimmering mirage below the end of the horizontal bar of Lawrence Kocher's polemically floating but ultimately more earthbound building. **fig. 21** A glowing geometry and a new optics was finally taking off and leaving modern architecture behind.

When the skin was finished, three women on the platform, including Fuller's wife, Anne Hewlett, were lifted up by Fuller and nine students holding the dome above their heads to demonstrate the combination of lightness, strength, and integrity in instantly adjusting itself to the different amount of force used by different students before it was set back on the posts. **fig. 23** One of Merce Cunningham's students danced on the platform to demonstrate the new sense of freedom offered by the space. **fig. 24** She was photographed from below to show the lightly defined web of the plastic envelope surrounding her as she floated above the ground, dancing in a new kind of open space suspended against the backdrop of the natural world.

Fuller jumped up too and beams proudly at the photographer looking down from the adjacent school building as he stands on a hidden student's shoulders and sticks his head up through the one uncovered hexagon for ventilation at the top of the dome, firmly grasping the geodesic frame with both hands. **figs. 26 and 27** More than simply being inside the structure, it is as if he is wearing it like a skirt, becoming part of it in this key image which would be almost the only one he would publish of this crucial first dome.[4] In fact he would eventually publish three slightly different versions of the same basic shot—the apparently spontaneous image having been carefully staged and selected like so many of the key images throughout his career. Yet this image may be the most important of all. Fuller later describes Black Mountain as the place where he realized the pivotal idea that to be at the center of such a transparent dome allows one to understand one's

The First Dome Lands and Levitates at Black Mountain

17 RBF students Jeffrey Lindsay, Joseph Manulik, Ysidore Martinez, Harold Young, and Louis Caviani demonstrate the lightness of the dome, Summer Institute at Black Mountain, 1949. Photo by Masato Nakagawa

18 Necklace Dome frame being carried to site by RBF students, Summer Institute at Black Mountain College, 1949

19 Students demonstrate the strength of the Necklace Dome

20 Plastic skin being inflated with Fuller lying down inside

21 RBF and students inflating skin. Photo by Hazel Larsen Archer first published in *Architectural Record*, January 1952

17

18

19

20

21

22 RBF sitting on suspended platform watching the sky as Joseph Manulik inflates the plastic skin. Photo by Masato Nakagawa

23

24

25

26

A New Dance Liberated by a New Lightness

23 RBF and students demonstrate lightness, strength and resilience of Necklace Dome by carrying Anne Fuller and two other women

24 One of Merce Cunningham's students dances inside completed Necklace Dome

25 Necklace Dome at Black Mountain at night

26 RBF stands on shoulders of student to be photographed from above

27 RBF photographed from above by Hazel Larsen Archer. Version of photo first published in cropped form in *Architectural Forum*, August 1951

27

place in the universe, and therefore to act in the world. The minima plastic skin defines both a protected interior and an active engagemen both a shelter for the body and a prosthetic extension. The omnidirection al window floating above the ground turns architecture into a persona observatory, a panoptic platform that allows people to visualize the pa tern of their world and thereby take responsibility for it.

As soon as the dome was up, Fuller and his closest colleagues wrot to friends about the successful test of the inflated vinyl skin on its frame declaring that it was simply "the most beautiful bubble imaginable anc what a place to be when it rains!"[5] It remained up for the whole summe being both studied and used as a study. When later showing slides of i during lectures, Fuller described being thrilled by the thermal performanc of the heat-sealed plastic (saying that it measured 10 degrees cooler insid than outside and was even throughout), its resilience (surviving stone being thrown at it by students to simulate the danger of hail), its structura integrity with the frame (especially the discovery that alternative vertice could be pushed inward and outward to produce an even more rigid "invc lute" form), but above all its optical performance in both daytime anc nighttime.[6] **fig. 25** The solidity and immobility of conventional architectur is replaced by a single omnidirectional window. To occupy the space is tc occupy a window. Weight gives way to the eye. The stars enter, or, mor precisely, are entered.

INHABITING THE SKY

The success of this first plastic-encased dome acted as the launching pac for decades of geodesic experimentation. The "Fuller Research Founda tion" formed in the same year gathered a team of collaborators arounc him, mainly a set of his most committed students. His major innovatior was not only the geodesic structure as an interconnected system of equa elements sharing all loads, but the idea of an interconnected system o researchers distributed across a series of nodes in different cities to work ir parallel on domes—an interlaced network to study interlaced networks Immediately after Black Mountain, one of the Chicago students at th heart of the Black Mountain experiments formed a key node in Montrea with a friend who had attended a Fuller lecture. Another, entitled Skybreal Carolina Corp., was formed in Raleigh in 1951 by a group of teachers anc students at a new school of design where Fuller was invited to teach on th basis of the Black Mountain work, and others were formed in Detroit anc Cambridge. When Fuller received the patent for the geodesic dome in 195

5 On August 24 Fuller and two of his team report that "The 14-footer has been erected right outside Bucky's windows for purposes of observation and many tests, the vinyl skin is on and has been inflated [...] the most beautiful bubble imaginable and what a place to be when it rains! This phase of test we have had much opportunity to observe since rain is something we have plenty of! [...] With three ladies seated on platform, namely, Anne Fuller, Mary Jo, and Jane, [...] the structure was loosed from its moorings and held aloft by ten of the boys! Lifting by the ten constituted a continually varying stress as one lifted a little harder than the other. This demonstrated that the total integrity of the structure was very great in that it automatically equalized the uneven stressing." Buckminster Fuller, Jano Walley, and John Walley to "Daisy and Polita," 2 August 1949, BFP Series 2, Box 72, Folder 9.

6 Buckminster Fuller, audiotape of lecture (Detroit Museum, April 9, 1952), BFP Series 17, Box 1, Reel 4d.

7 Buckminster Fuller, "Dymaxion Comprehensive System: Introducing Energetic Geometry," 15-page manuscript dated January 1944. BFP Series 18, Box 119, Folder 16.

8 Buckminster Fuller, "Cosmopolitan Homes Corporation: Lightful Products," BFP Series 8, Box 2, Folder 1, p. 41. Fuller's diary records that: "After much philosophical thought while walking about worked out theory of spheres." Entry for Wednesday February 1, 1928, BFP Series 2, Box 16.

9 "Matter if existent at all (and we cannot fallaciously assume *a truth that is not*) must be spheroidal." Buckminster Fuller, *4D Time Lock* (self-published, 1928), 17.

and the first commissions for domes from the military, the Raleigh group formed Geodesics, Inc., to produce the designs, and a similar venture, Geodesics, Inc., was set up in Cambridge by students who had been inspired by the original Institute of Design experiments in Chicago. In the same year, Shoji Sadao, who had been yet another student of Fuller at Cornell in 1952, became the closest collaborator of all, working in all of the nodes and eventually forming an office with Fuller to carry out their shared design for Expo 67, assisted by many of the other former students operating in the network. The plastic sphere in Montreal emerged out of almost twenty years of research following the summer experiment with plastic at Black Mountain, a collaborative research program that was carried out in a distributed array of dozens of different schools where Fuller was a guest professor. A smaller set of schools (North Carolina, MIT, Princeton, and Southern Illinois) acted as the key nodes in the research network but the strength lay in the ever-growing array of venues. Fuller would typically give a lecture at a school that would go for hours and so amaze that he would be invited back to do a three- or four-week workshop with the students which invariably involved building a geodesic dome or sphere. Each of the major questions being asked could then be investigated simultaneously in different places, with much of this experimentation involving plastic.

In fact, the plastic skin was always at the heart of the research. Fuller kept buzzing around in his usual attention deficit mode, pollinating all the dispersed nodes and sustaining the feedback loops between them that steadily built up a huge archive of continuous overlapping and mutually reinforcing investigations of plastic architecture and the architecture of plastic, even if it never appears in the massive literature about Fuller. His whole teaching career and its unique methodology was literally launched at the intersection of geometry and plastic.

Fuller had received his first teaching appointment from Serge Chermayeff, the director of the Institute of Design in Chicago, after giving a hugely successful lecture at the school in February 1948 when he was right in the middle of six months of manic effort at his home office in Forest Hills trying to master spherical geometry—what he had been calling "Energetic Geometry" since 1944.[7] In a frenetic flurry of drawings, models, and calculations, he was obsessed with the possibility of a "comprehensive system" based on the idea of the entire universe being constantly in motion through waves of spherical radiation rather than the "tyranny" of straight lines and the resulting illusion of solid objects. He was finally developing, testing, and refining the theory he had presented in his very first text—when launching his first house—that everything in the universe is made of nested ever-expanding spheres. "Cosmopolitan Homes Corporation: Lightful Products," the unpublished manuscript of early 1928, had argued that "all matter (visible or invisible) is naturally a perfect sphere or spheroidal in shape" and elaborated the concept at length as the basis of the four-dimensional radiation approach to the universe and therefore to the house.[8] The argument was repeated shortly afterward in the self-published text *4D Time Lock* when Fuller was making his house public for the first time.[9] In a sense, his houses had always aspired to the perfect sphere. "Cosmopolitan Homes Corporation: Lightful Products" pointed out that none of the spheres in the world are perfect because of all the dynamic contacts with other spheres, but Fuller kept thinking of an unconstrained sphere from which all these dynamic interactions would become visible. Home would no longer be understood as a withdrawal from the world but precisely the opposite, the deepest possible engagement with the world. It would literally be suspended within radio.

It is not by chance that the intensity of Fuller's months of work on spherical geometry at the end of 1947 and beginning of 1948 echoed the manic intensity of the months of writing twenty years earlier that led up to the manifesto for his first 4D House and to the house itself.[10] The thought of housing was again in the air—literally. It was not a particular shelter but shelter itself that was to be found within the geometric waves of radiation that pulsated across the pages of Fuller's notebooks. The countless drawings, calculations, notes, and analytical commentary culminated in a set of remarkable, dense documents in February 1948 that combined all of the findings in complex summary images of his abstract geometric system that were covered in detailed calculations and notes. **figs. 28–31** The most stable geometric figures were shown to be produced by patterns of spheres, and spheres were shown to be produced by patterns of such geometric figures. This attempt to finally master the sphere was once again inseparable from the idea of house. The turning point was when Fuller had finally been able to calculate the "31 great circle" geodesic geometry with a sphere defined by the networked lattice of 31 circles with 12 vertices, and he promptly converted the analytical drawings into potential construction documents. The analysis of spheres immediately turned into an analysis of hemispheres. Unconstrained geometry turned into geometry fixed on the ground. As Fuller put it, the rest of the sphere would now be completed by the Earth, as he successfully tested with a self-supporting 4-foot-diameter hemispherical model of overlapping circles made out of the aluminum strip stock used in venetian blinds. In a set of sketches on a notepad of March 1, 1948, the great circles would be made of perforated aluminum or plastic strips to form curved triangular pans that would lock together to form a dome and be covered with a wire or plastic net as a shelter.[11] **fig. 34** In a play on the word *bungalow*, Fuller conjured up the idea of an Atomic Bulkalow made of this extremely lightweight construction technique. He detailed the connector for the pans and did all the calculations of the angles for each element and devised a triangular system for the floor. By May 4 he had done the calculations for hemispherical buildings of diameters ranging from 10 to 400 feet with an ever-increasing number of balconies inside them, but his analysis ended up zooming in on the scale of a house with a 50-foot diameter dome and a single 500-square-foot balcony. Drawings of abstract nested geometrical systems had given way to detailed

10 "For 3 months he was like a man with ague. He carried blocks of paper and fasces of pencils with him everywhere. He wrote so fast that, as soon as the writing was done, he had to go over it and print atop it. If he let it cool too long, he couldn't read it. [...] At the end of three months the compulsion [stopped] as suddenly as it had begun. By this time it had totaled some 5,000 double-spaced typewritten pages." Buckminster Fuller (in third person) to Joe Bryant, 1 July 1939, BFP Series 2, Box 29.

11 Buckminster Fuller, drawings on notebook, dated March 1, 1948, BFP Series 18, Box 119, Folder 15.

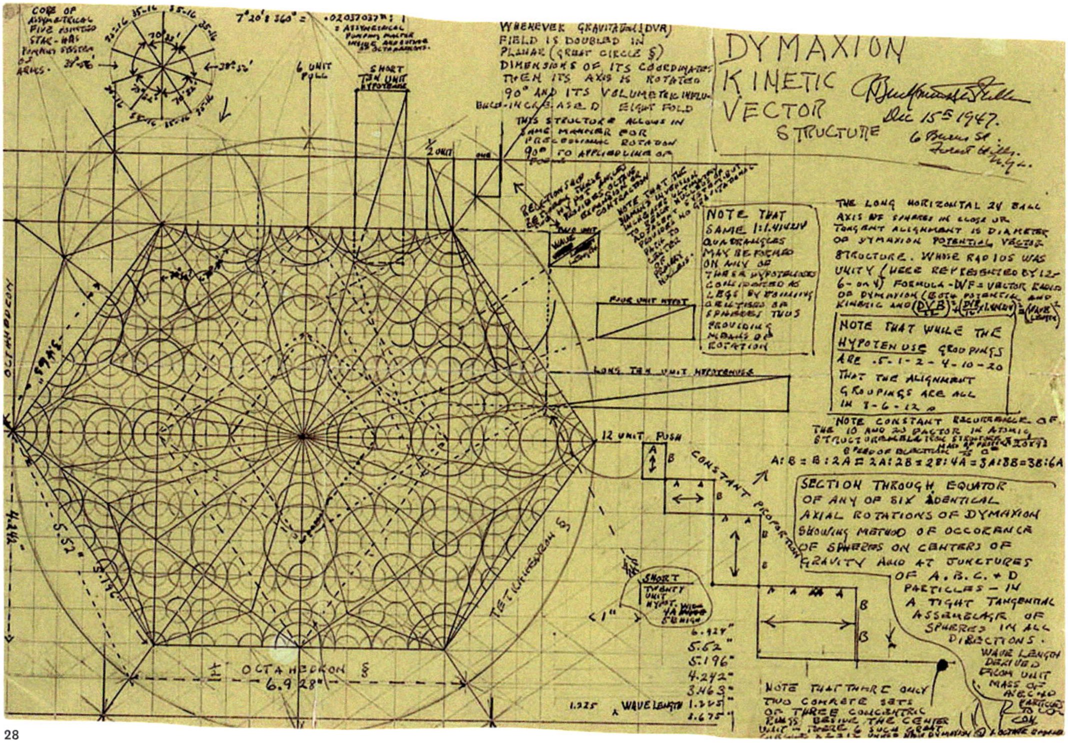

28

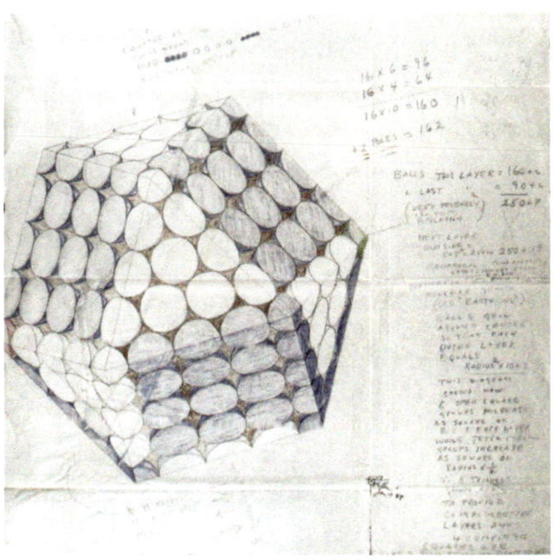

29

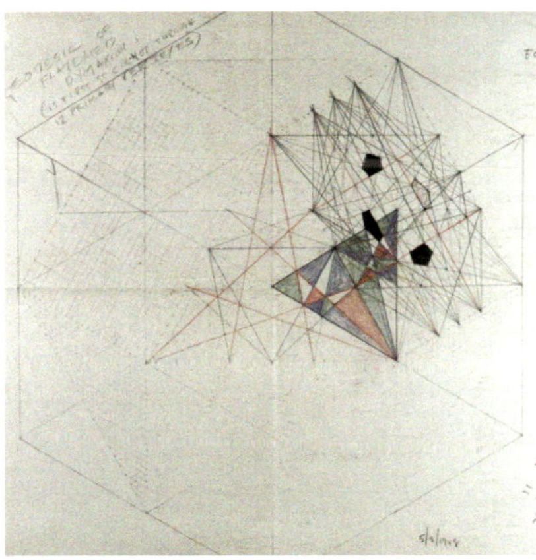

30

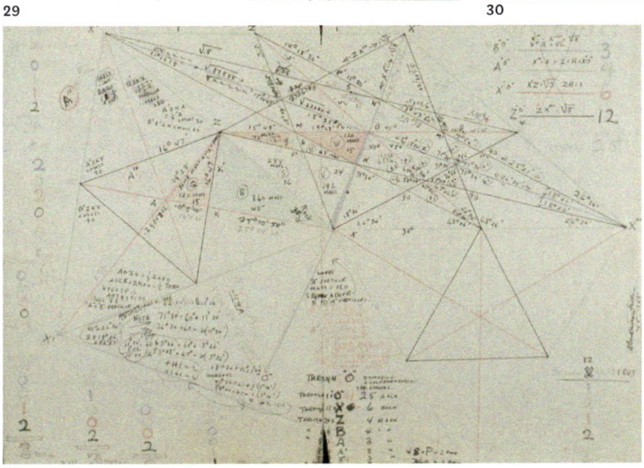

31

Energetic Geometry

28 RBF “Dymaxion Kinetic Vector Structure” drawing, dated December 15, 1947

29 RBF “Vector Equilibrium” drawing, dated January 10, 1948

30 RBF “Geodesic of Flattened Dymaxion” drawing, dated May 3, 1948

31 RBF Energetic Geometry drawing, dated February 5, 1948

calculations of all building materials, the weight of the structure, skin, floor, and balcony, along with the total cost.[12]

Symptomatically, it was right then in mid-May that Fuller did a pencil sketch of a double-skinned dome with a revolving shading system of three layers of shells suspended between the two fixed transparent layers to produce what he called a "Private Sky" effect for its occupants.[13] **fig. 32** A second drawing on the same day imagines a system of "gills" in this Private Sky Dome to reduce wind drag and toys with the label "Privisky."[14] **fig. 33** What the hemispherical house encloses is not a private space—there being little nostalgia for privacy in a transparent bubble—but the sky, and ultimately nothing less than the cosmos itself. Transparency here is not the absence of material but simply the accentuation of the fact that all material is porous, made of geodesic webs that are themselves mobile wave fronts. Drawing the skin of the dome implied the geodesic web just as drawing the web had already implied such a "spherical surface." This is not a surface in the traditional sense of the limit of a solid or even the limit of a void. Rather, it is the lightest, most ephemeral line possible to be held by plastic, a seal to the weather but simultaneously an opening to all forms of radiation. The geodesic sphere concept and that of the shelter and that of plastic were intimately tied to one another. Fuller told a writer for *Science Illustrated* that he was working in his apartment in Forest Hills on a 50-foot-diameter double-shelled Sky Fence House that would overlap two of these domes made of one-inch-thick aluminum strips in great circles with a three-foot space between them.[15] A new polemical Private Sky sketch of June 15 shows the new type of house resting on the curve of the planet and engaging with the full sky. A handwritten text with the same date is attached to the drawing and describes this ephemeral transparent dome made of aluminum strips as a highly protective shelter, such that "inhabitants of 'Sky'" would be safe from explosions, violent storms, and electronic phenomena like lightning—noting in the margin: "not first occurrence of this idea which is old 'dymaxion' 1928 thought but worth recording here."[16] The core aim of the original house, to do the most with the least, was about to be realized.

Fuller unsuccessfully tried to raise a 48-foot-diameter version of just such a dome a month later on a rainy day in the grass with the artists and students at Black Mountain at the very end of the summer session. He stood in the middle of the stubbornly flaccid aluminum strips, tensely clutching his set of crisp drawings with his 4-foot version sitting in the

12 Buckminster Fuller, "Laws of Dymaxion Shell Structuring on Great Circle or Geodesic Principles," analysis on notebook pages, dated May 4, 1948, BFP Series 18, Box 119, Folder 15.

13 Buckminster Fuller, "Private Sky" drawing dated May 22, 1948, BFP, Series 18, Box 119, Folder 15.

14 Buckminster Fuller, "Private Sky Dome," drawing dated May 22, 1948, BFP Series 18, Box 119, Folder 15.

15 Robert Marks, "Bucky Fuller's Dymaxion World," *Science Illustrated*, November 1948, 31.

16 Buckminster Fuller, handwritten text dated June 15, 1948, attached to Private Sky drawing of June 15, 1948, BFP Series 18, Box 119, Folder 15.

17 "The book on Plastics goes off with this mail. Willie is sending immediately the rest of your treasure." "Bobby" at Black Mountain College to Buckminster Fuller, 14 October 1948, BFP Series 2, Box 69, Folder 4.

18 Marks, "Bucky Fuller's Dymaxion World," 30 (see note 15).

19 Beaumont Newhall to John Whiting at *Science Illustrated* responding to requests of 27 July 1948, BFP Series 2, Box 69, Folder 8.

20 "Our dwellings in nature have essentially the characteristics of the urban dwelling. We don't live in direct, physical contact with nature. Would it be possible to develop a dwelling type which would virtually be a green-house enclosure, a living garden, interior space zoned for various activities including a 'cave,' an enclosure within the enclosure, for special privacy. Such a problem would require fundamental research in terms of light control, acoustic control and would find its solution in completely unprecedented forms and structure." Serge Chermayeff to Buckminster Fuller, 28 April 1948, BFP Series 2, Box 68, Folder 17.

grass as a model of what was supposed to happen. **fig. 36** He clearly had a house in mind when making this attempt and was even thinking about plastic—being very concerned after leaving Black Mountain that he had left his "Plastic Book" there, and agitating until it was sent to him in mid-October before any of the rest of his "treasure."[17] The Sky Fence House concept was eventually published in the November 1949 issue of *Science Illustrated* alongside a photograph of him in his Black Mountain studio surrounded by the models he had brought from Forest Hills and some geometric calculations floating on the blackboard. **fig. 35** The image would become one of the canonic portraits of Fuller. It was taken by Hazel Larsen Archer, who had been photographing life at the school since 1944 and audited Fuller's classes. He is staring thoughtfully at a small model in his lap. Hanging above him is the 4-foot great circle hemisphere that he placed on the grass outside as the model during the failed construction of the 48-foot dome. The caption has no doubt about the intimate relationship between the geometric investigations, the model dome, and the question of the house: "Through study of intersecting arcs, he developed [a] new kind of geometry (model above him) dome for new house."[18] The magazine had asked for photographs showing Fuller assembling or dissembling the model of his house in late July but his assistant responded that he did not have it with him, recommending they ask Hazel Larsen Archer for an image showing him with his teaching models.[19] Avoiding the fact that no house had been developed, the idea of such a house was reinforced as the real horizon of the conversation for the readers and for Fuller's colleagues, but crucially also for Fuller himself. The Bubble House is the tantalizing promise of the ultimate end point of doing more with less. Or, to say it the other way around, it was the foundational mirage. Nothing could be more real for Fuller than the promise of this barely visible image.

When the issue of *Science Illustrated* finally came out in November, Fuller had already taken the intersection of geodesic geometry and house to his first class in Chicago in October. Energetic geometry was understood to contain a new idea of house and vice versa. Both architecture and its occupants were finally to be suspended within radiation, which is where they originally came from and fundamentally belong.

Serge Chermayeff had sent Fuller the transcript of the February lecture in Chicago that had inspired the teaching appointment just a couple of weeks before the first Private Sky sketch was done in May. He suggested that the studio brief for the fall semester be a kind of "green-house enclosure" in the country, a "living garden" with an "enclosure inside the enclosure" for privacy.[20] Although Chermayeff would later make suggestions of other projects that could be done that semester, Fuller stayed with this first idea, presumably because it simply echoed the original ambitions of the Dymaxion House. He wrote back four days after doing the Private Sky sketch saying that the title of the class would be "Design Mutations in the Industrial Complex." The students were to develop prototypes for mass production and their case study would be "'the private sky' i.e. facilities of high standard deployed living without isolation" but they should not picture" the outcome when they start, as happened in the traditional

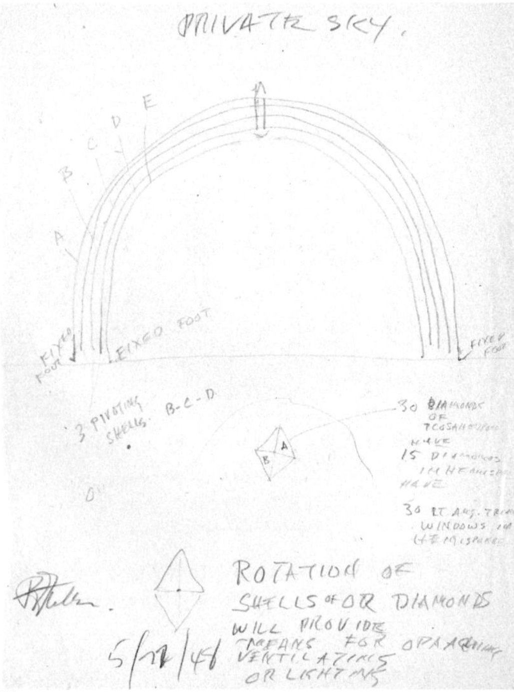

32

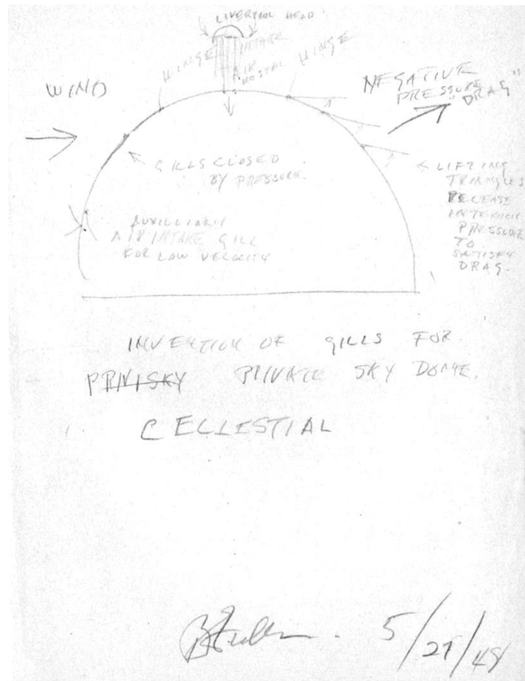

33

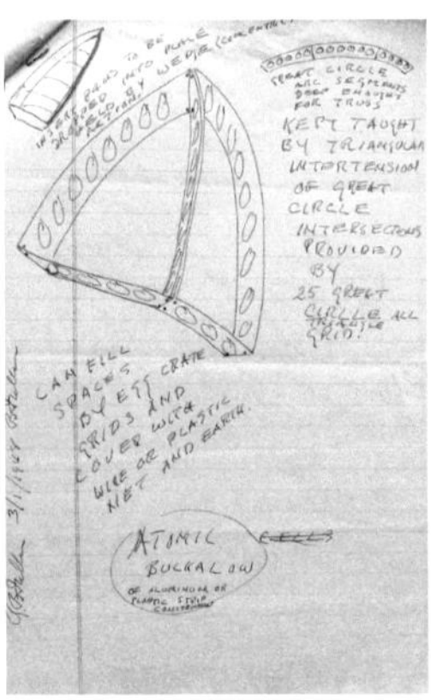

34

35

Drawing to Model to Collapse

32 RBF, Private Sky, drawing of rotating shells, dated May 21, 1948

33 RBF, Invention of Gills for Private Sky Dome, drawing, dated May 21, 1948

34 RBF, Atomic Bulkalow, drawing, dated March 1, 1948

35 RBF at Summer Institute of Black Mountain College, 1948. Photo by Hazel Larsen Archer

36

36 RBF with Elaine de Kooning and Josef Albers with collapsed dome, Summer Institute of Black Mountain College, 1948. Photo by Beaumont Newhall

architectural curriculum. The design cannot come out of a predetermined image, even the experimental image already implied by the label "Private Sky."[21] The draft for the letter indicates that Fuller had already mentioned "the 'Private Sky' or 'little house that was not there' idea" to Chermayeff making it unclear if the concept reacted to Chermayeff's suggestion or vice versa. It also goes into more detail about the idea and about wanting it to emerge logically out of the student research rather than be the evident goal from the beginning.[22] In a sense, the mirage was productive only inas much as it was a mirage, a tantalizing but unclear goal that forced both students and teachers to produce the thing that might lie ahead—a "little house that was not there." If a house is usually thought of as the opposite of a mirage, being a fixed image of the known point of departure rather than the unknown destination, the Private Sky idea tries to dissolve the house both literally and conceptually. Even the word *house* must be dis solved to open up the more radical potentials.

Fuller's eventual syllabus for the fall semester, his first ever, offered a formidably dense fourteen-page analysis of the evolution of technology and the uniquely transformative role that could be played by students within it.[23] The industrialized expansion of human capacity and the result ing global systems of transport and communication have reduced all dis tances in a planetary-sized network. Mankind now finds itself engaged in an another enormously bigger world beyond vision, without knowing how to handle it because of a lack of understanding of the simple principles of radiation at the heart of everything in the universe. Only students in the new role of artist-engineer can explore the voids in conventional under standing that science, industry, commerce, engineering, and politics stay away from and thereby act as an invisible and therefore effective "histori cal blockage" to further evolution. This exploratory work is needed to close the chasm between inventions in the lab and transformative applica tions in society. It took World War I "to launch the wire-less and track-less radio and aircraft industries" but war is no longer an efficient excuse to upgrade industrial capacity. It is a matter of taking advantage of the radiant condition of the "all energetic motionfull-limitless universe" understood as an "omni-directional network" in which the intellect can produce use ful patterns by modulating the length, frequency, phase, and direction of waves. Science and design are treated as inherently collaborative and pro active forms of radiation, acts of broadcasting rather than the consoli dation of existing systems. Educational institutions like the Institute of

21 Buckminster Fuller to Serge Chermayeff, 26 May 1948, BFP Series 2, Box 68, Folder 17.

22 "Wish to refer specifically to the 'Private Sky' or 'little house that was not there' idea which I mentioned, in our exploration, — of the summer project, — in order to clarify between ourselves, that the general could be reduced to the specific while opening up whole vistas of value to the engineer-architect student and his client the public — Ergo — prefer to suppress references to these items though it is to be presumed that they will emerge of their own natural logic when we get underway." Buckminster Fuller to Serge Chermayeff (draft), 26 May 1948, BFP Series 2, Box 68, Folder 17. Chermayeff replies two days later thanking him for the course outline, saying "Will try to digest this at leisure in the next few weeks." Serge Chermayeff to Buckminster Fuller, 28 May 1948. BFP Series 2, Box 68, Folder 17.

23 Buckminster Fuller, "Comprehensive Design: Synopsis of course to be conducted by Buckminster Fuller at the Institute of Design, Chicago, Ill. Oct. 4, '48-Jan.29, '49," BFP Series 8, Box 8, Folder 3.

24 "Emergency situation is the lever that overcomes man's inertia. The city is to be evacuated. All residential and industrial concentrations of 50,000 persons or more are in immediate danger of annihilation. Consumable goods now directed toward these areas will be diverted to smaller, decentralized communities. You have seven days in which to gather all living mechanics necessary to maintain a high standard of living for a family of six, two adults, two children and two guests. Everything not decentralized from big cities will be destroyed." Spring 1949 studio assignment at the Institute of Design, Chicago. Buckminster Fuller, "The Autonomous Dwelling Facility," unpublished manuscript dated May 2, 1949, BFP Series 8, Box 8, Folder 13, p. 2.

Design are described as being in a unique position to design the comprehensive integrated scientific packages that could be purchased by the always too cautious worlds of private industry and public agencies. Students would find themselves on the very frontlines of change.

As Fuller had insisted to Chermayeff, the syllabus didn't say anything about what the students would specifically focus on, other than that it would be a group project engaging an unsolved and politically bypassed social problem—one causing economic distress across a broad geographical and population base. They were to develop prototype mechanisms that could contribute to the overall standard of living, then test these prototypes technically and conceptually. The method would be to start with a 'Trial Balance' taking of the inventory" of the available technologies, a list of essential equipment for sheltering the species that would be continuously updated until prototyping begins. There was to be a ruthless self-monitoring throughout the whole process in notes and diagrams. This would safeguard each student's all-important creative ability to defeat conventional expectations in their crucial role of "radar long-distance range finders," the artist side of the critically needed hybrid figure of the artist-engineer.

This is of course a self-description. Fuller saw himself as a form of radar, devoted to scanning and charting the evolution of technology in order to anticipate its future, always looking beyond what can be seen to what might come next, but equally devoted to relentlessly charting every detail of his own activity. The expansive view beyond the horizon depended on the ruthless inspection and maintenance of one's local mechanism—in the same way that the ability of a new kind of house to engage with the electromagnetic spectrum would depend on the ecological self-sufficiency of its compact electromechanical core. Teaching would be the effort to multiply the Fuller effect, producing a kind of radar network out of interlinked students and focusing their collective capacity on a very precise set of questions.

RADAR CAMP

The question of the house was never mentioned in the syllabus but the assignment for the forty students in both the fall and the spring inevitably became the "Autonomous Living Facility," a unit that could be assembled in the countryside with all the equipment for modern life in the event that urban life was about to be annihilated in just seven days by atomic destruction.[24] The students were divided into teams. One set of teams focused on the Trial Balance Inventory of all the essential living equipment that could be integrated into a single package that could have wheels and a trailer hook attached to it. Another set of teams worked on the lightweight portable enclosure to shelter that equipment when it was unfolded—although the work on the shell quickly gathered momentum and dominated the fall, while the work on the living equipment to be housed within it became the main focus in the spring.

Fuller told Chermayeff that he had no need for traditional drawing tables and his basement studio space became a laboratory with a dense array of spheres hanging from the ceiling inspiring the domes being buil on the floor. **fig. 37** The space was a perfect image of Fuller's world, dome on Earth that dream of being spheres in the air, literally escaping the gra ity of architecture's clumsy attempt to pretend that there are straight line in the universe. In a pattern that would be repeated in countless project in countless schools, Fuller lectured in a torrent for seventeen hours ove the first days, with the students earnestly taking notes before he insiste that they take the lead with him as just the oldest team member:

> We start our class with the assumption that we are working as a group in development project. I have never been a teacher and I am sure that I woul not be good at conventional teaching as I was exposed to that practice. [... We are a team and I am the older man on the team.[25]

The students quickly felt themselves to be a collaborative able to do mos of the work without Fuller's direct involvement and soon had the sens of being independent from the school in which they were working. The started to call themselves Spheres Inc. as a self-styled research and deve opment group with an eye on real commissions. Fuller was particularl touched when the group gave him a wire recorder at the end of the sprin semester so that they could continue to listen to him wherever he was an transcribe and analyze the latest arguments.

Such machines were even part of the project. The autonomy of th Autonomous House was once again dependent on receiving, recordin and broadcasting media. The list of essential equipment in the Trial Ba ance Inventory included an FM-AM receiving set, television set, publi address system with microphone inputs, alarm-sounding devices, signa ing equipment, short-wave radio set, wireless telephone set, and wir recorder set. One of the research teams continued the original concept c the 4D House by devoting itself to the design of "a special area inside [the autonomous dwelling structure in which all equipment selected to deve op awareness of human progressions can be used with maximum eas comfort and efficiency. [...] Within this area, man will extend intellect ally his comprehension of dynamic world processes going on outside hi immediate empirical scope."[26] This unfolding "Kenning Space" would b carefully integrated into the heart of the overall unfolding package an receive broadcasts of all political activity and allow continuous electroni referendums on any political issue. The detachment of the shelter from th city was again to be enabled by a reattachment by radio and the radio se itself was again the model for the shelter that it serviced. Fuller had alread pointed to radio when doing charts of economic and technological trend at *Fortune* magazine in early 1939. He argued that all the acceleratin gains in technical advantage would finally lead to the mechanization c the home, using the example of going from the "old and careless concep

25 Buckminster Fuller, unpaginated transcript of lecture (Institute of Design, Chicago, Saturday, November 9, 1948), BFP Series 8, Box 8, Folder 3. Even the sequence of lectures at the Institute of Design was based on notes summarizing the lectures at Black Mountain College that students there did after Fuller had left on his request to help organize the Chicago course. This pattern of student notes on both the lectures and student reports on the prototypes acting as the raw material for the next course became the basic mode of Fuller's teaching.

26 Undated student report on the Spring semester, 1949, BFP Series 2, Box 70, Folder 3. The political section of the Autonomous Dwelling Facility brief includes a "system of individual dual balloting relayed into central agencies to permit universal referendum on every political issue and "24 hour a day radio and television broadcasts from all central legislative bodies." Ibid.

27 Buckminster Fuller to Russell Davenport, 17 March 1939, BFP Series 2 Box 39.

f standard of living" embodied in thinking of radio as a large wooden onsole to the new concept implied in carrying a radio in one's vest pockt. He predicted an "eventual mechanical package" servicing all technical eeds that could be enclosed in any shell, or even a tent.[27] The Stanlard-of-Living-Package and camping structure assignment given to the tudents in Chicago had actually been formulated a decade earlier, and vas anyway embedded within the electromechanical core of the 4D House nother decade before that. Fuller was teaching for the first time but the ubject was his oldest and most continuous obsession. The class itself vas simply a form of magnification and acceleration.

The class involved parallel investigations of parallel investigations—gain setting the pattern for all Fuller's subsequent teaching projects and or the tight interrelationship between those projects. The fall semester urned Fuller's 4-foot great circle hemisphere in venetian blinds of six nonths earlier into a viable shelter. The first Necklace structure was sucessfully developed by the end of the semester and constructed by the chool's technicians in a 10-foot-diameter version. **fig. 39** When it was noved from the workshop to an auditorium for the final steps of construcion, Fuller sat in front of it, seemingly transfixed, as if waiting and wonlering about the transparent vinyl skin that would complete it but was never made. **figs. 40 and 41** It stayed up for a while but was then photographed n the floor in its collapsed form as a beautifully portable, wrinkled bunle with a matching set of blueprints. **figs. 38, 42, and 43** Alternative structural ystems had also been rapidly prototyped during the semester, starting vith a 14-foot-diameter, noncollapsible, open-framed dome in venetian lind material folded into a U-shaped channel that a beaming Fuller and ome of students held proudly aloft on their fingertips in celebration f the radically lightweight future and a closed dome made of triangular luminum metal "pans" riveted together. The space filled up with metal rototypes but plastic was always understood as the key step in realizing he concept.

One of the first tests tried to combine the virtues of the collapsible Necklace and the fixed pans through the idea of a foldable plastic dome f six concentric rings of hinged triangular pans that would initially lie flat ut could be pulled up into shape on a mast, with the flanges of each pan ocking together to form a stable structure before the mast was removed nd the final triangles of plastic filling the hole at the top would complete he hemisphere. One of the students, Jeffrey Lindsay, drew the blueprints ull-size and a successful 40-inch-diameter working model was made in lastic. **figs. 44–46** It was photographed in each step of being pulled up from lat to final dome and then from multiple angles to understand its structurl and optical quality—with the geodesic lattice of great circles becoming ghostly trace marked within the plastic itself. The idea of such a selfupporting plastic pan house had already been incubated when Fuller ad finally managed to tame the great circles in the first months of 1948. n a few pages of notes, he had calculated that 150 standard transparent lastic ice boxes with tapering sides from Woolworth could be attached to ne another to form a 50-foot-diameter hemisphere held together by

37

38

39

40

41

Engineering the First Dome in the Lab

37 RBF in his studio at Institute of Design, Chicago. Photo by Charles Eames, February 1949

38 Collapsed Necklace Dome package, Institute of Design, Chicago, Spring 1949

39 RBF and technicians assembling 10-foot Necklace Dome in workshop at Institute of Design, Chicago, Fall 1948

40 RBF and 10-foot Necklace Dome in auditorium of Institute of Design Chicago, Fall 1948

41 Completed 10-foot Necklace Dome in auditorium, Fall 1948

42–43 Blueprints for construction of Necklace Dome, Spring 1949

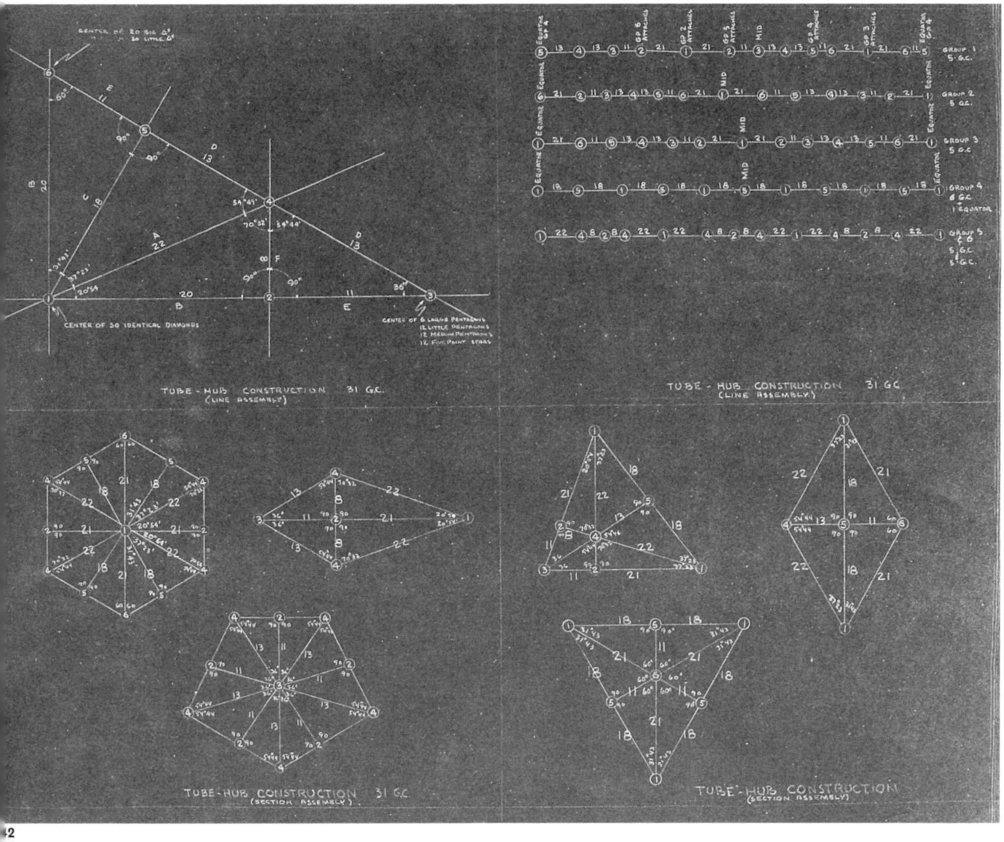
TUBE-HUB CONSTRUCTION 31 G.C.
(LINE ASSEMBLY)
CENTER OF 30 IDENTICAL DIAMONDS
TUBE-HUB CONSTRUCTION 31 G.C.
(LINE ASSEMBLY)
GROUP 1 5 G.C.
GROUP 2 5 G.C.
GROUP 3 5 G.C.
GROUP 4 5 G.C. 1 EQUATOR
GROUP 5
TUBE-HUB CONSTRUCTION 31 G.C.
(SECTION ASSEMBLY)
TUBE-HUB CONSTRUCTION
(SECTION ASSEMBLY)

42

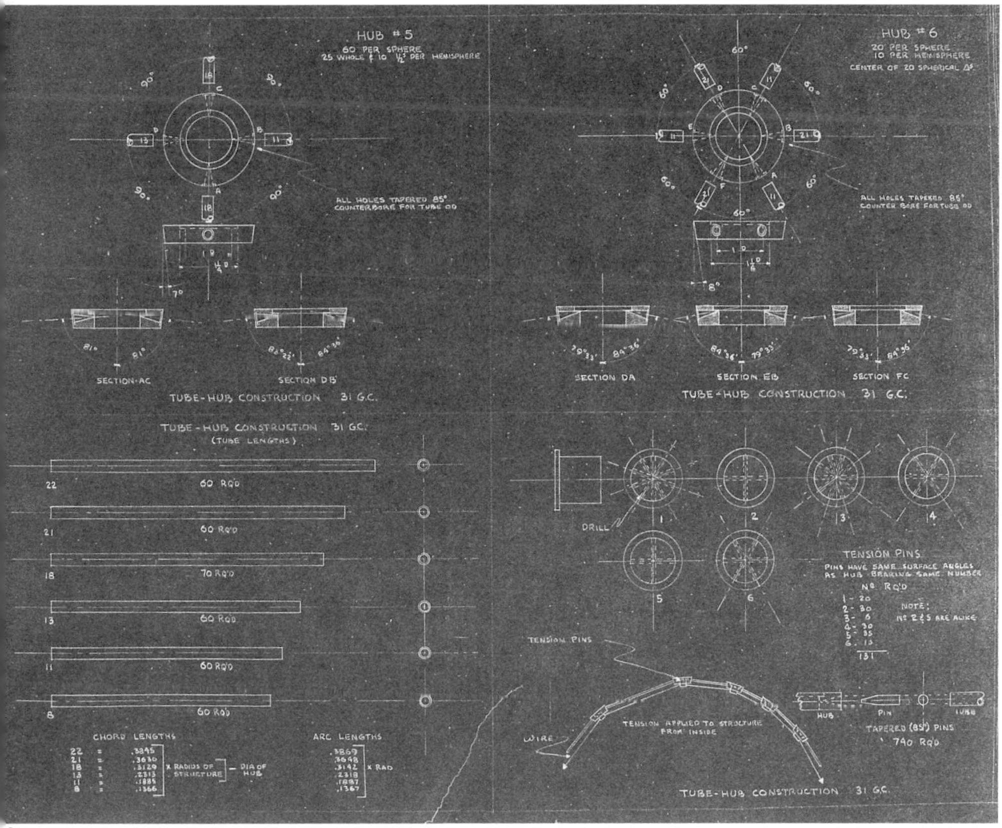
HUB #5
60 PER SPHERE
ALL HOLES TAPERED 85°
SECTION AC
SECTION DB
TUBE-HUB CONSTRUCTION 31 G.C.
HUB #6
20 PER SPHERE
10 PER HEMISPHERE
CENTER OF 20 SPHERICAL Δs
ALL HOLES TAPERED 85°
COUNTER BORE FOR TUBE OD
SECTION DA
SECTION EB
SECTION FC
TUBE-HUB CONSTRUCTION 31 G.C.
TUBE-HUB CONSTRUCTION 31 G.C.
(TUBE LENGTHS)
60 RQ'D
60 RQ'D
70 RQ'D
60 RQ'D
60 RQ'D
60 RQ'D
CHORD LENGTHS
ARC LENGTHS
DRILL
TENSION PINS
TENSION PINS
WIRE
TENSION APPLIED TO STRUCTURE FROM INSIDE
HUB
PIN
TUBE
TAPERED (85°) PINS
740 RQ'D
TUBE-HUB CONSTRUCTION 31 G.C.

3

2-inch-wide aluminum great circle strips.[28] **fig. 48** Detailed working drawings of such a plastic structure without the metal bands were done in Chicago and the idea at Black Mountain College in the summer of 1949 was to test both a plastic-skinned Necklace frame and a self-supporting plastic structure. Plastic had been divided into two promising trajectories. Or rather, plastic itself was the promise. If there is an architecture of, in, or from radio, then plastic would be its medium.

The team had devoured any information about plastic they could find, assembling an array of samples and technical manuals. Fuller repeatedly insisted that architecture, like all technology, was ultimately a matter of chemistry. A representative from DuPont was invited to the class to describe the latest plastics in November 1948, and the understanding of what plastic could do was dramatically transformed as Fuller and the students learned about the performance of fiberglass, a material that seemed destined to be both skin and structure.[29] They desperately contacted the industry looking for the latest information just before heading off to Black Mountain for what would turn out to be an unsuccessful attempt to make a self-supporting 20-foot-diameter fiberglass dome out of double-skinned, double-curved triangular panels held together with fiberglass plastic splines.[30] **figs. 49 and 50** It turned out to be a too ambitious test based on the unexpected "involute" idea accidentally discovered early in the summer session when some of the vertices of the plastic-covered Necklace Dome were popped outward and the others inward. In what would again become the pattern of the research on geodesics, each plastic experiment was affected by the others. Plastic itself seemingly flowed through all the spaces of Fuller's work, acting as the ever-evolving limit of his thinking. Plastic was literally his medium. It is as if the very figure of Fuller was molded in plastic.

After their experiments alongside the regular Black Mountain students within Fuller's so-called Philosophy of Measurement class, Spheres Inc. intended to fuse the two ways of using plastic by testing a 60-foot-diameter "prototype house" with a fiberglass skin. In the very last week of Fuller's stay at Black Mountain, Jeffrey Lindsay, the student who along with Don Richter had the greatest interest in plastic and was setting up the research node in Montreal with his friend Ted Pope, already proposed to act as the

28 Buckminster Fuller, undated 2-page manuscript with drawings, notes, and calculations in Fall 1948 files, BFP Series 18, Box 119, Folder 15.

29 "Each of our days we are going to learn a little more about our chemistry and technical abilities. We are going to know that our tensile strength is just gone up just this last week. DuPont man came here and showed us new insertion of a fiberglass into plastic and he showed us we now have 300,000 tons of strength in this little piece. You put it under the sledge hammer and it wouldn't break." Buckminster Fuller, "Structure" (lecture, Institute of Design, December 2, 1948), BFP Series 8, Box 8, Folder 3, p. 10.

30 Fuller wrote to his brother at General Electric in early July asking for very detailed information about size, performance, availability, and cost of the latest plastics including fiberglass, and whether they could buy the materials from GE through him as "we wish to make an experimental structure whose outside skin is comprised of triangular molded pans whose vertical flanges coincide geometrically with great circle planes in such a manner that each pan consists of a rigid 3-way keystone in a comprehensive compound curvature dome." Buckminster Fuller to Woody [Wolcott] Fuller, 4 July 1949, BFP Series 20, Box 71, Folder 7. Three days later, the students sent a version of the same letter to another industry figure.

31 "I propose that when the Chicago group have worked on a prototype house, and have done all the lab work on the plastics etc., and when they feel that fabrication should begin on their own and agreed design, and that if at that time they wish to build the house in Montreal and if no money will finance it at some better place, then I would offer to be their first customer." Jeff Lindsay to Buckminster Fuller, 6 September 1949, BFP Series 2, Box 71, Folder 13.

32 Eleanor Cannon to Buckminster Fuller, sent 23 September 1949, BFP Series 2, Box 74, Folder 2.

33 Buckminster Fuller to Eleanor Cannon, undated but sent between 23 and 28 September, 1949, BFP Series 2, Box 72, Folder 9.

34 Eleanor Cannon to Buckminster Fuller, 30 September 1949, BFP Series 2, Box 71, Folder 1.

35 Robert Richter, Don Richter, and Louis Caviani to Buckminster Fuller, 6 December 1949, BFP Series 2, Box 71, Folder 12.

36 Drawings and notes dated January 6, 1950, BFP Series 2, Box 71, Folder 11.

37 "Dome – Aluminum Slat and Pneumatic Bag," 1949 blueprint, BFP Series 16, Map Folder 65.

client and build the house in Canada once the rest of the group in Chicago had "done all the lab work on the plastics, etc."[31] Equally promptly, Fuller started trying to persuade potential patrons of the unique advantages of such a house. Just a week after leaving Black Mountain in September, he visited the "Cannon's Landing" property in the "remote wilderness" of Woodstock with its owner, Victor Cannon, who made an on-the-spot deposit for him on 3 acres of the land. The Cannons were building a new largely glass-walled house (despite being unimpressed when visiting Philip Johnson's recently completed glass house in New Canaan) and they were excited about the possibility of having Fuller and an extreme building as a neighbor. Eleanor Cannon wrote to Fuller welcoming "A radical designer!"[32] He wrote back describing in detail the proposal for a 60-foot-diameter, plastic-covered aluminum Necklace Dome with an unfolding Standard-of-Living-Package within it. There would be a set of living space enclosures "blossoming within the enclosed garden." Radiation was again the key. Fuller compared the dome house with its compact mechanical package to the glass spheres of lightbulbs and electronic tubes that shelter their respective technical elements from the immediate world so that those elements can better do their job of reconnecting with the world beyond.

After floating this tantalizing image in the air, Fuller said the structure first needed to be tested inside another building (presumably a reference to the Spheres Inc. research), and then on site in the isolated countryside of Woodstock where "its bugs could be worked out under the indulgent protection of the creatively disposed who could tolerate the temporary shortcomings in view of its partially fulfilled promise."[33] What would be built in Woodstock is an intermediate "experimental structure" to explore a concept that has the potential to transform housing worldwide if refined under real-world conditions. Eleanor Cannon responded in excited capitals: "DEAR-RADICAL-COMPREHENSIVE-DESIGNER, NO ONE EVER TALKED TO ME THAT WAY BEFORE! I READ AND RE-READ. WHAT A THING TO DO WITH WORDS AND THEN TO PUT THEM UP PHYSICALLY!!! SINCE IT IS POSSIBLE TO HAVE THE FUTURE NOW WHAT A CRIME ONE MUST WAIT!"[34]

Yet it turned out to be much more than a wait. The work of Spheres Inc. went very slowly after Black Mountain. They were pleased to have the most up-to-date information from plastic manufacturers and fabricators by December 1949, along with samples of a "near transparent fiberglass polyester plastic" that offered both the strength and optical properties they desired.[35] Their idea of an involute dome with a double skin of fiberglass was finally being described in detail in January.[36] But a whole catalog of alternative plastic techniques was developed in parallel by the different groups of ex-students, as can be seen in drawings of domes with "pneumatic bags" made of "inflated plastic bag filler" between the aluminum slats of a structure,[37] and drawings comparing the use of strips of nylon in diamond shapes with zippers on the edges to presewn nylon "pillowcases" for each diamond unit of a Necklace structure. **fig. 47** Each new plastic idea would be sent to Fuller as a kind of offering and he would feed and reenergize the collective obsession with the elusive capacity of the elusive

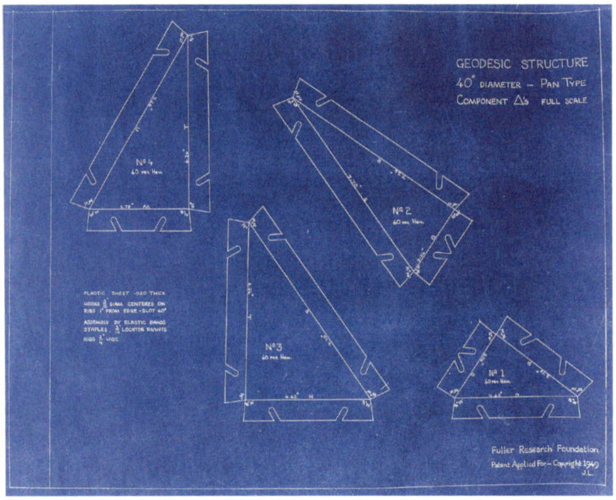

44

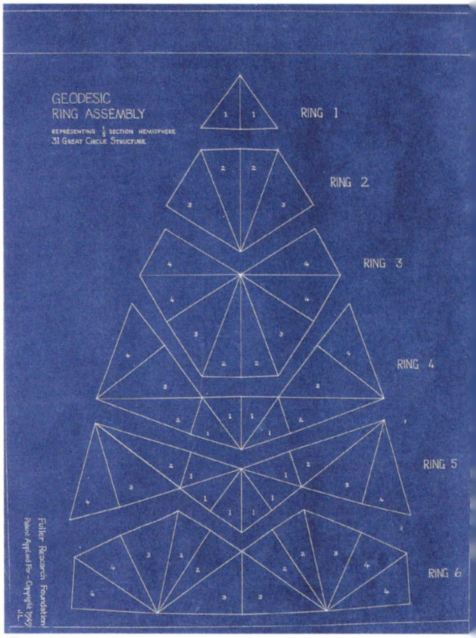

45

Detailing the Desire for a Self-Supporting Plastic Architecture

44–45 Blueprints for construction of plastic pan great circle dome drawn by Jeffrey Lindsay, 1949

46 40-inch Foldable Plastic Pan Dome, Institute of Design, Chicago, Spring 1949

46

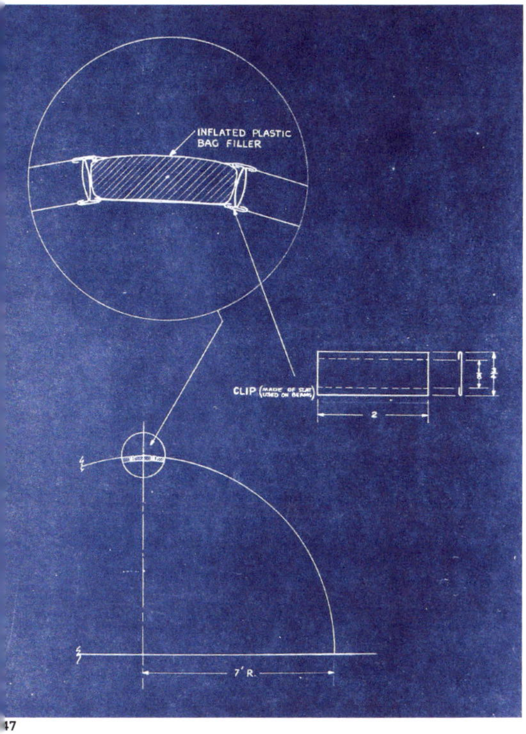

47

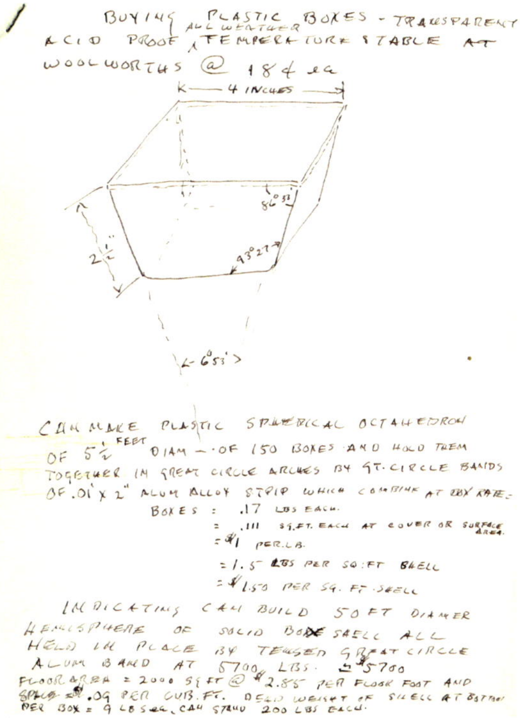

48

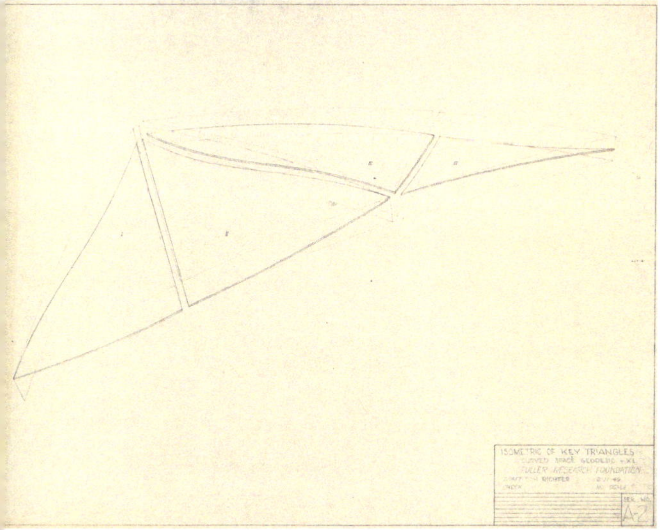

49

47 Blueprint detail of Aluminium Slat and Pneumatic Bag Dome, 1949

48 RBF, notes on dome constructed out of plastic boxes from Woolworth, early 1948

49 Isometric drawing of panels for Curved Space Geodesic involute dome by Don Richter, August 11, 1949

50 Louis Caviani, Don Richter and Jeffrey Lindsay working on fiberglass panels for involute dome, Summer Institute at Black Mountain College, 1949

50

material. In August 1950, for example, Don Richter in Chicago, who had maintained a regular correspondence with Fuller about fiberglass, sent drawings of a new kind of structure using inflated hexagon pillows for a dome and expressed his gratitude for the *Plastic Encyclopedia* that Fuller had recently sent him.[38] Jeffrey Lindsay had similarly written a week earlier describing working with plastic manufacturers on the possibility of an external structure made of inflated triangular cushions of three layers of Vinylite or neoprene-coated nylon and talking with tent manufacturers who could sew bags of the materials to hang on the inside. He was studying all the options of vinyl, nylon, fiberglass, Vinylite, and polyethylene.[39] By November Lindsay was zooming in on Orlon, a translucent acrylic fabric that had just been introduced by DuPont, and he regularly updated everyone on the ongoing analysis.[40] There were clear rivalries between the groups and an always palpable confusion about Fuller's role and associated difficulties in the ambiguity of authorship, but a kind of shared loyalty to the promise and seductive mystery of the material itself that was almost more significant than loyalty to Fuller.

Lindsay and Pope finally erected a 49-foot-diameter aluminum Weatherbreak Dome in spring 1951 that was tensioned by external cables and internally skinned with Orlon. **figs. 51–55** A few months later, they built the first plastic-glazed wooden dome as a possible commercial Skybreak prototype with 76 translucent fiberglass panels contributing to its structural stability and two rows of acrylic panels forming a 360-degree window—followed by experiments with a skin of transparent saran and an Orlon sunshade suspended over it.[41] The promise of plastic could finally be seen with the first images of a family happily encased in the almost invisible skin. *Architectural Forum* devoted its cover and seven enthusiastic pages of its August 1951 issue to these experiments with a "spidery new framing system."A fragment of Fuller's argument about energetic geometry was included and a description of the plastic on each dome, even showing the deftness of the attachment of the skin to the Weatherbreak frame in Montreal in a cinematic sequence of seven photographs—starting with the students earnestly holding the bundle of the plastic tent between them in front of the geodesic frame and concluding with the smooth white plastic bubble.[42] The fascination with the images of young builders suspended in the lightweight metal frame as it went up, one of which was featured on the cover of the magazine, is matched by a fascination with the plastic skin. The very openness and abstract geometry of the frame is seen to invite the plastic. The article also referred to a new project for a huge 411-foot-diameter dome with "a skin of a new type of plastic, glass fiber-reinforced polyester styrene." The state of the art of structure was

38 Don Richter to Buckminster Fuller, 21 August 1950, BFP Series 2, Box 72, Folder 6. Richter points out that the group has been limited to "only theoretical work" on these different plastic systems and that even that work needed minimal financial support.
39 Jeffrey Lindsay to Buckminster Fuller, 14 August 1950, BFP Series 2, Box 72, Folder 6.
40 Jeffrey Lindsay to James Fitzgibbon, 21 November 1950, BFP Series 2, Box 73, Folder 3.
41 "Panels of translucent fiberglass reinforced polyester resin laminate [...] are structural, providing the lateral stability for the frame members, thereby reducing the required frame section." Jeffrey Lindsay, report on dome, BFP Series 18, Box 147, Folder 1.
42 "Geodesic Dome: Bucky Fuller's Spidery New Framing System," *Architectural Forum*, August 1951, 144–151. Once again, what is being enclosed is the sky above the dome: "We knew that it was light, knew that it was strong, but we did not know that it was going to do just that to a blue sky." Buckminster Fuller, "Architecture Out of the Laboratory," *Student Publication*, Michigan College of Architecture and Design, 1 no. 1 (1955): 17.

51–55 Installation of plastic skin inside the frame of Jeffrey Lindsay and Ted Pope's Weatherbreak Dome, Montreal, spring 1951

51

52

53

54

55

seen to be inseparable from the state of the art in plastic. Confirming the foundational role of the Black Mountain experiment, the final page shows the ecstatic Fuller wearing the first plastic dome at Black Mountain and the plastic model of the imagined house within the surrounding vegetation there alongside a description of the "The Autonomous House" and a listing of all the trustees and fellows of the Fuller Research Foundation. The antiarchitectural experiment with plastic had successfully infiltrated the most-read architecture magazine.

This was not simply a case of reporting on a new development in the field. The article was part of the development, negotiating between idea and realization. What is crucial about the image of the Black Mountain dome, the very first realized dome to be published, is the sense that when the mirage is realized, it will precisely look like a mirage, a shimmering ambiguous space. Fuller had made a private lecture in April to the editorial staff of *Architectural Forum* at their offices in New York, giving a long account of the evolution of technology before describing the history of his own projects. His history of technology culminated in the accelerating evolution of plastic from 1927 onward to the latest fiberglass with its fantastic strength that would only increase in the near future to produce structural components with the spectacular properties of "insect legs."[43] The account of the architectural research that then began, using slides of all the projects, likewise culminated in an extended discussion of the plastic dome at Black Mountain. Before showing the first slide, Fuller had said that the ambition of his work was to make a valve, again using the transparent sphere of the electronic tube sheltering its specialized elements from the environment as his model. He told the magazine that a new kind of architectural enclosure would likewise have its specialized elements inside for radiation, like the large valve that is a television tube. The last slides showing the Black Mountain dome were seen to finally realize the ambition of life inside a radio tube:

43 "Mr. Buckminster Fuller Presentation April 19, 1951" (transcript of presentation to *Architectural Forum*), BFP Series 8, Box 11, Folder 4, pp. 12, 14.
44 Ibid., 35.
45 The students sent Fuller periodic updates by telegram while he was traveling around the country, confirming on March 7 that they had finished the model, were sending it along with the blueprints, and "will forward plastic structure as soon as possible." "Marty" [Ysidore Martinez] to Buckminster Fuller, 7 March 1949, BFP Series 2, Box 70, Folder 2. Three days later, Martinez confirms "Structure assembled and plastic cover supported very well. Assembly of structure approximately 3 hours for well experienced crew." "Marty" to Buckminster Fuller, 10 March 1949, Series 2, Box 70, Folder 16. Later the same day, he confirms that the model is finished and is on a flight to Washington along with blueprints, the plastic cover, and other equipment. "Marty" to Buckminster Fuller, 10 March 1949, Series 2, Box 70, Folder 8.
46 Fuller later claimed that the dome was made at 14-foot diameter rather than full-size only because they had assumed that it would be demonstrated inside a large Pentagon office rather than outside. Buckminster Fuller, audiotape of lecture (Yale University Department of Architecture, October 16, 1952), BFP Series 17, Box 4, Reel 3k.
47 When Fuller was at Black Mountain Chermayeff asked if there was a Vinylite cover for the 10-foot Necklace Dome that had been left behind or whether one could be made and Fuller responded that a plastic skin had never been made for the Necklace ("spaghetti") Dome left at the school, territorially detaching the whole concept from the school in which it had been developed: "there is no Vinyl cover for the 10 foot spaghetti type,—you are probably thinking of the Vinyl pneumatic skin of the Fuller Research Foundation's 14 foot model prepared for and erected at the request of the Air Corps in the Pentagon building." Buckminster Fuller to Serge Chermayeff, 11 July 1949, BFP Series 2, Box 71, Folder 7.
48 General Grandison Gardner to Buckminster Fuller, 15 March 1949, BFP Series 2, Box 73, Folder 9.
49 The military was also interested in different kinds of covering. The official report already raised the possibility of using the frame "as a basis for a form for use with expandable, self-setting plastics." US Quartermaster Report by Mr. Griffing and Mr. Millard on "tube and cable structural framework," March 14, 1949, BFP Series 8, Box 8, Folder 2.
50 Buckminster Fuller to General Grandison Gardner, 25 March 1949, BFP Series 2, Box 73, Folder 9.
51 "So the summer school plans rest mainly on me and I was wondering whether you can come this summer and build a dymaxion science lab—where you want and how you want." Natasha Goldowski to Buckminster Fuller, 25 February 1949, BFP Series 2, Box 70, Folder 1. On March 19 Cynthia Floyd wrote to say that she had sent the "plastic tent for the structure" back to Chicago but "The Plastic tent for the structure is in Hal's [Brigadier General Harold Watson] office." Cynthia Floyd to Buckminster Fuller, 19 March 1949, BFP Series 2, Box 70, Folder 16. Fuller responded that he had received the plastic skin back and had been invited to direct the summer course at Black Mountain, where "We will carry out development there of some larger structure. I have had a most friendly letter from General Grandison Gardner suggesting the six next tactical moves including test of the fourteen-foot structure in the Air Corps cold hangar during its next rundown to –75 degrees." Buckminster Fuller to Cynthia Floyd, 28 March 1949, BFP Series 2, Box 70, Folder 16.

> The structure was used then for study all summer long. Monitors were placed at many points around the outside of it and inside of it and we had a very hot summer sun at the Black Mountain, so we could really get some good study of what it would be like being inside of a transparent enclosure or an electronic cell. In other words, remember that we are dealing with this concept as a valve. [...] so, you're doing a whole lot structurally and it's a matter of being a valve, of letting the radiation through. You're going to get a whole lot of control for very, very little.[44]

MIGRATING MIRAGE

A key point in the story that was not overlooked in Fuller's lecture or the resulting coverage in *Architectural Forum* was the military dimension. With the success of the 10-foot-diameter prototype of the Necklace structure at the end the fall semester in 1948, Fuller promptly contacted the US Air Corps about the promise of this rapidly deployable structure and they agreed to take a look. The students started to build a new 14-foot version of the Necklace structure and a vinyl cover for it in February and sent them to Washington in early March. They also sent the blueprints, an air pump to inflate the plastic skin, and a plastic-covered model showing it with an internal garden and a two-level dwelling for a family (with all the furniture, grass, plants, and trees), each of which was shipped on the day it was finished in a frenetic attempt to have it on site when Fuller would be there.[45] **fig. 57** The dome was temporarily assembled in a courtyard of the Pentagon by Fuller himself, a passing GI, and a young intrigued civilian visitor, getting a lot of attention during the day before being formally inspected.[46] **fig. 56** The frame and its plastic cover (which Fuller did not attempt to demonstrate on the structure) were refolded and sent back to Chicago.[47] But the "plastic tent" model of the family residence stayed for a while in a Pentagon office with its faceted plastic surfaces that had been taped to the metal frame catching the light from the window and attracting many visitors. **fig. 58**

The general in charge of the inspection of the courtyard and office models wrote that he was "intrigued by their possibilities," asking for more tests with the plastic cover installed as intended, with a specific focus on the thermal performance of the envelope in extreme heat and cold.[48] He also wanted photographs of the small model to be done outdoors to appear as if it was already realized, and for its interior fittings to be built to scale inside the 14-foot dome for another set of photographs, suggesting there could also be versions for two or even four families. His advisors added the possibility of using the latest "expandable, self-setting plastics."[49] Fuller replied that his team would do all the things that had been asked for when continuing the testing at the summer program at Black Mountain College.[50] He had been invited just a month earlier to direct the summer program there and set up a "dymaxion science lab" in whatever way he wanted.[51] The new version of the small model taken to Black Mountain for the requested photographs outside—and put on a sophisticated metal-and-wire display mount in Fuller's studio classroom **fig. 59**—sustained both the military and civilian agendas in showing a new internal

THE PLASTIC LINE

56

57

Putting the Dome on the Road

56 Necklace Dome installed in courtyard of Pentagon, March 1949

57 Student with first plastic Skybreak House model, Institute of Design Chicago, photo by fellow RBF student Iris Steinmuller, circa February 1949

58 Skybreak House model on display in Pentagon office, photo by David Floyd, March 1949

59 Skybreak House model on display in RBF's studio, Black Mountain College, summer 1949

60 Students with their Standard-of-Living-Package model, Institute of Design, Chicago, April 1949

61 Don Richter holding up plastic-covered dome of the Skybreak House model, Black Mountain College, summer 1949

62 Standard-of-Living-Package model encased in plastic on the grass, Black Mountain College, summer 1949

58

59

61

60

62

63

63 RBF with Skybreak and Standard-of-Living-Package models, Black Mountain College, summer 1949

64 Photograph of Skybreak House model used by RBF to represent the "omni-directional translucent" setting for the plastic skin, 1949

›**65** Photograph of Skybreak House model used by RBF to represent the "omni-directional clear" setting for the plastic skin, 1949

64

organization for accommodating three officers and the option of using the unfolded Standard-of-Living-Package for a typical family which had been finalized shortly after the Pentagon demonstration. All the equipment for sustaining domesticity was packed by the students into a transparent plexiglass box, ready to be unfolded within the plastic dome (which had now been upgraded with doors and schematic indications of internal curtains). **figs. 60 and 62** Fuller was photographed proudly beside the model in the grass in both its military and domestic modes **fig. 63**, while Don Richter waved the plastic dome in the air like a kind of net to catch some sky just as they would soon triumphantly hold the 14-foot Necklace Dome up in the air to grasp the whole sky. **fig. 61**

Fuller had no interest in the plastic bubble shelter being a secret project in either its military or domestic modes. He responded to a newspaper editor's questions in early February by saying that the Sky Fence House concept that had first been published in November was a research and development project that had the possibility to be manufactured in the near future and that the beginning of April would be the right time for its publication since the final plans would be available them, as if only the rest of the spring semester were needed.[52] A month later, just a few days before the Pentagon visit, he showed images of the prototype Necklace structure in a lecture at the University of Illinois and optimistically said "we are making right now" a 50-foot-diameter Necklace Dome with a transparent, inflated double skin of vinyl quilted in triangles. The plastic dome would be a "very light capsule" offering protection from unwanted elements while admitting wanted radiation and be so efficient that it would allow for a transformative separation of the design problems of enclosure and activity. Architecture would be liberated from the usual constraints and a dense mechanical package, a garden, automobile, mobile partitions and mobile ceilings could be installed below the "complete capsule sky."[53] Once again, plastic is seen to have the unique ability of housing the sky. A plastic capsule would literally launch its occupant into space itself. The most elemental shelter becomes a launch pad.

Fuller used a major architectural conference held at the University of Michigan immediately after the Pentagon demonstration to promote the idea of living in a 50-foot-diameter hemispherical dome made of great circles with an inflated "transparent plastic skin of double wall construction." He described the military's interest in the studio assignment at Chicago and presented two photographs of the original model taken at the

52 Buckminster Fuller to Milton Amsel, *New York Star*, 9 February 1949, BFP Series 20, Box 9, Folder 7.
53 Buckminster Fuller, lecture (University of Illinois, March 4, 1949), BFP Series 8, Box 8, Folder 11.
54 Buckminster Fuller, "Preview of Building" (lecture at *Time for Change* conference, University of Michigan, Ann Arbor, April 1, 1949).
55 "I think it made it acceptable because you didn't seem to be talking about architecture and we were able to get away with quite a lot under the momentum of the tent concept. At any rate when it was over [...] a great many students indicated enthusiasm." Buckminster Fuller, wire recording of lecture (Institute of Design, April 2, 1949), BFP Series 17, Box 130, Tape 13.
56 Jeanne Rockwell, "Fuller Describes Unusual Ideas of Future Home," *Ann Arbor News*, April 5, 1949, 10. "The top photograph shows Fuller's 'Autonomous Geodesic Structure' with its transparent shielding of plastic material set at 'omni directional clear' (by means as yet undisclosed). [...] Smaller photograph shows this package as seen from the inside. It is assumed here that controls are set at 'omni directional translucent' so there is privacy from prying as if the interior were 'surrounded by sunlit mist.'" "Fuller's New Super-Tent," *Architectural Forum*, May 1949. "The double walls of plastic are inflated to withstand rain, hail, snow, hurricane, and all other onslaughts, and allow '100% variable optic control. [...]'" "Everyman's Eden," *Interiors*, June 1949, 19.
57 "Bucky Inc," *Time*, November 7, 1949, 61.
58 Buckminster Fuller, "The Behavior Characteristics of the Autonomous house," manuscript, BFP Series 2, Box 71, Folder 9.

Pentagon showing that the transparency of this "super camping structure" could be adjusted with an unspecified system of shutters—the concept that he had sketched in the very first Private Sky drawing ten months earlier.[54] An image of the dome from the outside was used to represent the "omnidirectional clear" setting and another showing the internal architecture against a white background without the dome represented the "omnidirectional translucent" end of the range. **figs. 64 and 65** Three students from Chicago came that evening and exhibited their freshly made model of the unfolding Standard-of-Living-Package, which was positively received for an hour after the conference dinner. Fuller felt that the presentation of the transparent dome enclosure plus the compact equipment package concept was a very important announcement, the beginning of a major transformation of the field. He confided to the students a few days later that the initial reception by the leading architects and architectural journalists had been conservative and hostile, due to the extreme "nakedness" of the architecture: "This did represent the first impingement of the idea on the academic world and on the architectural publishing world and had sort of a shock factor." But he thought he had managed to deflect the negativity by referring to it only as a "tent," a "camping structure" rather than a house, portable equipment for the times away from architecture rather than architecture itself.[55] This was accurate in the sense that his lifelong polemic was exactly to address what comes after architecture, without any interest in a return trip. He was happy that the enthusiastic reaction from the local students seemed to convince the journalists that something significant was happening and the two images of the Pentagon model were highlighted in newspapers and professional magazines like *Architectural Forum* and *Interiors* in the following months.[56] On an even bigger stage, a November issue of *Time* magazine published the photograph of the transparent model at the Pentagon, predicting that Fuller's "plans for a new house he calls 'Geodesic'" that would be 1,000 times lighter than a conventional house" might be the one to finally earn the respect of architects in the coming years.[57]

None of this media exposure was accidental. Fuller told his students that he had persuaded the journalists not to overexpose the concept before it was fully developed, but he was working closely with the different magazines and had even sent images of the student model to the editor of *Arts + Architecture* magazine before the Ann Arbor conference in the hope it would be published along with a text on "The Behavior Characteristics of the Autonomous House." The short essay argued that such an enclosure would be but one of the multiple widely dispersed shelters that people would nomadically occupy in the near future.[58] It is not a mobile house in the simple sense of a lightweight enclosure that moves. Rather, it was mobile in the more radical sense of the distribution of the very idea of house across a network of dispersed ephemeral structures that are continuously updated or simply replaced whenever the technology advances. Charles Eames, one of the founding trustees of the Fuller Research Foundation, helped organize the images for the article. He must have seen the prototypes when photographing Fuller's studio at the Institute of Design in early February, sending Fuller a slide showing him as a kind of ghostly figure lurking almost unseen at the back of the thicket of models to "give the smell of the space in which you work."[59] **fig. 37** There was similarly a lot of dialogue back and forth with the editor of *Interiors* magazine and Jano Walley, one of Fuller's close associates who would be a crucial part of the team at Black Mountain. She wrote a long text for *Architectural Forum* that summarized the presentation at Ann Arbor, with the same two images of the model that had been taken to the Pentagon showing the "all year garden" with its dome adjusted to clear and translucent.[60]

The two images accompanied a summary text on "Everyman's Eden" produced by Fuller's office that quoted passages of his program for the summer session at Black Mountain and was used by a number of magazines and newspapers.[61] When the associate editor of *Interiors* responded enthusiastically to the text and images, Fuller was very quick to reply with a long letter addressing each of her questions but began by describing the care with which they had to shepherd the "critical early phase" of the project and therefore to "carefully consider each item of first mention and exposure" and protect the "very tentative, though cordial" relationship with the Air Corps.[62] He said that the full-scale tests that were about to start included those asked for by the military but would also "out-distance" their requirements. He again tried to avoid the more traditional idea of the mobile apartment, insisting that what they were doing was simply removing all compromise from "extended living." He enclosed some additional images of the latest model of the Standard-of-Living-Package and asked that the students be credited for all the work on the dome and package as independent researchers who are operating under their own initiative before finally insisting that the magazine "adhere to the precise phraseology within which I have presented it."

The tone and timing makes it clear that all of this management of the publicity was extremely important to Fuller. He wrote to the editor of *Architectural Forum* to insist that the text of Jano Walley be published in full to avoid any misunderstanding,[63] and devoted a lot of work to her

59 Charles Eames to Buckminster Fuller, 9 February 1949, BFP Series 2, Box 70, Folder 9. Already on February 15 Entenza had confirmed an interest to publish one of Fuller's lectures to the Institute of Design, and Eames wrote in the week of the Pentagon demonstration that Entenza was delighted with the article and suggested that Fuller's black-and-white images would be better than his own Kodachromes. Charles Eames to Buckminster Fuller, 11 March 1949, BFP Series 2, Box 70, Folder 1. In the same week, Chermayeff wrote to the editor of *Progressive Architecture* for advice about a proposed Institute of Design-sponsored book on energetic geometry, saying "I am pretty sure myself that this is a revolutionary publication." Serge Chermayeff to Thomas Creighton, 14 March 1949, BFP Series 2, Box 70, Folder 1. In October Fuller would pursue the idea of doing the book with Entenza, saying that "Black Mountain produced some important gains," and that he had rewritten the essays he had sent earlier in the year. Buckminster Fuller to John Entenza, 20 October 1949, BFP Series 2, Box 71, Folder 4.

60 Jano Walley, "Report to Architectural Forum, R. Buckminster Fuller Lecture—Ann Arbor Conference, April 1, 1949," BFP Series 2, Box 72, Folder 1.

61 "Building and Housing: Everyman's Eden," BFP Series 8, Box 21, Folder 4, pp. 410–414. See "Everyman's Eden," *Interiors* (June 1949).

62 Buckminster Fuller to Deborah Allen, Associate Editor, *Interiors*, 8 May 1949, BFP Series 2, Box 71, Folder 5. The letter responds to one from Allen to Fuller, 4 May 1949.

63 Buckminster Fuller to Douglas Haskell, 17 April 1949, BFP Series 2, Box 72, Folder 1.

64 The text is longer by "one-third, accounted for by necessity to incorporate communication that is coincidentally effected during my speech by gestures, whose picturings are a part of the continuity of meaning. This gesture picturing is particularly employed in describing structural interactions, and dynamic properties." Buckminster Fuller to Dean Wells Bennett, University of Michigan, 14 May 1949, BFP Series 2, Box 72, Folder 8.

65 "Called Geodesic Structure, Actually It's New House," *Toronto Daily Star*, December 15, 1949. Dorothy Howarth, "Glass Garden Homes His Aim for World," *The Telegram* (Toronto), December 14, 1949.

66 "Designer of Futuristic Buildings Shuns Conventional for 'Geodesic' Pattern," *Christian Science Monitor*, June 15, 1951, 13.

67 *Housing: A National Security Resource* (Cambridge: Bemis Foundation and the School of Architecture and Planning, MIT, 1951). *Architectural Record*'s report on the conference included one of the rare published images of the completed Black Mountain plastic dome. "MIT Conference Shows Need for Long-Term Housing Research," *Architectural Record* 111, no. 1 (January 1952): 22.

68 The design for the so-called Brewer House was published in Bruno Leon, "Tensile Integrity," *Student Publication of the School of Design, North Carolina State College* 1, no. 2 (1951): 30–39.

transcript of the Ann Arbor lecture, cannily explaining to the Dean of the Architecture School that the final text was a third longer than the original transcript because a third of the content of the lecture had been delivered by the "gesture picturing" of his body that "is particularly employed in describing structural interactions, and dynamic properties."[64] He inevitably recommended the images to use and described the upcoming tests in the summer. A carefully crafted micronarrative of the evolution of the plastic bubble is inserted into the macronarrative of the evolution of technology over the previous century that Fuller was always repeating and refining. His experiments are portrayed as being at the very frontlines of the evolution of human capacity. They are a kind of window onto the future of the species.

Fuller was obsessively devoted to media coverage throughout his career. He continuously cultivated relationships with editors and journalists, agreeing to almost every interview, sending unsolicited texts, ghost-writing articles, developing close relationships with writers who would dedicate many articles to him in a wide range of publications, encouraging others to work on books about him or of his writings and always having several book projects being simultaneously proposed to different publishers by friends and associates. He monitored the results of all this effort by relentlessly charting every single reference from the beginning of his career to the end. **fig. 68** But his tone throughout 1949 is more intensely that of having finally accomplished a real transformative breakthrough. The plastic Bubble House was seen as the ultimate revolutionary act, the culmination of more than two decades of polemical designs and statements, even if many "bugs" would have to be eliminated on the way to the first million units. Each public lecture and newspaper interview was treated as a chance to move the concept forward.[65]

Fuller was still talking to newspapers about the concept in the same way, using the same two images, in the summer of 1951, despite having been continuously working on the idea for more than two years.[66] In the fall of 1950, for example, he had advised students at MIT who were developing two variations of a dwelling within a transparent dome. The results were exhibited in a plastic-skinned model at a January 1951 conference on industrialized housing at MIT sponsored by the Bemis Foundation alongside research on "plastics in housing" and an "autonomous core package" by one of the students who been part of the original team in Chicago—with Fuller giving the keynote on how to "stretch resources."[67] Meanwhile, James Fitzgibbon, the young teacher who had seen the first plastic-covered dome at Black Mountain and helped bring Fuller to teach at the new school nearby at Raleigh, was completing his own 90-foot-diameter Skybreak House design with an internal garden using a version of the aluminum dome that Jeffrey Lindsay was developing in Montreal.[68] A huge amount of research was dedicated to the technical performance of the plastics, involving a number of manufacturers, and a continuous exchange between Raleigh, Chicago, Montreal, and New York on the role that would be played by the different layers of plastic and the transformative capacity of finally building such a house. The plastic line that would define shelter was never simple. It was a high-performance series of layers addressing structure, weather, light, and temperature. Plastic was discussed in almost every communication between the different research nodes.

Fitzgibbon's house design looked like it would be the first serious application of plastic architecture. Lindsay was proposing in early November 1950 that it have an outer safety net of saran with a two-inch gap before another saran layer then an eight-inch gap before another three layers of saran spaced three-quarters of an inch apart with perhaps an additional layer hung inside—an expanded sandwich of six layers to produce the desired "highly translucent dome."[69] **fig. 66** By February, Fitzgibbon was drawing a translucent fiberglass skin lined internally with four layers of saran half an inch apart.[70] The idea was to complete the plastics tests using the 48-foot frame they were making in Montreal, build everything using the same dies, and fly it to Raleigh as a kit set to be constructed in three days, with an imagined media launch in the summer of 1951 when the weather would be favorable.[71] Fuller abruptly brought everything to a halt by rejecting the idea of sharing any rights with the proposed client.[72] But the project was revived to such an extent that Lindsay expressed concern in late April about proceeding without having tested the saran.[73] As if in response, Fitzgibbon redrew the envelope in late May as an exterior skin in fiberglass or plexiglass triangles with three inner layers of saran built into each triangular pan and not stretched very tightly to avoid all the complications of zippers and seams in the saran.[74] **fig. 67** Lindsay finally received the saran to test the following week and the chemists at the manufacturer agreed to make a version of saran with fiber embedded in it.[75] Fitzgibbon had a new client by June and was proposing a double skin of fiberglass and addressing the problems with saran with the chemists. Once again, the first plastic house was about to appear, but the project soon faded completely.

A whole series of such projects that were never realized acted as incubators for testing the possibilities of plastic. Around the same time, for example, Charles and Ray Eames started collaborating with Fuller on the idea of a temporary Bubble House for one of their clients in the Mojave Desert that would have a wooden geodesic frame and a plastic skin. The Eameses reacted to Fuller's photographs of the latest plastic experiments in August 1951 by saying that they wanted to build a test model next to their own house.[76] It was impossible for Fuller just to apply a known material in a known way since plastic was a threshold to a new set of potentials, a question rather than an answer with each evolution in plastic moving the inquiry forward. He suggested a few months later that the Eameses use a

69 Jeffrey Lindsay to James Fitzgibbon, 9 November 1950, BFP Series 2, Box 73, Folder 3.

70 Sections of building envelope in pencil by James Fitzgibbon, BFP Series 2, Box 73, Folder 3.

71 In late January 1951 Jeffrey Lindsay reported that the saran has arrived so tests could begin on the "4 films spaced with fiberglass cuticle," and that the Air Corps was interested to see it after it was skinned, with a media launch in summer being best. Jeffrey Lindsay to James Fitzgibbon, 20 January 1951, BFP Series 2, Box 73, Folder 3.

72 For the most detailed analysis of Fuller's relationship to the question of rights and authorship in regard the Brewer House, and also the wider field of geodesic domes, see Yunn Chii Wong, "The Geodesic Works of Richard Buckminster Fuller, 1948–68 (The Universe as a Home of Man)," PhD diss., Massachusetts Institute of Technology, 1999.

73 Jeffrey Lindsay to James Fitzgibbon, 25 April 1951, BFP Series 2, Box 73, Folder 13.

74 James Fitzgibbon, drawing dated May 22, 1951, BFP Series 2, Box 73, Folder 17.

75 Jeffrey Lindsay to Buckminster Fuller, 25 May 1951, BFP Series 2, Box 73, Folder 17.

76 On August 10 Eames responded to Fuller's latest photographs of the dome experiments. Charles Eames to Buckminster Fuller, 10 August 1951, BFP Series 2, Box 74, Folder 3.

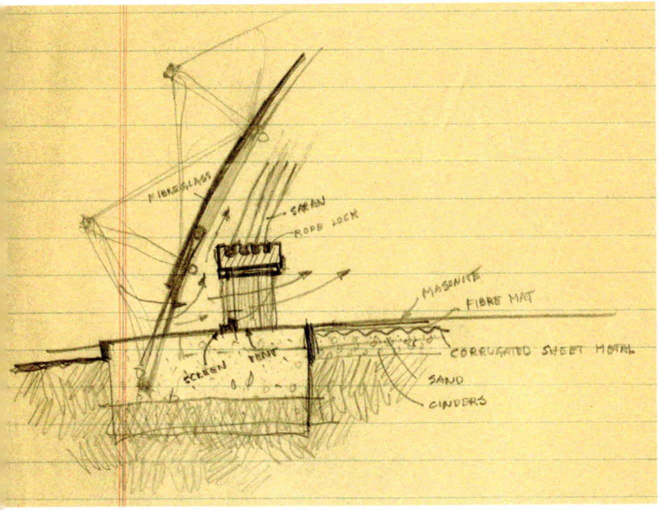

66

The New Anatomy of Plastic Membranes

66 Jeffrey Lindsay, detail of fiberglass outer layer and inner layers of saran, November 9, 1950

67 James Fitzgibbon, detail of joints between plexiglas or fiberglass pans and loose saran films, May 22, 1951

68 Chart of published references to RBF in "Basic Biography," 1975

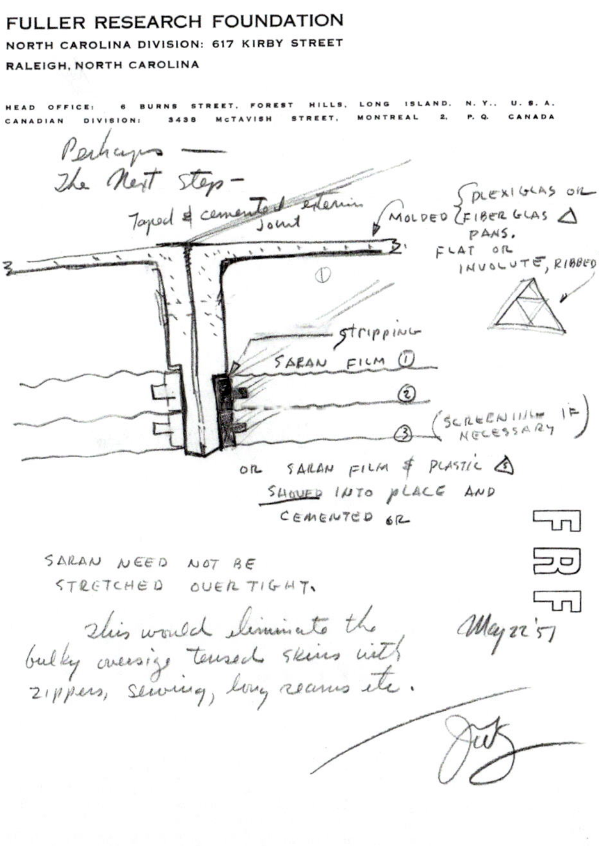

FULLER RESEARCH FOUNDATION
NORTH CAROLINA DIVISION: 617 KIRBY STREET
RALEIGH, NORTH CAROLINA

HEAD OFFICE: 6 BURNS STREET, FOREST HILLS, LONG ISLAND, N. Y., U. S. A.
CANADIAN DIVISION: 3438 McTAVISH STREET, MONTREAL 2, P. Q. CANADA

Perhaps —
The Next Step —
Taped & cemented exterior joint

MOLDED {PLEXIGLAS OR FIBER GLAS △ PANS.
FLAT OR INVOLUTE, RIBBED?

stripping
SARAN FILM ①
②
③ (SCREENING IF NECESSARY)

OR SARAN FILM & PLASTIC △ SHOVED INTO PLACE AND CEMENTED OR

SARAN NEED NOT BE STRETCHED OVER TIGHT.

This would eliminate the bulky oversize tensed skins with zippers, sewing, long seams etc.

May 22 '51

FRF

Fitz

67

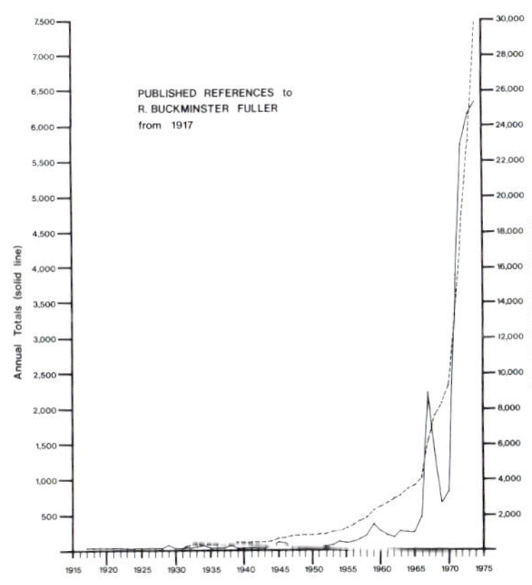

68

new plastic called cast-optics no.3 since it had properties between those traditionally associated with plastic and glass, quoting the latest issue of *Modern Plastics* magazine.[77] As always, the team sat right at the evolving edge of the material, using the very latest polymers in unanticipated ways.[78] New plastic was being used to pull architecture into new territory. It was precisely the instability of plastic that allowed it to hover so seductively yet ambiguously. Plastic was not a material like any other. It was more like a shimmering vibrating hint of the future of the material world, a hint of the world to come at the very intersection of chemistry and radio.

ACCELERATING THE DOME

Nothing could matter more to Fuller. He started to accelerate the concept that fall with his students at MIT, who now imagined a geodesic frame skinned in transparent saran and expanded the role of plastic to include thin sheets of polyester fiberglass laminate for the demountable floor, ceiling, and wall panels. Their designs were presented at the January 1952 conference on housing at MIT in the same series on industrialized housing sponsored by the Bemis Foundation and were referred to by newspapers and *Architectural Record* before being published in detail in the first issue of the Yale student magazine *Perspecta* that summer, still under the name "Autonomous Dwelling Facility." Fuller's introductory text, which was simply extracted from his April 1949 lecture at Ann Arbor that presented the bubble shelter experiment for the first time publicly, repeats the core point that an aluminum dome with an inflated transparent plastic skin could establish a whole new kind of space and that there was no limit to its possible size.[79] The architectural ambitions of plastic were growing exponentially.

Plastic detailing had become the critical art in the ever-expanding dome. Jeffrey Lindsay had already calculated the fiberglass covering for the 411-foot-diameter dome shopping center project in 1950 and the following year Duncan Stuart in Raleigh developed a proposal for a 150-foot diameter Skybreak Dome using fiberglass to replace the existing tent for the Aspen design conference. Meanwhile, Fuller had been working with Duncan Stuart and students at the school in Raleigh on the design of a seven-story-high automated cotton mill housed in a three-quarter sphere. **figs. 69–71** Once again, a double-walled skin of plastic sheltered a dense package of interconnected equipment, a complete technological metabolism with a network of transparent saran plastic tubing integrated into the geometry to handle the flows.[80] For Fuller, plastic was quite literally the space of advanced technology. He portrayed the sphere's "plastic envelope" as sustaining flows like those within the human body, electrical distribution systems, and the movements of contemporary industry.[81] The

77 Buckminster Fuller to Charles Eames, 14 October 1951, BFP Series 2, Box 75, Folder 15.
78 Jeffrey Lindsay to Buckminster Fuller, 25 May 1951, BFP Series 2, Box 73, Folder 17.
79 Buckminster Fuller, "The Autonomous Dwelling Facility: The Geodesic Dome," *Perspecta* 1 (1952): 30.
80 "Cotton Factory Student Report," January 2 to February 2, 1952, BFP Series 18, Box 107, Folder 1.
81 Buckminster Fuller, "The 90 Per Cent Automatic Factory," synopsis of the program given to twelve students. *Student Publication of the School of Design, North Carolina State College* 2, no. 1 (1952): 29–33. Fuller later republished the same synopsis alongside the resulting design. Buckminster Fuller, "Textile Mill of Tomorrow," *American Fabrics*, Spring 1953, 100–106.

69

70

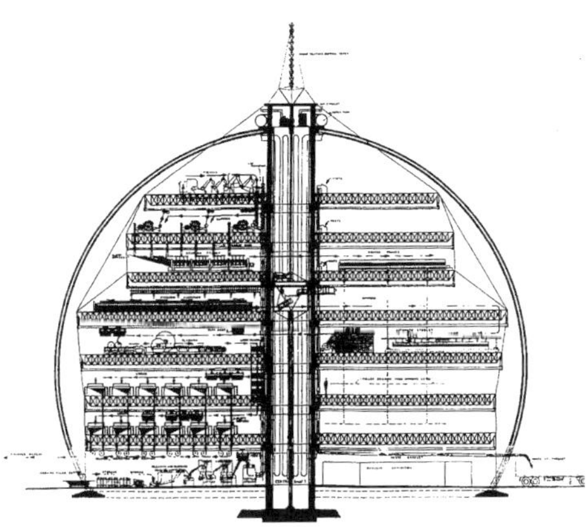

71

Lattice for the First Bubble

69 Students with Automatic Cotton Mill model, College of Design, North Carolina State College, Raleigh, 1951

70 RBF behind Automatic Cotton Mill model under construction, 1951. Photograph by Duncan Stuart

71 Section of Automatic Cotton Mill as metabolic valve, 1951

intricate design was finished in January 1952 and published a few months later in the ever loyal *Architectural Forum*, with the magazine noting that the crucial "stretched plastic skin" was missing from the otherwise precisely detailed demountable model.[82] But Fuller always saw plastic and thought valve, and therefore house, when looking at any intricate geodesic frame. The project was also highlighted in the article "You May Live in a Bubble House" that appeared a month later in the Sunday supplement to the *Washington Post* and a number of newspapers around the country—with domestic space symptomatically remaining the reference point, no matter how large the dome being discussed. The article interviewed Fuller's key collaborators in Raleigh and Montreal and concluded that the "biggest stumbling block" to dome houses is "the fact that FRF [Fuller Research Foundation] men have not yet found a suitable, light-weight transparent (or translucent) 'skin.' [...] But they're hoping that the right form of plastic will turn up any day."[83] Once again, plastic is the key to the geodesic experiment. Fuller orchestrates a continuous cascade of plastic, understood as an urgent stimulating quest to undo architecture from the inside.

A few of Fuller's students from Raleigh (including T. C. Howard, one of the third-year students who would become a key designer in the Raleigh node with James Fitzgibbon and Duncan Stuart) worked with him that summer in the New York office of George Nelson (another founding trustee of the Fuller Research Institute) to develop the plastic-and-metal model of the Skybreak House that was exhibited in August at the Museum of Modern Art, along with twenty-eight color slides of the earlier dome experiments.[84] **fig. 72** The basic 19-inch-diameter plastic dome had already been finished and published in March in what would quickly become a canonic image of Fuller staring thoughtfully at it on a table in his Forest Hills home.[85] The students concentrated on the interior fittings during the early summer. The house would now be lifted off the ground on hydraulic posts, with a floating transparent floor made out of an Octet Truss covered with plastic to produce an even more minimal sense of shelter as the landscape flowed underneath, complete with a tree again rising up into the space of the dome, Fuller's latest car design, and a compact technical equipment package on the ground connected by umbilical tubes reaching up to the suspended living units. Furniture and domestic equipment for cooking and bathing floats on the transparent floor and a set of three white rails running around the interior of the skin allow Orlon curtains to adjust the light so that once again, the plastic skin "ranges from transparent to opaque," as the wall text put it, with rails on the inside of the dome to suspend a plastic curtain, and, on Nelson's suggestion, internal

82 "Vertical Textile Mill," *Architectural Forum*, May 1952, 137–141.
83 S. A. Schreiner, "You May Live in a Bubble House," *Parade* (*Washington Post* Sunday supplement), May 25, 1952, 6–7. Don Richter immediately reacted that he thought the right plastic was already there: "The article in *Parade* is good, not too elaborate but still informative. About the problem of a satisfactory plastic to be used as a glazing in cold weather, this was not too clear. I believe it is available. [...] Convair is interested in a new plastic which develops much more of the fiber-glass strength in laminated. They are just receiving information on it now so I will keep in touch with this project to learn what I can." Don Richter to Buckminster Fuller, 25 May 1952, BFP Series 8, Box 11, Folder 1.
84 *Two Houses: New Ways to Build*, MoMA exhibition #518, August 26–October 13, 1952. Curatorial Exhibition Files, The Museum of Modern Art Archives, New York.
85 The image appeared with the caption "Fuller ponders over some structural designs at his home in Forest Hills," in Anthony Adams, "He'd Like to Rip the World Apart ... And Make It Over Again," *Long Island Sunday Press*, March 9, 1952. The text argues that a plastic dome "can enclose not only your house but your gardens too. It will act as a sky fence in keeping out the elements."

72

Plastic House Hovering into MoMA

72 Skybreak House model, 1952

73 Installation view of the exhibition, *Two Houses: New Ways to Build,* August 26 through October 13, 1952. The Museum of Modern Art, New York. Photographer Soichi Sunami. Photographic Archive, The Museum of Modern Art Archives, New York

74 RBF and Skybreak House model at MoMA, photograph published in several newspaper reports on the exhibition

73

74

divisions could be temporarily made with colored plastic fabric stretched over aluminum poles.

The model was raised near eye level on a white pedestal alongside a huge blowup of the 1950 aluminum dome in Montreal with its white Orlon skin standing in the snow alongside trees without any other manmade objects in view. **fig. 73** The wall text and museum press release repeated the formula that geodesic frame plus plastic plus mechanical package equals nature: "a dome 80 feet in diameter, constructed with aluminum tubes and covered with a plastic skin that is weatherproof. [...] Total mechanization, in Fuller's vision, would enable a return to man's earliest recorded home: The Garden of Eden."[86] The students had photographed the model against the sky on the roof of Nelson's office in what would become Fuller's usual published image of the project, but the museum released another photograph with his head lurking behind the model that was used by several newspapers.[87] **fig. 74** He proudly appeared with the model in two television broadcasts around the opening of the show.[88] Newspaper reviews were captivated with the idea of life in a plastic house and celebrated the "brilliantly engineered bubble" with its mobile Orlon skins that would transform the traditional heavy house into a "transparent umbrella," as the MoMA curator Arthur Drexler put it.[89] The first simple test in the countryside at Black Mountain had been turned into a sophisticated model house on display at the very heart of the metropolis, the art world, and public debate in the mass media.

This was just the beginning for Fuller. There was no option but to go ever deeper into plastic. Each new polymer had to be absorbed—often within a few weeks of being released—and quickly pushed to the point of failure to find the precise line where shelter is provided with the minimum resources and the maximum engagement with the extended environment. The continuous refinement of the domes was inseparable from the evolution in plastic. As Fuller recalled decades later:

> I would organize the students into aeronautical production. [...] The President of DuPont happened to be a friend, he had a student, son, up there at Cornell. He was interested. One reason and another there would be somebody you could get in touch with, and you said we are going we are making an experiment, and we really, really there is no use in going through this without using the most advanced materials, and we understand you have a little better clear Plexi-Glass, or whatever it is, and these men would send you a special airplane of materials.[90]

Fuller and his students at Raleigh extended the research during the first months of 1953 by building a 36-foot-diameter experimental greenhouse as a wooden geodesic frame with a double-skinned bubble of transparent

86 "Two Houses of the Future to Be Exhibited," MoMA press release, August 22, 1952.

87 See, "Designers Dream Houses," *The Youngstown Vindicator*, September 7, 1952; and *Washington Star*, August 30, 1952.

88 On August 5, 1952, Fuller was interviewed on CBS by Durward Kirby with the Skybreak model, and in September he was interviewed by Arthur Drexler on the "Mike and Buff" talk show on CBS. He had already been interviewed on the same show on February 12, 1952, about the advantages of the "thin plastic bubble" for housing.

89 Alice B. Louchheim, "New Ways of Building: Modern Museum shows Fuller and Kiesler," *New York Times*, August 31, 1952, 6. Harriet Morrison, "New Concepts of Housing Are Put on Exhibit," *New York Herald Tribune*, August 27, 1952.

90 Buckminster Fuller, "Everything I Know" (videotranscript of lecture, Bell Telephone Studios, Philadelphia, PA, January 1975), Session 8, Part 3 (Buckminster Fuller Institute, 1997).

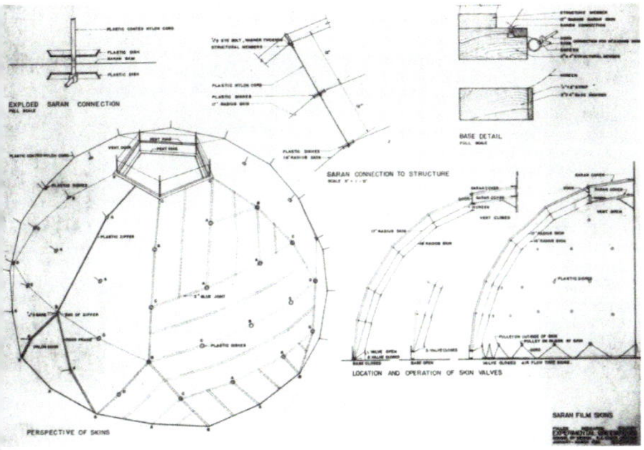

75

76

77

78

Testing to Failure

75 Installation details for saran film skins and raising and lowering of Experimental Greenhouse as plastic valve, North Carolina State College, Raleigh, January to March 1953

76 Students unrolling the first samples of Mylar, North Carolina State College, Raleigh, early 1953

77–79 Installing and testing polyethylene skin on Experimental Greenhouse, North Carolina State College, Raleigh, early 1953

79

saran suspended within it on nylon cords attached to hard plastic disks on each of the vertices and a door made of Orlon. It tested the idea that the internal climate could be controlled by raising and lowering the bubbles to adjust the passage of air between the two layers of plastic. **fig. 75** The idea of the valve finally became literal. Not by chance, Fuller had lectured the students on why a house operated like an electronic valve and vice versa showing slides of his earliest house designs to show that they looked "quite a lot" like an electronic valve and directing attention to the key role of the skin.[91] Plastic was being asked to play an increasingly active role. When the saran skins lasted only long enough to be photographed, a single skin of polyethylene was tried but failed after eighteen hours, and eventually Mylar, which had only just been invented by DuPont, was able to survive for ten days before the adhesives gave out, so was seen to show the greatest promise.[92] **figs. 76–79**

Forty University of Oregon students were by then building the first geodesic dome successfully covered with Mylar, which was not yet available on the commercial market. Fuller had personally solicited the cooperation of DuPont immediately after hearing that there was a new experimental material and they offered to donate some. For Fuller, this donation of plastic was a pivotal moment, as it was the very first support from industry for his research, which up till then had been sustained by "very meager personal funds and "such wonderful gifts of time, unsparing time" from a very large roster of students in different schools.[93] He asked for samples on the day he started teaching in Oregon and did the calculations of how much was needed after getting them a couple of days later, promptly ordering 1,000 feet of film for the project, "which I am convinced will demonstrate the feasibility of using Mylar for the exterior skin of our dome structures," as he put it to DuPont.[94] He intently supervised the production of each lightweight wooden diamond element with the stretched Mylar already built into them and their incremental assembly over just four hours into a 36-foot diameter dome on the lawn outside the school on the afternoon of April 14—only eight days after he had arrived.[95] **figs. 80–82** Solid

91 "When I first tried to talk about valve to people about house they seemed to think that it was an offensive word but it seemed to be the only really accurate technical word. You can see how this looks quite a lot like an electronic valve. It's going to have a skin on it and like an electronic valve you control the environment in the center of the controlled environment you set up some mechanism for valving energy to give you special results [. . .] the energetic environment valve, a house." Buckminster Fuller, audiotape of lecture (School of Design, North Carolina State College, Raleigh, February 18, 1953), BFP Series 17, Box 4, Reel 1a.

92 Kenneth Goldfarb and John Nina, "The Architect and Agriculture — Two," *Student Publication of the School of Design, North Carolina State College* 4, no. 1 (1954): 12–15.

93 Fuller, lecture at School of Design (see note 91). During his opening lecture on April 6, Fuller told the Oregon students that "The DuPont company has written me saying that they would be willing and glad to give me some material for the transparent skin part of it. The amount of material we would receive from them would be about 250 dollars, and is a special new research plastic that hasn't been available up till now. [. . .] Each one of the schools, up to this project I have paid for all the materials myself; in this instance the industry seems to be willing to pay for it which is a new kind of experience for me." Buckminster Fuller, audiotape of lecture (School of Architecture, University of Oregon, April 6, 1953), BFP Series 17, Box 1, Reel 2a. Fuller said that he had paid for the materials for the Yale, Raleigh, and Minnesota domes with his fees from the Ford Company, "my first project in 25 years research work, my first customer." Ibid. He had reached out to DuPont on March 16 asking about their new "V-Film" which he had heard about, and which could outperform polyethylene and saran, reminding them that the president of the company had seen his work at Cornell. Buckminster Fuller to Mr. Fake, Plastics Division, DuPont, 16 March 1953, BFP Series 18, Box 107, Folder 3. On April 6 he asked for samples of Mylar and data sheets to be sent to himself, James Fitzgibbon in Raleigh, and the student group at Yale, which they did. DuPont wrote to the Yale group, for example, describing Mylar as a "new product which the Film Department is currently producing on a semi-works scale," with the first factory not ready till 1954, enclosing the technical bulletin on the material and a number of sample sheets — indicating its willingness to provide more samples for experimental work. R. C. Krueger, Film Department, DuPont, 10 April 1953, BFP Series 8, Box 107, Folder 14.

94 Buckminster Fuller to W. R. McNeil, Film Department, DuPont, 9 April 1953, BFP Series 8, Box 107, Folder 21. The project for a Mylar-Covered Dome was promoted in the university newspaper with the concluding comment that "The students who are assisting Fuller will gain firsthand experience in the use of plastics and also in making the elements from the dome." "Fuller Directs Installation of Dymaxion-Type Dome," *Oregon Daily Emerald*, April 10, 1953, 7.

95 Jean Godknecht, "New Plastic, Plywood Building Demonstrates New Architecture," *Oregon Daily Emerald*, April 15, 1953, 17.

80

81

Assembling the First Mylar Jellyfish

80–82 Students installing Mylar-skinned wooden panels of 36-foot dome, University of Oregon, April 1953

83 Oregon dome at night, April 1953

82

83

architecture was polemically replaced by a veneer of delicate reflections floating over the thin wooden frame—a seamless, barely visible skin of a new material integrated into the structure of each panel and broken only by the triangular section of the dome removed for an entrance. From the inside, people saw themselves floating as reflections as if suspended in the space beyond. From the outside, the sky was doubled and even the frame dematerialized into the reflections. The students seemed to be simultaneously on the lawn and bracketed off from it, hovering in a superlight spaceship that acted as a kind of observatory of everything around it. As always, Fuller was photographed inside the dome checking progress for the newspaper reports along with images of the "futuristic" completed dome.[96] At night, the dome had an ethereal glow like that of a jellyfish. **fig. 83** The otherworldly optics of Expo 67 had its first serious prototype and magazines like *Business Week* used it to push the idea that contemporary homes were obsolete.[97]

Fuller pulled all his students at the different schools into the evolving joint between geodesic frame and plastic skin. "An Experimental Project" that had started at the University of Minnesota immediately after the greenhouse in Raleigh had developed another plastic-skinned 36-foot-diameter Demountable Dome but with a much lighter and more open wooden frame held in place by a diamond-shaped web of cables of Dacron (a fiberglass neoprene cord recently introduced by DuPont). The mission was a Skybreak House, although the term was never used. The student report described it as: "The question of being able to project yourself in any desired direction and to be able to take your environment along with you or have it sent there ahead without compromising any conveniences or advantages but rather would enable you to be more intimate with the earth."[98] The structure was thought of as a house and the original idea had been to design the package of living equipment to go inside it but it was decided there was not enough time.[99] After Fuller had spent a week lecturing, there were only three weeks for the twenty-six students to complete the project. Different teams intensely studied the three ingredients of wood, fiberglass cable, and plastic sheet, assembling "charts and diagrams relating the properties of various plastics." The first test of the structure on the roof of a university failed after two days of steady rain and a lot of research and testing went into the fragile "polyethylene hemisphere" which required the expertise of the team in Raleigh, where it was sent to be worked on but still needed to be recut when it was returned.[100] Fuller had responded to the news of the original problems of the skin by saying that he was having success with Mylar at Oregon and could prepare the skin for them. He even asked the three thesis students in the class to work out a version of the structure as a house for himself and his wife with an equipment

96 "A Mushroom of Wood and Plastic Sprouts on UO Campus," *Register-Guard* (Eugene), April 16, 1953.

97 "The Changed America You Will Be Living in, Doing Business in," *Business Week*, June 6, 1953, 111.

98 "Fuller Project University of Minnesota, Spring Quarter 1953," 129-page student report, BFP Series 18, Box 147, Folder 12, p. 12.

99 "Consideration was given to the problem of the 'core' of the unit—the kitchen, heating and lavatory facilities which would be required to make our environment control a complete system in terms of providing all the desired facilities. It was decided that this would require too extensive a study in and of itself and was also a further development from our consideration which could not be made within our limited time of three weeks." Ibid., 21.

100 The "polyethylene hemisphere" was sent to Raleigh to be worked on. It turned out to be too large when it was sent back and a section had to be removed to make it fit the structure.

84

85

86

87

The Aspen Experiment in Translucency

84–85 Plastic skin being lifted up, unfurled, and fixed onto 36-foot Demountable Dome, Aspen, June 1953

86 RBF explaining Demountable Dome, Aspen, June 1953

87 RBF seen through plastic of Aspen dome, June 1953

› **88** Demountable Dome at night, Aspen, June 1953

package complete with plastic plumbing.[101] It was again as if the Skybreak House concept was finally to be realized. Fuller called the team a day later with a change of plan, announcing that the dome was going to be erected at the third Aspen Conference on Design in a few weeks where he was speaking and that the delicate skin should be attached for the first time there. But newspaper reports of the final test of the structural frame on the lawn of the university on May 13 still described it as a small "plastic-skinned model of the "house of the future" which Fuller "believes may soon be housing families, and which may someday cover an entire city."[102]

The color-coded kit set was trailered to Aspen and assembled by the students in the grass field near the main conference tent with all the attendees paying close attention, even more so when it was covered in the crucial layer of translucent polyethylene—a difficult operation, as it threatened to blow away with all the force of a spinnaker. **figs. 84–86** Charles and Ray Eames were particularly animated and filmed Fuller inside and through the plastic skin as it went up.[103] **fig. 87** The students used it as their dormitory during the conference, using sleeping bags to complete the environmental control. Daytime and nighttime photographs by Fuller himself captured the glowing bubble against the background of looming mountains and sky, with the structural frame turning into a blurry ghostly trace. **fig. 88** The plastic dome had migrated over five years from the basement studio laboratory in Chicago to the landscape of an isolated experimental school in Black Mountain through a series of other schools to arrive at the site of the most advanced debate of the international design community—still in the countryside withdrawn from visibility in the city but highly visible in the media as a prototype of a new kind of house.[104] The whole point of the Skybreak from the beginning had anyway been such a disconnection from the city.

The dome was repacked after the conference and trailered to Woods Hole, Massachusetts, where it was temporarily reassembled to house twenty students from ten universities that had come to assemble another wooden dome designed, milled, and packed into a truck by a group of MIT students. After it was discovered that the plastic skin from Aspen had ripped it was replaced with a tightly fitting white fabric that Fuller found in a nearby town.[105] He lectured the gathered students inside the first dome, was filmed during the construction of the second dome, photographed deliriously swinging from a rope hanging inside it on the night it was finished and gave a short public lecture inside it on a Sunday afternoon. **figs. 89 and 90**

101 "I would deeply appreciate your working out a living arrangement for my wife and me with a 4-guest capacity which specifically identifies high standard living apparatus to be purchased and installed with open plastic plumbing and flexible electric cable etc., with a minimum of space screening design. I am eager to see pictures of the work." Buckminster Fuller to J. P. Damberg, 9 April 1953, BFP Series 10, Box 107, Folder 2.

102 "A new architectural design that may be the house of the future—a 36-foot in diameter plastic-skinned, wood-framed dome that resembles a transparent hemisphere—was erected in the Main engineering court yesterday. The dome [...] is really a small model of what Fuller believes may soon be housing families, and which may someday cover an entire city." Dick Elsberry, "IT Seniors Erect Architect's Dome," *St. Paul's Pioneer Press*, May 14, 1953. The same paper reported a day later that the plastic skin provided by General Mills to be installed at Aspen was usually used for weather balloons. "Dome of the Future Built by U Students," *St. Paul's Pioneer Press*, May 15, 1953.

103 Eames had photographed Fuller's very first studio at the Institute of Design in 1947 (see *Architectural Forum*, January–February 1972, 62–63) and would publish "the first images of the Expo 67 dome under construction" (see *Domus* 446 [January 1967]: 8–16).

104 Fuller once again used images of the dome under construction to support the idea of a new kind of lightweight house "covered with polyester fiberglass, a tough plastic" that enables home owners to "live inside a garden." "House of the Future?: $15,000 Homes Predicted for $5,000 in Future," *Denver Post*, July 1, 1953, 17.

105 "Fuller and His Disciples to Make History with Plastic Dome," *Falmouth Enterprise*, August 7, 1953, 19.

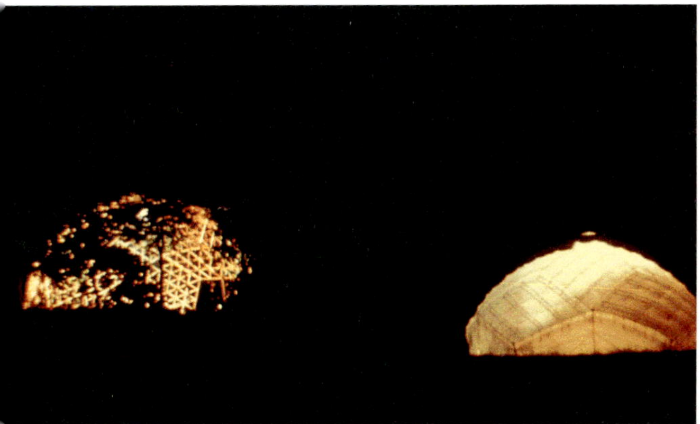

89

90

91

92

96

93

94

95

Permanent Plastic Finally

89 Woods Hole domes at night, summer 1953

90 RBF having dinner inside Woods Hole structure to celebrate the completion of the wooden geodesic dome soon to be covered in Mylar

91–95 Testing strength of fiberglass triangles, joining them together into bigger triangles and installing on aluminum frame on Ford Rotunda, summer 1953

96 Kaleidoscopic effect of fiberglass skin of Ford Rotunda Dome, summer 1953

After a series of tests on the skinning technique, the wooden frame was covered in transparent Mylar to house a restaurant among the trees.[106] Fuller later proudly recalled that the stretched plastic skin was so strong that it could be walked on and expressed disappointment that much of it was later replaced by opaque plastic.[107]

It is not by chance that this first permanent functioning building by Fuller that emerged out of the continuous series of temporary rapid prototyping experiments was ultimately just a transparent plastic skin held in place by a geodesic frame that tries to do the most with the least. Fuller's first large-scale commercial project completed in the same months with the Raleigh team was again a plastic line between inside and outside that had been modeled and even tested in plastic. The 93-foot-diameter dome for the Ford Rotunda was a lightweight aluminum Octet Truss frame covered with thin translucent polyester fiberglass panels provided by a company whose factory Fuller had visited two years earlier as part of his relentless research into plastic.[108] Fuller's team tested the strength of the first samples of the 1/25-inch-thick triangular panels by throwing objects at them as hard as they could before they were overlapped to form larger triangles that were then screwed onto the frame with tape covering the joints and Fuller, covered with several cameras as always, relentlessly photographed every step of the fabrication and installation of the plastic skin. **figs. 91–95** There was originally also going to be layers of Orlon suspended across both the inside and the outside of the frame, but the feedback from Fuller's various teams experimenting with the plastic fabric led to its being abandoned at the last minute.[109] Its omission produced a kind of kaleidoscopic effect of the exposed fiberglass from below that was immediately celebrated in professional magazines like *Architectural Forum* and popular magazines like *Life*.[110] **fig. 96** Fuller's plastic dream was becoming a reality magnified through the lens of the mass media. Images of workers suspended in the sky, silhouetted against the seemingly infinite lattice

106 The owner of the structure had been inquiring about the qualities of the plastic as early as May and requesting that it be transparent at least up to seven feet. Richard Hamilton to Buckminster Fuller, 15 May 1953, BFP Series 18, Box 107, Folder 14. A very detailed description of the attachment of the skin was sent to him in October after a successful test panel had been constructed. A "tight smooth skin that will not loosen and wrinkle" would be produced by stretching the Mylar a particular percentage. This specification was to be tested in a week on a larger part of the structure on site before the whole skin was applied. Cambridge Office to Gunnar Peterson, 18 October 1955, BFP Series 8, Box 107, Folder 14.

107 Fuller, "Everything I Know," Session 11, Part 6 (see note 90).

108 In October 1951 Fuller had toured the facilities of Molded Fiberglass Sheet Company, Ashtabula, and the Dow Chemical Company on his way back from a lecture in Michigan. Anne Fuller to Don Richter, 30 October 1951, BFP Series 2, Box 75, Folder 4. The renamed Reinforced Plastics Corporation of Ashtabula provided the fiberglass for the Ford Dome. Reinforced Plastics Corporation to Buckminster Fuller, 6 March 1953, BFP Series 2, Box 76, Folder 13.

109 One of Fuller's collaborators at MIT, for example, explained to Fuller that the material was hard to clean, formed wrinkles, had variance in the width of material, had melting due to high friction, creeping in machines, and light brown stains due to waterproofing. Dick Soderlind to Buckminster Fuller, 23 February 1953, BFP Series 18, Box 107, Folder 15. The decision to abandon the Orlon layer was communicated on April 10, 1953, but other dome projects continued to experiment with the material.

110 "Exhibition Housing," *Architectural Forum*, May 1953; "Tape, Plastic & Aluminum: Ford Builds a Geodesic Dome," *Life*, June 8, 1953, 67–70.

111 The teachers and students had built the 30-foot Wooden Lattice Dome in Fitzgibbon's backyard in 1951 as a test and had covered it with plastic in 1952, even if the genesis of the dome, along with its plastic skin, would never be mentioned by Fuller. An undated photograph of the dome under construction along with an interview of Fitzgibbon appeared in May 1952 in "You May Live in a Bubble House" (see note 83). It was also featured on the cover of *Student Publication of the School of Design, North Carolina State College* 3, no. 1 (Fall 1952).

112 Just as in early 1949 Institute of Design students had successfully made a 40-inch dome of curved plastic "pan" elements attached to one another and unsuccessfully tested the idea at a larger scale with molded fiberglass panels at Black Mountain College that summer, the students at MIT in 1951 had likewise included a version of a hangar dome made of superimposed "diamonds of fiberglass laminate" alongside versions with metal frames.

113 From late 1949 on, Eleanor Cannon kept suggesting that Fuller and his wife visit again, and continued to do so after offering that her husband could reduce the price of the property, and did so again after her husband's death in September 1950. She would give Fuller the land at the end of 1951. Agreeing with her that his first geometric structure on her site was not a success and thanking her for the gift of the land, Fuller expressed excitement about the "experiments" that they would collaborate on there. Buckminster Fuller to Eleanor Cannon, 30 January 1952, BFP Series 2, Box 75, Folder 3.

being covered with plastics, again acted as icons of a new way of occupying the world—life within geodesic geometry enabled by the almost nothingness of plastic. But in an uncanny premonition of the fate of Expo 67, a worker repairing the waterproofing on the afternoon of November 9, 1962, set fire to the alluring plastic skin, engulfing and destroying the building.

INSIDE THE EYEBALL

In the iconic image of January 1954 in which Fuller stands with his back to us watching a dome being carried aloft by a Marine helicopter a few months after the completion of the Ford Rotunda Dome, it is not by chance that the flying form representing the mobility that he had dreamt of for a quarter of century is yet again plastic. **fig. 97** The image of the flying white dome, which first appeared in newspapers like the *New York Times* and was highlighted in most subsequent Fuller publications, is an image of Fuller's strongest desire, as can be seen as he runs after it with his camera. **fig. 98** It was yet again realized by mobilizing a group of students. The wooden lattice structure had been built in late 1951 by James Fitzgibbon, Duncan Stuart, and Manuel Bromberg—the founders of the Raleigh node—with their students at North Carolina State University and was eventually covered in chicken wire to support a sprayed-on rubber-plastic neoprene material.[111] **fig. 99** The interior had the effect of a plastic skin reinforced by the web of the geodesic frame embedded within it. There was no evidence of the web on the exterior except for two sets of horizontal windows with the wooden framework covered with a single film of translucent plastic like pairs of eyes and a similar circular window at the apex filled with triangles. Students carried the white dome to the middle of a field, a helicopter descended, and the structure took off. **figs. 100 and 101** The lightweight Magnesium Domes that were commissioned by the Marines on the basis of this successful flight, and were already prototyped by Geodesics, Inc., in Raleigh a few months later, were inevitably refinements of plastic, with a stretched skin now attached to the inside of the frame at each of the vertices. The pattern of this plastic garment was more complex than the geodesic structure holding it up. The art of geodesics now lay in the plastic itself. **fig. 102**

Plastic was no longer seen as just skin. Fuller had been actively pursuing the idea of having the structure itself in plastic, with plastic panels folded on the edges simply attached to one another to form a self-supporting dome—the concept he had first modeled with the students at the Institute of Design in Chicago in early 1949, unsuccessfully tried a few months later at Black Mountain College, and explored with Spheres Inc., in 1950.[112] When Fuller had finally returned to the property in Woodstock with some of his students to give a lecture in 1951 at the invitation of Eleanor Cannon, they had a model of a shallow dome made solely out of plexiglass that had been developed with students as part of a whole series of self-supporting transparent plastic domes ranging up to three-quarter spheres.[113] Cannon was again very excited by the idea and even gave Fuller the property to build it on, but was disappointed to hear from him that such a plastic structure could not be realized yet. Ultimately

97

98

99

100

Plastic Takes Off

97 RBF watching Marine Corps helilift 30-foot wood and plastic dome, Orphan's Hill, North Carolina, February 1, 1954

98 RBF photographing helilift

99 Plastic skin being sprayed on James Fitzgibbon, Duncan Stuart and Manuel Bromberg's wooden geodesic dome, 1952

100–101 RBF photographs of preparation for helilift

101

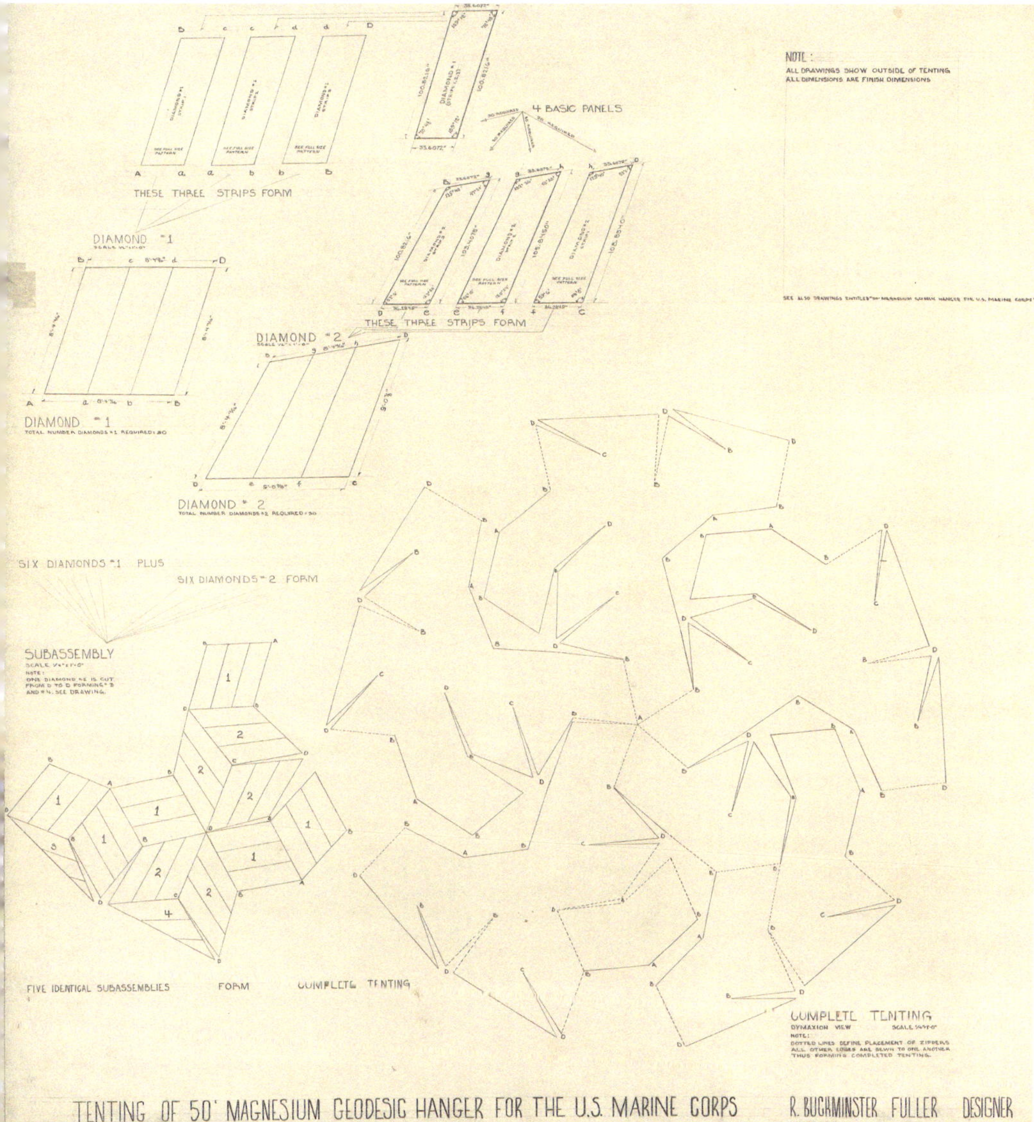

102

103

104

The New Plastic Geometry

102 Plastic tenting for 50-foot magnesium hangar for US Marine Corps, June 1, 1954

103 Don Richter and Monohex plastic dome

104 Involute plastic dome

there was only one unsuccessful wooden "globe" structure put up near her house in 1951 which she quickly asked to be removed.[114] There had been two years of relentless research into geodesic frames since Black Mountain, with plastic skins steadily evolving toward plastic being the structure itself, but the idea of the all-plastic dome was still more advanced than the reality.

A new group in Detroit committed themselves to the goal with Fuller periodically visiting to pass on all the lessons from the other research nodes. Don Richter in Chicago, the student who had been most engaged in making the double-curved panels for a fiberglass dome at Black Mountain, had developed a series of increasingly sophisticated all-plastic involute models since 1949. **figs. 103 and 104** He did a huge amount of research into the possibility of structural plastics, consulting with companies, technical manuals, and conference proceedings—with Fuller again pushing things along by identifying the best contacts in the chemical industry that had agreed to support his work.[115] The hope was to build a full-scale self-supporting translucent plastic Skybreak House in the garden of the Museum of Modern Art. The idea was accelerated by George Nelson, who had written to Fuller in October 1951 asking if he could provide a plastic dome with an all-plastic structure for a house project he was working on for his own family based on the Private Sky concept—saying that *Interiors* magazine wanted to devote an issue to the concept as they had previously discussed.[116] He soon reported that MoMA was already interested in

114 Eleanor Cannon to Buckminster Fuller, 21 January 1952, BFP Series 2, Box 75, Folder 3. Fuller kept a photograph of the all-plastic "involute" dome with her letter from Paris of early 1951, BFP Series 2, Box 73, Folder 3. In a 1952 lecture at Yale, Fuller refers to the unused property as a place they could continue their experiment: "I have a piece of land up in New York State and I'll put it on there and live in it. I haven't been able to use this land because I have been so busy that I never get time to get anything on it, so I could use this next summer or something like that." Buckminster Fuller, audiotape of lecture (Yale University Department of Architecture, October 17, 1952), BFP Series 17, Box 4, Reel 4b.

115 "I have just finished mailing some letters to the plastics and Fibreglas people to get the latest physical properties. I am sure my data is obsolete. One letter was sent to the Society of the Plastics Industry to obtain a copy of the report on the reinforced plastics conference held in Chicago last April. I will use this information to design and analyze the form we hope to build in Ft. Worth." Don Richter to Buckminster Fuller, 3 May 1952, BFP Series 2, Box 76, Folder 1. Fuller responded by recommending the technical director of the Fiberglass Reinforced Development unit of Owings-Corning, who had "pledged" to help their work. Buckminster Fuller to Don Richter, 12 May 1952, BFP Series 2, Box 76, Folder 1. Fuller formally confirmed that Richter was his consultant on the development of fiberglass domes in January 1953.

116 George Nelson to Buckminster Fuller, 2 October 1951, BFP Series 2, Box 75, Folder 13.

117 George Nelson to Buckminster Fuller, 27 November 1951, BFP Series 2, Box 75, Folder 10. "I had a meeting with a Monsanto representative last week, and he gave me good reason to hope his company would become first sponsor in the design research program. He was, naturally, most interested in the Museum's proposal to put up the fibre glass dome as 'The House in the Garden.' He also showed real interest in the possibility of developing uses for plastics in houses of conventional design. Regarding the fibre glass dome, he brought up a number of points. [...] It was his proposal that the whole matter be discussed with Monsanto's technical committee." George Nelson to Buckminster Fuller, 4 December 1951, BFP Series 2, Box 75, Folder 9.

118 George Nelson to Arthur Drexler, 25 February 1952, Curatorial Exhibition Files, The Museum of Modern Art Archives, New York. Nelson goes on to describe the technical challenges of "a plastic shell without supporting framework." In early 1952 Nelson had developed a 78-foot-diameter version of the house for his own family using a model of Fuller's geodesic frame in which both the skin and the geodesic frame were in transparent plastic. His lecture on the design in Chicago in mid-June was covered by the *New York Times* the following day (Betty Pepis, "Architect Offers Bubble for House," *New York Times*, June 18, 1952, 23) and formed the basis of a detailed illustrated article in the July 1952 issue of *Interiors*, in which Nelson described his hope for a plastic skin that could be adjusted from transparent through to opaque depending on mood or season and announced that his office would work with Fuller and some students on a new model "suitable for use as a scale prototype [...] a laboratory experiment at working scale." George Nelson, "After the Modern House," *Interiors* 111, no. 12 (July 1952): 80–89.

119 Drexler had agreed to build the dome in the summer of 1953 but said that MoMA needed a model to raise money. George Nelson to Buckminster Fuller, 6 March 1952, BFP Series 2, Box 74, Folder 14. At the beginning of April Fuller advertised for a small group of students to make the model in Nelson's office. A month later, he agreed with Serge Chermayeff's offer to do a review of the "museum bubble," having "been fairly close to various stages of foetal development from aluminum 'spaghetti' to fiberglass 'armadillo.'" Serge Chermayeff to Buckminster Fuller, 5 May 1952, BFP Series 2, Box 74, Folder 13.

120 "The Cardboard House," *Perspecta* 2 (1953): 28–35.

121 Fuller, lecture. Yale University (see note 114). The Yale students did a huge amount of research into plastics in the fall of 1952, and in the spring of 1953 seven of the thesis students formed themselves into the "Fuller Study Group," complete with its own letterhead, that continued the study of plastic in an attempt to realize their Cardboard Dome as a commercial project, studying many different kinds of film and impregnation techniques. "We are investigating with great interest the plastics industry and its possible application to our product. [...] We have been overwhelmed by the extent of the paper and plastics industry and of the still undeveloped possibilities of these industries." Roy Ferguson to Buckminster Fuller on behalf of the Fuller Study Group, 31 March 1953, BFP Series 18, Box 107, Folder 17.

122 Betty Pepis, "People in Plastic Houses," *New York Times Magazine*, November 28, 1954, 50.

constructing the dome in their garden, and promptly met with Monsanto to address the technical issues with fiberglass.[117] His February 1952 summary letter to Arthur Drexler at the museum makes it clear that the plastic itself had again become the main issue:

> Discussions with Buckminster Fuller revealed on his part a special interest in a new kind of dome—a kind of plastic eggshell, without the wood or metal framework shown in earlier models, and much larger, 90' in diameter. [...] We therefore decided that if possible the house in the garden was to be a complete dwelling, constructed as a translucent plastic shell, designed as a quarter sphere with a 45' radius. A model of this structure is being built in my workshop. [...] At this point it seems advisable to concentrate on the technical problems posed by the plastic shell, and to put aside consideration of the fascinating possibilities created by the space it would enclose [...] a meeting of the Technical Council of Monsanto was set up, and consultation with it created more problems than were solved.[118]

The problems with construction, weatherproofing, and the unknown aging of plastic turned out to be overwhelming, and the model exhibited at the MoMA that August (still with the idea of raising funds to build a full-scale model in the museum garden the following year) returned to the metal frame with plastic skin.[119] But Fuller remained dedicated to the possibility of an all-plastic dome, steadily increasing the structural role of plastic in his projects. The first Cardboard Dome, erected on the roof by Yale students a few months later in November 1952, had the structure itself made of a new type of cardboard composed of thin layers of paper and plastic bonded together with resin. The outermost layer had a thin polyethylene film as the weather seal and any open triangles were meant to be covered with clear plastic.[120] Fuller had explained to the students that the "tough grade" version of Dow Chemical Company's saran is "very clear, stretched tightly it is very transparent. You hardly know that it is there."[121] The idea was to laminate a layer over the outside and the inside of each opening to produce windows with a high degree of insulation. The cardboard structure of Fuller's two domes at the Milan Triennale in February 1954, having been quickly developed by Shoji Sadao at Raleigh, was likewise covered by a tightly fitting translucent Vinylite "bathing cap" that had been carefully designed and was spread out on the grass while the dome went up then stretched over it, turning all the triangular openings in the geodesic web into sealed windows for the space, which was minimally furnished as a bachelor's house. **figs. 105 and 106** The effect was that of two glistening plastic bubbles in the gardens supported by triangulated cardboard. Architecture publications symptomatically only referred to the cardboard but the structure was labeled a "plastic dome" in "People in Plastic Homes," a *New York Times* magazine report on the *Plastics in Building* conference in Washington that year.[122] In fact, the cardboard itself was meant to have been impregnated with plastic for strength.

The idea was realized a month later when the cardboard struts of the dome built by students at the University of Tulane to model a hangar for the military were treated with plastic, using techniques that had been developed at Raleigh and would also be tested in the coming weeks in domes at the University of Michigan and at Cornell.[123] Fuller talked to newspapers about how such plastic-coated Cardboard Domes "would avoid radar detection, too, but could house radar equipment."[124] Not by chance, the design that was done at the same time with the students at Tulane for the huge Sky Eye radio telescope had the geodesic frame itself made of lightweight fiberglass-reinforced polyester resin struts—continuing the successful experiment using such hollow plastic struts in the 40-foot-diameter Tensegrity Hemisphere built by University of Minnesota students in December 1953 in the usual spillover of research from one school to another. **figs. 107 and 108** The Minnesota students had become expert in rolling "cigars" of fiberglass dipped in resin (after advisors from chemical companies and the aircraft industry spent a week with them) Fuller kept converting architecture schools into plastic production factories with the spatial freedom offered by the resulting structures being directly associated with the chemistry of the different polymers. He thought the ability to produce plastic should be just as comfortable for architects as the ability to make drawings.[125]

The September 1954 issue of *Architectural Forum* even used Fuller's domes for the Triennale as a model of the new "plastic order" that would be brought about by atomic processes. Materials would be greatly strengthened by being subjected to intense radiation in an age in which "chemical electronic, radionic manipulation" will replace handcraft and mechanical processes to become the dominant techniques in building. The magazine calculated that a dome made of irradiated polyethylene would be one third the weight of Fuller's current plastic-skinned prototype. Fuller suggested that "his favored material for atomic irradiation is something like a new DuPont sandwich of extra-thin plastic sheets with foam plastic filler These would be rolled out with an impression of all structural components printed on."[126] The molded skin would become the structure. Architecture would more than house radio waves and pattern itself as a set of such waves. It would be literally formed by radiation.

It was not by chance that Fuller finally managed to do away with the distinction between frame and skin with the fiberglass-reinforced resin panels of the Radome to house the continental radar defense system in 1955. In fact, he had already approached the Headquarters of the Signal Corps Engineering Laboratories in the spring of 1951 about the possibility of using his domes to house their radar equipment. He had been given the contact name and numbers when visiting his students at MIT, which was just then starting to set up the Lincoln Laboratories to develop the Cold War SAGE (Semi-Automatic Ground Environment) continental defense system. He promptly went to the Signal Corps labs in Belmont

123 The small 14-foot-diameter dome with a set of triangular plastic film windows constructed by students of the School of Architecture at the University of Michigan on April 23 was made of cardboard "covered with a thin coating of strength-giving plastic." Fran Sheldon, "Transparent Dome to Be Erected Today," *The Michigan Daily*, April 23, 1954. Similar experiments were carried out with a 36-foot-diameter dome at Cornell a month later.

124 "Cardboard Domes to Replace Tents?: Marines Interested," *Christian Science Monitor*, June 4, 1954, 17.

125 "I figure it would be very proper from this time on for anybody coming into our kind of work to have just as comfortable a feeling about making polyester fiberglass and knowing how to set up production yourselves as you would feel about setting up a drawing board just to make any drawing. It is such an important art." Buckminster Fuller, audiotape of lecture (North Carolina State College, School of Design, Department of Architecture, January 6, 1954), BFP Series 17, Box 7, Reel 4a.

126 Douglas Haskell, "In Architecture Will Atomic Processes Create a New 'Plastic' Order," *Architectural Forum*, September 1954, 101.

Plastic Wraps, Infiltrates, then Becomes Structure

105 Translucent Vinylite "bathing cap" on grass in front of 42-foot Cardboard Dome for Milan Triennale X, 1954

106 Vinylite-covered Cardboard Dome at Milan Triennale X, 1954

107 Suspended 40-foot Fiberglass Tensegrity Hemisphere, University of Minnesota, December 1953

108 Students constructing fiberglass cigars for dome, University of Minnesota, December 1953

105

106

107

108

New Jersey to show pictures of his latest experiments with domes. The Signal Corps kept the pictures in their files and Fuller kept a July clipping from the *New York Times* of the latest radar equipment in his files.[127] **fig. 110** Four years later, the two would definitively come together on the roof of the Lincoln Labs building as a fiberglass Radome was lowered by crane onto a functioning radar system, like an eggshell being put back together with the egg still inside. **fig. 109**

The project had officially got under way in January 1953. Fuller's two young associates (once again ex-students of his from MIT) took advice from the "Plastics Lab" at MIT and a local plastics manufacturer, before ordering the first set of 27 diamond panels in February 1953 from the same company that would do the panels for the Ford Rotunda Dome.[128] They were overlapped into a triangular section of an 18-foot dome and tests with microfrequency radar waves indicated that the overlaps and all angular surfaces needed to be removed. The design was revised for the fabrication of one-third of a dome, which in turn led to prototyping a full-sized version.[129] The chain of tests culminated in a 31-foot dome wrapped around a radar unit on the roof of the Lincoln Labs in April 1954 and Fuller promptly gave a keynote at an MIT conference, *Plastics in Building*, arguing that the global economic impact of air-deliverable reinforced plastic architecture would actually be greater than the other seemingly more dramatic twentieth-century developments in technology.[130] The Radome on the roof impressed the scientists by surviving a major hurricane a few months later without any damage and was taken apart and reassembled on the peak of Mount Washington at the end of the year to test its performance in extreme cold and wind. A final revised prototype was then installed around an AN/FPS-8 antenna on the roof of the Lab in 1955 to finally confirm that it did not interfere with the radar signals. Architecture and electronics had become one system with radio as the ultimate client. In a perfect image of Fuller's concept of valve, the detailing of the plastic had been steadily adjusted in response to the needs of the radar inside and the pressure of the environmental forces outside. **fig. 112** The goal was to produce an "electromagnetically transparent" architecture still able to protect the radar equipment under extreme conditions. It was the ability of plastic architecture to be invisible to radio at a certain thickness and angle that would liberate the full capacity of electronic technology. Fuller's

127 On June 12, 1951, the Signal Corps responded to Fuller's letter of June 4 and the meeting took place on June 20, with Fuller noting that they wanted more pictures. Signal Corps to Buckminster Fuller, 12 June 1951, BFP Series 2, Box 75, Folder 8. Fuller's radar clipping is from the *New York Times*, July 8, 1951, BFP Series 2, Box 75, Folder 8. In an October 1952 lecture Fuller reported that one of his contacts in the general's office at the Air Force had apologized that nothing had happened with what they had discussed and informed him that another company had taken the idea of the great circles and was making 20-foot-diameter domes of polyester fiberglass pans as a Radome to house radar in Alaska in the Artic but was unable to control the geometry to scale it up beyond that dimension. Fuller, lecture, Yale University (see note 46).

128 The early work on the Radome was carried out by John Williams at the instigation of Bill Ahern, another ex-student of Fuller's who was part of the Lincoln Labs facilities group. In early 1953 Lincoln Labs ordered the first test sections and was already talking about the need for larger domes of 25–30 feet diameter. Invoice for fiberglass diamonds from Lincoln Labs to Buckminster Fuller, February 9, 1953; and John Williams to Buckminster Fuller, 2 February 1953, BFP Series 18, Box 107, Folder 18.

129 "John Williams has been preparing an 18 foot dome of the standard diamonds received from Morrison [President of Molded Resin Fibre Products] in response to request made to me by MIT's secret defense (Lincoln) project. [...] After trying out individual pieces of the polyester with various types of overlapped and angled reinforcing with their micro-frequency radar waves, they discovered that they had to eliminate all modulated angular surfaces and to employ either circumferential or pure radial components. [...] They ordered a one third sphere which has just been completed and will receive further testing by their laboratories. Upon completion of these tests, if they are satisfactory, it is proposed that they order one whole dome." Buckminster Fuller to Don Richter, 9 March 1953, BFP Series 2, Box 76, Folder 2.

130 Buckminster Fuller, "A Glimpse into the Future" (keynote address at *Plastics in Building* conference, MIT, April 15, 1954).

109

110

Rendezvous with Radar

109 Radome being lowered over radar on roof of the Lincoln Lab building, MIT, 1955

110 Early warning radar, clipping from *New York Times*, July 8, 1951, in RBF's Chronofile

111 Structural test of Radome, Long Island, August 1955

112 The overlapping geometries of Radome and radar

113 Plastic panels awaiting assembly, Bell Laboratories, Whippany, 1956

111

112

113

obsession with architecture as a form of frequency modulation had finally become literal. Or, to say it the other way around, plastic pulled architecture into the space of radio.

The first sphere on the on the roof in 1954 had only some of the fittings holding the plastic panels of the spheres together in metal. William Wainwright, Bernard Kirschenbaum, and Peter Floyd, the partners of Geodesics Inc., which was formed that year in Cambridge to carry out the project soon developed a way of even making those connections in plastic, too Wainwright and Floyd had been working on the use of plastics in housing at MIT and Kirschenbaum had been a student at the Institute of Design in Chicago where he fell under the spell of a lecture by Fuller. Their definitive design of a 55-foot-diameter Radome, fabricated in August 1955 by Lunn Laminates in Long Island, had 361 plastic components and a huge slab of concrete was hung inside to confirm its strength. **fig. 111** A year later, the first production model was assembled on top of a dedicated radar tower above the trees at the Bell Laboratories in Whippany, New Jersey. **fig. 113** Fuller and a group of scientists watched on a rainy day as the stacks of translucent plastic pans were quickly fitted around the radar equipment like a simple kit set in a final demonstration before being rapidly installed in 63 radar stations to form a 10,000-kilometer defensive line running across the Arctic at the upper border of North America.[131] **fig. 115** The plastic line no longer simply defined a domestic shelter as first imagined in 1948 but now defined domestic security for an entire continent. The architectural responsibility of plastic had reached a whole new level.

Newspapers, architecture and industrial design magazines, news magazines, and journals of the plastics and electronics industries promptly celebrated the construction of "the world's largest rigid plastic structure. The first full-size prototype Radome of August 1955 was immediately and repeatedly reported on with detailed images of the molding and cleaning of the fiberglass elements, their step-by-step assembly into a dome, the structural testing with large weights hung from the frame, and the visual effect of the structure at night.[132] Fuller took his usual photographs of workers holding up the plastic diamonds on fingertips to demonstrate their lightness and standing on them to demonstrate their strength. But more than anything, it was the optical effect of the translucent dome that fascinated him. His files are full of photographs building up a kind of aesthetic portrait of the material in images of technicians seemingly suspended within the glowing plastic surface of the prototype, whether in nighttime photographs from the outside or daytime photographs from the inside. **fig. 114** Shadowy human figures tattooed into the surface of the plastic come to represent the idea of shelter, an idea that was intensified when

131 Far from secretive, all the final steps in the progress of the Radome were publicized. In January 1956 the "security-conscious" Lincoln Laboratory held "its very first press party" to discuss the new continental radar defense system and released a photograph of the Radome on the roof. "Lincoln's Sage," *MIT Observer* 2, no. 4 (January 1956). See, for example, the use of the photograph, captioned "Radar Antennas Atop Highly Secret Research Building at Lincoln Laboratory," in Robert Cown, "US Welds Defense Link with Computer Key," *Christian Science Monitor*, January 18, 1956. The installation of the first production model was likewise covered. See, for example, W. J. McFadden Jr., "'Radome' at Bell Labs Seen DEW Line Help," *Newark Sunday News*, July 8, 1956. Companies playing a major role in installing the overall system, like Western Electric, regularly featured Radomes in their advertisements.

132 Already by November 1955, the dome was covered by *Modern Plastics Plastic News*, *Architectural Record*, *Industrial Design*, *Materials and Methods*, etc., with titles like "The Biggest Thing in Plastics" and "Lightweight Plastic for Heavyweight Work." See, for example, "Bucky Fuller Builds an All Plastic Dome" *Architectural Record*, November 1, 1955, 235.

114

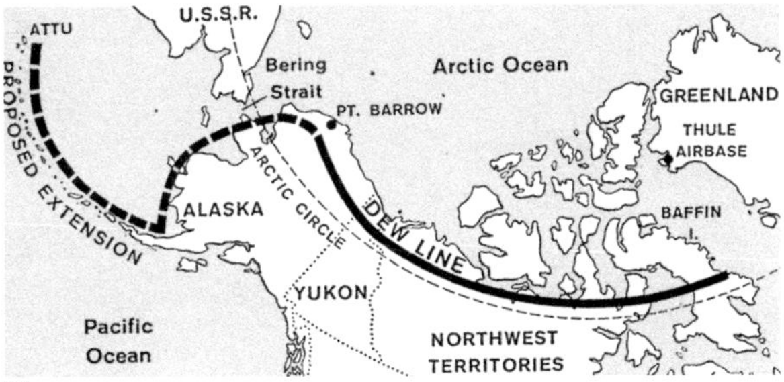

115

Plastic Architecture as the Frontline

114 Radome at night, Long Island, August 1955

115 Distant Early Warning (DEW) Line map in RBF files, 1957

116

117

116 Bomber flies over Radome in *National Geographic*, July 1958

117 Model of plastic dome over Ebbets Field, Princeton University School of Architecture, November 1955

the Radomes were dispersed across the most deserted border of the continent. Articles in popular magazines like *Life* and *National Geographic* celebrated the construction and operation of the buildings in their isolated locations, with scientific details always mixed with aesthetic appreciation.[133] **fig. 116** It was never a secret project. On the contrary, the ability of Fuller's plastic to capture the sky was flaunted as a weapon.

The surprising strength of the prototype Radomes had already inspired the owner of the New York Dodgers baseball team to commission Fuller in 1955 to design an enormous 750-foot-diameter translucent plastic dome to cover Ebbets Field in Brooklyn. The idea was to make a dome more than twice as big as the largest previous clear-span construction in the world. Fuller developed the design with Princeton students and their large plastic model showed the soaring translucent polyester resin skin internally reinforced with a triangulated web of fiberglass and aluminum. **fig. 117** A lot of media coverage was devoted to the 300-foot-tall plastic dome, and the fact that many of New York's skyscrapers would fit within it. Plastic architecture was firmly in the public eye, redefining both private and public space, getting itself ready to swallow the city itself.

POLYMER DELIRIUM

The last and most sophisticated version of the Skybreak House in March 1956 combined all of these evolving plastic techniques for an unrealized "Homestyle" theme park by the Home Research Foundation in Grand Rapids, Michigan, that was meant to feature fifty full-scale houses by leading designers like Paul Rudolph and George Nelson.[134] The design for the Fuller house, led by James Fitzgibbon in Raleigh, started in late 1955 as a variation of the Radome, with domestic equipment rather than radar housed inside a transparent polyester fiberglass sphere, and was exhibited as a large see-through model with floating platforms inside with some of the character of the Expo 67 design.[135] It ended up in mid-1956 as a hemisphere raised off the ground like the version exhibited at MoMA in 1952. **figs. 118 and 119** A translucent fiberglass paneled dome was to be hung from a geodesic frame of magnesium and protected by a polyester fiberglass skin stretched between dome and frame. Environmental control was achieved by regulating air passage between the plastic layers and additional white plastic skins and moveable translucent frames hanging within the space as sun shades. The intricately detailed model showed domestic life suspended in the air and supported by a set of independent equipment packages resting on an elevated platform made of a spidery Octet Truss—with the whole scene glimpsed through three layers of plastic. The simple Black Mountain dome that positions its occupants in the universe has become a complex technical instrument with an equally complex layered aesthetic. **fig. 120** The highly sophisticated project that absorbed many of the environ

133 See, for example, "Sprouting Domes on DEW Line: US Builds a Radar Warning Net in the Arctic," *Life*, April 30, 1956, which shows the first full-sized "Golden Dome" under construction but also the construction of one of the first radar sites. See also "DEW Line: Sentry of the Far North," *National Geographic*, July 1958.

134 Sixteen architects were chosen and each led a four-person team with an interior designer, landscape designer, and builder to "present a complete panorama of the nation's needs in home architecture." "Architects Chosen to Design Grand Rapids Homestyle Center," press release of Homestyle Center Foundation Inc., October 29, 1955.

135 The large transparent model of the first version of the Homestyle house was exhibited at a regional conference of the AIA and published as a "Futuristic Home," in the *Durham Morning Herald*, April 12, 1956, and *The Florida Architect*, May 1956, 28.

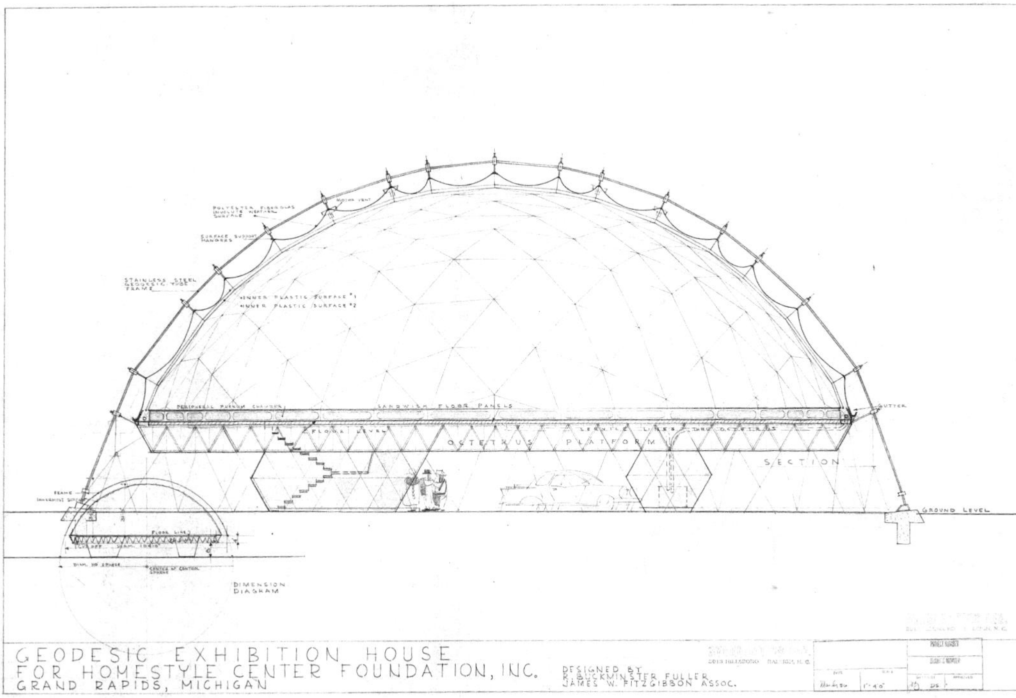

8

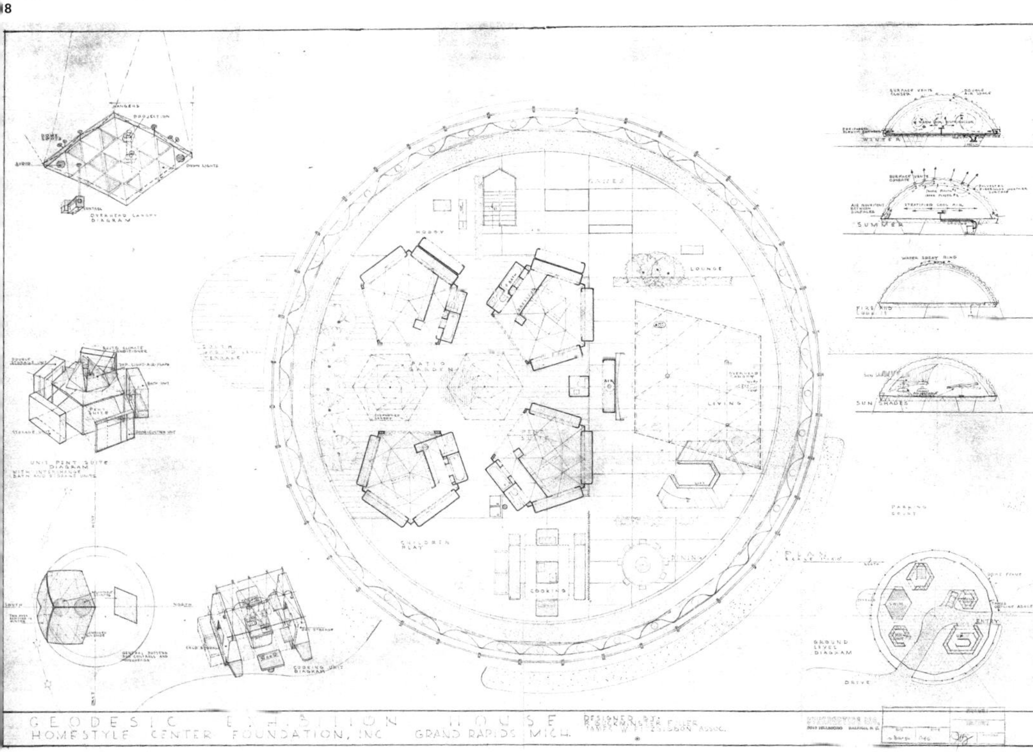

9

118–119 RBF and James Fitzgibbon, Geodesic Exhibition House for Homestyle Center Foundation, March 1956

mental control techniques tested over the previous seven years was highlighted in newspaper articles as the centerpiece of the proposed theme park and the image of the model was published in magazines like *Arts and Architecture*, *Interiors*, *House and Home*, *Architectural Design*, and *Architectural Record*, even if Fuller himself would almost never refer to it.[136]

Such plastic buildings were not simply exhibited and publicized but were themselves a way of publicizing things, a communications device. The plastic-covered Milan Triennale domes of 1954 toured a series of international expositions in Europe and Asia until the end of 1956. The numerous exhibition domes that were again designed by Fitzgibbon and Howard at Geodesics, Inc., in Raleigh for the United States Information Agency (USIA) were lightweight, easily assembled metal frames internally skinned with stretched tent of translucent, plastic-coated nylon. They started with the 100-foot-diameter version assembled in Kabul in 1956, which traveled to a whole string of global fairs, and was perfected in the dome for the 1957 Milan Triennale, which won the top prize that year (as had the plastic-covered Cardboard Domes in the previous Triennale). The geodesic geometry of these structures is minimal on the outside with a very open metal web that almost disappears on the inside where the geometric pattern of joints in the translucent plastic skin dominates the sensuous effect. **fig. 121** The plastic glows on the inside during the day and on the outside at night. Once again, to enter the triangulated geodesic world is actually to enter the softened space of plastic. The geodesic web is turned into a ghost, reinforcing Fuller's claim from the beginning that the structure of things is ephemeral. In March 1958, Fuller worked with architecture students at the University of Texas, Houston, in an unsuccessful attempt to assemble a self-effacing barely-there 25-foot dome as the first unsupported structure made only of transparent plexiglass.[137] The heavily publicized exhibition of one of the original green-tinted all-plastic Radomes within the garden

136 The model was published in a newspaper article about Geodesics, Inc., Raleigh. Jay Jenkins, "Dome Structures Doing Wonders," *The Charlotte Observer*, November 18, 1956. The detailed drawings of the project were published for the first time in 1985 in *The Artifacts of R. Buckminster Fuller*, vol. 3, *The Geodesic Revolution, Part 1, 1947–1959*. The design had been carried out by Geodesics, Inc., in Raleigh, under James Fitzgibbon and Thomas C. Howard (one of Fuller's first students at the School of Design in North Carolina). Having worked on the Skybreak House model for MoMA in 1952, Fitzgibbon and Howard played a key role in the evolution of the geodesic role of plastic. The 175-foot-diameter Climatron building in St. Louis of 1960, for example, featured 4,000 triangles of plexiglass (having originally been envisaged with a suspended Mylar skin). It took the original goal of the Skybreak House to produce a "Garden of Eden" effect to a new level of sophistication by creating 12 different internal climates regulated by a central "brain." The public was offered its own low-tech version of climate control through plastic in 1966 when *Popular Science* made plans of a "sun dome" covered with transparent vinyl skin available, with 80,000 of the blueprints licensed to Fuller being sold within a few years. Charles E. Rhine, "Amazing Sun Dome," *Popular Science*, May 1966, 108–112.

137 Due to breakage, the overlapping sheets of plastic bolted to each other were finally reinforced with a steel frame. "Fuller Guides Architecture Student's Geodesic Dome," *The Cougar*, March 7, 1958.

138 Fuller was, for example, the keynote speaker at the "General Products Division Engineering Conference" of the Fiberglass division of Owens-Corning at Newark, Ohio, September 25–27, 1957.

139 "This is still a confidential product, but I could not help but think of you and the time we were discussing fiber-fabric behavioral patterns. [...] I know you are constantly looking to new materials which will tie in with your basic thinking of using the least amount of energy and material to produce the largest amount of physical form." DuPont Advertising Department to Buckminster Fuller, 31 July 1959, BFP Series 2, Box 104, Folder 9.

140 Peter Floyd to Buckminster Fuller, 19 October 1959, BFP Series 2, Box 105, Folder 2.

141 "Design Seminar 1957," unidentified student report, BFP Series 18, Box 147, Folder 15.

142 Buckminster Fuller, "Conceptuality of Fundamental Structures," in *Structure in Art and Science*, ed. Gyorgy Kepes (New York: George Braziller, 1965), 75. Fuller compares an image of the model to recent electron microscope photographs showing the "geodesic dome structures" of plant and human biological structures, including the cornea of the eye. In fact, the similarity of the structures had been pointed out to Fuller by the Canadian doctor who took the images and sent them to him. "The regularity of this arrangement struck me and I was quite sure that this triangular pattern with the six pointed stars, is an architectural 'Maximum-Minimum' construction which provides a maximum of strength with a minimum of material. [...] Since then I have often found in the morphological literature pictures of the same geodesic pattern and derivatives of it in various organs of various animals. All these are, so to speak, incarnations of the laws you have found. [...] Even the most regular dome structure in our body the Cornea, has until now unsuccessfully resisted any revelation of the secret of its structure. Nevertheless, I was successful in finding slight but remarkable indications that the Cornea too is built according to a geodesic dome structure." Arthur H. Ch. Von Hochstetter, Professor of Anatomy at University of Western Ontario faculty of medicine, to Buckminster Fuller, 27 June 1962, BFP Series 8, Box 27, Folder 7.

of MoMA in 1959 (finally realizing the ambition of 1952), with its interior used for events, fashion shoots, and as an artist's studio, demonstrated the ability of a plastic bubble to put things on show. **fig. 122** More than a space to be occupied, plastic was understood as a way of seeing things, and seeing through and beyond things.

These countless layers of plastic with which Fuller relentlessly looked for the ultimate material with which to dematerialize architecture ultimately produce a kind of psychedelic delirium, a swirling kaleidoscopic haze of different polymers. There is an astonishing dedication to plastic in Fuller's work. He was likely the single designer of the twentieth century most obsessed with the material, with an extraordinary intensity of research and testing in continuous dialogue with manufacturers and fabricators. He had even become the keynote speaker at plastics industry conferences.[138] A decade of continuous exploration went, for example, from Fuller's personally reaching out to DuPont to get samples of the latest plastic to DuPont's reaching out to him to see if he wanted to use new plastics that were still confidential products.[139] And this was no longer a private obsession. The discipline of architecture could find ways to not see the plastic in Fuller's work but the Radome put the material unambiguously at the very center of public vision. By the time it became the most visible plastic architecture of all when exhibited at MoMA in 1959, it was already spreading itself across the planet. Even as the show was being prepared and Arthur Drexler was not yet sure if the Radome offered by the Lincoln Lab could be installed in the garden, Marconi was ordering Radomes of different sizes for the NATO early warning system, as was the Canadian Military, and the US Navy in addition to the Signals Corps.[140] For the first time, Fuller had a real taste of the mass production of globally mobile plastic buildings installed beyond the limits of conventional urbanization—which only whetted his appetite for more evolution in the concept.

Fuller soon went even further with the all-plastic strategy of the Radome. He presented a transparent plastic model of a Fly's-Eye Dome in 1962 to his client Matsutaro Shoriki in Tokyo, who as a baseball team owner had initially been attracted by the huge plastic dome for Ebbets Field. **fig. 123** The new model was based on the Monohex structure that Fuller's students had already calculated, detailed, and named in his seminar at Southern Illinois University in 1957.[141] It was to be another 5/8 sphere but now punctuated by a network of plexiglass-covered eyeholes. Although a different structural system was finally chosen, Fuller tested the concept with his new client at a variety of scales and in 1965 compared the plastic Monohex model to the first electron microscope images of the hidden geodesic dome structure of the human eye taken in 1962—a connection that the doctor who took the photographs had made.[142] The omnidirectional plastic eye was now seen as a visible echo of the invisible structure of the eyeball itself. The prosthetic viewing instrument literally expanded the body's own viewing instrument to create a new self-awareness of one's position in the universe. Fuller would polemically return to the idea in 1977. He acknowledged that he had just spent fifty years unsuccessfully trying to revolutionize domestic shelter and turned the Fly's-Eye Dome into yet another prototype

The Bubble Goes to Washington

120 Model of Homestyle Center House project, *Architectural Record*, September 1956

121 US Pavilion at night, Kabul, 1956, 100-foot dome flown in as a package and assembled with skin in 48 hours

122 Radome, Octet Truss, and Tensegrity Mast displayed in MoMA garden, 1959

123 Model of Fly's-Eye Dome presented in Tokyo, 1962

120

121

122

123

124 Plastic model of Expo 67 Sphere in *Domus*, August 1966

125 RBF presents Expo 67 project to President Johnson in the Cabinet Room of the White House, December 1966

126 RBF with larger metal and plastic Expo 67 model for testing design in *Look*, August 23, 1966

24

25

26

for the autonomous air-deliverable 50-foot-diameter house, claiming that the fiberglass-and-plexiglass project drew on all his experiments from 1927 onward.[143] The plastic house was called into action one last time.

By then, the sphere for Expo 67 commissioned again by the USIA had already fused all of the relentless plastic research into a single spectacular monument to the new material, intensifying the imagery of an enormous multifaceted eyeball. The design was first publicized in 1965 with a model that had the geodesic geometry of triangles and hexagons inscribed into the outer and inner surfaces of an acrylic sphere. **figs. 124 and 125** The basic idea of a shimmering plastic architecture supported by a spidery web was emphatically established. Fuller repeatedly appeared alongside the model from its press launch in June 1965 to its official presentation to President Lyndon B. Johnson in December 1966 to an exhibition in New York just a few months before the building opened that featured a new 8-foot-diameter model much taller than himself that the designers had been using to test the aesthetic effect of the dome from inside and outside with countless photographs—including images focusing on the shiny ripples of plastic within the frame that would be seen by the visitors looking upward before entering. **fig. 126** The model included all of the 1,900 plastic domes forming the envelope and was featured at the dedication of the Boston Architectural Center in May 1966, where Fuller spoke.[144] He literally embraced it for *Look* magazine and at press conferences echoed the original polemic launched at Black Mountain College by once again describing it as a "geodesic skybreak bubble" that produces a "Garden of Eden" interior that allows one's position in the world to finally be grasped.[145]

Even the plastic surface was itself now meant to be an intelligent organism, with an array of six motorized silver Mylar retractable shades inside each hexagon activated by computer in response to the angle and intensity of the sun. The June 1966 issue of *Architectural Forum*, the magazine that had so closely monitored each step in the evolution of the geodesic domes since the first one in 1949, devoted the most attention to this system of environmental control. After a full-page photo of the first plastic model detailed technical drawings of the mechanism of the "animated surface appear alongside a sequence of close-up photographs of the shimmering aluminized Mylar shades in operation on the first working prototype **figs. 127–129** The text even anticipates the sensuous aesthetic of these overlapping mobile layers of technologically advanced plastic: "the effect should be little short of fantastic. For in the course of each day, as the rays of the sun light up the dome from different angles, the plastic skin will slowly change from complete transparency to polished 'chrome!'"[146] The promise

143 Buckminster Fuller, *Critical Path* (New York: Macmillan, 1981), 310.
144 The model appeared alongside an ever-bigger model of the system of fitting the acrylic domes into the metal net. Donald Boyer, *Dedication: The Boston Architectural Center* (Boston: The Boston Architectural Center, 1966).
145 "R. Buckminster Fuller: Dean of the Dome," *Look*, August 23, 1966, 58; Wolf Von Eckardt, "Bucky's Big Bubble Isn't Full of Just Air," *The Washington Post*, March 5, 1967, B4.
146 "Bucky's Biggest Bubble," *Architectural Forum*, June 1966, 74–79. This sensual effect was clearly part of Fuller's promotion of the advanced use of plastic, as, for example, in his presentation of the model two months before the fair opened. "The effect from the outside, according to the designers, will be of a many-hued dome, sometimes silvery and sometimes rainbow colored." Kathleen Teltsch, "A 20-Story Bubble by Fuller to Hold US Expo 67 Display," *New York Times*, March 1, 1967, 45. The newspaper reinforced the point in its preview a few days before the opening: "The skin is real, breathing if not living skin, composed of nearly 2,000 vari-proportioned acrylic hexagons that throb and change color. [...] As a result of all of this, the bubble changes all day long and looks different from one angle to another—here clear, there silvery, elsewhere like a rainbow." David Jacobs, "An Expo Named Buckminster Fuller," *New York Times*, April 23, 1967, 32–33.

127–129 Mylar sunshades for Expo 67 Sphere in *Architectural Forum*, June 1966

130 Circuit for controlling automatic sunshades on Expo 67 Sphere, April 30, 1966

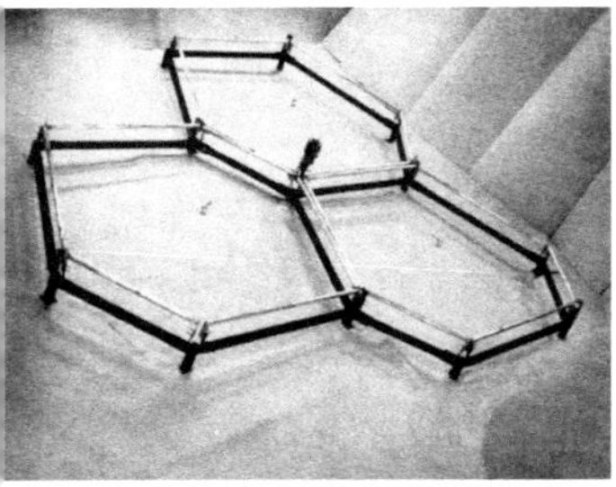

127

128

129

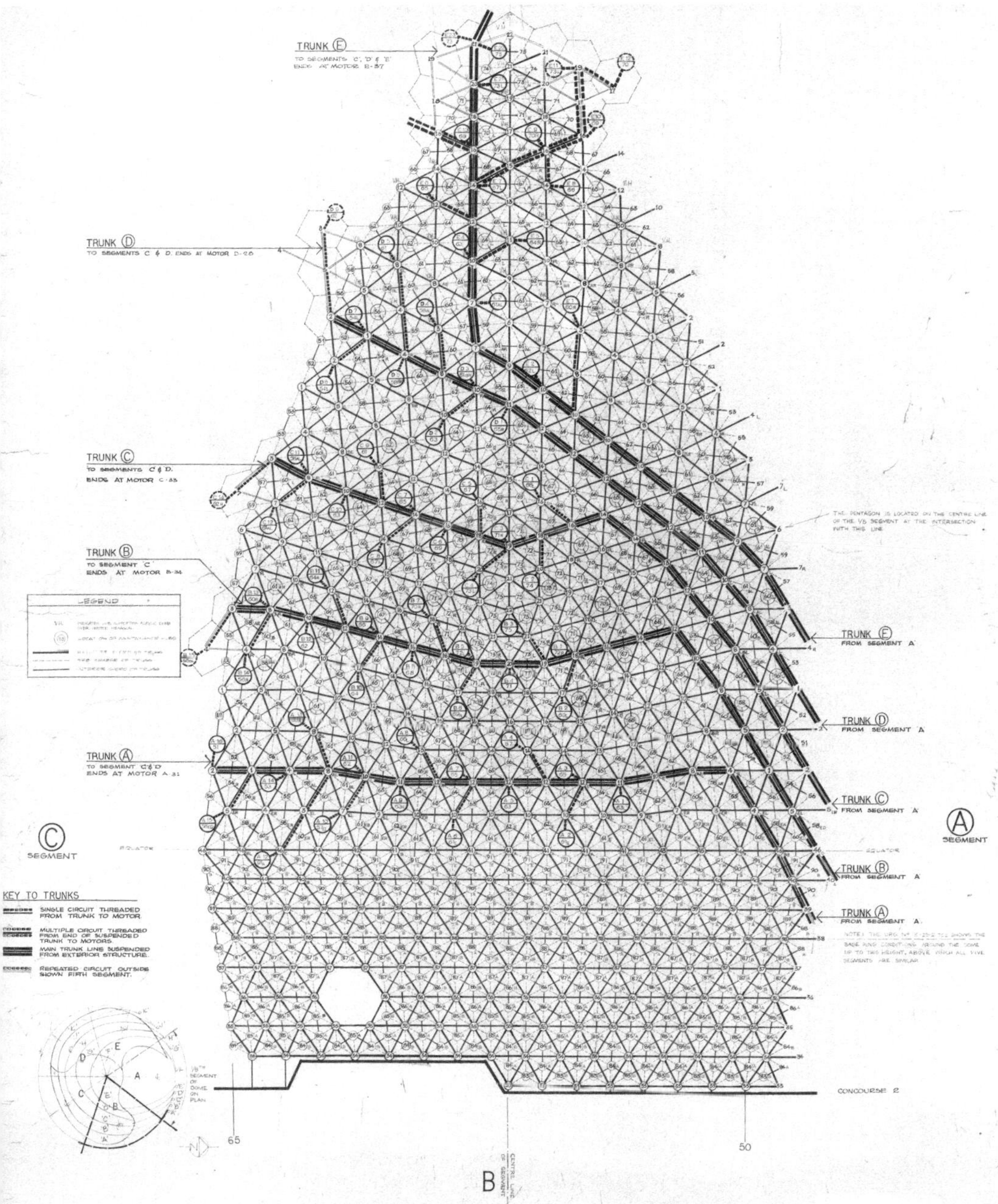

of the very first Private Sky drawing that was repeated in each version of the bubble idea would finally be realized by computer. fig. 130 In fact, the whole mechanism froze shortly after the building opened, with an idiosyncratic pattern of Mylar shades in different degrees of opening permanently suspended within the eyeball, which was all the more attractive to the camera—returning the idea to the world of promises magnified by the media. Jack Massey, who hired Fuller to do the Expo 67 building and had been commissioning the USIA domes for a decade, had not by chance been working at *Architectural Forum* at the time that Fuller's first plastic domes were published. The exposure of each plastic step had led to an even larger step in a relentless and increasingly global project of magnification.

It is as if the Expo 67 sphere was the inevitable result of a single obsessive trajectory of research, the product of almost twenty years of experimentation at the intersection of geodesic geometry and plastic. The geodesic experiment literally took place inside plastic. If anything, it was the plastic line that remained constant while the geodesic props of the line evolved.

THE ARCHITECTURE OF ANTICIPATION

In fact, Fuller's entire career was encased in plastic. His Lightful/4D/Dymaxion House of 1928–1929 was already defined by it. The house is a 360-degree viewing platform hung on a central mast. Traditional outer walls have been replaced by triangles of double-skinned vacuum-sealed plastic suspended in a triangulated cable net, which is itself suspended in a larger net of cables. The plastic wall flexes and can be adjusted by pulling down larger triangles of plastic behind it to block the light or provide privacy when necessary. The ceiling is likewise in plastic, evenly distributing the light that has been reflected onto it by mirrors after coming in through the top of the central mast that is sheathed in translucent plastic. In fact the whole mast including the exposed section below is wrapped in plastic and glows. The house appears from the outside to be a plastic space suspended halfway up a plastic mast with just thin floating bands of metal held in place by cables to in turn hold the plastic planes in place. Every surface on the inside is plastic and the bathrooms are molded in colored plastic as independent units. Fuller prescribes a wide range of plastics from transparent outer walls to translucent ceiling and bathroom surfaces. Such plastics were not even available at the time. The only plastic in 1927 was

147 Fuller, "Everything I Know," Session 9, Part 11 (see note 90). "But I also had to assume in 1927 the largest clear plastic we had was the watch crystal, and it was celluloid, and it was not a water-tight at all, and it got yellow very rapidly, and it scratched very badly. And this is simply what they made celluloid dolls and things like that, and it was highly inflammable. It was not until, well, in 1927 I started these things. That's all I really had to [...] they had at that time poker chips which were opaque, made out of casein from milk." Ibid.

148 Buckminster Fuller, "The Ballistics of Civilization," unpublished manuscript dated March 13, 1939, BFP Series 8, Box 3, Folder 11, p. 14. The text was produced by reworking the February 22 manuscript "Investment and Invention." BFP Series 2, Box 30.

149 "It is a careless viewpoint that construes objective manifestations of the new society such as a new plastic or a new alloy as constituting unique discoveries of the individual designer, as though he personally had made an original finding of a basic chemical element, whereas he has but naively encountered a compound of isolated elements only after years of operative effort by the army of anonymous laboratory workers has provided that latest status quo of materialization." Buckminster Fuller, "Architecture from the Scientific Viewpoint" (paper given at NYU on May 12, 1939), *Student Publication of the School of Design, North Carolina State College 3*, no. 3 (1953): 6.

150 E. J. Applewhite, ed., *Synergetics Dictionary: The Mind of Buckminster Fuller* (New York: Garland, 1986), 296.

151 "Mr. Buckminster Fuller Presentation April 19, 1951," transcript of presentation to *Architectural Forum*. BFP Series 8, Box 11, Folder 4, p. 12. "However in 1927 I made many assumptions based on 21 year interim gains to be reasonably expected. [...] I planned in the terms of plastic materials being available for windows in 1948, though 'plastics' was an industry which by record only starts in 1926 and no such windows were known to exist." Buckminster Fuller, *Designing a New Industry* (Wichita: Fuller Research Institute, 1947), 25.

casein, made from milk. It didn't have the properties Fuller wanted, but he specified it for the house in all his presentations and articles. His architecture aimed beyond the current performance of materials. Materials were used to reimagine their own future. Almost half a century later, Fuller described how the Dymaxion House anticipated and waited for plastic to transform what is possible:

> But there were great indications of developments in the plastics, and so I made the working assumption that I would come eventually to clear material, that you could see through, that would not be glass, that would be lighter than glass, and would be almost as scratch-proof as glass and so forth. I made really a lot of working assumptions like that, and tried to use the curves of already developed phenomena, to give me some idea of how fast I could expect the others. So when I was really designing a structure, a house, the Dymaxion house to have windows all around I was not planning the weight of glass. Glass is very heavy, and so I was waiting on a plastic, and finally a plastic that I would be able to have hermetically sealed.[147]

This anticipatory mode defined all Fuller's work. His "Ballistics of Civilization" manuscript of March 1939 described the strategic approach of closely monitoring and charting the evolution of technologies to predict their future performance, using plastic as a key example. Plastics is described as a new industry that had started to gather speed in 1925 but would only achieve its potential in the near future when reinforced plastics took over from traditional building materials to realize a whole new combination of delicacy and strength, an aesthetically complex and high-performance architecture that would finally embody the ephemeralization that defined the new age:

> The next decade will see the birth of an architecture delicate as flower petals, transparent, translucent, or opaque, in an infinite variety of shades of color, and yet far more resistant to stresses than any structure to date conceived. It will be the dawning of the idiom of universal architecture. The architecture of the age of ephemeralization.[148]

Two months later, Fuller argued that it was not a matter of waiting for new materials like plastic to be invented in the laboratory. Rather, materials are successively found by continuously and collectively exploring the world.[149] Any distinction between natural and artificial is rejected. Synthetic chemistry is seen as the most natural space in which architecture could grow: "There is an unfortunate tendency to abhorrency of the plastic. Our fingernails are plastic. Our eyes are plastic."[150] In a private lecture of 1951, Fuller associated the beginning of his research on the first version of his house in 1927 with the fact that the plastic industry had begun the year before yet the evolution of the material had already promised that in another twenty-five years "I could actually be dealing in fairly large films, enclosures, membranes, and plastics very successfully—perfectly logical."[151] The house was both inspired by plastic and waited for plastic. Plastic flings the house forward, then has to catch up.

In this way of thinking, architecture is not made of materials. Rather it floats in an evolution of chemistry. Or, more precisely, it is constructed within an evolution in the perception of the invisible chemical world.

Design is simply a taking advantage of chemistry. Materials are always suspended between fact and desire. Each technical development stimulates the thought of yet another development and architectural projects appear within this kind of flow of thinking about material. They feed technology, or should. This is why Fuller always made a double argument. Architecture must finally engage with the universe of radio and thereby join the waves of industrialization transforming all dimensions of an ever more global society. But equally, global industrialization is waiting for architecture in order to realize its radical potential. A truly networked wireless shelter industry will fling technology itself into a whole new orbit.

Symptomatically, one of Fuller's last books recalled the foundational moment in 1927 when the absence of the right plastic provoked both the desire and expectation for an imminent architectural transformation: "Quite clearly plastic materials of many kinds were desirable substances, as transparent and waterproof as glass but not easily breakable and of much lighter weight. [...] Wanting better materials and looking at one's own fingernails, one could say that such and such a material is ostensibly feasible, so it will be developed."[152] Fuller was so committed to his predictions that following "Dymaxion Theories" of ephemeralization in 1928, he invested what little he had inherited in shares of casein in addition to the shares in radio and airlines that he had strongly recommended to his mother. Plastic was the inevitable future as the very image of doing more for less.[153] The display model of the Dymaxion House with which he promoted the concept in department stores, galleries, magazines, and movies in mid-1929, like the larger version completed in early 1930, had the outer walls of the living spaces made of thin sheets of transparent plastic, with the triangulated pattern of the cables etched into their surface, and the mast made of translucent casein illuminated from within by an electric lightbulb. **fig. 131** The inhabitants were to float in the reflections and glow of plastic. Fuller favored photographs in which the presence of the plastic in

152 Fuller, "Critical Path Part Two," *Critical Path*, 267 (see note 143).
153 "The $300 he had inherited from his aunt Edith he invested in the stock market according to Dymaxion Theories, specifically in Casein, according to the theory of ephemeralization. Casein was a plastic and had previously been used largely for poker chips and fountain pens. 1927 was the beginning of the growth of plastics. B saw the Oct. crash coming and sold out in June and financed the trip east." Buckminster Fuller, "Family and Career," manuscript attached to Fuller to Joe Bryant, 1 July 1939, BFP Series 2, Box 29, p. 6. The record of the shares in casein can be seen in Mrs. R. B. Fuller's account with F. M. Zeiler & Co., BFP Series 2, Box 19.
154 BFP Series 2, Box 21.
155 Loretta Lorance, *Becoming Fuller* (Cambridge: MIT Press, 2009), 164. Fuller described the background of each of the four young architects working on the 4D project. Buckminster Fuller to Paul Nelson, 10 August 1928, in Fuller, *4D Time Lock*, 86 (see note 9).
156 When the patent application for the Bathroom was being drafted Fuller insisted: "I think it is extremely important that the phrase 'or thin-walled plastic material' be employed throughout the claims in conjunction with your phrase 'sheet metal' as plastics might readily be employed in the future and economically so only by virtue of the same curvature and integral structuring features." Buckminster Fuller to W. P. Churchill, 15 April 1938, BFP Series 2, Box 38. "I had not designed it to be in copper, you see, I designed it to be in polyester fiberglass, which was in the laboratories. But the setting temperatures were at that time, where you had the temperatures 2,3-400 degrees, not room setting, and so forth. But I was assuming that we'd get to where we could. So it would have been ideal in it." Fuller, "Everything I Know," Session 10, Part 16 (see note 90).
157 Patricia Fitzsimons, Editorial Department, Doubleday, to Buckminster Fuller, 15 March 1939, BFP Series 2, Box 39.
158 "The first prototype of the Dymaxion dwelling machine, a complete housing unit actually designed to take advantage of the engineering improvements offered to the building industry by plastics [...] this circular postwar house will make full use of various types and weights of plastics and plastic finishes in both interior and exterior construction. [...] 'In the Dymaxion we do not replace former wooden or glass parts by prettier plastic parts,' states R. Buckminster Fuller, inventor and chief engineer. 'Dymaxion employs plastics with new high tensile micro-reinforcements in its structural engineering just as concrete was employed with steel reinforcing to create a new structural phase a generation ago. In 1927 when I constructed the first model of the Dymaxion house, plastics played a major role in my presentation of how the structure would eventually be built,' Fuller points out. 'Although the manufacture of the plastics had not yet grown to the proportion of an industry, the dwelling machine was none-the-less engineered for the ultimate use of those light-weight synthetic components.'[...] The postwar Dymaxion house will include electronic household appliances and plastic bathrooms and wall surfaces which will be easy to clean, and even special furniture may be designed." "Postwar Housing Unit to Use Plastics," *Plastics News: The Weekly Bulletin of the Industry*, March 2, 1945. The house was again given extensive coverage by the industry in "Building Compact Efficiency in Housing," *Plastics*, December 1945.
159 See, for example, "Dymaxion Dwellings Form One of Wichita's New Postwar Firms," *Wichita Eagle*, August 26, 1945.
160 "Beech to Build Homes of Aluminum, Plastic," *The Wichita Sunday Beacon*, November 12, 1944.

the outer skin, ceiling, and mast was clear, like the one he used in the catalogue of the exhibit at the Harvard Society for Contemporary Art in 1930, and he kept samples of the plastic from the models alongside the early drawings of the house in his archives.[154] **figs. 132 and 133** Much of the thinking of the plastic-skinned house of 1948/1949 as nothing but an omnidirectional window was already in place twenty years earlier—even the fact that the design and models of the Dymaxion House were developed with a group of recently graduated students in an informal "designing class" that Fuller was running.[155] He both waited for plastic to catch up to his designs and used plastic to radicalize the designs further, relentlessly absorbing each new form of the material into his redefinition of the house.

The 1932 model of a ten-story version of the Dymaxion House encased the already plastic-skinned building in a rotating acrylic weather vane to reduce drag. **fig. 135** When plexiglass came to the market a year later, Fuller immediately used it to form the wraparound window of the Dymaxion Car. **fig. 134** The ceiling of the different versions of the Dymaxion Bathroom from 1936 to 1938 were in translucent plastic, as first sketched in 1931, and the whole unit was meant to be in plastic as soon as the material developed further.[156] Fuller was even going to write a book on plastics and synthetics in 1939 and had assembled one of his huge scrapbooks of clippings on the theme, but the commission fell through.[157] He was proud of the fact that his Dymaxion Deployment Units of 1940 were the first houses to have plexiglass windows and that the version of Dymaxion House developed from 1944 to 1946 with Beech Aircraft featured a 118-foot-long 360-degree window made of two layers of plexiglass with fiberglass curtains and a Lumite plastic screen for ventilation below. The ceiling was a fiberglass neoprene tent and two plastic versions of the Dymaxion Bathroom formed the core of the house. There was such a wide range of different plastics between the inner skin of the bathrooms and the outer skin of the windows that *Plastics News* could hardly contain its excitement as Fuller explained why plastic had been so central to his work from the beginning—even arguing that the whole point of the new house was "to take advantage of the engineering improvements offered to the building industry by plastics."[158]

The publicity for the house started with the obligatory photo of a naked woman bathing in the plastic version of the Dymaxion Bathroom, an image associating nudity, fluidity, modernity, and plastic that appeared in newspapers and architectural journals before the design of the house itself had been worked out.[159] Once again, the bathroom precedes and stimulates the house. But plastic also played less glamorous technical roles behind the scenes. The curved aluminum roof, for example, was lined with hidden molded plexiglass panels and a see-through plastic model was used for the extensive wind tests. The house was defined by the play between metal and plastic, with typical newspaper headlines since late 1944 like "Beech to Build Homes of Aluminum, Plastics."[160] Plastic had become a basic building material rather than an accessory.

The precisely detailed model of the final design had all its aluminum and plastic elements accurately rendered in the corresponding materials

THE PLASTIC LINE

The Dream then Reality of Architecture as Plastic Lens

131 RBF and Dymaxion House model with plastic skin etched with triangles to represent the wire net, 1929

132 Sample of plastic used in Dymaxion House model, kept in RBF Chronofile, 1929

133 Photograph used in *4D: Buckminster Fuller's Dymaxion House*, Harvard Society for Contemporary Art Inc. exhibition catalogue, 1930, showing glowing translucent plastic mast and ceilings, along with reflections off the plastic skin

134 First prototype of Dymaxion Car with plastic windscreen, 1933

135 RBF and plastic model of 4D Tower, *Vanity Fair*, December 1942.

131

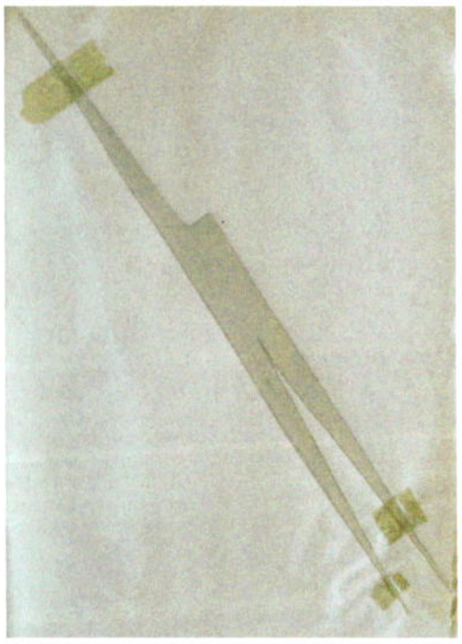

132

133

134

135

136

137

138

136–137 Plastic window panels being hung on Wichita Dwelling Machine prototype, 1946

138 360-degree plastic window and fiberglass curtains in second Wichita Dwelling Machine prototype, published in *Plastic* magazine, December 1946 and was photographed from every angle both with the roof and without as the centerpiece of all promotions of the house in 1945 and 1946. It appeared in countless articles in newspapers and magazines and received high-profile full-color treatment in *Fortune* magazine. It was exhibited in New York in March 1946 and when it was put on display in a department store alongside other housing designs built "for tomorrow," the accompanying text proudly announced that "The unique Fuller house, like an airplane, is made of aluminum and plastic and produced on the assembly line."[161] The full-scale prototype of the house that had been completed in a field in October 1945 was an "aluminum and plastic job" as *Fortune* put it.[162] After the circular floor was constructed, the curved ring of the metal roof was suspended in the air and the large sheets of plexiglass were hung from it in a full circle broken only by the doorway (which would have its own plexiglass window) before another ring of metal was added below forming a kind of basic sketch of the house that was completed when the prototype was rebuilt indoors with all the other plastics added. **figs. 136–138** The modernity of the design was inseparable from its plastic. The prototype was even constructed at Krehbiel Plastic Products, a major subcontractor to Beech Aircraft. From the outside, the building appeared to be an aluminum house with a continuous plastic window but from the inside it was a plastic house with only a small amount of metal trim. Most of the surfaces were in plastic. The role of the metal was simply to protect and hold in place the plastic that would in turn hold the inhabitants in place

Plastic was not simply added to the geodesic frame with the first successful dome a few years later in 1949 at Black Mountain. The new frame simply allowed plastic to take over the whole architecture—permanently Fuller never let go of plastic. **fig. 139** It was not by chance that his very last book retold the story of anticipating the future structural role of plastic in 1927.[163] When doing the first version of the 4D House in 1928, he had kept a clipping of a DuPont advertisement, a company he admired for basing itself on research and was then accelerating the move of its chemical expertise from explosives to plastics with a new laboratory devoted to polymers.[164] Likewise, one of the working documents on Fuller's desk when he died was a photocopy of the article "DuPont *Tefzel*: Successor to Mylar" describing the 1970 upgrade to his favorite material.[165] In every version of his architecture, it had been the plastic line that defined both the interior space for modern life and the research space in which geodesic geometry was incubated. Fuller's architecture was made with and within plastic. His work alerts us to the possibility that we have gone from the dream of plastic houses to the reality of plastic housing architecture, which is precisely why we don't see it anymore.

161 Photograph of *America Builds for Tomorrow* exhibition at Lord and Taylor department store, BFP Series 13, Box 21, Folder W2008.
162 "Fuller's House," *Fortune*, April 1946, 169.
163 "I foresaw the ultimate development of a large plastics industry producing materials similar to our fingernails that would be opaque, translucent or lucent and as relatively unbreakable as poker chips and fountain pen barrels, which in 1927 were among the only plastic products. At the time there were no plastic products larger than celluloid dolls. Anticipating products as large as our present-day seventy-foot-long yachts of reinforced fiberglass hulls, I predicted large, strong, and lightweight all-weather plastic reinforced by high-tensile-strength steel rods." Buckminster Fuller, *Cosmography: A Posthumous Scenario for the Future of Humanity* (New York: Macmillan, 1992), 114.
164 DuPont advertisement, June 1928, BFP Series 2, Box 20.
165 "DuPont *Tefzel*: Successor to Mylar," BFP Series 7, Box 5, Folder 11.

139 RBF testing strength of plastic film at College of Design, North Carolina State College, Raleigh, 1953

IX

IX RBF as skyscraper,
New York rooftop, 1931

PLANETARY HOMEBOY

It has become hard to look in any direction without seeing numbers. Inside, outside, on the move, flying or hiding, we increasingly imagine ourselves to be living inside layer upon layer of information. Our tangible surrounding environment is experienced as the tip of vast hidden mountains of data, an endless depth of bits that has to be mined to carry out even the simplest act. We see our world through the visualization of data. Domestic spaces are filled with little screens presenting continuous readouts of an ever-increasing set of parameters. It's no longer just a clock on the wall, a thermometer and a set of water, gas, and electricity meters in the basement monitoring invisible flows that are read and understood only by utility companies. Every space now has multiple data displays treated as vital signs to be monitored before, during, and after any action. Action itself is increasingly understood as whatever impacts data. Even when we sleep, our domestic environment literally glows with flickering galaxies of color-coded numbers, pilot lights, and display patterns—all of which can be monitored remotely when we move out into the world. Even the step outside is usually preceded by consulting the screen of a computer or mobile phone to check on a few things about the exterior. The line between inside and outside is now drawn within the protocols of information transfer. The transition to the outside occurs in the space of data before it happens in the physical world and the outside is itself turned into an inside by the structuring of information. The portable architecture of the car, for example, becomes another domestic space filled with glowing information on the resources, condition, and performance of its own mechanical systems, the interior, the immediate exterior, and the world beyond. Even the outside environment seen through the windshield is itself covered with numbers, color codes, and coded patterns. Data is not just superimposed on the visual field. It has become a fundamental part of that field.

It is no longer clear that we can imagine a world before or beyond data—or even imagine ourselves denuded of numbers. The body itself is increasingly a source of real-time information. Occasional measurements of weight, periodic checkups, and massive detail in moments of medical crisis have given way to continuous streams of precise forensic detail about the movements and status of the body. The wristwatch has become a sophisticated medical instrument delivering a continuous biometric readout of a range of physiological conditions and biorhythms streamed to the cloud to compare with our personal patterns which are compared to the patterns of others. Every movement of the body and within the body is earnestly recorded, visualized, and analyzed. Likewise, all personal, social, financial, and legal interactions are experienced as patterns in vast data sets. Identity itself has become something that is literally generated online and can be multiplied or stolen there.

The ever-present mobile phone with its every movement located precisely in time and space has become the most important architectural window, superimposing countless layers of data onto the perceived world. It tells us more about what is in front of us than our eyes can see. We literally see the world through this thin networked computer that has become a part of our body and thereby made our body part of so many invisible webs. It is a set of sophisticated eyes but also a vehicle as it shows us what is not in front of us. Or, to say it the other way round, it moves us by pulling distant or deeper things toward us. Distance itself is transformed as all phones are connected to one another and to countless embedded devices in an incomprehensively massive collective global net. The very idea of movement evolves, as does the idea of depth, when all the interconnected devices generate and receive data at an ever-increasing rate in a steadily accelerating spiral. The data world expands exponentially as it relentlessly feeds on itself. The term *big data* is completely inadequate to the colossal scale of digital landscapes. Anyway, the density of data now defines scale so the scale of data itself is, by definition, beyond scale. It will always exceed imagination even as imagination tries to think of little else.

To say the least, the production, organization, maintenance, evolution, and experience of cities, buildings, institutions, and bodies is understood in terms of data management, as are professional, social, and personal lives. Which is not to depersonalize experience. On the contrary. Everything, including the planet itself, has become extremely personal. It is as if our world, even the unconscious, is filled with measurable flows that need to be unlocked by seeing patterns and the relationships between patterns—the pattern of patterns in what we see or expect to see. The data is never in an ethereal cloud as advertised. It is on the ground and in the ground, infusing the systems of objects and the objects themselves. Despite the exponential increases in miniaturization and efficiency, a massive infrastructure is required to store data and sustain the illusion that it floats in an ephemeral and accessible cloud. This ever-growing global infrastructure of data management has been constructed at a scale that dwarfs all the previous waves of industrialization. Data itself is physical in the end—starting with the binary logic in which all the 0s and 1s are physical states at the nanoscale within a chip but equally at the scale of the planet. If all the elements responsible for data collection, flow, storage, and presentation would momentarily be visible as the only thing you see, then the form of buildings, cities, and the planet itself would be completely clear, shaped by a dense but usually hidden physical fabric of information technology sustained by unthinkably huge amounts of energy. It would even appear to be a single continuous tightly woven three-dimensional fabric, a planetary architecture, a colossal interior which most of our species inhabits, a physical space dotted by billions of little data displays, fixed or mobile interfaces that are usually the only visible trace of this hidden architecture. Data is not just superimposed on the environment but is part of the environment itself, even as its substanc More important, the visible world is understood to be suspended in a larger world of information. Information about the world has giver way to worlds within information.

The constitution and behavior of objects and people is infused by data which is never seen. Indeed, data can never be seen as such. Rather, it can only be visualized. The very word "data" is already a visualizatio What is experienced is not bits but images. We see the world through and as image. What we see is never simply in front of us, and has neve been. The world of images is neither superficial nor artificial. On the contrary. Images are deep and fully tactile. It is as if the experienced world is itself a prosthetic device, an interface, a screen through whic we connect to what we cannot see. The surface of the phone and the surface of the world are touched to unlock secrets, or add to them The mobile phone works so well because it is an evolution of the complexity of experience rather than a revolution. After all, nothing is mor human than prosthetics. The use of tools is what defines our species. We at once extend ourselves with tools and live inside the extensions There is finally no clear line between ourselves and the spaces we inhabit, no clear line between inhabitation and the way we see the wor

What does it mean for architecture when a set of data visualizations is no longer suspended in an interior but the interior is suspended in a set of data visualizations? The expertise of the architect, since the firs formulation of Vitruvius in the time of Augustus Caesar—and still very much alive, even urgently relevant today—has been to combine incompatible forms of information. The architect gathers together heterogeneous forms of knowledge in a loose basket, developing a simple formal organization, like a house, that allows complex and heterogeneous flows to coexist and be sustained in all their complexit and heterogeneity. The architect has always been something of a data visualizer—starting with the classical idea of simultaneously revealin the hidden harmonic patterns of the cosmos and accommodating the hidden patterns of everyday life. Architecture, in this sense, has alway been carved into and out of what is now called information. It is an expertise in revealing or constructing a sense of pattern, offering a single visible inhabitable pattern as a nest for a multiplicity of hidden patterns, and, most crucially, making this offer in the very sites of the greatest mystery. The architect is only invited in when the problen is unclear, with multiple incompatible sets of information preventing the use of any existing toolbox. The real task of the architect is not to solve a problem but to visualize it. The architect suspends a sense c pattern right there in the gaps in collective understanding, not simply

1 "New York is a continual evolutionary process of evacuations, demolitions, removals, temporarily vacant lots, new installations, and repeat. This process is identical in principle to the annual rotation of crops in farm acreage—plowing, planting the new seed, harvesting, plowing under, and putting in another type of crop." Buckminster Fuller, "New York as a Focus of Energy," in *The New York Guidebook*, ed. John A. Kouwenhoven (New York: Dell Publishing, 1964), 27.

2 Buckminster Fuller, "the summer session...Black Mountain College, North Carolina 1949. (An Outline by r. buckminster fuller, Dean of Session)," typescript manuscript. BFP Series 2, Box 71, Folder 6.

accommodating the everyday but interrupting it in a way that allows the world to be seen. Whether asked to or not, the architect crafts a hesitation in the name of overlooked patterns in information. Architecture is both window and mirror.

BLUEPRINT FOR A CLOUD

Buckminster Fuller, who surrounded himself with statistics, tables covered with models, endless sentences, animated hand gestures, and captivated audiences, was first and foremost an artist, an image-maker. Each of his projects is an artistic manifesto—despite his professed disinterest in the look of his projects, the crudeness of his drawings, his condemnation of architects for their dedication to visible surfaces, and his call for the earnest figure of the "design-scientist" interested only in efficiency. All the layers of data and analysis of efficiency are carefully organized to produce an aesthetic effect. Science is to be deployed as an art form. Not just any art. The art of housing. More precisely, the art of ecology.

Consider the ever so smoothly photomontaged megastructures that Fuller and his partner Shoji Sadao produced in the 1960s. The Tetrahedronal City of 1965 is a 9,000-foot-tall pyramid with a million inhabitants living inside its faces and a vast park on the inside. **fig. 1** A floating city that would circumnavigate the planet, it is hyperrealistically rendered visiting San Francisco and Tokyo Bay—the new city dropping in on old ones, towering over them like something from another planet. Nothing produced by ancient Egypt could compete. The huge structure even heads onto land to commune with Mount Fuji in a 1965 issue of *Playboy*. Likewise, the Cloud Nines of 1960, a couple of giant flying spheres one mile in diameter, would carry thousands of people around the world and occasionally anchor themselves to mountaintops to enjoy each other's company and swap passengers without any urbanization in sight. **fig. 2** Science fiction is rendered as if already realized. These are precisely crafted images of huge floating houses conceived from an ecological point of view. Each is based on an idea of radical efficiency, housing many more for much less. They extend the logic of the 1959 proposal to house three million people more economically by planting a two-mile-diameter transparent dome on the unsuspecting island of Manhattan. **fig. 3** For Fuller, the buildings of New York are "but crops in a farm that needed to be rotated, turned over, ploughed under, and the elements reused and replanted, recycled into a new crop."[1] The dome that would enclose them is a colossal greenhouse. It is meant to cultivate both the recycling of materials and the recycling of ideas—an ecologically balanced physical environment and an ecologically balanced environment of design thinking.

The Manhattan Dome was in turn just an extreme version of the idea launched ten years earlier with the artists at Black Mountain College in 1949 when Fuller wrapped his very first dome in plastic and called for "creative artist-scientists" to concentrate on new models of housing for the whole planet.[2] The huge bubble is again a sophisticated artwork, a conceptual and aesthetic provocation that became his single most iconic image as it rapidly spread through every possible kind of publication and continues to do so today. Symptomatically, the project was first exhibited in an art gallery, appearing in October 1959 at the Museum of Modern Art in New York as part of a supplementary exhibition to the *Three Structures by Buckminster Fuller* that had been built in the MoMA garden in August 1959.[3] **fig. 4** A 2 × 4-foot aerial photograph of Manhattan was displayed on its own wall with the white geometry of a vast geodesic dome superimposed on Midtown. It was a polemical image of a new triangulated architecture taking over from the old gridded one of the island, magnified by the fact that MoMA itself would be covered by the structure. The viewers—whose eye level was positioned at the center of the massive dome—literally saw Manhattan through the porous structure and could recognize themselves already housed within it.

Immediately to the left of the photomontage was a small print of one the most reproduced photographs of Fuller staring thoughtfully at a model of a transparent plastic dome on the desk in his Forest Hills home office in early 1952. The print was attached to the text panel written by the curator Arthur Drexler that introduced the whole exhibition, including the trio of structures in the adjacent garden. The text was reproduced in the belated exhibition brochure of early 1960, where the photomontage now appeared alongside Fuller's own photograph of the glistening plastic-covered dome at Aspen in 1953, as if to demonstrate the capacity of a delicate translucent dome to simply expand its responsibility from temporarily sheltering a few people in the countryside to permanently sheltering a whole city.[4] But Drexler's text insists that the aesthetic effect is just a consequence of the underlying principle rather than any concern for the visible surface:

> Obviously, Fuller does not think of himself as a designer, architect or engineer as those terms are normally understood. [...] Although he is not directly concerned with esthetics, Fuller is quite aware that many of his designs are extraordinarily beautiful. But he observes that their beauty is incidental, because each of his designs is merely a local pattern embodying pure principle. It is our awareness of the principle, however incomplete, that makes the pattern so pleasing to us.[5]

This directly echoes Fuller's own statements since the thirties. In 1934, for example, he had said that "the surfaces most evident to the eye are the least important in the contemplation,"[6] and his first formal book in 1938 criticized the visual fixation of architects, insisting that beauty does not belong to the surfaces we see but is an effect of a deeper principle of economy and only arrives if it is not aimed for.[7] Yet the surfaces of both the realized plastic Radome in the museum garden and the imagined dome for

3 "Models, photographs and drawings of Buckminster Fuller from early house and car schemes to a recent proposal for a dome covering half of Manhattan will be on view in a first floor gallery of the Museum of Modern Art from October 27 through November." MoMA Press Release, October 27, 1959. The exhibition also included the plastic model by T. C. Howard of Synergetics, Inc., in Raleigh, of a 650-foot-diameter dome to be skinned with plastic panels to cover an athletic center with an array of sports fields and associated facilities, and a hanging model of a plastic pan sphere structure.

4 The conclusion of Drexler's wall text for the original display of the Radome had already hinted at the possibility of scaling up from house to city: "They might also be adapted to make giant 'houses' enclosing gardens and lakes. And, with variations of the structural principles Fuller has developed, domes might also be used to enclose whole cities on the Earth or the Moon." "Text of Wall Label: Structures By Buckminster Fuller," MoMA Press Release, September 22, 1959.

5 Arthur Drexler, *Three Structures by Buckminster Fuller* (New York: MoMA, 1960).

6 Buckminster Fuller, "Industrially Reproducible Architecture," *Trend: An Illustrated Bi-Monthly of the Arts* 2, no. 3 (May–June 1934): 122.

7 "They start with an arbitrarily predetermined aesthetic of design, rather than counting on the inevitable design beauty that develops with pure economy." Buckminster Fuller, *Nine Chains to the Moon* (Philadelphia: Lippincott, 1938), 337.

Minimalism on Steroids

1 Tetrahedronal City, 1965

2 Cloud Nines, 1960

3 Dome over Manhattan, 1959, as rendered in 1962

1

2

3

Manhattan on the wall inside were so carefully produced, controlled, described, and circulated. In fact, the photomontage of the colossal dome was featured again in the museum's highly publicized *Visionary Architecture* exhibition of 1960, in which Drexler celebrated utopian projects freed from technical, social, and economic restraints—idealized designs that parallel realistic ones but "may bring forth ideas that make history."[8] The supposedly antiaesthetic image was even published alongside the introductory text of a *Vogue* fashion shoot by Horst P. Horst of the latest women's suits inside the exhibition, with the already "built" and occupied enclosure of the suits juxtaposed against the unbuilt visionary architecture—the look of today framed by the possible look of tomorrow.[9] **fig. 7**

The photomontage toured the world for eight years with the MoMA exhibition, **fig. 8** visiting more than forty-nine cities in twenty-two countries, but a new image that started to appear in early 1962 quickly became the iconic representation of the project. The dome was now rendered three-dimensionally on another aerial photograph of Manhattan. The gigantic building is no longer seen as a triangulated metal net but as a transparent surface that is visible only because of the reflection of light off its curves. The one-mile-high structure sits ever so lightly, appearing like a huge water bubble or contact lens, an image of ephemerality that is at once vast and insubstantial. Despite Fuller's supposed indifference to aesthetics, he again concentrates on the optics, arguing that the bigger the dome gets, the less visible its structure gets, even adding an arrow to the image the first time it is published to point to an invisible element:

> In fact, we are approaching building structures with altogether invisible components. [...] The thickness of structural members would be about the thickness of the mast for the steamship *Queen Mary*. In that picture, *Queen Mary* is in the harbor, but you cannot see her masts; therefore you could not see the structural components of that dome. The dome is invisible—just as invisible as a fly-screen when you get far away from it.[10]

8 "Introductory Statement on the Visionary Architecture Exhibition," MoMA press release, September 29, 1960, 1.

9 The opening text, alongside the image of Fuller's "daring plan," reads: "Beginning here: new suits for spring, 1961—shown against vanguard designs by American architects from the Museum of Modern Art exhibition called 'Visionary Architecture.' Some of its designs—for buildings, roads, cities—were done as early as 1916, some only last year; but they have one thing in common—all of them are still visions. The suits, on the other hand, have been built, beautifully—and they're all ready to move into, right now." "New Suit Architecture for Spring," *Vogue*, February 1, 1961, 187.

10 Buckminster Fuller, "A New Approach to the World's Housing Problem," *New Scientist*, February 8, 1962, 315.

11 "If we make a microscopic inspection of a pneumatic balloon, we will find that the balloon skin is a system of holes. The balloon skin is really a subdivisible spherical netting rather than a flexible solid film." Buckminster Fuller, "A Philosophy of Space and Shape," *Consulting Engineer*, December 1959, 90–96, here, 94. Fuller repeats the point in a 1961 article again alongside images of the MoMA exhibition. Buckminster Fuller, "Tensegrity," *Portfolio and Art News Annual*, no. 4 (1961). The article is an expanded version of a manuscript dated December 22, 1958, entitled "Tensegrity: Excerpts from Buckminster Fuller's Discourse on Structural Expression and Invention," BFP Series 25, Box 1, Folder 24.

12 Fuller discusses the two-mile-diameter dome on Manhattan as a $200 million project and speaks of a two-mile-diameter Tensegrity Sphere that could "rise and float in the air like a balloon. We could have sky islands going around the world." Calvin Tomkins, "Architecture: Umbrella Man," *Newsweek*, July 13, 1959, 87. The quote was repeated in Robert Marks, "Double-Dome Bucky and his Dymaxion World," *True: The Man's Magazine*, October 1959, 99. The concept was already embedded in Fuller's 1958 proposals for structures in outer space. On January 2, 1959, Fuller had responded to a question about his proposed satellite and Moon structures from *Engineering News Record*. He reworked the "Tensegrity" manuscript of a week earlier to again make the point that a balloon is full of holes, describing his projects as "spherical nets" that echo the microstructure of atoms and the macrostructures of celestial bodies. Adjusting the porosity of the net by adjusting the frequency leads to an "air-floatable" structure equally at home in orbit, in outer space, or on the ground. Buckminster Fuller to David B. Hill, *Engineering News Record*, 2 January 1959, BFP Series 18, Box 144, Folder 1.

13 Buckminster Fuller to Pieter Brattinga, 24 January 1958, quoted in *Buckminster Fuller*, by Buckminster Fuller and Pieter Brattinga (Hilversum: Steendrukkerij De Jong & Co, 1958), 5.

14 Buckminster Fuller, "Invisible Buildings," text prepared for a press release for the March 6, 1958, opening of the ASM dome, BFP Series 8, Box 15, Folder 13, p. 14.

15 Ibid., 19. Fuller's text was printed in a reduced form for the opening as "Remarks by R. Buckminster Fuller, President, Synergetics, Inc., at the March 6 Luncheon announcing the new ASM headquarters building." BFP Series 8, Box 15, Folder 13.

16 "England under an Electronic Dome," Buckminster Fuller interviewed by Reyner Banham, BBC Third Programme, August 1, 1958. Fuller Papers, New York Public Library, p. 6.

Fuller is paradoxically focused on an aesthetics of invisibility. The structure is no longer drawn because it is meant to disappear. The idea that the structural web becomes invisible from a distance is the reverse side of his earlier point that the perforated structure of a seemingly continuous skin becomes visible the more closely you look at the surface. Immediately after the 1959 exhibition, he had published an image of his structures in the MoMA garden and argued that the seemingly continuous film of any inflated balloon turns out under a microscope to be "a system of holes," a "spherical netting."[11] **fig. 5** The plastic film of a balloon is the most efficient structure of all. It is the very image of sheltering the most with the least. It is not by chance that the Manhattan Dome immediately evolved into the huge Cloud Nine balloons. Fuller was already talking about two-mile-diameter Tensegrity Spheres as "sky islands" orbiting the world when he first discussed the dome over New York in the months before it appeared at MoMA.[12] The visual sense of their seemingly smooth skin is but an effect of a structural system that is too fine to be seen. Space is defined by perforations rather than lines.

In his usual contrarian way, Fuller reverses conventional assumptions and the default mantras of modern architecture by arguing in January 1958 that structure is actually less visible as it gets stronger and that form will never follow function: "Here both the form and the function are invisible. [...] If the function is to be *strong*, that function is invisible—which is to say it has no aesthetic form."[13] What is modern is precisely the engagement with that which cannot be seen. The point was repeated two months later in a text called "Invisible Buildings," prepared for the opening of the polemically skinless ASM building outside Cleveland (with the design led by T. C. Howard in the Raleigh node). Fuller begins with the stark assertion of "buildings trending towards invisibility." He says his office had already completed calculations for one-mile-diameter domes covered with glass or plastic where the structural elements would be invisible and predicts that the decade ahead will see multimile-diameter domes covering whole cities with transparent or translucent skins that cannot be seen, "causing merely a mild light-diminishing quality with the otherwise unobscured sky."[14] The enormous structures would be as unconscious to humans as the Radomes are invisible to the microwaves of radar. Geodesic structure is once again understood in terms of the unseen world of radiation. Fuller corrected the manuscript after the building opened, changing the dimension of already calculated domes from one mile in diameter to two miles and adding a sentence using radio tubes as the model, as he had been doing since his very first dome experiments: "The mechanical package will be to the Geodesic dome what the electronic valving elements are to the enclosing electronic tubes."[15] The wireless world in which and for which the dome is built is one in which built architecture is not seen. It disappears so that we can fully engage the architecture of the unseen electromagnetic spectrum.

Fuller returned to the argument a few months later in a July radio interview with Reyner Banham in London, pointing out that the plastic skin covering his domes was actually filled with holes.[16] He responded to Banham's curiosity about the status of the plastic layer by systematically undoing the apparent difference between a metal frame and its skin. The skin itself is a web and each of the elements of the web are themselves filled with holes in a nesting of different frequencies. The appearance of solidity, even in such a thin, translucent material, is an illusion, the product of a particular set of wavelengths. Buildings are not built of materials but of frequencies and those invisible frequencies are the real source of strength. Architecture will get stronger and less visible the more that architects operate directly with frequencies. The mission of the designer is to dissolve the illusion of solid objects. Modernity is the trajectory away from the visible. Once again, the real architecture of domes is that of radio itself. Fuller even predicts that eventually the whole of England could be covered in an invisible "radio dome" that completely transforms the environment:

> We're really working towards an invisibility of environment controlling. [...] In handling things on this frequency basis, we may really be able to develop some kind of inference patterns. We could put a radio—a radio dome—an electronic event dome over England and make it a whole Garden of Eden.[17]

When Fuller first introduced the more modest and therefore more visible idea of the two-mile dome idea in a March 1959 lecture at Michigan, he started by saying that Detroit could be covered with an eight-mile diameter dome within ten years. After just two years, a city in the United States could already be covered with a two-mile dome covered with clear plastic and spheres two miles in diameter would be able to float 30,000 feet above the Earth through subtle adjustments of porosity.[18] By June Fuller was telling an English newspaper that the two-mile dome would be over Manhattan with such a delicate frame and a transparent synthetic skin that it would "defy" eyesight and take shelter out of the visible: "We are all set for invisible architecture."[19] He explained all its technical advantages a few weeks later to the huge readership of *Newsweek*, including the weight, construction, and projected costs—even making the remarkable argument that the savings from the absence of common cold and respiratory illnesses alone would quickly pay for the whole project. Any interest in aesthetics is again denied because "I like to work on invisible architecture," and yet the aesthetic effect of the project is described. The huge aluminum and plastic structure would be "so delicate as to be nearly invisible."[20] The goal was the aesthetics of invisibility and the magazine published a photomontage trying to capture the barely-there effect of an enormous plastic bubble superimposed on an aerial photograph of Manhattan. **fig. 6**

This image of a fragile plastic cloud marked only by the radial pattern of some fine pseudostructural lines done by a graphic designer for the magazine clearly acted as the model for the photomontage that was shown at MoMA a few months later. As can be seen from the documents in the MoMA archives, the montage was made for the exhibition with an image

17 Ibid., 15.

18 Robert R. d'Arcy, "Ah, June the Year Round—That's Life in Giant Dome," *Detroit News*, March 13, 1959.

19 "I'll Put a Dome over Manhattan," *Daily Mail*, June 18, 1959.

20 Tomkins, "Architecture: Umbrella Man," 84 (see note 12). Fuller clearly looked for an orchestrated buzz to animate the reception of the dome over Manhattan. One report just before the exhibition opening did refer to *Newsweek*'s comments about the project under the heading "New York Roof," "Domes and Dymaxion" (*Observer*, August 2, 1959, 3), but almost all of the media coverage of the exhibition concentrated only on the built structures in the garden.

4

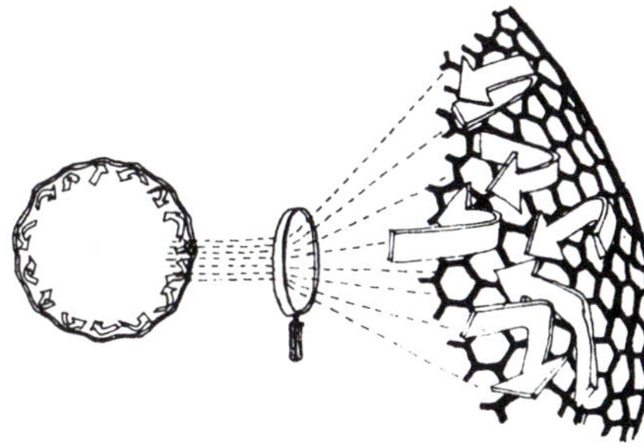

5

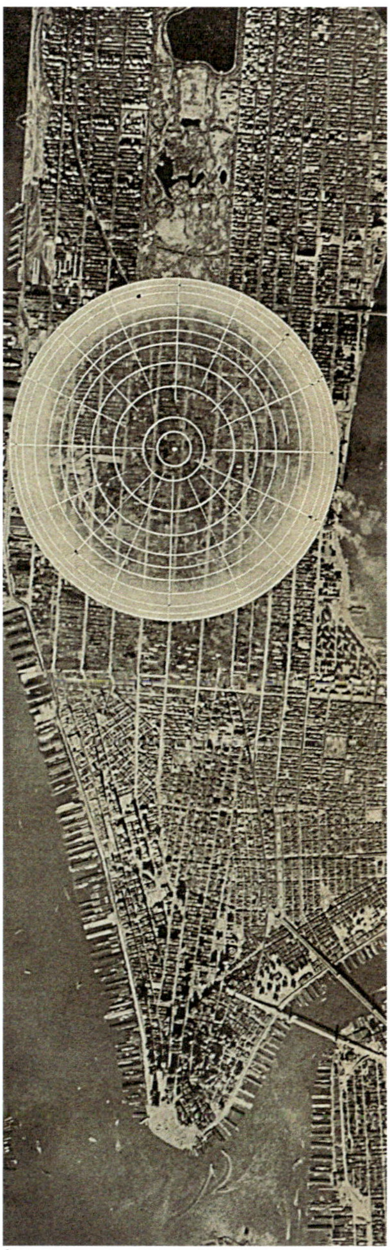

6

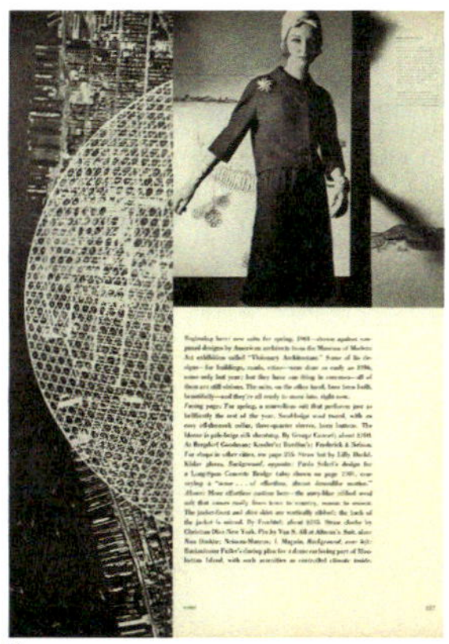

7

8

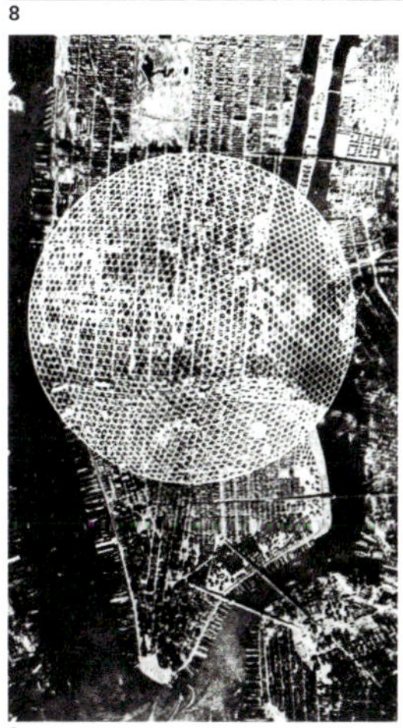

9

Archeology of an Iconic Image

4 Installation view of the exhibition *Buckminster Fuller,* October 27, 1959, through November 22, 1959, the Museum of Modern Art, New York. Gelatin-sliver print, 8×10" (20.3×24.4 cm). Curatorial Exhibition Files, Exhibition #652. The Museum of Modern Art Archives. Photographer: Kenneth Snelson

5 Image of holes in balloon from RBF lecture to UIA congress in Mexico City, October 10, 1963

6 Dome over Manhattan, *Newsweek*, July 13, 1959

7 "New Suit Architecture for Spring," *Vogue*, February 1, 1961

8 Opening of *Visionary Architecture* exhibition, Southern Illinois University, April 11, 1961

9 Dome over Manhattan, photomontage constructed for exhibition at MoMA, October 1959, and published in *L'architecture d'aujourd'hui,* June 1962

of a geodesic net on transparent acetate placed onto two aerial photos, with the superimposition of net and island then rephotographed and blown up into a wall-sized print. **fig. 9** The white net was dramatically opposed to the darkness of the city, whereas the three-dimensional version of 1962 was seamlessly airbrushed onto an aerial photograph to show what happens when even the net becomes invisible.[21] **fig. 3** In this definitive image, the effect of a transparent hemisphere is added with great precision as a subtle white cloud marks where the face of the dome nearest the viewer embeds itself into the fabric of existing buildings and an even more subtle black cloud marks where the face furthest away is embedded. The result is an uncanny confusion of monumental and ephemeral, a visual manifesto of the most for the least that was explicitly launched to reinforce a polemic about the general "trend to invisibility" in contemporary life.[22]

The new image was first displayed in January 1962 in an exhibition of Fuller's work in Eero Saarinen's recently completed American Embassy building in London, and his lecture at the opening again described mankind's ever-deeper engagement with the invisible universe since World War I. We are "approaching building structures with altogether invisible components" as represented by the shimmering structure over Manhattan: "The dome is invisible. [...] I come from an art that is becoming essentially an invisible one—we are dealing in invisibles."[23] Fuller polemically ended the lecture with a slide of the new image and the airbrushed ephemeral bubble was promptly published in several British magazines and quickly started to spread in international magazines.[24] It appeared alongside the MoMA image for the first and last time a few months later in a section on "visionary architecture" in an issue of *L'architecture d'aujourd'hui* before it

21 In 1975 Fuller refers to the two-mile dome as a "theoretical study": "Because I had calculated it, I wondered what it looked like in terms of something I was familiar with. It turns out that Manhattan Island is two miles wide at 42nd Street. [...] Now it happened that the size of the compression members on this dome were the diameter of the mast of the *Queen Mary* [...] you can't see her mast from this altitude therefore you could not see my compression members in this dome from this altitude. Therefore it would really be like looking at an aluminum kitchen sieve from a great distance where you would not be able to see the individual wires. You would just see a glistening reflectivity of the aluminum. So that's what we have here. So the airbrush of this was perfectly valid." Fuller had often used the *Queen Mary* as an image of a floating city, and noted that there was enough material in the ship to build his dome. Buckminster Fuller, "Everything I Know" (videotranscript of lecture, Bell Telephone Studios, Philadelphia, PA, January 1975), Session 8, Part 7 (Buckminster Fuller Institute, 1997).

22 "In the advanced technology form is not following function. All the form is where you can see it. The functions are invisible. There are not forms following function at all [...] the trend to invisibility." Buckminster Fuller, Lecture #1 (Oregon University, July 1, 1962), BFP Series 8, Box 27, Folder 9. The theme of the series of nine lectures was "Trends to Invisibility" and symptomatically began with the discovery of X-rays and radio.

23 "If you look downstairs there is a picture of New York City with a proposed two-mile dome. The structural members for that have been carefully computed; it is a possibility to do such a dome. The size of the structural members would be about the size of the nest of the steamship *Queen Mary*. In that picture, the *Queen Mary* is out at dock in New York and you can see her very clearly, but you cannot see her mast, therefore you could not see the structural components of that dome. The dome is invisible—just as invisible as a fly-screen when you get quite far away from it. Thus form is not following function." Buckminster Fuller, lecture at exhibition opening (US Embassy, London, January 30, 1962), BFP Series 8, Box 27, Folder 8, p. 9.

24 Fuller, "A New Approach to the World's Housing Problem," 315 (see note 10); "Richard Buckminster Fuller in London," *Architect's Journal*, February 1962, 352; "Buckminster Fuller: He Can Put a Dome over Anything!," *Junior Scholastic*, April 1962, 10.

25 "Architectures Fantastiques," special issue, *L'architecture d'aujourd'hui*, June 1962, 103. The traveling *Visionary Architecture* exhibition featured the 1959 collage of the Manhattan Dome, as can be seen in photographs of Fuller looking at the image when the exhibition was installed at Southern Illinois University in April 1961.

26 John McHale, *Buckminster Fuller* (New York: George Braziller, 1962), 110. The first version of the Cloud Nines marked with the geodesic structure was likewise replaced by one with an unmarked white surface like that of a balloon.

27 "The Dymaxion American," *Time*, January 10, 1964, 124.

28 "As inspection will reveal the 3 way-geodesics allow of economical treatments even in unprecedentedly enormous structures, whose interstices may be arranged to conform to the same economy as that arrived at in the 50 foot structure already described. A dome one mile in diameter, 2500 feet high at center [...] and large enough to enclose a major city magnitude of planned and integrated activity and facility may be (can be) immediately realized." Buckminster Fuller, "Project Noah's Ark #2," in *Your Private Sky: Discourse*, ed. Joachim Krausse and Claude Lichtenstein (Zurich: Lars Müller, 2001), 209. The original sketch for the dome over New York City page includes the idea that the depth of the dome is "less than 100 foot." BFP Series 8, Box 11, Folder 2.

29 "A hemispheric dome one mile in diameter comprised of ninety-three intersecting great circles is now possible." Buckminster Fuller to Major General Follett Bradley, 25 March 1949, BFP Series 8, Box 8, Folder 12.

30 "A dome one mile in diameter appropriately skinned may, in the future, economically encompass the activity of a city. Such a city would require no weather walls for its individual buildings and yet could be entirely air conditioned." Buckminster Fuller, "Preview of Building" (lecture at *Time for Change* conference, University of Michigan, Ann Arbor, April 1, 1949), 13.

took over as the iconic representation of the project.[25] It was published in a book for the first time in late 1962, when it was added without discussion to the end of John McHale's monograph on Fuller in a book series that legitimized him by placing him alongside the key postwar architects Louis Kahn, Eero Saarinen, Philip Johnson, and Kenzo Tange.[26] The image was somehow both his most ambitious fantasy and the seal of his legitimacy as a contemporary practitioner. Not by chance was it featured in the issue of *Time* magazine that completed the canonization by putting him on the cover in January 1964 with the chirpy caption "Dome over Manhattan! Why Not."[27]

This delicate image of invisibility would not just shelter the dense bustling city below it. The city would now be suspended within the image itself. As with a balloon, even the lightest membranes have an internal three-dimensional geodesic net, a space that can be occupied. The first captions of the image argued that the 100-foot depth of the structure would accommodate twice the volume of buildings within it than the ground below it, so all the buildings and transportation systems of the city would move into the shell, with the ground left as an enormous tropical garden—the Garden of Eden that Fuller had aspired to since the first Private Sky drawings in early 1949. Even if the discourse is about invisibility, Fuller doesn't stray from the optics. There are no accompanying technical drawings of how this vast inhabitable surface installed by a fleet of helicopters is actually going to be constructed. Fuller's presentation of the dome is as ethereal as the dome would be for those underneath it—as if it has no weight.

Some basic calculations of the overall geometry for a one-mile-diameter dome for Manhattan with a four-foot depth covered in translucent fiberglass-reinforced plastic had been done a decade earlier in the summer of 1950. Fuller prepared a private manuscript with calculations of the stress (live, dead, and wind loads), total weight/cubic feet enclosed, and total cost using 2-inch-diameter aluminum tubes for all the elements—insisting that such "unprecedentedly enormous structures" enclosing a major city "may be (can be) immediately realized."[28] The dome over New York would be one thousand times the volume yet one fiftieth of the weight of the Empire State building that "would appear as a relatively small spike reaching up but one half the way to its 'sky.'" Even more remarkably, the concept of such a colossal dome had already been discussed the year before during the construction of Fuller's very first successful dome, the 14-foot-diameter Necklace Dome fabricated in the Institute of Design in Chicago, demonstrated at the Pentagon, and covered with its plastic skin at Black Mountain College as a model of what a 50-foot-diameter Autonomous House for domestic or military use might look like. Fuller referred to the possibility of a one-mile-diameter dome in a March 25, 1949, letter that summarized the Necklace Dome research to the retired general who had facilitated the demonstration at the Pentagon two weeks earlier,[29] an idea he repeated a week later in the April 1 conference presentation of the Autonomous House idea at the University of Michigan.[30]

The Manhattan Dome of 1959, with the Empire State Building again at the center but now reaching only a third of the way up, simply demonstrated the point Fuller had been making for a decade that the efficiency of housing a family in a 50-foot dome would be exponentially greater when housing a whole city. If the dome is the most minimal structure, its leanness increases as the structure gets bigger. In a spiral of ever-increasing efficiency, less energy would be used to house more people that would now need less to sustain them. Architecture itself would mirror the evolution of thinking and technology in trending toward the invisible.

The emphasis on the optical only increased as Fuller started including the definitive airbrushed image in his books and lectures. In his major speech to the 1963 congress of the Union of International Architects (UIA) in Mexico City, for example, the whole project was even described as an exercise in optics. The dome was "theoretically superimposed" on Manhattan because:

> I wanted to see what that would look like relative to familiar structural undertakings of man. [...] The structural members are so relatively small as to be as invisible as an aluminum, fine mesh, wire, fly screen, as seen from a distance. Therefore we find that as we get larger and larger, geodesic, tensegrity structures we get to the point where the structure itself tends to become invisible at any distance away from it at which the whole dome may be seen, simultaneously,—without moving our eyes or head.[31]

This paradoxical image of invisibility was presented at the end of a sequence of seventy-six slides of almost all Fuller's projects understood as a career-long rejection of appearances. Before asking for the lights to go down to show the slides, he insisted that "I made up my mind tonight to try to talk to you about what seems to me to be fundamental and not just to show superficial pictures of forms."[32] The illusion of solidity was dismantled by illustrating in detail the argument that the skin of a balloon is really a net, a system of holes. The point was again crucially extended by saying that even the elements of this "webbing" that defines the array of holes are themselves porous, being constellations like the Milky Way that only appear to be some kind of object from a vast distance away. As a result, "there is no such thing as a continuous 'solid' skin or 'solid' anything in the universe. But we *do* have a network pattern—a network of energy actions which is interspersed with vast spaces or lack of energy events."[33] Even the first close-up photograph of the structure of the cornea of the human eyeball, done just a year earlier, was presented to show its geodesic net. Vision itself depends on a hidden net within the seemingly transparent gel of the eye. Such nets are visible in the slides of the translucent plastic dome for the Ford Rotunda of 1953 and the Woods

31 Buckminster Fuller, "World Design Initiative," speech given to UIA congress, October 10, 1963, in *World Design Science Decade 1965–1975, Phase 1, Document 1: Inventory of World Resources, Human Trends and Needs*, ed. John McHale (Carbondale: Southern Illinois University, 1965), 93.

32 Ibid., 30.

33 Ibid., 45.

34 Ibid., 68.

35 "For the same reason, the structural members of the dome also are invisible. They are as invisible as are the wires of a screened-in porch when viewed from 100 feet distant. For this reason the appearance of the dome would be as seen in the picture—that is, as a glistening translucent form. One would get the same effect if he photographed an ordinary kitchen wire strainer, turned upside down and placed 100 feet away. [...] The lower edge of the dome over the city would be at such a height above the city as to make it appear as a high umbrella, with plenty of blue sky visible under its rim. The dome would appear from below as a translucent film through which the sky, clouds and stars would be visible. It would not create a shut-in feeling any more than carrying a parasol above one's head on a summer day. The dome's skins, consisting of wire-reinforced, one-way-vision, shatterproof glass, mist-plated with aluminum, will have the exterior appearance of a mirrored dome, while the viewer inside will see out without conscious impairment." Buckminster Fuller, "The Case for Domed Cities," *St Louis Dispatch*, December 26, 1965.

Hole restaurant dome of the same year that was covered with such a thin skin of transparent Mylar that "it began to seem that we were approaching a time when the construction would become entirely invisible."[34] But it is only with the airbrushed dome over Manhattan, the very last of the slides, that the illusion of solidity has finally given way to the unmatched efficiency of invisible nets with which the universe is organized. The effect of the image is the ambition or horizon of all the work that preceded it.

The basic argument about efficiency is repeated alongside the canonic image in "The Case for a Domed City," a three-page article in the Sunday supplement to a major newspaper in 1965, but again Fuller offers the basic technical rationale without any technical detail and ends up going even deeper into the aesthetic effect. The article describes the desired invisibility of the structure but also its "glistening translucent form" with the sense of a "translucent film through which the sky, clouds and sun would be visible" from the inside and the appearance of a "mirrored dome" from the outside.[35] Fuller continuously obsessed about the supposedly unintended aesthetic effect of a systematic attempt to avoid aesthetics.

The viral success of the image, promoted in numerous lectures, interviews, articles, books, and exhibitions, does not simply derive from the uncanny sophistication of the montage, in which the dome appears to have already been constructed, or the reassuring cadences of the technical polemic about energy and structural efficiency surrounding it, or the detailed description of the optics. It is the combination of all of these that gives a sense of realism to the project, making the huge dome appear to be more than an image, more than a fantasy. They suspend the viewer between fantasy and reality, leaving the sense of a fantasy realized. The brilliance of the photomontage is to show the dome as realized but realized as a kind of ghost. Architecture becomes the most delicate optical distortion, a slight interruption of the visual field. The minimal ghostly surface acts as the trace of architecture's disappearance. It marks the absence of solidity, the departure of buildings as normally understood. The hovering, barely visible surface (initially described as plastic, then glass, and eventually as plastic again) marks the final detachment of architecture from the land and from vision—leaving both site and sight behind. It literally absorbs architecture into itself, digesting traditional buildings and enabling the Garden of Eden to be restored below it as itself a kind of image, a framed technological image of a pretechnological world.

The photomontage of the dome hovering over the buildings of Manhattan and about to absorb them is an image of Fuller's lifelong mission. A barely-there floating surface marks the disappearance of solid forms, the dissolving of traditional architecture, and the arrival of a sensitive medium for registering traces of the invisible world. It is an optical instrument for looking at the largely unseen environment we inhabit. The delicate, suspended transparent or translucent film in all his work is where solid architecture has just left and information about the unseen is about to arrive. All of Fuller's countless words prop up this lighter-than-air yet supercharged surface. Far from abandoning aesthetics, Fuller was singularly dedicated to the paradoxical question What does the invisible look like? All the plastic surfaces attached to barely visible geodesic frames are ultimately images of a single fantasized surface through which to look at the unseen world—a lens that superimposes data onto the world.

EXPANDED TELEVISION

The geodesic dome always remains a fantasy, no matter how many thousands of them have been built in every corner of the globe. It is above all an image, the image of a single world, following the single world/single house/single human family polemic that Fuller cultivated throughout his career. He portrayed the planet as a house for a global family and each house as a surrogate planet. It is not by chance that so many of the projects take the same shape as the planet itself. They are images of Earth placed on Earth as a kind of simulacrum that allows people to see themselves in their world as if from the outside for the first time, but also to see from the inside out. If your shelter is a miniature Earth, you can only approach it as an astronaut. Anything outside its seemingly ephemeral envelope is already outer space. The Manhattan Dome is but the tip of a spherical iceberg that wants to float free of the land and of solidity, a delicate spherical image that can be occupied.

This concern for a singular domestic image of the world is most explicit in Fuller's lesser-known Geoscope project, which transforms geodesic structures into a literal image of Earth. The planet's geography is precisely marked on a transparent sphere to act as a new kind of mirror in which people see themselves in their total environment for the first time. The Geoscope is fixed in the same orientation as the planet it simulates so that the observer at its center sees the stars in their exact location above each geographic point and feels the planet's spinning trajectory within the starscape. The sphere's surface is graphically encoded with layers of information about the flows of resources around the planet to produce a hypermap, a totalizing view that is unavailable with any other technology of representation. Fuller argued that the most efficient form of analysis of complex data is visual and offered the Geoscope as a mechanism for producing visual images of an otherwise invisible global scene, a compact accounting of planetary flows. The Geoscope is a data visualization project in which the visualization and the world being visualized are literally juxtaposed. Diverse interacting phenomena become aesthetic patterns. Constant observation of these evolving patterns will supposedly enable a more equitable and efficient distribution of resources.

36 The two articles that launched the image—"A New Approach to the World's Housing Problem" (see note 10) and "Richard Buckminster Fuller in London" (see note 24)—begin with the Geoscope proposal.
37 Buckminster Fuller, "International Exhibition Among Students of Architectural Schools," 1961 proposal submitted to the Executive Committee of the International Union of Architects (UIA). *Inventory of World Resources Human Trends and Needs: Document 1*, 1963, unpaginated. Fuller republished the text of his proposal to the committee, with a few minor changes, as "World Planning" in *Ideas and Integrities: A Spontaneous Autobiographical Discourse* (New York: Prentice-Hall, 1963), 256–263.
38 Buckminster Fuller, "The Architect as World Planner," *Architectural Design*, August 1961, 235. The portrait of Fuller accompanying the publication of the speech was by Monica Pidgeon herself and was also used in a 1962 newspaper article interviewing Fuller about the project and the Geoscope's ability to visualize the world: "When the various schools in the world begin to plot their data on the model worlds, patterns that we do not at present see will become visible." Diana Rowntree, "The World of Buckminster Fuller," *The Guardian*, January 27, 1962, 5.
39 "Whereas doctors deal with the interior organisms of man, architects deal with the external organisms of man. Architects might thus join forces as do scientists with the integrity of inter-self-accrediting of the respective abilities of each individual on the team. Architects might begin the laboratory pooling of the resource capabilities at the university level." Buckminster Fuller, "The Comprehensive Man," *Northwest Review*, April 1959, 33.

t is not by chance that Fuller was talking about the Geoscope concept n January 1962 when launching the airbrushed image of the dome over Manhattan in London.[36] He had first promoted the concept to an interna- ional audience in London six months earlier at the July 1961 congress of he UIA with the self-consciously shocking proposal that all architectural schools around the world should stop traditional design teaching and join ogether for ten years to study how to "render" the total resources of the vorld on a sphere.[37] **fig. 10** In fact, he had not been invited to speak at the ongress but came with a speech prepared about "The Architect as World Planner." He went to the congress ball and danced with Monica Pidgeon, he legendary editor of *Architectural Design*, who had not been looking orward to seeing him for fear of encountering the idiosyncratic and end- ess density of his writing. She was charmed and promptly offered her nagazine as a media platform for the ongoing project, publishing the speech a month later, helping to persuade the executive committee of the JIA to formally accept the proposal in 1962, covering the project with her own photographs of Fuller and the ongoing experiments over the next decade, and providing her photographs to newspapers that were writing about him.[38] Her magazine was effectively part of the project, even listing tself as the project's official mailing address.

Fuller's speech was a call to arms in the face of ecological and therefore social disaster. The world was unable to support more than forty percent of its citizens and urgently needed to see itself as a world. Looking for a "dramatically communicated solution" to act as the focal structure of a najor world city, as the Eiffel Tower does for Paris, Fuller gave up on the dea of using the entire façade of a skyscraper or mountain cliff and pro- posed that the rendering be a "Minni-Earth," a 200-foot-diameter trans- parent globe which inventories all available planetary resources and their nistorical and contemporary movements. Schools of architecture were to develop working models and photograph the resulting "data array" for an exhibition four years later at the 1965 UIA congress in Paris. The overall nission was to launch a ten-year effort by the international architectural education community to design the means to visualize and thereby real- ocate global resources in real time. The usual emphasis on individual students would give way to coordinated teams subdividing the problem of inventing a new means of representing the world. Schools producing a Geoscope would even become schools within a Geoscope, since "the vorld architectural students may if they wish employ it as their design acility." The Geoscope is both a tool to be designed and a tool for design- ng. Architectural programs would eventually inhabit the data visualiza- ion instruments they had developed. Education, design, research, visual- zation, communication, and architecture would become one thing.

Fuller had systematically attended regional conventions of architects over the previous three years, repeatedly calling for professional architects o work collaboratively like scientists in the laboratory setting of the uni- versity and likewise calling for schools of architecture to focus on research rather than practice.[39] The UIA congress was the opportunity to magnify and globalize this insistence on a "laboratory pooling" of resources. The attempt to harness the research capacity of all schools of architecture simply intensified his working method since 1949 of networking dispersed schools by coordinating parallel teams studying different dimensions of the same problem. In a sense, he had only ever been addressing this one problem since starting to teach. The question of the dome and of the Geoscope were inseparable. Fuller had already sketched the idea of lining the inside of a transparent dome with an accurately aligned global map in June 1948, just before unsuccessfully trying to raise his first proto-house dome with students at Black Mountain College, and a year later saw his first successful plastic-covered dome there as a personal observatory for seeing one's place in the world. He had been experimenting with what he would later call the Geoscope since the early 1950s, moving from school to school to develop a series of increasingly sophisticated prototypes. The goal was to build up a comprehensive data display out of layers of information superimposed on the flat, triangulated surfaces of a geodesic sphere. The challenge was to perfect both the surface receiving the information and the lightweight structure that held it in place. The structure developed more quickly than the surface. The basic geodesic principles had just been established when Fuller first formulated the project but the imagistic surface was to remain somewhat speculative. By the time of the formal submission of the 1961 proposal to the executive committee of the UIA, he predicted that:

> Its interior and exterior surfaces could be symmetrically dotted with ten million small variable intensity lightbulbs and the lights controllably connected up with an electronic computer. [...] At 200 ft. minimum distance away from the viewer, the lightbulbs' sizes and distance apart would become indistinguishable, as do the size and distances between the points in a fine half-tone print. Patterns introduced into the bulb matrix at various light intensities through the computer, would create an omni-directional spherical picture analogous to that of a premium television tube whose picture could be seen all over its surface both from inside and outside.[40]

The Geoscope is a glorified television set. This 200-foot TV does not sit in your living room. It is your living room. Furthermore, everyone else's house is inscribed in it. The scale of the sphere is determined by the fact that at that particular size, with 35 mm aerial surveillance images spread across its surface, each individual house on the planet would be discernable as a one-hundredth-inch speck, the smallest dimension the human eye can detect.[41] Fuller calculated that if you looked at the sphere from 1,000 feet away with good binoculars, your house would be visible but not your car. The representation of the global house is only possible at the moment that it can account for every single house. It is reliant upon both

40 Fuller, "International Exhibition among Students of Architectural Schools" (see note 37).

41 "If we use the 35 mm contact prints of the photographs taken by the aerial surveyors at their lowest altitude of operation, in which individual houses, as home of men, may be discerned by the naked eye, [...] he could pick out his own home. Thus Minni-Earth becomes a potent symbol of man visible in Universe."Ibid. "In designing the optimum public Geoscope in 1950 I chose the 200-foot-diameter, approximately transparent, gossamer-structured sphere because at that time the United States Air Force was, wherever possible, engaged in making radio-triangulated, geographically accurate photographic maps of the whole Earth's surface [...] known as the aerial (photographic) mosaicing of the world. [...] The diameter of such a spherical picture 'globe' made up of contact prints of the lowest-level mosaicing is about 200 feet [...] of such detail that you could, with your naked eye, identify your own home grounds and even your house, which would be a 1/100th-of-an-inch speck—the smallest speck seen by human eye." Buckminster Fuller, "The Geoscope," in *Critical Path* (London: Hutchinson, 1981), 175.

10 RBF at opening of UIA congress in London, 1961

11 Minni-Earth above the East River, drawing by Winslow Wedin, 1955

0

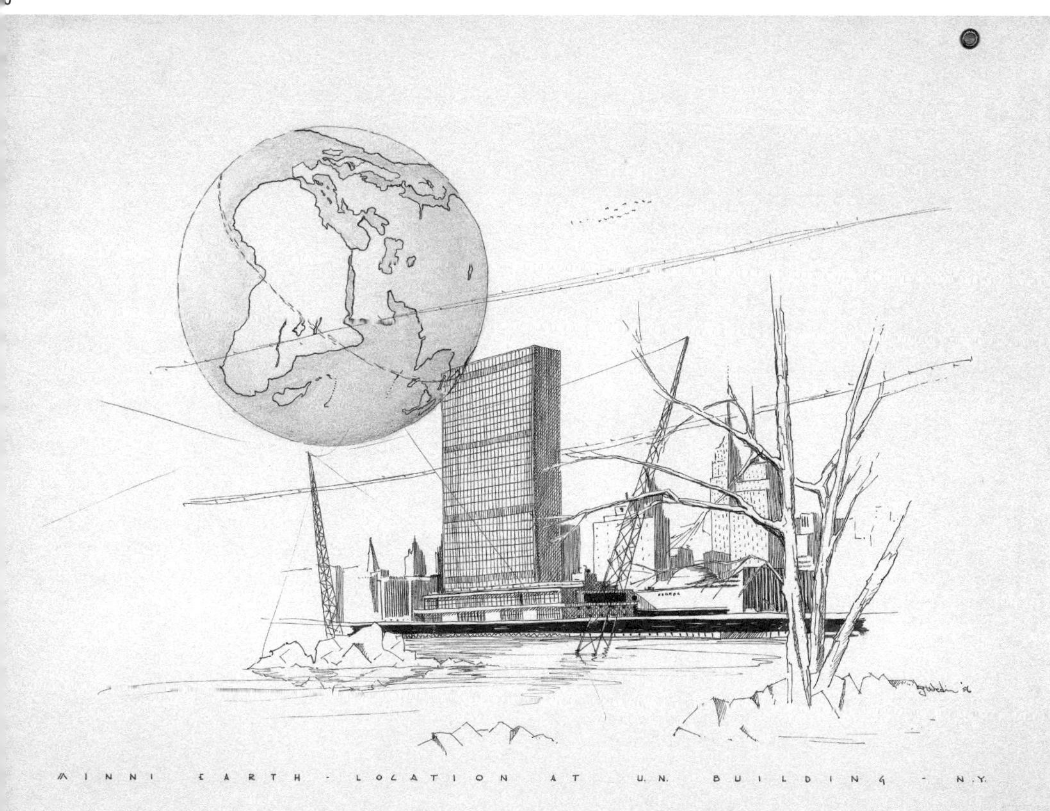

a new lightweight structural system that aspires to be invisible and a new sophistication in surveillance photography, the ability to register a certain level of detail on film. The extreme thinness of the structure and the extreme detail in the images were linked.

The Geoscope is born of a technological advance in which the visible structure of a house begins to disappear at the same moment that the house itself finally becomes larger than the grain of surveillance film. You can only see the outside of your own house, the world outside, the whole world, when every other house is visible. The modern architect's dream of bringing the outside in and taking the inside out makes a quantum leap when the view from the inside is bigger and more complex than from the outside, giving the viewer the world in a glance, an immediate and comprehensive awareness of "man in the universe." The huge TV set displaces traditional architecture to provide a total picture. It becomes the paradigmatic architectural project, transforming the world into a single space, an interior with a domestic economy to be monitored and regulated. Turning the planet into a TV set reinforces the polemical idea of Earth as a house. It is the final implication of Fuller's repeated description of how the arrival of television into houses completed the invention of a global world by radio. And this ability to visualize the world as a world for the first time sets the stage for visualizing its hidden structure. The understanding that the universe is predominantly invisible initiated by radio demands new technologies of visualization, new instruments "that can inform humanity about its invisibly trending evolutionary challenges."[42] The new design task is to bring the enormous bandwidth of the invisible into the narrow bandwidth of the visible, and within that limited range to bring it onto the even narrower space of a single "gossamer" spherical surface. The transparent plastic skin of a geodesic sphere is invested with the whole future of the human species. The most minimal plastic takes on the most monumental of tasks.

Fuller nominates two strategies to the UIA to maximize global focus. The Geoscope could either be installed as the central urban focus for whatever city is holding the Olympic Games and be reinstalled in each successive Olympic city or it could be permanently suspended on wires over Blackwell's Ledge, a set of rocks in the East River directly opposite the United Nations headquarters, to "serve as a constant confronter of all nations' representatives of the integrating patterns, both expected and unexpected, occurring around the face of man's constantly shrinking 'one world town.'"[43] **fig. 11** As with the two-mile-diameter dome project of two years earlier, the focus is on Manhattan because it is the international center for the production and redistribution of images, the world's "most concentrated pattern-processing and exchanging center," as Fuller would

42 Fuller, "The Geoscope," 162 (see note 41).
43 Fuller, "International Exhibition among Students of Architectural Schools" (see note 37).
44 Fuller, "New York as a Focus of Energy," 30 (see note 1). "New York is not an idea factory, nor an idea mine, nor an idea garden, but is the world's point of highest velocity in idea exchanging." Ibid. "New York City is, for the moment, the most radiant communication-relaying center on planet Earth." Ibid., 34.
45 Buckminster Fuller, *New Approaches to Structure*, The Voice of America Forum Lectures no. 5 (Washington, D.C.: Voice of America, 1961), 2.
46 A photograph of Wedin looking at the drawing while Fuller points to it appeared in "U Students Plan Huge Globe for Use by UN," by Reub Monson, *St. Paul Pioneer Press*, November 1955.
47 Fuller, "The Geoscope," 175 (see note 41).

later put it.[44] After all, the mantra of doing the most with the least also applies to doing the most with the least amount of images. For all his massive production and self-documentation, he maintained a compact set of images (the so-called LECO set) with which to make his case in lectures, essays, newspapers, magazines, books, and exhibitions. Each of the experiments is typically known through one or two carefully selected and endlessly reproduced images. The drawing of the Geoscope floating over the East River is no exception, and the absence of visible structure within the sphere in the drawing is no accident. It floats as a see-through image, with clouds seen passing behind it. The invisibility of structure and the visibility of pattern is the whole point. The mission of the Geoscope is to offer an image of that which cannot be seen. In a radio broadcast on Voice of America the same year, Fuller rejected the commonsense idea that architects "build buildings out of materials," insisting that this idea dates back to the era of man's thinking of matter as solid. What I tell architecture students is that what they do is build visible modular structures out of sub-visible modular structures."[45] Architecture should be a visible echo of the hidden molecular and atomic structure of nature.

The Geoscope is a TV set for the world that looks like the world or, more precisely, gives the first sense of what the world really looks like. Elevators would lift people up from ferries, bridges, or tunnels into its center where they could witness the presentation of stars, satellites, earthquakes, electromagnetic and astrophysical patterns, economic, demographic, and sociological displays, or world news twenty-four hours a day, with all the images being generated in a remote computer housing. The huge, open, animated sphere floating over the water is meant to be in continuous active dialogue with the monumental closed oval of the General Assembly Hall with its dense, opaque wrapping. The global exchange of ideas inside would now be dependent on the global images outside. The basis for decisions and the effect of decisions would be registered on the sphere's hyperpublic surface. The project was presented to U Thant, the secretary-general of the United Nations, who liked the idea and organized a presentation of it to all the ambassadors in a New York hotel. Half of them attended Fuller's talk, but nothing came of it.

PROTOTYPE PLANETS

The rendering of the flying spherical TV presented to the ambassadors was drawn in 1955 by Winslow Wedin, an architecture student at the University of Minnesota.[46] A group of thirty of his fellow students had worked on the design, detailing a 160-foot-diameter transparent "Minni-Earth" with a weight of 35,000 pounds to be hung over the East River on cables strung from five poles so that "It will almost look like a big ball hovering low over the Earth" or "as though it were a small celestial body that had come in very close to Earth."[47] The project was part of the three-year Design-Science program launched at the Department of Architecture in November 1954 (after developing the plastic-covered dome temporarily installed at Aspen and Woods Hole the year before). Following his normal pattern, Fuller attended for a number of weeks each year. The idea was to build a

12

13

14

The Minnesota Minni-Earth

12 Cover of *Time*, January 10, 1964

13 "Buckminster Fuller with Minni-Earth Model," *Minneapolis Sunday Tribune*, November 6, 1955

14 Architecture students assembling 80-inch pilot sphere, University of Minnesota, 1955

15 Photomontage of Minni-Earth suspended on steel wires over University of Minnesota building, *Architectural Record*, June 1957

16 RBF with pilot sphere and Ralph Rapson, head of the School of Architecture

5

6

50-foot-diameter plastic globe with a magnesium frame one-millionth the size of Earth that he argued would be "infinitely better for studying the world than the Earth itself."[48] **fig. 13** The traditional globe that sits on the table would be progressively enlarged into a globe that could be entered. Students drew a geodesic net onto a small globe and took measurements off it to make an enlarged "pilot model" at the end of 1955 with an 80-inch diameter and a transparent surface of acetate to be packed with global information arranged on triangular vinyl sheets marking every small lake, river, railroad, and highway.[49] **fig. 14** Once again, the plastic surface takes over from the frame, with the geodesic pattern built into the surface itself. The whole point of the structure is that it is meant to disappear so that the information suspended in the layer of plastic literally hovers in the visual field, the invisible global patterns now superimposed on the visible world—vision itself transformed by an enhanced plastic lens. When Fuller was photographed in front of the shiny transparent sphere the sense that it is a kind of glistening magnification of his almost hairless head is far from accidental and is a central trope organizing countless photographs that would be taken to the logical extreme in 1964 when the cover of *Time* magazine portrayed his head as a dome propped up on little legs like those of a space capsule. **figs. 12 and 16** After all, the animated sphere was precisely understood as a brain magnifier.

The goal of the Minnesota team was to suspend their 50-foot-diameter version on wires above a university building with a stairway to an observation platform at its core passing through the Indian Ocean. The sphere in the air would have 2,160 triangular openings in its surface corresponding to each of the triangular subdivisions of the 1943 Dymaxion Map of the planet that had recently been revised by Fuller and Sadao. Each opening would accept an easily removable, 5-foot-deep, triangularly sectioned drawer (a truncated tetrahedron), producing an interior sphere of 40 feet in diameter to represent Earth's surface (at a scale of 1:1,000,000) and a five-foot depth to represent the successive layers from ocean floor to outer atmosphere. The silhouette of all landmasses and geopolitical organizations would be drawn "as an open lace like pattern" on the inner surfaces and the drawers would be sectioned into concentric layers to display

48 Buckminster Fuller, cited in "'U' May Help Build Giant Model of Earth," *Minneapolis Sunday Tribune*, November 6, 1955.

49 "Four-Story High Globe to Be Constructed at U," *The Minnesota Daily*, January 5, 1956.

50 Buckminster Fuller, cited in "'U' May Help Build Giant Model of Earth" (see note 48).

51 "Fuller Group Completes Study of Geodesic 'Minni-Earth,'" *Architectural Record* 121, no. 7 (June 1957): 16. When the three years of study had been concluded at the end of the Fall 1956 semester, Fuller proposed that the students would benefit from its realization. "minni earth inc. would be established as a corporation with a third of the shares going to the students who had worked on the project, another third to the ex-students that had worked on the Dymaxion Map and a third be held for the future associates who would help with the full scale realization." Handwritten document signed by Buckminster Fuller and witnessed by Winslow Wedin, dated November 14, 1956, BFP Series 18, Box 107, Folder 2.

52 Fuller argued that such a "regenerative circuit of information" through the "device" that "made it possible to feel yourself in the universe" should be the appropriate first step for all design activity. Buckminster Fuller, audiotape of lecture (Yale University Department of Architecture, September 26, 1952), BFP Series 17, Box 2, Reel 2e.

53 Fuller had described the "true planetarium" effect of superimposing a wire outline of the continents to the inside of a 20-foot-diameter steel wire three-quarter sphere like the one designed by Don Richter and assembled with Fuller in Lawrence, Long Island, in 1951. With the head of a 6-foot-tall person being at the exacter center of the sphere and the geography accurately aligned to that of the planet itself, it would for the first time give such a precise sense of orientation in the cosmos and of the Earth revolving that "I feel one of these ought to be installed in every school to help the young life get these proper orientations in their own right." Buckminster Fuller, audiotape of lecture (Detroit Museum, April 9, 1952), BFP Series 17, Box 1, Reel 1e.

54 "Fuller Notes Artist's Relation to the Pattern of Technology," *Cornell Daily Sun*, April 26, 1952.

55 Walter Johnson, "Architects Build Giant Experimental Sphere," *Cornell Daily Sun*, May 21, 1952.

56 "Aspen Conference on Design," *Fortune*, September 1952.

57 Dave Behrens, "Science or Symbolism ... A Reporter and a Visitor Speculate on Rand's Rooftop Sphere," *Cornell Daily Sun*, October 15, 1952.

information. Neon tubes and colored lights would provide a "spectacular display" of global events to be followed "like a great big baseball game," as Fuller told a reporter toward the end of 1955.[50] The transparent surface of the sphere, like the Manhattan Dome of 1959, has an inhabitable depth, hosting layers of information rather than people and producing continually evolving dynamic patterns. The proposal was well publicized in local newspapers and the June 1957 issue of *Architectural Record* summarized the recently completed three years of "preliminary studies" with a photomontage showing how the sphere would look floating above a Minnesota campus building alongside Wedin's rendering of how the final expanded version would look alongside the UN.[51] **fig. 15** The information ball would bounce from university experiment to permanent global center, expanding exponentially in size and sophistication.

The proposed pilot project above a campus rooftop was itself a development of the first prototype miniature Earth done at Cornell University in May 1952. Ten of Fuller's students, led by Sadao, had assembled a 20-foot-diameter, wooden geodesic sphere on the rooftop of the engineering school. **fig. 18** They painted it blue, covered it with chicken mesh, and wove in strips of bronze-colored screen to mark all the landmasses at the scale of 1:2,000,000. The sphere was propped up with Ithaca at the top to give it the same orientation as Earth and thereby "a true picture" of the planet when viewed from the inside. As soon as the basic wooden geodesic grid was finished, Fuller climbed inside and posed with a small globe in his hands marked with the same geodesic grid. **fig. 17** There is nothing accidental about the image. His head is suspended between two globes. He looks down on the surface of the smaller globe as if from outer space while standing inside the larger globe that will present the view through the same surface as if from the center of the planet. The blue of the wider sky resonated with the blue of the oceans on the more compact globe before the translucent landmasses were added to the wooden frame in a shimmering image that could be seen from all over the campus. When the see-through globe was complete, Fuller spent most of the day and the night on top of the ladder with his head at the center excitedly looking at movement of Earth relative to the Sun and the stars as if through a huge spherical helmet.[52] He had already described such a project for a 20-foot-diameter "true planetarium" with the viewer's head at its center in an April 9 lecture in Detroit, saying one should be installed in every school to provide proper orientation.[53] His opening public lecture at Cornell just two weeks later was devoted to the key role of the artist as "articulator of the great pattern,"[54] and the new sphere constructed at the intersection of art and science attracted considerable publicity.[55] Photographs were published in *Fortune* magazine alongside a sequence of images of Fuller energetically lecturing to the annual Aspen design conference.[56] Local and national newspapers covered it and speculated on its symbolic meaning.[57] The sphere was supposed to be a permanent installation but at the end of October, a week before *Life* magazine's extended photo shoot was to take place, seven students decided to move it to a quadrangle as a Halloween stunt. They climbed up a nearby elm tree, sawed through the wooden

Inside and Outside the Globe Simultaneously

17 RBF looking at globe inside prototype miniature Earth under construction, Cornell University, 1952

18 Students constructing prototype miniature Earth on rooftop, Cornell University, 1952

19 RBF with students beside 80-inch prototype Geoscope, Princeton University, published in *New York Times* article "Princeton Builds Large Globe Map," April 6, 1960

20 Prototype Geoscope with landmasses marked on plastic skin, Princeton, 1960

21 RBF inside 40-foot Tensegrity Sphere, Princeton University, 1953

17

18

19

20

21

tripod, and cut the securing wires. The "delicately balanced" 200-pound sphere fell to the roof, crushing the bottom third.[58] The university announced that it was damaged beyond repair and the original student team reassembled it as a hemisphere on a raised platform in a more accessible site to demonstrate Fuller's concept of geodesic structure rather than the Minni-Earth concept.[59]

In fact, the idea of the geodesic sphere and the idea of the Minni-Earth were inseparable. When fifteen students at Princeton University built the first large discontinuous Tensegrity Sphere out of aluminum struts a year later, for example, the 40-foot sphere suspended on wires outside the architecture school's laboratory building (with Fuller yet again posed inside it) was publicized as "a sort of scale model of the world, at 1:1,000,000."[60] **fig. 21** Fuller's spheres are always surrogate planets. Indeed, he described Earth itself as a Tensegrity Sphere. The sense of the planet as a solid has to be abandoned along with the very idea of solidity. Fuller promptly told the *New York Times* that the tensegrity principle exhibited at Princeton was the "characteristic structural principle of the universe" and that the floating sphere could easily contain an eight-room, two-story residence, once again linking the idea of house to the task of representing the universe.[61] The Geoscope simply exemplifies the overall mission to transform the discipline of architecture by reconfiguring the relationship between structure, image, and house—as became clear when the ongoing Minni-Earth project made another leap forward at Princeton in March 1960 and was called a "Geoscope" for the first time.

Twelve Princeton students constructed an 80-inch-diameter transparent sphere of plastic (suspended within an 84-inch-diameter aluminum geodesic frame) onto which the map of the world had been printed, with revolving sputniks to be added later and a baseball-sized Moon to be put on top of a building 213 feet away. **fig. 20** As soon as the basic structural frame was completed, but before the clear vinyl skin was installed inside it, Fuller once again had himself photographed beside it (both alone and with two of the students) for a series of newspaper statements promoting it as the largest and most accurate globe map in the Western world. **fig. 19** The ultimate goal was now a 200-foot version, with which "the dream of all geographers will be realized. A mapmaker will then be able to look on his globe and find a dot representing his house."[62] The ability for every

58 "Globe Atop Rand, Japes Scene of Vicious Pranks," *Cornell Daily Press*, November 7, 1952.

59 Taking the action to be that of a "fanatic" attempting to steal the project, the ten students who built it wrote to the editor of the local newspaper, noting the "considerable skill" with which their "inside-out planetarium" had been destroyed while lamenting the loss of "good publicity" for Cornell, the College of Architecture and, above all, Fuller. Letter of the Editor, *Cornell Daily Press*, November 7, 1952. The demolition experts were soon identified. They claimed to be unaware of the value of the sphere and offered to help reconstruct it but the sphere was seen to be beyond repair. See Axel Hochkoeppler, "Geodesic Design ... Architects to Remodel Sphere," *Cornell Daily Sun*, May 20, 1953.

60 "The Sphere of Ideas," *Princeton Alumni Weekly*, November 27, 1953.

61 "New Giant Sphere May Alter Homes: Princeton Architecture Project Aims to Bring About Lighter and Cheaper Housing," *New York Times*, November 15, 1953, 74.

62 Henry McLaughlin III, "Scientist Builds Model Earth in Princeton Lab," *The Daily Princetonian*, March 24, 1960.

63 "Princeton Builds a Large Globe Map," *New York Times*, April 7, 1960, 17.

64 "Your World: An Architect's Dream will Help You Understand It," *New York Herald Tribune This Week Magazine*, September 11, 1960, 16.

65 Buckminster Fuller to John McHale, 11 October 1961, John and Magda McHale private archive, Buffalo.

66 "It is not a practical matter for architectural students to make an inventory of world resources and to learn how to reorganize these total resources to the highest advantage." Buckminster Fuller, "Redesigning World Resources," *UIA: Review of the International Union of Architects*, no. 26 (April 1964), 27–29.

67 "SIU Staffer Builds Miniature Globe that Tells Story of Earth and Man," *The Daily Egyptian*, August 5, 1964, 8.

68 John McHale, "The Geoscope," *Architectural Design*, December 1964, 632.

house on the planet to be individually marked was already the crucial dimension of the project. The *New York Times* cited the prediction that the Princeton prototype would "help architects plan their work in a larger perspective."[63] Every future architectural project would be based on the patterns revealed on the ephemeral surface of the sphere. The little sphere carried a heavy load. The Sunday magazine of the *New York Herald Tribune* published a photograph of an excited couple looking up at the completed Geoscope hanging in the glass box of the laboratory of the School of Architecture, announcing that the globe with all the translucent landmasses floating in its geodesic plastic grid "may well revolutionize our understanding of the planet in which we live."[64]

The compact Princeton sphere would be the last test of the concept before Fuller's speech the following year in London trying to recruit all schools in the world. A few months after the speech, he told Monica Pidgeon that the priority for the first year would be the "design, maintenance and installation of a Geoscope for world planning controls."[65] When the proposal was eventually accepted by the UIA in 1962 with Pidgeon playing a key role in getting it approved, he looked forward to the next congress in Cuba to further the project. Because of the Cuban Missile Crisis, the event was partially diverted to Mexico City where Fuller, very unhappy not to be in Havana, returned to the concept in his keynote speech and later that year devoted chapters to the Geoscope in his 1963 book *Ideas and Integrities*, which was not by chance the first of his books to feature the new airbrushed image of the Manhattan Dome. Geodesic research was ultimately optical research.

The most sophisticated prototype of the Geoscope was produced a year later by eleven students at the University of Colorado under the supervision of John McHale, the director of the World Resources Inventory that had been launched in 1963 at Southern Illinois University in Carbondale to gather all the global data to be displayed on the new data visualization device—freeing architecture students to concentrate on the design of the device itself.[66] Fuller had already announced the need for such a data gathering and distribution center when in London for the UIA congress and persuaded McHale to join him at Carbondale, where he had received his first permanent professorship in 1959. McHale became a full-time faculty member in early 1962. Within a year, his students had made a very schematic, unpublished 9-foot-diameter model of a Geoscope but the more compact, high-resolution Colorado Geoscope that was unveiled in the amphitheater at the Aspen Design Conference in August 1964 was considerably more advanced.[67] **fig. 22** McHale published an article on this prototype for a "giant spherical television screen" a few months later in *Architectural Design*.[68] As when Fuller had first published the Dymaxion Map as a do-it-yourself globe kit in a 1943 issue of *Life* magazine, McHale's team had folded the map into an icosahedron. **fig. 23** It was formed by twenty triangles of sandwiched layers of plexiglass with the oceans in blue and the land in white. Layers of information on Mylar sheets were inserted between the two layers of these triangular surfaces or above and below them on additional surfaces supported by telescoping extension tubes. **fig. 25** This accumulated layering of plastic "data planes" (along with hinged planes at right angles providing sectional information where needed) produced a complex record of atmospheric, ground, underwater, and subterranean conditions. The information could be scrutinized from outside or by stepping inside where there was room for one person to put their head and the effect was like an all-plastic data helmet offering a spherical multidimensional image. **fig. 24** The Dean of the School of Architecture at Colorado happily described this data visualization device as "architecture in the broadest sense."[69] It prototyped a new conception of architecture as fluid pattern. The Geoscope was both a scientific instrument and the projector of a new kind of artistic image to be broadcast to a global audience.

If Fuller cultivated "total design," the title of one of McHale's first essays on him in 1958, the Geoscope clearly aspires to be a total work of art, an image of the whole world that approaches the detail of the world.[70] Not by chance, McHale had been an artist in London in the fifties and first met Fuller when studying under Josef Albers at Yale in 1956. He became Fuller's main propagandist in Europe, with a series of essays after returning to London that year, facilitating the 1961 UIA intervention, and curating the 1962 exhibition at the American Embassy that launched the iconic image of the Manhattan Dome. While McHale was supervising the Geoscope project at Colorado, his speaker bio for the annual Conference on World Affairs there in April 1964 symptomatically listed him as a "designer artist and writer" who is currently "a Research Associate with the World Resources Inventory."[71] The inventory project was itself the engine of a computer-generated artwork, an attempt to visualize pattern in data that is "slow to become visible to man."

Twelve years of Geoscope research had gathered momentum and the planned exhibition of prototypes at the 1965 UIA congress took place in the Tuileries Gardens in Paris with contributions from seventeen different schools displayed around the Colorado Geoscope and a 20-foot-diameter transparent plastic Geoscope by the University of Nottingham that again visitors could put their head inside to use as a kind of information helmet **fig. 26** Two months before the exhibition, Fuller had prepared a text that described the way the new device brings the invisible world into visibility as a political earthquake. It pretended that the whole impetus, title, rationale, and organization of the Geoscope project derived from the students themselves.[72] Fuller went out of his way to insist that the project had nothing to do with technocracy, the idea of "an engineer's dictatorship" born in the Depression years, which he regarded as highly suspect and unthinkable, as engineers make poor politicians. He is often retroactively criticized for being a technocrat through his early friendships with leading members of the technocracy group and his lifelong associations with the

69 Dean Devon Carlson, quoted in "For a World View: Prototype 'Minni-Earth' Built by Architects," *The Colorado Alumnus*, June 1964. "The inventory [of information in the globe] deals with every kind of resource available to man, including man himself. That is what architects deal with every day." Ibid.

70 John McHale, "Total Design," *Architecture and Building*, July 1958.

71 "Speaker Bios for Seventeenth Annual World Affairs Conference April 13–17, 1964," University of Colorado.

72 Buckminster Fuller, *In the Tuileries Garden* (self-published 8-page brochure), May 1965, 2. Even more remarkably, Fuller would later say that the whole Design Decade was the idea of the students "There is actual activity under way in what they call the 'Design Decade,' which is five two-year increments of progressive design activity initiative by the students, not being told what to do." Buckminster Fuller, "An Address, given at the 2nd Annual Meeting of the Industrial Designers Society," *Journal of Environmental Design* 2, no. 2 (1967): 21.

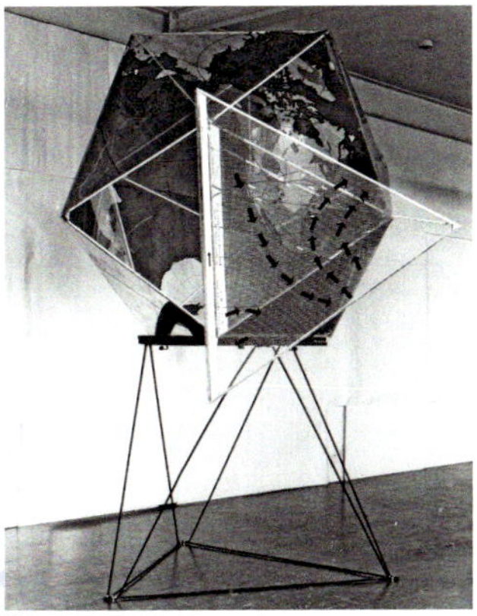

22

Life Presents
R. BUCKMINSTER FULLER'S
DYMAXION WORLD

23

24

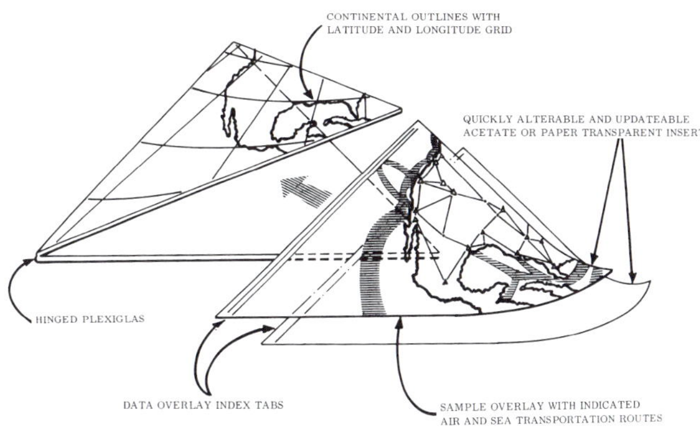

25

26

The Geoscope as Heads-Up Display

22 Geoscope, University of Colorado, 1964

23 RBF holding Dymaxion globe, *Life*, March 1943

24 Student inside Colorado Geoscope, 1964

25 Insertion of transparent "data planes" into Colorado Geoscope, *Architectural Design*, December 1964

26 Head inside university of Nottingham Geoscope, Tuileries Gardens, Paris, 1965, in *Unesco Courier*, July–August 1965

military, big business, big media, and transnational organizations—along with his belief in the capacity of singular technical designs to circumvent political problems. Usually overlooked is the fact that he had explicitly opposed technocracy since his early writings and repeatedly called for radical forms of bottom-up collaborative decision making.[73] Yet the very decision to make a technical instrument act as the medium for this democratic process and the basic concept of the instrument comes from Fuller himself. He had always called for "self-captaincy" and the Geoscope project was precisely the attempt to give citizens the kind of information a genuinely collaborative self-captaincy needs to steer the planet but the project itself was clearly steered by him alone.

The original speech to the UIA in London calling for architects to rise above politics insisted that "the students themselves tend always to transcend political bias."[74] In a complex identification that marked all his work as he only ever did projects with students, Fuller projected himself onto the students, imagining that he saw the world with their eyes. He saw himself as exposing rather than imposing and even argued that the students of the sixties could carry out the necessary "revolution" because they were the first generation "to be raised by the *third parent*—television," and were therefore the first generation to "now think only in terms of the world."[75] The generation that sees the world through television is building the ultimate television set to overcome the barrier between scientists and the public, trying to avert the imminent destruction of the planet through nuclear war triggered by conventional politics and conventional disciplinary specialization. Fuller insisted on the urgent practical necessity of utopia. "Utopia or Oblivion" quickly became one of his mantras and the title of one of his books. The Geoscope is a utopian project for a new form of realism.

THE ART OF THE INVISIBLE

When the world *Geoscope* was being used for the first time to describe the concept at Princeton University, Fuller asked the engineer Donald Moore to determine the electronic needs for a 200-foot-diameter version in March 1960. Moore had temporarily left his job with the Radio Corporation of America, where he worked on circuit design for color television and radar, having just completed projects for the Home Electronic Center automat-

73 In 1932 Fuller appreciated the "time-energy-studies" of the technocrats but was already criticizing the "distasteful insinuations about iron-hand dictatorship which, aside from its incompatibility to the evolutionary trend, is transitionally impossible of establishment in the US without much machinegunning and gassing, which the current personnel of their staff seems unsuited to command." Buckminster Fuller, "Putting the House in Order," *Shelter* 2, no. 5 (November 1932): 6. In 1938 Fuller added that technocracy would always fail because it "made no allowance for passion, fashion, chance, change, intuition, the mysticism of harmony, and most of all, for—*'it happens'*" along with "the essential major forces" of speculation, initiative, superstition and emotion. He counters with a call for the equal distribution of energy that allows for "active self-captaincy." Fuller, *Nine Chains to the Moon*, 102–104 (see note 7).
74 Fuller, "The Architect as World Planner," 235 (see note 38).
75 Fuller, *In the Tuileries Garden*, 2 (see note 72).
76 Moore had visited Southern Illinois University six months earlier to discuss the Autonomous Dwelling Project, along with another RCA Whirlpool engineer. Harold Cohen to Buckminster Fuller, 23 May 1959, BFP Series 2, Box 103, Folder 9. Whirlpool then hired Fuller as a consultant, with Moore as the liaison. "We feel we are ready for more discussion on Min-Max-Fam-Fax and the use of the tetrahedron. We have been using these in describing various systems and would like to perfect our use of these powerful tools." Donald G. Moore to Buckminster Fuller, 4 November 1959. BFP Series 2, Box 105, Folder 7.
77 D. G. Moore, "Preliminary Investigation of Electronics for the R. B. Fuller Geoscope Information Display," March 31, 1960, BFP Series 18, Box 110, Folder 3.
78 Donald G. Moore to Mr. W. L. LePage, Franklin Institute, 18 September 1960, BFP Series 18, Box 110, Folder 4, p. 7.
79 Ibid., 8.
80 John McHale to Monica Pidgeon, 20 October 1961, John and Magda McHale private archive, Buffalo. McHale reported that the electronic scanning facility concept was under review by RCA and the Ford Foundation.
81 Don Moore, "Geoscope," final draft dated October 15, 1961, BFP Series 18, Box 110, Folder 4, p. 8.

ing every dimension of domestic life.[76] His preliminary investigation, developed in consultation with his colleagues at the RCA laboratories in Princeton, called for ten million pixels of resolution with one lamp and magnetic storage unit per pixel lining the inner surface of the sphere to construct the image that could be seen from inside or outside.[77] Each million lamps would need two thousand wires to control them and the system would perform better than a television since only updates to particular pixels would be made rather than refreshing the whole image thirty times a second. This system, which had recently been developed by RCA and first published in the November 1958 *Proceedings of the Institute of Radio Engineers*, would enable the Geoscope to use the variable intensity in each pixel to produce a seamless half-tone picture without the pixels' being evident from the center of the sphere. **fig. 27**

Moore and Fuller soon imagined the formation of a "Dymaxion Institute" to carry out the task. Radio receivers and the human brain are limited in the range of frequencies and signal strengths that they can tune in to, so a Conning Tower Facility would need to be built to widen the respective bandwidths of body and electronics on the way to a full-fledged Geoscope that would "allow us to use our brains to the fullest extent possible in solving our many complex problems."[78] This in turn would allow an automated geodesic education system by organizing "the aggregate of all man's apprehended and communicated experiences into a geometric pattern" that could be transmitted onto each student's private television screen with the computer monitoring and responding to the student's responses.[79] The huge television set would give birth to countless little ones dispersed around the world in a single endlessly pulsating network.

Such a "'Geoscope' electronic scanning facility" would form the heart of a Geoscope science headquarters to house architectural world planning activity that Fuller and McHale described to Monica Pidgeon after the overall initiative had been presented in London the following year.[80] Moore promoted the concept to the organizers of a proposed International Science Center in Berlin. He sent the final version of his report along with an extended summary of Fuller's arguments, saying that the computer-driven electronic image would not be on when people enter the sphere, just the world map inscribed on the semitransparent surface of the sphere. People would become aware that their home planet is a spaceship before the computers were activated to feed the much more sophisticated technology of the brain itself: "The Geoscope's dynamic electronic display is intended to bring more of the patterns affecting mankind in significant ways into comprehensible focus of the most powerful tool of all, the human brain."[81] The point of the image is not the visible content but the brain's unique ability to recognize complex patterns within the image. The task of the Geoscope is simply to bring all the unseen data into the "conceptual tuning range" of the human body. It is meant to be an extension of the human body's own radio.

It is in terms of this brain expansion ambition that the 1965 exhibition of prototype Geoscopes in the Tuileries Garden was faithfully publicized by *Architectural Design* in two articles but described there as "not as striking as Fuller may have wished."[82] **fig. 29** He denied this and circulated enthusiastic reports, but even the best Geoscope prototype produced at Colorado fell far short of the dream. McHale had already worked with students at Carbondale to film the dynamic trends in human population since 4000 BC at 30 years per second against the Dymaxion Map as an alternative test of the "dramatic picture" the Geoscope should present. Ideally the data would be electronically recorded and retransmitted by precisely mapping it to coordinates on the triangular surfaces on which it is displayed, thereby enabling his small Geoscope to be linked by radio in real time to similar ones in schools around the world. He used film to model the future of television. With each successive prototype, Fuller and McHale ended up focusing on alternative technologies of representation, studying multiprojection devices, flat-screen data displays, triangular-faced television tubes, new kinds of photography, multislide machines, microfilm, 8 mm cinema units, videotape mechanisms for film or data storage, and so on. They deployed state-of-the-art image making, storing, and distribution while dreaming of the 200-foot version that would be made possible by much more advanced forms of computer and display.

The vision of an all-powerful computer that had driven the project since the early fifties started to be realized in 1963 when the World Resources Inventory used the computers at the University of Southern Illinois to coordinate and expand all the data from Fuller's previous attempts to make an inventory of global resources.[83] McHale even published some of the IBM computer cards recording the data, the computer code being used, and the resulting printout.[84] **fig. 28** An idealistic image of a computer network underpinned the series of six reports that he produced for the Inventory between 1963 and 1966. The emergent world of networked information technology acted as the paradigm. The 1965 outline of the ten-year timetable for the whole project repeated Fuller's basic argument since the late twenties by calling for a phase devoted to "general extension of dynamic network operating principles into formerly 'static' areas of environmental control both internal and external."[85] Immobile solid objects had to give way to dispersed ever-evolving networks. McHale elaborated the point a year later when giving more detail on the timetable. He insisted on the transformative prosthetic extension of the body and the mind with the latest technologies. This "organic extension" of the human species is exemplified by communication electronics and the computer. Their exponential miniaturization toward invisibility and increase in power approached the "dimensional complexity and performance per unit of nature itself."[86] The representation and what was represented were seen to be merging. The ability to gather and coordinate vast amounts of

82 "Outsize UIA Congress," *Architectural Design*, August 1965.
83 The data had been collected unofficially in Fuller's personal archives since 1917, was named "Inventory of World Resources" in 1927, updated and officially presented in reports for the World Copper Industry between 1936 and 1938, updated again for *Fortune* magazine special issues in 1940 and the Board of Economic Warfare from 1942 to 1944. Eventually the files were moved to Fuller's office at Southern Illinois University.
84 John McHale, "Data Conversion and Per Capitalizing Program Report," in *World Design Science Decade 1965–1975, Phase 1, Document 1: Inventory of World Resources, Human Trends and Needs*, 64 (see note 31).
85 "The Five Two-Year Increment Phases of the Ten-Year World Facilities Redesign," in *World Design Science Decade 1965–1975, Phase 1, Document 1: Inventory of World Resources, Human Trends and Needs*, 108 (see note 31).
86 "Tool Evolution," in *World Design Science Decade 1965–1975, Phase 1, Document 4: The Ten-Year Program*, ed. John McHale (Carbondale: Southern Illinois University, 1965), 69.

27

Data Architecture

27 Illustration of RCA pixel technology for Geoscope in 1960 report by Donald Moore

28 Computer punch card from World Resources Inventory Project published by John Mchale in 1963

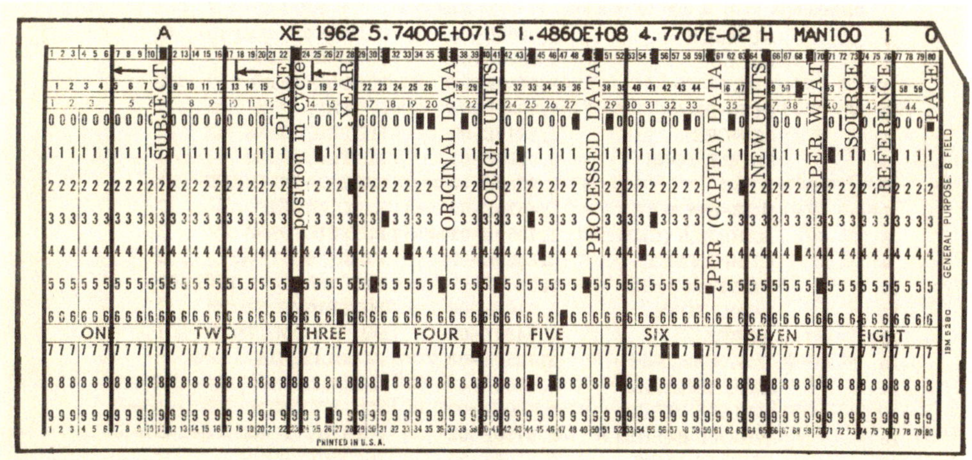

28

29

29 RBF photographed inside Colorado Geoscope, Tuileries Gardens, Paris, 1965, by Monica Pidgeon

30 Electronic organism on the cover of special issue on "The Computer Age," *Fortune*, March 1964

30

information supposedly would enable the designer to deal once again with the "design of the whole."[87] McHale echoed arguments made at some recent conferences and a number of 1964 features in architectural magazines on the possible transformative role of computers in design and their wider promotion in mass circulation journals like a recent series on "The Computer Age" in *Fortune*. **fig. 30** He argued that sketching directly onto a display with a light-pen would soon allow design work to be done on a computer that would then directly control the production and distribution of whatever was being drawn. The computerized designer would become an "overall 'systems' and 'pattern' creator."[88]

Once again, the dominant criterion is aesthetic. It is all a question of pattern. Science makes possible a new form of art. Or rather, science is the means of art's survival in an exponentially expanding and confusing world, the way of detecting or imposing pattern on unseen or apparently chaotic flows. Despite the computer, humans are needed to recognize the patterns. Fuller used the third document in the series, on *Comprehensive Thinking*, to advise "the design-science artist" that the technological extension of the human body into the farthest reaches of the electromagnetic spectrum would lead to a historical era of "invisible architecture" that is only detectable by an aesthetic instinct located somewhere between the unconscious and the conscious. His model of this instinct is the appreciation of the female body: "the subconscious measuring capability of man's eye to judge, at considerable distances, to a sixty-fourth of an inch accuracy, the diameter of the female leg."[89] Throughout his career, Fuller employed sexual analogies. *Hook-up* is his term both for sex and for prosthetic expansion of the body through networked tools. The world of high technology is itself an erotically charged body. When the essay goes on to describe his work on the "ecological problems" of lightweight geodesic domes, it is as if the goal of comprehensive design is a spontaneous discharge of sexual energy in the face of a visual image that walks right out of the nonvisual realm of calculation:

87 Ibid., 72.
88 Ibid., 74.
89 Buckminster Fuller, "The Prospect for Humanity," in *World Design Science Decade 1965–1975, Phase 1, Document 3: Comprehensive Thinking*, ed. John McHale (Carbondale: Southern Illinois University, 1965), 74. The article was originally published as a set of three articles in *Saturday Review*, August 29, September 19, and October 3, 1964.
90 Ibid., 75.
91 When McHale revised his article on the Geoscope for publication in the *World Science Decade* document series, he also published a text giving more emphasis to "large interlinked facilities data processing systems spread over a continent and with possible international hookups," "world networks" and "educational service networks," and "the continuing global spread and vast interlinkages of such computerized communications and control systems." John McHale, "The Service Industries," in *World Design Science Decade 1965–1975, Phase 1, Document 4: The Ten-Year Program*, 79 (see note 86).
92 "The local university may be considered as already functioning as part of a large network extending around the Earth. Within this net, ideas, discoveries and new configurations of knowledge are constantly in flow. It may be viewed as a kind of extension of the individual intellectual consciousness into a global consciousness." John McHale, "Toward a World University," in *World Design Science Decade 1965–1975, Phase 1, Document 4: The Ten-Year Program*, 100 (see note 86).
93 John McHale, "Information Explosion—Knowledge Implosion," *Campus Dialogue* 1, no. 8 (1966): 1. In the same year, Fuller was trying to set up a "World Man" conference in a dome in Cyprus, with the Geoscope referred to in the press releases. "Statement Issued by President Makarios at the Presidential Palace in Nicosia, Cyprus," July 7, 1966, sent by Fuller to Arthur Drexler. Buckminster Fuller file, Department of Architecture and Design archives, MoMA.
94 Ibid.
95 "In discussing the mind, I find it helpful to think back to my earlier formative experience as an artist. In art, in creative work, the mind often seems to work best when you are least conscious of it. [...] Progressively, we are off-loading the mind from functions for which it is not the best instrument. [...] Turning over much of our mental functioning to computers and other kinds of instruments. [...] You have to learn to work with your mind almost as a self-directive organism—in which you occupy the cockpit but do only part of the steering." John McHale, "The Future of the Mind: A Dialogue with Futurist John McHale," *University Review* (State University of New York) 3, no. 3 (1970): 8–13, here, 8. "Let's go back to the case of the artist. A visual artist places himself in the position of trying to receive as much stimuli in the visual environment as possible. He's striving in a sense for information overload and his reaction is to increase his pattern recognition as he confronts the disorder of his environment. [...] Using the analogy of the artist, our own period can be characterized particularly by disorder. I'm suggesting that much of that disorder, rather than being negatively connoted as in future shock, may be much more positive [...] a period of creative disorder." Ibid., 10.

> I deal with the hows of mathematics and economics, the hows of industrial production and distribution, assembly, and service. I don't even consider how any structure is going to look until after it is finished. If, when finished, the structure seems beautiful, I know it is all right. To me 'beautiful' apparently emerges as an ejaculation, spontaneously released by my total set of subconscious control coordinates. 'Beautiful' is probably ejaculated when my entire chromosomic neuron bank is momentarily in 'happy' correspondence with my entire experience (memory) neurons bank. I speak of my brain as if it were a computer. It is.[90]

A massive computer would likewise enable the Geoscope to extend the gaze beyond the visual, offering a visual image of the nonvisual world's architecture, an image as intoxicating as a well-organized chart, a veritable erotics of statistics. The computer is to be the basis of a barely visible yet deeply attractive architecture.

McHale argued that the Geoscope would take advantage of the networks that exist "embryonically" in universities, libraries, international agencies, and communications infrastructures to actively transform such institutions and deemphasize the role of buildings in an age in which cities and buildings have become but "terminals" in global computerized communication and control networks.[91] The network itself would become the architecture of a new kind of university that extends individual consciousness into global consciousness.[92] In a 1966 essay on the possibility of a global university orchestrated by communications satellites, transistor radios, telephones, and television sets, McHale again echoed Fuller in speculating that computers will facilitate the emergence of "world men" who "are not confused by the explosion of information about the Earth and its peoples but are able to conceptualize this whole as easily as one previously conceptualized one's hometown, neighbors and surrounding country."[93] The computer is the new means of domesticating the planet, satisfying the old demand for information to be converted into knowledge by being "simply and elegantly structured into new conceptual form."[94] The scientific project is again an aesthetic project. The computer is the new artistic medium. It is the "elegance" of the intellectual structure that counts.

It is not by chance that McHale turned to his own "formative" experience as an artist when advocating the transference of most mental functioning to globally interconnected computers to engage with the emergent planetary community. He insisted on the creative uses of unconscious perception and the artist's capacity to recognize pattern in disorderly environments.[95] Likewise, Fuller explicitly conceived the Geoscope as a mechanism for blurring the distinction between science and art. His original promotion of the project to the UIA called on the hybrid figure of the "scientist/artist." Just as the World Resources Inventory got under way at Carbondale, he submitted a text to a local student magazine describing himself as operating at the "threshold between art and science." He recalled that the images of the original Dymaxion House that had been designed only for mechanical performance were rebuffed by engineers and economists who said "women won't like it; to me it is aesthetically repulsive" yet the same images were enthusiastically embraced by artists, gallerists, and art critics, who "acclaimed my work on aesthetic grounds."[96] A dedication to science produces art and, in reverse, art can make possible new science. In 1954 Fuller stressed that art "embraces order without conscious measurement." The viewer senses order through "intuitive aesthetics, borderline tuning and feedback amplification" by feeling a desire to look in greater detail.[97] The plastic surface of the Geoscope is meant to trigger this desire, acting as a means for crossing the line between conscious and unconscious.

The whole project is finally nothing more than an attempt to transform the communication networks into an artwork. It reproduces, at the level of image, what is already in operation in numerous systems. In Fuller's hands, the diffuse architecture of the network, no longer easily distinguishable from the planet it wraps, is transformed into a singular aesthetic object. Even the technical drawings and analysis of the sphere have to be considered as artworks. They mark the obsolescence of preelectronic forms of building and urbanism itself. McHale once again echoed Fuller in arguing that when "the dissemination of knowledge has become established on a true *frequency modulation* basis as a form of radio, one may literally 'tune in' on knowledge" and the city would become "but one type of *way station* in an extended social and communication net."[98] Not by chance he became increasingly interested in "instant cities" when working on the Geoscope.[99] A few years later, he described the arrival of a phase of such transitory cities inaugurated by electronics, in which "a center can be anywhere—even in orbit around the earth."[100] Buildings and cities must be as mobile and ephemeral as the nomadic clusters of information that endlessly circulate. Indeed, they are constructed out of that information. The overlapping networks define a new space, a global ecology of subliminal rhythms and flows whose shape can only be made visible through the Geoscope's artistic synthesis of the information pouring in through its infinitely extended sensors. Fuller's original concept of the house as wireless interface constructed within a global communication net turns the net itself into an image that can be occupied.

TECHNICOLOR SURVEILLANCE

As Fuller and McHale's discussion of the Geoscope repeatedly acknowledged, the network, like the computer itself and the whole concept of systems analysis, is a military invention. The NORAD (North American Aerospace Defense Command) Center constructed inside a mountain in Colorado, with its colossal "Iconorama" display screens for online tracking of global troop movements and missile paths, acted as a key model for

96 Buckminster Fuller, "Art-Science Threshold," *Parallax*, no. 5 (1962): unpaginated.
97 Cited in John Dixon to Gyorgy Kepes, 20 December 1954, John McHale Papers.
98 McHale, "The Services Industry," 87, 91 (see note 91).
99 See for example, John McHale to Serge Chermayeff, 28 October 1964, which describes the idea of "instant cities" after discussing the progress on the University of Colorado Geoscope and the plans for the forthcoming exhibition during the UIA congress in Paris at which he and Fuller hope that Yale could participate. Serge Chermayeff Papers, Department of Drawings and Archives, Avery Architectural and Fine Arts Library, Columbia University.
100 John McHale, "The Future City(s): Notes on a Typology," in *The Postindustrial City*, ed. William Weismantel (Albuquerque: University of New Mexico Press, 1969), 92.
101 Barry Katz, "The Arts of War: 'Visual Presentation' and National Intelligence," *Design-Issues* 12, no. 2 (Summer 1996): 3–21, here, 5.
102 Arthur Krock, "The War in Pictures: Lighted, Marked Globe May Keep Top Officials Posted," *New York Times*, October 8, 1941, 4.

the Geoscope. **fig. 31** Even the scale of the sphere was taken from the resolution of the film used by the US Air Force in its ongoing Cold War project to produce a complete map of Earth's geography through a mosaic of aerial photographs, a map accurate enough to organize blind military operations. But there is another model that Fuller does not discuss. The NORAD display was itself derivative of displays that he had worked on during the war.

In 1941 Fuller had become part of a secret team of artists, filmmakers, designers, and architects (including John Ford, Raymond Loewy, Walter Teague, Henry Dreyfuss, Norman Bel Geddes, Louis Kahn, Bertrand Goldberg, Lewis Mumford, and Walt Disney) working for the Visual Presentation Branch of the newly formed Office of Strategic Services (OSS), the predecessor of the CIA. Their mission was to design a Presidential Situation Room that would coordinate and efficiently present "a panorama of concentrated information" during a war. Based on the principle that a picture conveys much more than a thousand words, the proposed two-story windowless space contained a central semicircular auditorium filled with numerous presentation devices, including semitransparent screens on which information could be projected from front and back, statistical charts in fluctuating panels of light, television monitors, topographic models, three-dimensional displays, and new forms of animation. The design for the building, code-named Q-2, was approved at the end of 1941, but the Combined Chiefs of Staff promptly asked for the same devices to be installed in their own buildings. Eventually they decided that their already proposed Situation Rooms would suffice and by June 1942 the spaces were under construction.

Interestingly, the team had been called in to elaborate a preliminary design by its leader, the Hollywood moviemaker Merian Cooper that was, as Barry Katz's study of the Visual Presentation Branch notes, "dominated by an immense illuminated globe on which could be projected everything from weather fronts and oil fields to the disposition of land, air, and naval forces."[101] Excited by the idea, the OSS publicized it in an October 1941 issue of the *New York Times*. "The War in Pictures" describes how the "huge globe, lighted from within" can make visible all the tactical, economic, and political consequences of any military action "blocked out in vivid color and measured in large numerals." A dense mobile image of all available facts can then be presented to the "tired mind" of the president: "If this ambitious hope matures, the light within the globe can be adjusted so that these pictures of facts will be projected in successive sets and in Technicolor. The sum will be an easy statement for the eye of the war's status quo."[102]

Is Fuller responsible for the idea of the illuminated globe as dynamic data display, or is the Geoscope project derivative of that idea? He may well have been involved in the formulation of the concept since he was an acknowledged pioneer in the presentation of global statistics, and most of the design team had long been friends and collaborated on projects like the 1939 World's Fair in New York. It is significant, given Fuller's eagerness to identify the origin of so many ideas with himself, that on the one occasion he spoke of the genesis of the Geoscope project, he located it in 1952 with the first "Minni-Earth." But the only crucial distinction between the Geoscope and the original design for the illuminated globe in the Situation Room is the transparency of the sphere that allows the entire surface to be seen in one glance and the option to view it from the inside, to literally inhabit the image. In fact, the illuminated globe was never built for the Situation Rooms. Information was simply projected onto a large curved steel map on which magnetized symbols could also be moved. The War Department did commission six 50-inch (1:10,000,000) globes "designed as a tool for strategic military purposes." Calibrated by fifty geographers and cartographers, they were the largest and most accurate in the world. Franklin D. Roosevelt, Winston Churchill, and each of the military services received one by the end of 1942. **fig. 32** The remaining globe went on display for two weeks at the Museum of Modern Art in the August 1943 exhibition *Airways to Peace: An Exhibition of Geography for the Future*, a show based on the thought that "there are no distant points in the world any longer [...] peace must be planned on a world basis."[103] Fuller was again involved. He had even introduced his Dymaxion Map in a March 1943 issue of *Life* by presenting the triangulated Dymaxion Globe alongside the "President's Big Globe," insisting that it met the same strategic objective of a "visually correct picture."[104] **fig. 33** Symptomatically, the previous issue of *Life* had featured a color spread on the "military holy of holies," the recently completed Situation Rooms.[105] The roots of the Geoscope are clearly to be found in the military command and control center.

The Situation Room project is the hidden context of Fuller's April 1955 letter to the commander of the Air Technical Intelligence Center of the US Air Force attempting to raise money for the Minni-Earth research then under way at the University of Minnesota. The letter gives a complete discussion of the concept, specifying the role of the computer in coordinating the input (from photoelectric cells and radar sites around the world) and networking the sphere to a series of identical "repeaters" in other centers using radio so that people would be able to study the same image on their spherical televisions in multiple places at the same time. The Minni-Earth would itself be a radio network broadcasting the patterns within "vast information" stored through IBM cards and printed circuits. The ability to see the comprehensive picture is the key to strategic and technical advantage in a time of peace. But these patterns cannot be detected by the computers that make them available: "It is all very well to have machines integrating details, but only humans may comprehend the significance *to humans* of the unprecedented, emergent, integrating, synergetic patterns."[106] The letter seeks more funding to develop the electronic interface to enable human perceptions and judgment.

No funding was forthcoming, but the Minnesota students completed a design for its installation at the Pentagon in addition to the one in

103 Wendell L. Willkie, cited in press release for *Airways to Peace* exhibition, MoMA, June 25, 1943.
104 "*Life* Presents R. Buckminster Fuller's Dymaxion World," *Life*, March 1, 1943, 42.
105 "US High Command Plans Strategy in Map-Filled Sanctum," *Life*, February 22, 1943, 72.
106 Buckminster Fuller to General Harold E. Watson, 19 April 1955, 9; Marquand Library rare books collection, Princeton University.

31

32

Globe Power

31 Iconorama display systems at Combat Operations Center at the NORAD headquarters in Colorado Springs, CO, 1964

32 President Roosevelt and 50-inch globe in the Oval Office, 1942

33 Photograph of Dymaxion Globe in *Life*, March 1943

33

Manhattan.[107] The electronic projection screens used at NORAD to monitor the real-time data coming in from the ever-widening net of Radomes from 1960 on huge maps became the role model for Fuller and McHale. But elsewhere they promoted the Geoscope's antimilitary capacity. The first proposal to the UIA in 1961, for example, repeats Fuller's career-long call to displace scientific research from "weaponry" to "livingry."[108] His 1932 issues of *Shelter* already treated his navy experience as both a model for design-science and for the need to divert valuable resources and intelligence away from the military. The Geoscope accomplishes this by understanding the communication networks of the military as a form of ecological sensitivity, where ecology includes all forms of technology. Fuller even advertises its peacemaking capacity in providing a real-time display of the global deployment of military forces and equipment immediately outside all the ambassadors' windows at the United Nations building. The technologies of command and control are to be turned against themselves by putting television on steroids.

THE ULTIMATE WINDOW

Fuller never stopped looking for hyperpublic sites for the Geoscope, and was undaunted by repeated rejections. The late 1957 proposal for a reduced 60-foot-diameter version in the 1958 Brussels World's Fair was as unsuccessful as the proposal to the UN. Just after the Princeton experiment in 1960 there was yet another failed attempt to persuade the organizers of the 1964 World's Fair in New York that a full-scale 200- or 400-foot version could be placed on helium bags or float in a pool of water located on Belmont Island in the East River during the fair before being pulled to locations all over the world by helicopters. In one version visitors would occupy an "orbiting space car," a glass sphere that would move along a track in the space between the animated surface of the planet and an animated map of the stars on the perforated "celestial sphere" at the edge of Earth's atmosphere—as if moving inside the moving image.[109] **figs. 34 and 35** In October 1961 there had been hope that it would become part of the proposed International Science Center in Berlin. It then became the orphaned centerpiece of the initial October 1964 proposal with McHale and Sadao for the US Pavilion at Expo 67, in which visitors were to ascend by elevator to a set of balconies under a vast truss resting on four pylons. **figs. 36–38** They would hover between the triangulated space frame above and the triangulated map below, as if having temporarily left the world in order to see it as a single dynamic image continuously responding to real-time data and their own collaborative inputs through computer terminals. A later version had the visitors ringing the interior of a 400-foot dome. Suspended above them, a glowing 100-foot Minni-Earth would be wired with computer-driven lightbulbs capable of displaying the data from the

107 "Fuller Group Completes Study of Geodesic 'Minni-Earth,'" *Architectural Record* 121, no. 7 (June 1957): 16.
108 McHale notes that the "most sophisticated systems for reviewing world data are employed mainly in weaponry" and that no similar investment has been made in "livingry." McHale, "The Geoscope," 633 (see note 68).
109 The design of the proposal was prepared by James Fitzgibbon at the Raleigh node, with a set of drawings dated March 1960; BFP Series 18, Box 107, Folder 11.

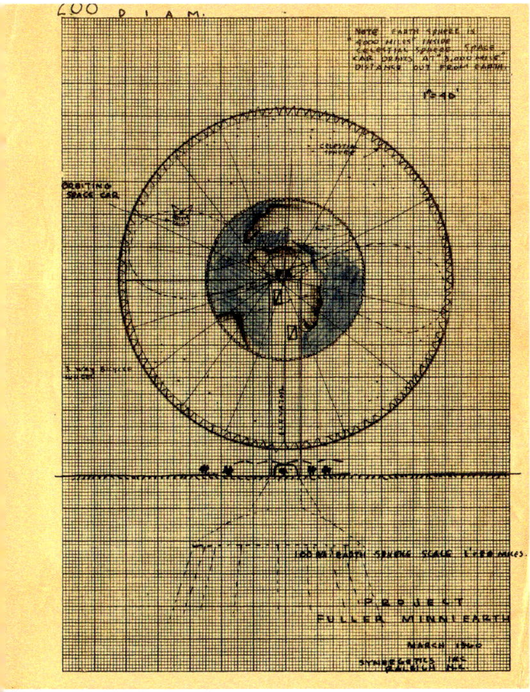

34

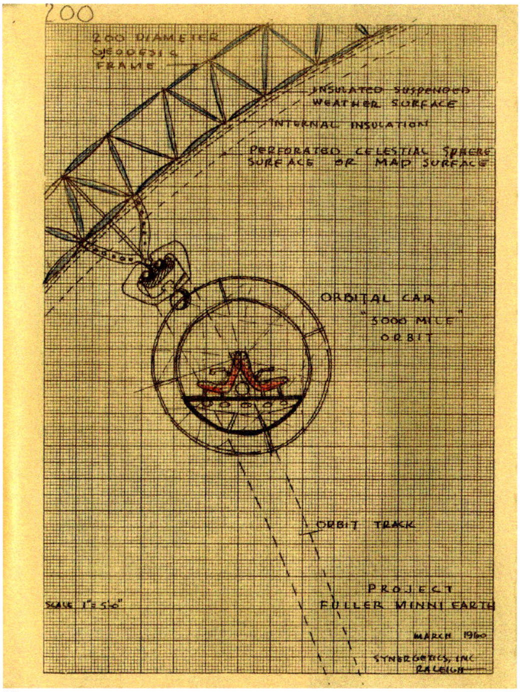

35

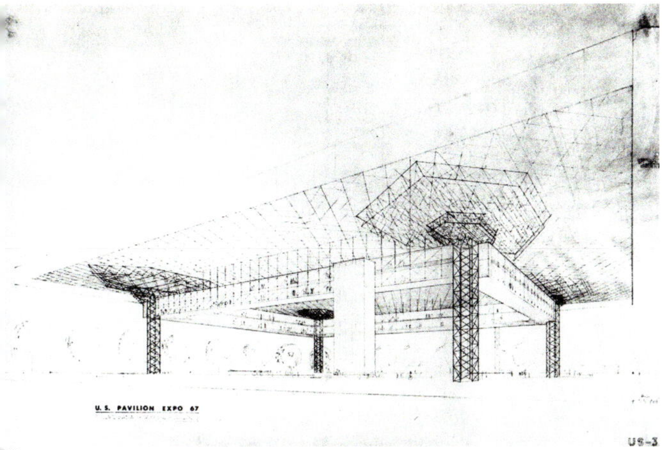

36

Interface as Public Space

34 Section of Fuller Minni-Earth proposal by James Fitzgibbon, March 1960

35 Section of "Orbital Car" in Fuller Minni-Earth proposal by James Fitzgibbon, March 1960

36 Geodesic truss covering map in original proposal for Expo 67 and containing television scanning for map, October/November 1964

37 Balconies overlooking Dymaxion Map in original proposal for Expo 67

38 Computer control panel in original proposal for Expo 67

37

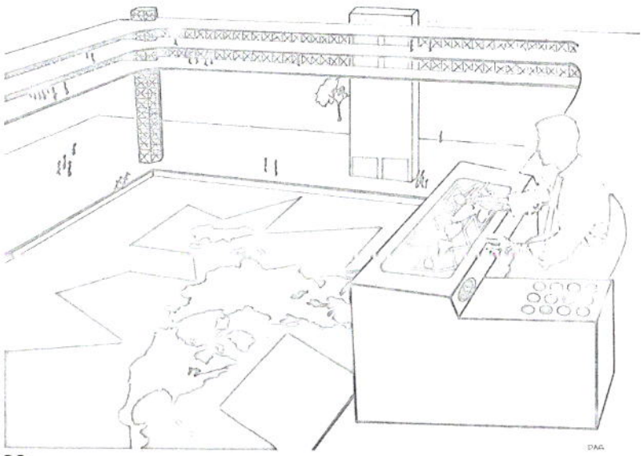

38

world inventory. The surface of this sphere would gradually turn into an icosahedron with twenty triangular facets which in turn would split along some of its edges before "the whole surface opens mechanically as an orange's skin or an animal's skin might be peeled carefully in one piece,"[110] progressively flattening itself out while descending to the floor. The spectators again end up looking down on a football-field-sized Dymaxion Map that displays global flows of resources, interacting with the huge image via numerous graphic display consoles mounted on the balconies that activate the "extraordinary computer facility" in the basement with unprecedented detail in the image like the movement of every airplane and ship being displayed in real time.

The Geoscope project was from the beginning based on this fluidity between plane and sphere, a fluidity at the heart of Fuller's geodesic geometry. Just as the crisscrossing wooden members of the first Geoscope at Cornell were assembled on the flat surface of a rooftop then drawn together to form the 20-foot sphere of diamond lattices, the surface of the Colorado prototype in 1964 was designed to unfold into a flat wall display of the Dymaxion Map—as was presented in the Paris exhibition. **figs. 39 and 40** The principle of geodesic structure and the principle of the map are the same. Indeed, the 1943 map was the very first application of Fuller's geodesic geometry. It is based on the possibility of a continuous topological transfer from the surface of a sphere to the faces of a polyhedron. The faces are simply unpeeled to produce a relatively distortion-free map. **fig. 41** When it was introduced in the 1943 issue of *Life* as a cardboard kit (with photographs that were actually used in the February 1944 patent application for the map), readers were invited to fold the flat surface of the cardboard into an icosahedron and then to unfold it into different layouts of the same map to reveal different global relationships. **fig. 42** The geodesic dome that eventually emerged from Fuller's 1944 concept of energetic geometry is based on the reverse possibility of projecting an icosahedron outward into a sphere. The Geoscope is exactly the figure of this coincidence of structure and map.

Fuller was dedicated to thinking of structure as map and architect as mapmaker or, in his favorite image, navigator. The planet is but a ship in the "celestial ocean," a spaceship that can supposedly be navigated from the Geoscope just as an ocean liner can be navigated from one of the lifeboats that is fixed to it, provided the lifeboat is open to the stars. To construct the Geoscope is to give Spaceship Earth a window. Reporters faithfully quoted the claim that "Minni-Earth can, if experienced and studied, give you 'feel'—as well as 'know'—of your passaging through Universe just as you would 'see' and 'know' from inside your windowed space ship."[111] Fuller is ultimately a window designer.[112] The dream of the Geoscope is the dream of the most sophisticated window possible.

110 Buckminster Fuller, "World Game: How It Came About," paper delivered to the Joint National Meeting of the American Astronautical Society and the Operations Research Society, June 18, 1969. Included in R. Buckminster Fuller, *50 Years of the Design Science Revolution and the World Game: A Collection of Articles and Papers on Design* (Carbondale: Southern Illinois University, 1969).

111 "'U' May Help Build Giant Model of Earth" (see note 48). "Fuller Plans Minni-Earth," *The Archi*, Winter 1956, 3.

112 "In the Geoscope we have the real stars in their real sky in exact zenith position as though the Geoscope's spherical triangle windows outwardly." Fuller, "The Geoscope," 173 (see note 41).

Unfolding the Planet

39 RBF beside miniature Earth under construction on rooftop, Cornell University, 1952

40 Folded and unfolded versions of Colorado Geoscope, *Architectural Design*, December 1964

41 Dymaxion Map, patent application drawing dated February 25, 1944

42 One of the unfoldings of the map in *Life*, March 1943, that was also used in the February 1925 patent application

39

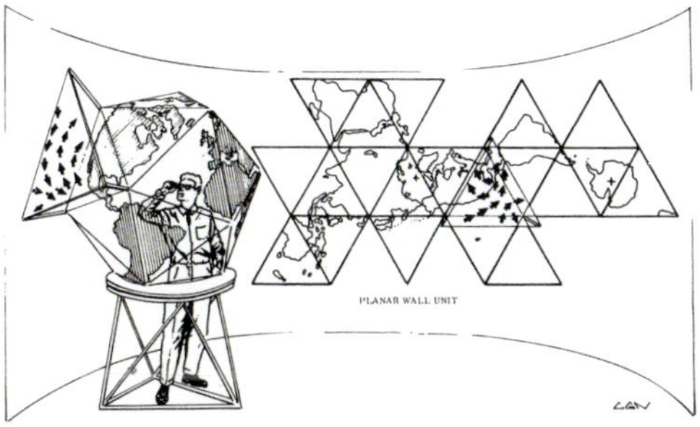

40

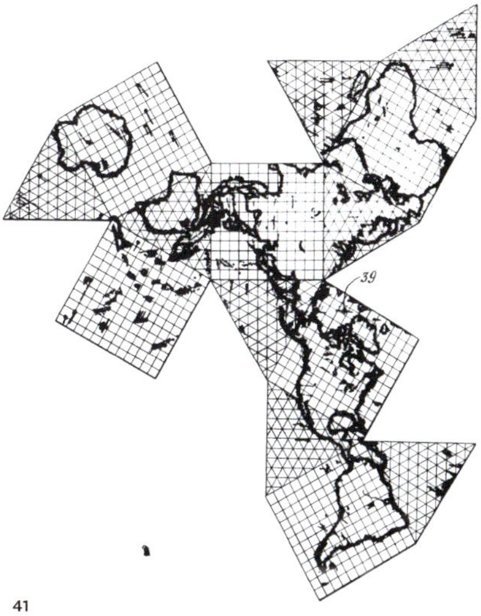

41

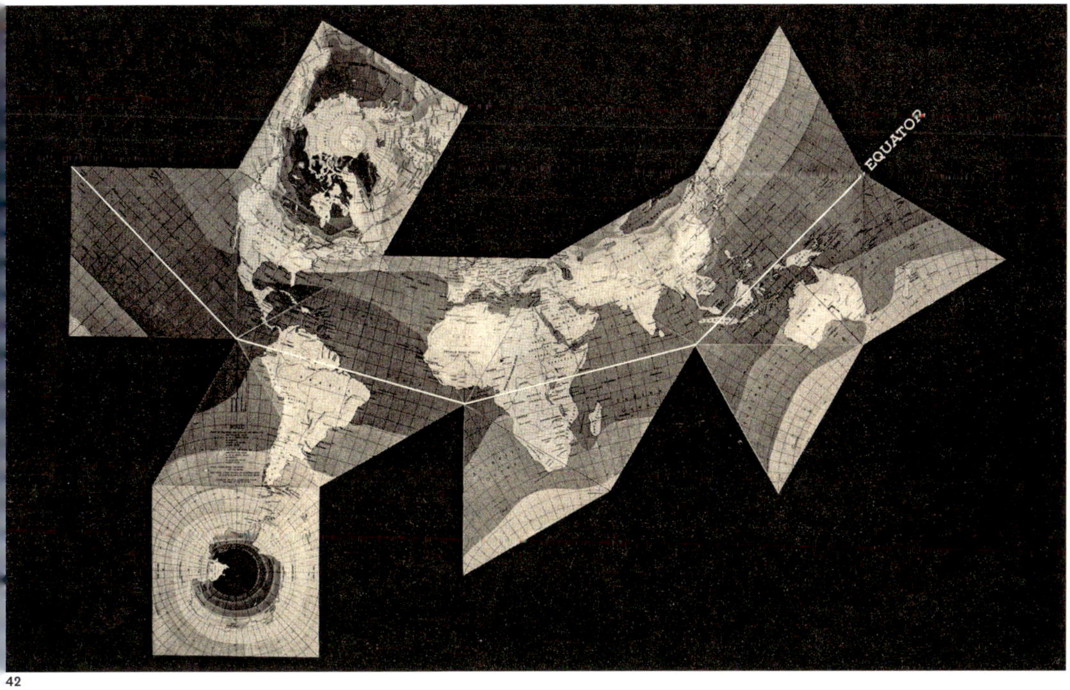

42

Fuller and Sadao eventually built a 250-foot sphere for Expo 67, but the Minni-Earth proposal had been rejected and the Geoscope concept had already migrated one more time. In a 1965 keynote lecture at Southern Illinois University, Fuller announced that the university was about to start a "computer feeding game" called "How to Make the World Work."[113] Teams of players would redirect the flows of global resources while a computer displayed the effects of their decisions on a huge Dymaxion Map using the design of the original Expo 67 proposal. By 1967 Fuller confirms that this "World Game" would take place on a high platform overlooking a football-field-sized map that is fed by historical databanks and live information from spy satellites.[114] He characteristically portrayed the project in autobiographical terms. He identifies the beginning of the idea with his 1917 awareness of the dawn of a single interconnected world through airplane and radio communication, which drew him into architecture in 1927, and which had now been exponentially accelerated by the latest computers and communications satellites.[115] The technological invention of a single world by radio was at the same time the production of an image that can be monitored and even used to proactively change the world through gaming techniques echoing those long used by the military. Fuller and his students started testing the idea in their own analog situation rooms in 1969, surrounded by images reporting global data on large wall-sized Dymaxion Maps while trying to develop their own counterimages through gaming. **fig. 43** Fuller would draw frenetically on the plastic-covered maps, and by 1972 they were generating new kinds of electronic image at the long-desired intersection of art and science that presented alternative scenarios for redistributing resources. **fig. 44**

Yet the ambition for new forms of electronic art was far more radical. Fuller presented the concept in detail to the US Senate in 1969, arguing that the computer that receives all the data from orbiting satellites picking up every event across the planet in all bands of the electromagnetic

113 R. Buckminster Fuller, "Keynote Address at Vision 65," *Utopia or Oblivion: The Prospects for Humanity* (New York: The Overlook Press, 1969), 133.
114 Buckminster Fuller, "The World Game—How to Make the World Work (1967)," in Fuller, *Utopia or Oblivion*, 159 (see note 113).
115 "This technological dawning, was manifest in the swift increase of the horsepower of airplane engines, accomplished with ever less pounds of material per horsepower and in the wireless radio communications across oceans displacing the earlier vast tonnages of cable." Buckminster Fuller, "Memorandum To All Those Inquiring About Or Concerned With The World Game," in *The World Game: Integrative Resource Utilization Planning Tool* (Carbondale: Southern Illinois University, 1971), 3. "A very important example today of the doing-more-with-less principle of the sea and sky craft evolution would be the 1¼-ton communication satellite which is now outperforming the transoceanic communication capacity of 175,000 tons of copper cable." Buckminster Fuller, "Statement of R. Buckminster Fuller," to US Senate, 1969, in *The World Game: Integrative Resource Utilization Planning Tool*, 9.
116 Fuller, "Statement of R. Buckminster Fuller," 26 (see note 115). Satellites exemplify the evolution of technology in their unprecedented ability to monitor the planet with sensors scanning the full electromagnetic spectrum and their ability to communicate: "A very important example today of the doing-more-with-less principle of the sea and sky craft evolution would be the 1¼-ton communication satellite which is now outperforming the transoceanic communication capacity of 175,000 tons of copper cable." Ibid., 9.
117 Ibid., 10.
118 Fuller, "World Game: How It Came About" (see note 110).
119 Buckminster Fuller, "Planned Implementation of the World Resources Simulation Center, Edwardsville, Illinois," 1969 manuscript, BFP Series 2, Box 194, Folder 4, p. 3. "[...] [A] visually continuous-surface picture equal in detailed resolution to that of a fine-screen halftone print or that of an excellent, omnidirectionally viewable, spherical television tube's picturing. It may well be that by the time the first 200-foot Geoscope is undertaken, we may be able to develop a spherical TV tube of that size or a complex of spherically coordinated TV tubes." Fuller, "The Geoscope," 174 (see note 41).
120 Buckminster Fuller, "Planned Implementation of the World Resources Simulation Center, Edwardsville, Illinois," caption to "Site Plan: Phase II (by 1978)."
121 "World-gaming will, in like fashion, engineer an environment which seeks to continually enhance sensory inputs to long-range planning strategies of decision-makers by as graphically and hypervisually, as skill and art will allow, presenting resource information on a total world, audience enveloping display. This display will be designed to elicit a stronger interface between planner and information than could be achieved under ordinary business office-confrontation procedures. The basic hypothesis of world gaming is: decisions of planners will be significantly increased in value in due ratio to the means by which information is presented to them in startlingly fresh visual manner." Thomas B. Turner, "World Game: State-of-the-Art Report," December 1969, 3. Department of Drawings and Archives, Avery Architectural and Fine Arts Library, Columbia University, AA 737 F96 F963.

spectrum and visualizing it for all citizens would act "as an enormously expanded and accelerated brain facility" that would permanently replace the always inadequate work of politicians.[116] The imagery "will be so photogenic that it will become popularly and repeatedly broadcast on the world's TV circuits."[117] Sketch proposals were prepared that year for the design of a "World Resources Simulation Center" for the game, restating Fuller's argument that decision making is best done on the basis of visual representations, with all available data being absorbed by computer and massaged and prepared for display." The space for the game has to be a total world audience enveloping display."[118] Image has become envelope.

The model is once again the massive installations of NORAD and NASA, now joined by the screens at the United States Meteorological Service Headquarters, with McHale being particularly fascinated with the first image of the whole planet's weather assembled from satellite photographs in 1965. **figs. 45–47** But Fuller argued that the state-of-the-art in control room displays are only computer-assisted and lack the speed and flexibility of traditional cathode ray tubes. Since computer speed was unavailable at the desired "Cinerama" scale, there was an interim proposal of a dome on the Edwardsville campus of Southern Illinois University with a 195-foot span in which a tiered auditorium faces a vast screen at one end on which traditional projectors would enlarge small-scale computer displays. When technology permits, this space would give way to a five-eighths geodesic sphere with a 400-foot diameter whose entire inner surface would act as a computer display screen "in a visual mode similar to color television screens of today" to produce "immense" on-line images.[119] The world's biggest TV had undergone yet another exponential leap in size. Now the audience would be literally suspended in front of the display, moving independently in the face of the moving images. Eventually, even this would give way to having the audience placed within the image itself:

> Data will be presented on the inner surface of the dome with audience and players electronically elevated one-hundred feet off the floor of the dome and with each sitting in a "pilot's" contour chair which can be omnidirectionally controlled by a computer—keeping the audience in line with images on dome surface that are important at any given moment and giving them a sense of "electronic" participation in image generation. This display will be even more effective when holography is perfected and audience and players are actually put inside of display image.[120]

Yet again, architecture as the space of images and the science of architecture as the art of the image. In a progress report, Thomas B. Turner (the director of research and development for the project) argues that the appropriate model is the development of the art of aesthetics in motion picture, television, and theater. The World Game is meant to "interface" the audience to incoming information by enveloping them in a "hypervisual" presentation.[121] Sophisticated pattern recognition software would give seemingly chaotic information an aesthetic form. Turner defends the production of such imagery by quoting McLuhan's hugely popular *The Medium Is the Massage* of 1967 on "the possibility of arranging the entire human environment as a work of art, as a teaching machine designed to

43

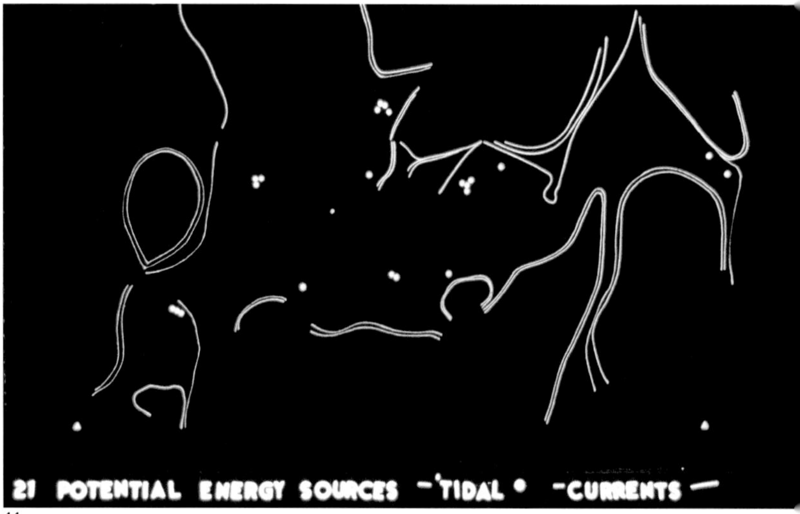

44

Designing a Technology for Collective Responsibility

43 World Game session, New York, 1969

44 Screen showing potential energy source of tidal currents, World Game Seminar, 1972

45 Cape Kennedy control center published by John McHale in *Architectural Design*, February 1967

46 Gemini 5 mission control room published by McHale in *AD*, February 1967

47 First complete image of the world's weather assembled in 1965 from 450 photographs sent by radio from an orbiting satellite, published by McHale in *AD*, February 1967

48 Religious Center, Southern Illinois University Geoscope, 1971

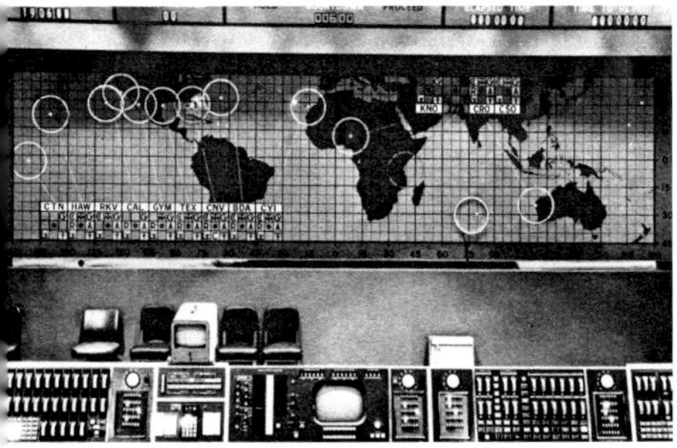

5

6

7

8

maximize perception and to make everyday learning a process of disco- ery."[122] The passage Turner quotes goes on to insist that:

> Application of this knowledge would be the equivalent of a thermostat co trolling room temperature. It would seem only reasonable to extend such co trols to all the sensory thresholds of our being. [...] Environments are no passive wrapping, but are, rather, active processes which are invisible. Th ground rules, pervasive structure, and overall patterns of environments elud easy perception. Anti-environments, or countersituations made by artist provide means of direct attention and enable us to see and understand mor clearly.[123]

The whole ecological movement was precisely such an attempt to turn th global environment into an antienvironment, an artwork. Particular ae thetic images of the planet played a crucial role. Turner refers to the famou photograph taken from the spacecraft looking back at Earth, paraphrasin Fuller in comparing the images produced at the World Resources Simul tion Center to the mind-expanding effect of "seeing for the first time th sapphire Earth against the black void of space."[124]

Without that image of Earth as an isolated sphere, the argument behin the ecological movement may well have floundered. Diverse group united around its preservation.[125] Having only been released to the medi because of the sustained efforts of Stuart Brand, a dedicated follower o Fuller's thinking, it is treated as a uniquely beautiful but fragile image tha can only be protected with ecological management strategies. It woul seem that the image can only ever be seen as beautiful. It supposedly tra scends and orchestrates the psychosexual system of aesthetic judgmen that Fuller places at the center of postelectronic space. A quasi-theologica view underpins the unquestioned sense of the beauty of "natural orde and the "harmony" of the universe. Ecology is a barely disguised form o theology. It is symptomatic that a final Geoscope (with a three-quarte sphere, 40 feet in diameter, with Earth's landmasses imprinted on its plex glass panels) was installed by Fuller and Sadao in 1970 at the Edwardsvill Religious Center of Southern Illinois University on the outskirts of S Louis, Missouri. **fig. 48** Fuller published a lengthy poem that credits th structure with the spiritual value of a cathedral:

> One goes inside to go outside one's self
> And into the center of the Earth
> And thence outward to the stars in seconds.[126]

To look through the Geoscope's window on the world is to stand in a co mic space. The role of the architect in an electronic age is to preserve a image of the universe, an image of its hidden architecture precisely.

122 Marshall McLuhan, *The Medium Is the Massage* (New York: Bantam Books, 1967), 68. Cited in Turner, "World Game: State-of-the-Art Report," 2 (see note 121).
123 McLuhan, *The Medium Is the Massage*, 68 (see note 122).
124 Turner, "World Game: State-of-the-Art Report," 2 (see note 121).
125 More recently, a space probe got so far away from Earth that it could turn around and produce the first family portrait of the solar system, looking back at all the planets, an image that could have a long-term impact in defining a new site for architectural operations.
126 Buckminster Fuller, "Go In to Go Out," in *Earth, Inc.* (Garden City: Anchor Books, 1973), 152. "It is a transparent miniature Earth. / Our plan et's continents can be seen / Accurately outlined against the transparen blue oceans / As they would be seen by X rays / If one descended by elevator from Edwardsville / To the center of the real Earth." Ibid., 145.
127 Buckminster Fuller, "Conning Tower—'Hoop-Skirt' Room," *Shelter* 2 no. 5 (November 1932): 64–65.
128 Fuller, "Putting the House in Order," 2 (see note 73).
129 Buckminster Fuller, "Earth Inc." originally published by the Fuller Research Foundation, 1947, republished in Fuller, *Earth Inc.*, 7 (see note 126).

Ecology is a question of images in the end, images of architecture and the architecture of images. To speak of ecology in architecture is already to raise the question of the image. The crucial technological issues are not those of energy conservation but those of the image, which include all the institutionalized technologies of discourse itself, of architectural discourse in particular. After all, the discourse is no more than the rhythmic exchange of certain kinds of image, an exchange whose politics need to be scrutinized.

Any inquiry into the contemporary mechanisms for the production and distribution of images, particularly the rise of data visualization, is already historical. The logic behind the Geoscope precedes the computer networks that it attempted to domesticate. Even the structure of its last holographic version is derivative of the Industrial Conning Tower design that Fuller published in the November 1932 issue of his magazine *Shelter*. fig. 49 He proposed that all industrial headquarters install a conference space organized as a set of tiered seats ringing a central mechanism that contains cameras, projectors, speakers, microphones, and three-way screens for "trans-lux visible displays." This mechanism, which emerges through the floor from a technical control and filing space below, can record and replay every meeting, "to see ourselves as others see us," or broadcast them by teletype, telephoto, and television to any other such space.[127] The space is understood as the bridge of a large ship, enabling industries to steer themselves toward the most efficient use of resources. What Fuller learned from the navy is the need for "conning capacity." Imagery management is the basis of resource management. Indeed, images become the most precious resource. It is not by chance that Fuller begins the same issue of *Shelter* by defining "shelter" in terms of ecology: "shelter represents the inclusive instrumental security and service of ecology and economy" where economy ("the management of household affairs") is "derived" from ecology ("the study of human relations, particularly as pertains to the home").[128] Shelter is literally the ecological preservation of image-making capacity.

For Fuller, shelter is provided by hooking into the networks of communication. It is the hookup that makes the ecological management of household affairs possible. Indeed, it is the hookup that domesticates a space. The Industrial Conning Tower idea is itself a derivative of the original Dymaxion House project with its "conning facility" in the form of a furniture unit combining desk, drawing board, filing cabinet, steel safe, typewriter, calculating machine, telephone, motion picture machine, radio-television receiver, Dictaphone, phonograph, revolving bookshelves, map, and globe storage. This networking and visualization instrument unit was located in the living room of the first version of the house in 1928 and in the library of the revised version of 1929. The house navigates itself through waves of information. Home is not a static point of withdrawal from the world but the site of the most active engagement with the world. Fuller's 1947 rejection of the traditional assumption that "man [...] isn't 'going' anywhere at home" is equally a rejection of the idea that "when at home he knows precisely where he is."[129] Home is the epicenter of movement itself. Home is precisely where bearings are most needed, where the most advanced radio-linked data visualization is crucial to individual and collective navigation. In this sense, the World Game is the ultimate extension of a domestic design. Radio constructs one hyperextended house.

The end game of the Geoscope remains as domestic as the first move. In a 1962 lecture at Southern Illinois University, Fuller envisioned a 200-foot Geoscope hovering 100 feet above the campus whose "dynamically viewable and picturable" data could be broadcast all over the world by radio to allow major questions to be thought through collaboratively in a global network. He argued that this "decontaminated" information could be "'piped' right into the environment of the home" by two-way television sets that allow people to select the information they want to see.[130] The small-tubed television set in private homes and the large-tubed Geoscope in hyperpublic spaces are presented as parallel inventions. Fuller had argued that home television should be the basis of all education ever since his own involvement in some of television's first test broadcasts between 1936 and 1938. In the spring of 1955 he devoted his studio class at North Carolina State College to the way television could "amplify and improve" education and what unique architecture could support that new and improved system of knowledge creation and transfer since traditional architecture is inadequate to the needs of the broadcast medium.[131] This concept was again already there in the Dymaxion House design, with television included in the set of essential equipment just a year after the first successful demonstration of a working television system. Unsurprisingly, the World Resources Inventory did detailed charts on the rising number of television sets in houses along with the number of radios in use. The students participating in the Geoscope project were inevitably encouraged to make movies to broadcast on television. In the first document for the World Resources Inventory in 1963, McHale predicts that education will use "the most highly advanced communication networks" and refers to the Geoscope as a prototype for the evolution of educational devices like two-way television.[132]

Architecture itself aspires to television. It is not by chance that Fuller and Sadao complete the design for the unbelievable 12,250-foot-tall tower in 1966 with housing inside its pyramidal base. The client, who owned the largest Japanese television network and asked for a structure taller than Mount Fuji, was also the client for the vast floating Tetrahedral Cities that took over from Fuller's flying Cloud Nine cities and the dome over Manhattan as the largest houses on the planet. The ever-expanding dream of broadcasting the highest definition interactive image of the whole world is linked to the ever-expanding image of housing.

The redesign of the planet into a single domestic space is bound to a specific redesign of the house. The original conception of the Dymaxion

130 Buckminster Fuller, *Education Automation: Freeing Scholars to Return to Their Studies* (New York: Anchor Books, 1962), 9. "All world data [on the Geoscope] would be dynamically viewable and picturable and replayable by radio to all the world, so that common consideration in a most educated manner of all world problems by all world people would become a practical event." Ibid., 46.

131 Buckminster Fuller to Dean Henry Kamphoefner, 11 January 1955, BFP Series 8, Box 9, Folder 3.

132 John McHale, "World Resources, Human Trends and Needs," in *World Design Science Decade 1965–1975, Phase 1, Document 1, Inventory of World Resources, Human Trends, and Needs*, 44 (see note 31).

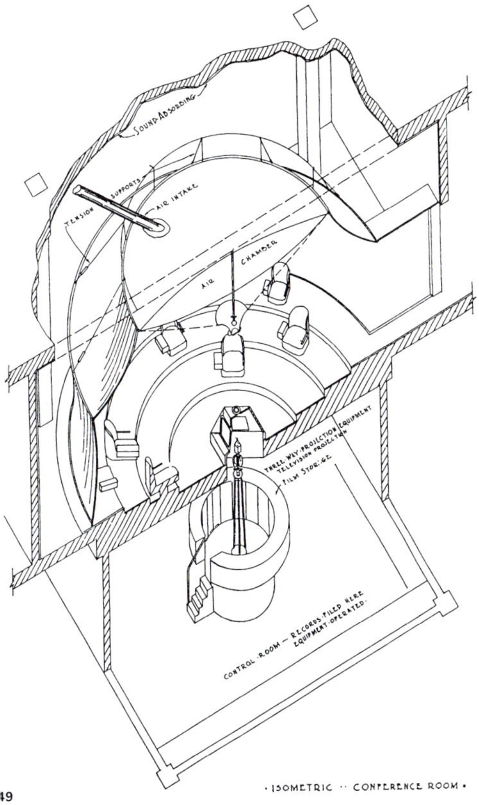

49

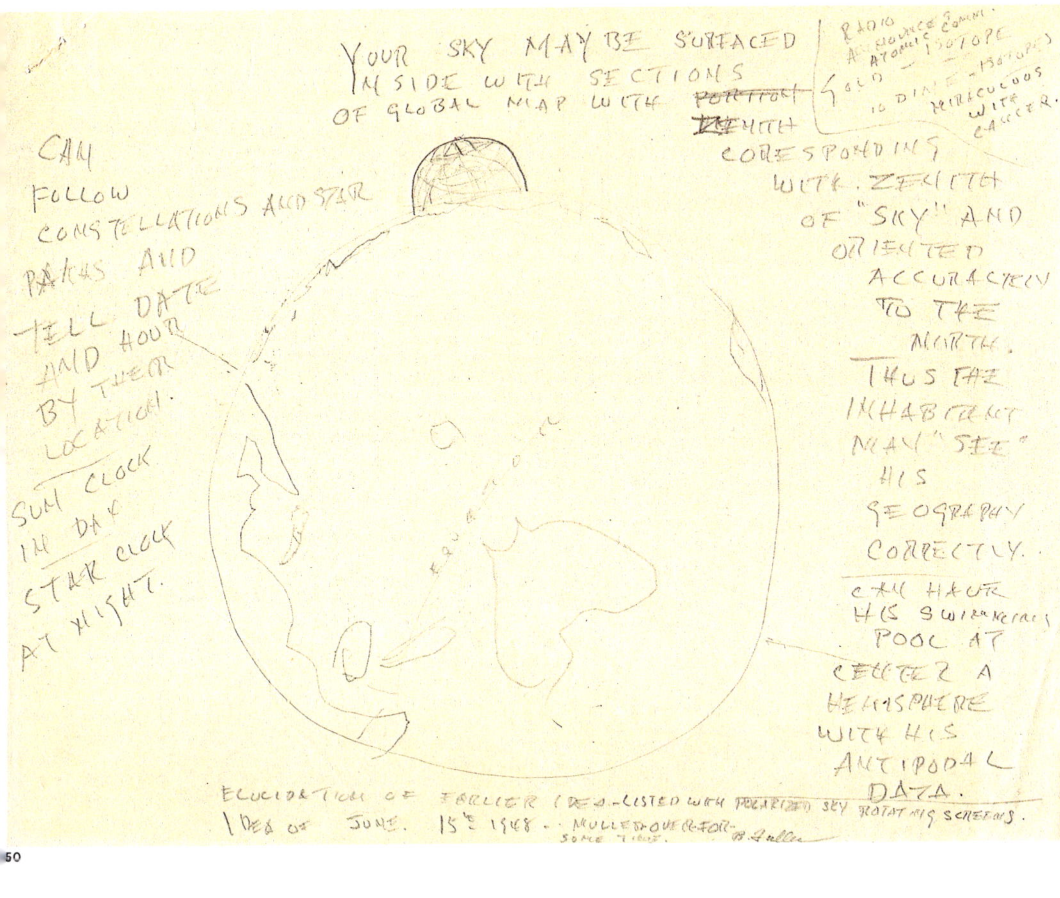

50

49 Industrial Conning Tower project, "to see ourselves as others see us," *Shelter*, November 1932

50 RBF sketch of June 15, 1948, with idea of house producing a spherical image of the world

House as a mobile-networked spaceship underpins the conception of th Spaceship Earth as a single house held together by invisible broadcas patterns. Indeed, the idea of the Geoscope is embedded in the very think ing behind the first designs. When the house was first published in *4L Time Lock*, Fuller describes the perspective of the manuscript itself as tha of looking outward through a glass globe: "The point of view, througl introspection, unlimited to the segmental area of our temporal eyes, is ou abstract central position in the center of the universe, looking or buildin from the inside out, as from the center of a great glass globe of the Earth."[13 The Geoscope was a domestically centered philosophy of design lon before it became a particular design. The idea of a transparent spherica map as an omnidirectional window onto the world takes over from that o the traditional house.[134] It is therefore no surprise that in June 1948, whe Fuller has started to literally talk about the geodesic dome as a house anc is on the threshold of trying to raise his first dome at Black Mountain, h already described in a sketch how the transparent surface of a Private Sk Dome could be lined with the global map, and even that the bottom of swimming pool, presumably also a hemisphere, could be lined with th other half of the map, enabling people to be suspended within a spherica image of their world—floating in information. **fig. 50** And not by chanc does he write a note on the sketch about a radio report of the success ir using radiation from newly isolated isotopes on cancer.[135] Fuller's nona chitecture is to be constructed at the very border of visible and invisible a a window onto that which cannot be seen.

After the first summer at Black Mountain, Fuller gave a lecture on th idea of an "invisible architect" constructing "thin gossamer shells" to th Institute of Design students who had just started working on the Autonc mous Dwelling project and would develop the plastic dome taken to Blacl Mountain the following summer. He described the way the experience o a house would be fundamentally transformed simply by having a maр overhead aligned with the planet.[136] With the very first potential opportu

133 Buckminster Fuller, *4D Time Lock* (self-published, 1928), 31.
134 This explains the otherwise incongruous carefully staged and lit photograph of Fuller and the president of Fuller Houses reverently holding the Dymaxion Map model over a plastic hemisphere in the *Fortune* magazine article on the Wichita House. "Fuller's House," *Fortune*, April 1946, 172. Fuller had bought personally a set of plastic spheres from B29 bombers and wanted to carve the land masses into them to make transparent 34-inch-diameter "world globes." Buckminster Fuller to Jake Butts, 11 January 1948, BFP Series 2, Box 68.
135 Buckminster Fuller, Private Sky drawing of June 15, 1948, BFP Series 18, Box 119, Folder 15.
136 Fuller describes a great circle dome with venetian blind material taped on "in regular latitudes and longitudes" to "put directly over your head in your house your own zenith on the world geodesic lines. Be very easy to outline continents up in here so that you had exact point on the continent where you are now located with your house. [...] This being so you would be in a true hemisphere like the planetarium and if you looked out though this network over your sky here and you saw a star in zenith over France that star would be over France. You would really be able to look out at your outer universe and have a very nice sense of its relationship to your own Earth. You would be able to see your own Earth turning in that space. It would be really quite exciting to you. Just as an educational device alone with the expenditure of a few hours that's just talking about houses you could begin to have such a very interesting relationship that life in the city wouldn't be particularly boring." Buckminster Fuller, lecture on Structure (Chicago Institute of Design, December 2, 1948), BFP Series 8, Box 8, Folder 3, p. 13.
137 Buckminster Fuller to Eleanor Cannon, undated but sent between September 23 and September 28, 1949. BFP Series 2, Box 72, Folder 9.
138 Fuller added the label "conning facility" to the requirements in the 1949 version published in *Architectural Design* in 1960.
139 Buckminster Fuller, "Universal Conditions of the Industrially Reproducible Shelter," *T-Square*, 2, no. 2 (February 1932): 37.
140 Buckminster Fuller, "Now and When," *Harper's*, April 1, 1972, 61. "All our vision operates as an omnidirectional TV set, and there is no way to escape it. That is all we have ever lived in. We have all been in omnidirectional TV sets all our lives, and we have gotten so accustomed to the reliability of the information that we have, in effect, projected ourselves into the field. We may insist that we see each other out in the field. But all vision actually operates inside the brain in organic, neuron-transistorized TV sets. [...] All we do is deal in brain images." Buckminster Fuller and E. J. Applewhite, *Synergetics: Explorations in the Geometry of Thinking* (New York: Macmillan, 1982), 440.
141 "Humanity's invention and adoption of the word *image* and its brain-formed employment as *image-ination* was occasioned by the need to describe to others the visual experiencing of structural conceptions—images 'Seeing' always and only occurs inside the brain." "Children: The True Scientists (1977)," in *R. Buckminster Fuller on Education* (Amherst: University of Massachusetts Press, 1979), 150.
142 Buckminster Fuller, "Guinea Pig B," in *Inventions: The Patented Works of R. Buckminster Fuller* (New York: St. Martin's Press, 1983), xxiv.

nity to build such a transparent dome house in September 1949, he again proposes to the hoped-for benefactor that "the sky-vantage geometry will carry an outline tracery of the world continents (the hemispherical portion thereof coinciding) oriented from the hemisphere's center, as they are oriented from the Earth's center" so that the precise location of body, house, and planet is revealed and "the Earth's rotation within the star-frame of cosmos will be far more apparent than it has hitherto been."[137] The idea of the house and the Geoscope were inseparable.

In these terms, the Geoscope is the ultimate house, the drawing of a domestic space out of computer networks. As such, it should be evaluated according to the "Universal Requirements for a Dwelling Advantage" that Fuller first published as "Universal Conditions of Industrially Reproducible Shelter" in a 1932 issue of *T-Square* and revised many times up until the adjustments he made in December 1959 for the version that McHale published in the March 1960 issue of *Architectural Design* and republished in the second document for the World Resources Inventory in 1964. In addition to fostering growth by providing a "conning facility" for communication channels with access to the past, the present, and the future,[138] the scientific designer of a house has to oppose the "internal destructive forces" of nerves, fatigue, and repression. The designer of the domesticating space of the network-driven holographic image in the Geoscope, like the designer of any house, has to satisfy Fuller's original psychic requirements of "nerve shock proofing," "fatigue proofing" and "repression prevention."[139] As these constraints apply to the architecture of the images themselves, they become aesthetic constraints.

After all, it is no accident that the Geoscope's visualization of the invisible logic of the computer network takes the form of a sophisticated television set. For Fuller, the computer is but an organic extension of the human brain and the brain is itself a kind of television set, with the mind acting as the TV studio production director selecting and sorting the incoming images:

> Because the brain's TV prime resource / Consists of Images, / We may call the total brain activity / Image-ination / All we have ever seen / Is and always will be / In the scopes of our brain's TV station. / All that humanity has ever seen / And will ever see / Is his own image-ination.[140]

In 1977, the year after his last unsuccessful Geoscope proposal with Sadao took the form of two drawings suggesting that the recently burnt-out Expo 67 Sphere in Montreal could be retrofitted like a planetarium with a new internal skin to have 2,500 people suspended inside a spherical image of the world, Fuller insists that thinking, whether conscious or not, is no more than the experience of "images," the "visual experiencing of structural conceptions."[141] No matter how dependent these pictures are on input from the sensors on the body or its numerous prosthetic extensions, they remain internal to the mechanism that displays them. In a strict sense, there is no outside of the brain. As Fuller put it at the beginning of his career, and repeats in one of the last manuscripts he wrote before his death in 1983, "all sensing occurs inside the brain's 'television control zone.'"[142] The brain is a thoroughly domestic space without an exterior. Likewise, there is no simple outside or inside to the Geoscope. To enter it is to enter a window, an image of the outside that is thoroughly internalized and yet portable, a mobile image that can be inhabited—an image without which any other form of inhabitation is supposedly impossible in the age of diffuse networks. But crucially it is an image of the invisible. Fuller was already telling art and architecture students at Yale in 1952 that the brain is a series of interacting television sets that allow for the construction, recollection, and evaluation of images with one set for recording previous experiences, another for present experiences, and another for generating possible future experiences. But he speculated that intuition is yet another kind of internal television set that constructs images out of the invisible by "dealing with the radio reporting that I am may be getting in my skin about things, the kind of thoughts I have been getting through my skin for all time," allowing an immediate unconscious "aesthetic appraisal" of things.[143] The Geoscope project that had got under way at Cornell earlier the same year likewise aimed to set up an aesthetic experience of countless radio signals, turning the brain into a house.

Fuller always insisted that his requirements for scientific shelter did not presuppose any particular visual form and that modern architecture's obsession with the visual had to give way to an invisible architecture.[144] But his actions suggest that it is only through the production of visual form, precisely when form itself seems to be dissolving, that electronic space can be constituted as a house. The Geoscope is the attempt to produce an inhabitable image, a fabulous and comfortable picture window. Its architecture is that of a graphical user interface. Fuller saw himself and the spectacle of his lifelong production as such an interface. At the age of eighty-one, he was still actively promoting the two-mile dome over Manhattan in 1977, using exactly the same arguments as in 1959 that he had first used to defend a one-mile dome for New York in early 1949, but now predicting that "In twenty-five years, we won't need buildings. We'll be sheltered by an electromagnetic field."[145] The barely visible structure inspired by and sheltering radiation will give way to radiation as shelter. Architecture will finally and happily disappear into radio.

143 Buckminster Fuller, audiotape of lecture (Yale University Department of Architecture, October 16, 1952), BFP Series 17, Box 3, Reel 3c.
144 "Forms are inherently visible and forms no longer can 'follow functions' because the significant functions are now invisible. That era of essentially visible 'modernism' is over. The architecture of superficial 'functionalism' is meaningless and dead. What usually we speak of as our everyday world is a stage set with visible props which are easily manipulated by ignorant people to exploit the equal ignorance of others. The unreliable, uninformative and often deliberately misinformative scenery of that stage is soon to be radically altered due to the inexorable trendings in the sub or ultra visible alterations of man's relationship to universe." R. Buckminster Fuller to all heads of architecture schools seeking institutional funding for film series on Fuller being prepared at Southern Illinois University, Serge Chermayeff Papers, Department of Drawings and Archives, Avery Architectural and Fine Arts Library, Columbia University.
145 Buckminster Fuller, cited in "$4,500 House Light Enough for Hand Delivery," *Canberra Times*, June 8, 1977, 21.

51

51 RBF during World Game seminar in *Architectural Forum*, January–February 1972

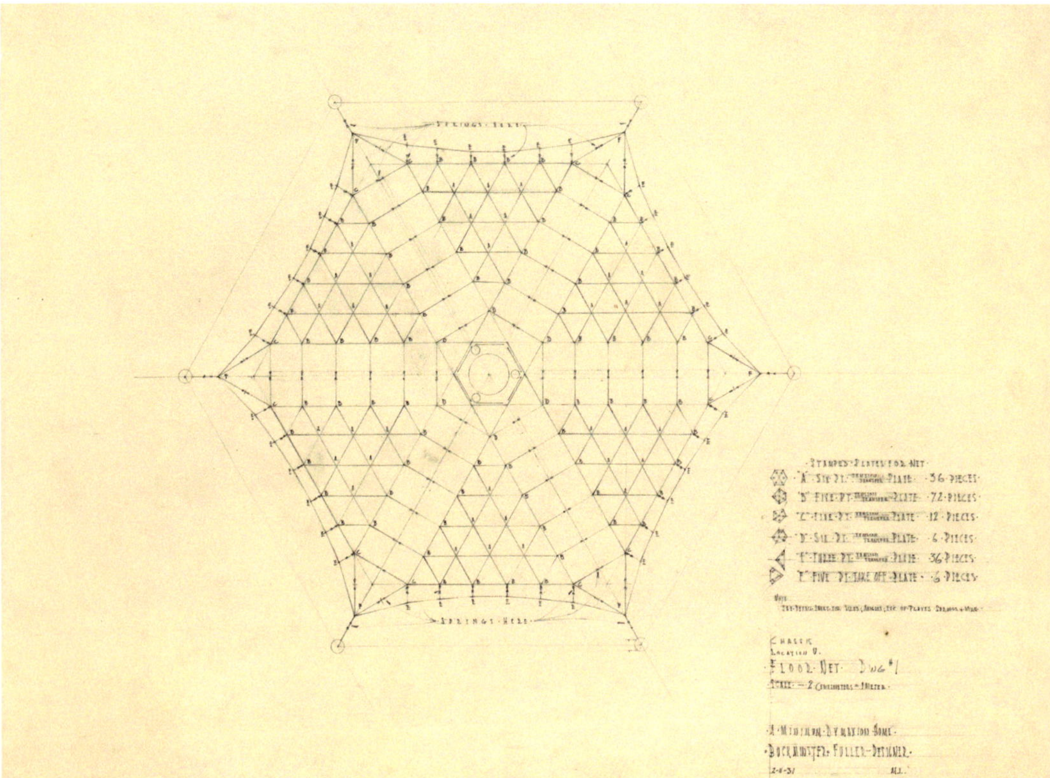

x

x Floor Net of Dymaxion House, dated November 2, 1931

NETWORK FEVER

We are constantly surrounded by talk of networks. Every third message article, and advertisement seems to be about one network or another. We are surrounded, that is, by talk on networks about networks. It is as if our technologies feed on a kind of narcissistic self-reflection. Everyone has become a kind of expert, ready to discuss the different types of nets (social, computer, television, telephone, airline, bank, business, healthcare, activist...) or scales (global, national, wide, metropolitan, infra, local, home...) or modes (open, restricted, anonymous...). And where would we be without our opinions about the Internet, the net of nets against which all others are now referenced? How many ways do we have to express our amazement at such a vast space in which any address is just a few clicks away from all the others? Attaching oneself to a seemingly marginal thread soon accesses an endlessly dense weave, as if a walk down a quiet country lane would suddenly bring one to the heart of a metropolis of unprecedented dimensions. In celebrating this new kind of territory, we recast questions of individual identity in terms of unimaginable levels of connectivity, ignoring the equally dramatic rise of new forms of inaccessibility to stage a collective institutionalized simulation of euphoria in which discourse about openness, democracy, free exchange, and speed dominates over that of control, surveillance, blockage, sedation, censorship, and crime. The proliferation of electronic forms of public space has been matched by the proliferation of highly restricted private networks. New forms of inaccessibility breed under the cover of our utopian image of infinite mobility. Half aware of this, since by definition one cannot be fully aware of the spaces one cannot enter, we all too eagerly celebrate new forms of connection in a highly ritualized cult of connectivity.

The message is clear. Nowhere escapes the net. A map of all the webs passing through any particular space would be impossibly dense Invisible networks seemingly threaten visible means of defining space, dissolving the walls of buildings. The architecture of borders, walls, doors, and locks gives way to that of passwords, fire walls, public key encryption, and security certificates. Indeed, the idea of a space occupied by networks or superimposed by them has been replaced by that of overlapping networks within which physical space only appears as a fragile artifact or effect. Space itself can only be seen when caught in the net. It is as if the modern perforation and lightening up of architecture in the face of speed, industrialized technology, and mass production at the turn of the twentieth century has gone a step farther as buildings dissolve into information flow, to be either discarded as a relic of a previous time or nostalgically preserved as a quaint memento.

The Internet is still relatively new, emerging out of ARPANET, a 1969 Cold War operation of the US Defense Department that combined the computers of four universities. It grew exponentially ever since

and now bounces from school to house to car to plane to beach. But what if we are actually at the end point of the network logic? What if contemporary discourse about the net simply realizes nineteenth-century fantasies that were acted out throughout most of the last century? What if the much-advertised dissolving of architecture occurred long ago? What if much of our net talk is just an echo? An echo of an echo.

DANCING GURUS

The radical confusion of architecture and electronic networks can be marked by the July 6, 1963, meeting of a short man in dark pants, close-fitting white jacket, crisp shirt, and tie with a tall man in light pants and a loose-fitting summer shirt covered with a geometric pattern. **fig. 1** The shorter man, born in the last decade of the nineteenth century, has been using communication networks as a model for architecture since the late 1920s. The taller one is a forty-year-old expert in communication who has just published a book on networks in which architecture plays a decisive but less obvious role. Photographed together on the deck of a boat, the architect is clearly no stranger to the sun but stands a little defensively, holding a text with two hands in front of him, as if about to deliver an important statement somewhere else. The communications expert is pale but leans casually toward the camera with his hands tucked behind his back, smiling openly as if he has nothing much to say and will stay on deck for as long as possible. Yet the odd couple took an instant liking to each other and quickly became a kind of intellectual tag wrestling team, tormenting colleagues and audiences around the globe until the younger man's death at the end of 1980. Both were regarded as entertaining but crazy in their respective fields. Both regarded their fields as crazy. But their mark is everywhere. They voiced so much of what is said today. They wrote a lot of our script.

Buckminster Fuller and Marshall McLuhan met for the first time after boarding the *New Hellas* in Athens for an eight-day boat trip around the Greek Islands. The two gurus of the electronic age had been invited on the trip, along with thirty-two other leading intellectuals from fourteen countries, by Constantinos Doxiadis, a Greek architect and urban planner. The idea was to have a "symposion," a radical mixing of intellectual activity and sensual pleasure as the boat traveled from island to island. Each morning, the group would have informal but intense discussions onboard about "the evolution of human settlements." In the afternoon and evening, they would leave the boat to go swimming, visit famous historic sites, eat in restaurants, see performances, go dancing, and shop. High-level theoretical discourse was well lubricated with retsina and ouzo.

McLuhan and Fuller admired each other's eccentricity. McLuhan liked to speak in aphoristic punch lines thrown as grenades into the morning discussions. **fig. 2** A pun was as likely as a formal statement. Fuller surprised the group by seeming uncomfortable with the rapid exchanges. Having difficulty following the conversation because of his bad hearing, he preferred to give speeches. **figs. 3 and 4** He would talk for hours on end, continuing his line of thought during meals, while drinking, and while changing

NETWORK FEVER

Gurus of the Net Tango at Sea

1 RBF and Marshall McLuhan aboard *New Hellas* in the Agean, July 6, 1963

2 McLuhan in discussion aboard *New Hellas*, July 1963

3 RBF giving “marathon” lecture aboard *New Hellas*, July 1963, in *DA Newsletter*, November 1963

4 RBF listening to discussion aboard *New Hellas*, July 1963

5 RBF singing aboard *New Hellas*, July 1963, in *DA Newsletter,* November 1963

6 RBF dancing with economist Barbara Ward aboard *New Hellas*, July 1963

1

2

3

4

5

6

in the cabin—enthralling yet ultimately exhausting everyone.[1] His "marathon" lectures, singing, and dancing blended into a single continuous onboard performance. **figs. 5 and 6** McLuhan said Fuller drank like a fish; Fuller said McLuhan danced like one:

> After dinner on the Doxiadis ship we used to dance and Marshall would dance with his wife all over the place, so much so that he took up the whole dance floor. He thought we had all stopped to marvel at his and his wife's performance, but that wasn't it; the way he was dancing there wasn't room for the rest of us and we had to leave the floor.[2]

Even if the others on the boat regarded McLuhan as "outlandish," as he later wrote to a friend, his arguments had a marked effect. The group included some prominent architects and planners, but most came from outside the traditional limits of architectural discourse. Led by superstars like Margaret Mead and Barbara Ward, there were representatives of psychiatry, engineering, economics, sociology, anthropology, political

1 "On a certain day, Bucky gave an afternoon presentation. [Norman] Cousins says: 'Then they adjourned for dinner, but Bucky kept right on talking, not eating himself, and resumed in the saloon after dinner. Then he walked with the individual participants to their cabins. Finally he ended up with Doxiadis and Jim Perkins in the former's cabin long after midnight. [...] Perkins and Doxiadis, totally exhausted, looked at this man, who by now had been on this talking marathon for nine hours. You can picture it—Doxiadis getting undressed, Jim Perkins slumped down in a chair, and Bucky sounding off his thoughts, exhilarated, fresh, energetic. And there was no doubt in either Doxiadis's or Perkins's minds that he could have kept on through the entire night, and he would still be fresh.'" Albert Hatch, *Buckminster Fuller: At Home in the Universe* (New York: Crown, 1974), 234.

2 Buckminster Fuller to E. J. Applewhite, 10 July 1973, in *Synergetics Dictionary: The Mind of Buckminster Fuller*, ed. E. J. Applewhite (New York: Garland, 1986), vol. 2, 592. The first report on the Delos meeting zooms in on the intersection of dancing and talking before juxtaposing images of Fuller singing and lecturing: "the tall and lean Marshall McLuhan, the Canadian professor of literature, who, one night danced merrily the twist and the next day talked about the electronic age and the implosion it produces, turning this planet of ours into a small, compact, village; or of the gay, like a student, world-famed Professor and engineer-inventor Buckminster Fuller, now dancing happily American popular dances and the next moment beginning a marathon lecture on his energetics and synergetic geometry that lasted until the early hours of next day." *DA Newsletter* 3, no. 7 (1963): 11–13.

3 "I realize of course that this is a rather belated time to invite someone on such short notice but I want to say frankly that I have just finished reading your wonderful book 'Gutenberg Galaxy,' in which I found so many of the things that we also believe in and so many of the ideas which I think are relevant and essential to human settlements and their problems." Constantinos Doxiadis to Marshall McLuhan, 29 May 1973, cited in Marshall McLuhan to Stewart Bates, 17 June 1973, in *Letters of Marshall McLuhan*, ed. Matie Molinaro et al. (Toronto: Oxford University Press, 1987), 289.

4 McLuhan to Stewart Bates, June 17, 1973 (see note 3).

5 McLuhan noted that "The electronic age with its tremendous speedup of communications has created a situation of 'implosion' rather than explosion. The technological age extended man's physical senses enormously, the electronic age is now extending the nervous system. Technology separated our different functions and distributed them widely in space; electronics fuses them together and overlays them. We have all become totally involved and—in terms of communication—the whole globe has been compressed to the dimensions of a village. This global extension of the human brain is as involuntary as seeing when one's eyes are open. It represents a new kind of continuous learning and an enormous upgrading of man. The task of the planner is to prepare the environment for the exploitation of this new tremendous opportunity." Notes from the second meeting, July 8, 1963, Delos Documents, Department of Drawings and Archives, Avery Architectural and Fine Arts Library, Columbia University. McLuhan's statement was cited in the introductory text to the coverage of the event in "The Delos Symposion," *Ekistics* 16 (October 1963): 206. McLuhan's presentation continued in a similar vein: "Electronic technology has extended the brain to embrace the globe; previous technology had only extended the bodily servants of the brain. The result now is a speedup of information that reduces the planet to the scale of a village—a global consciousness thus becomes the new human scale." *Ekistics* 16 (October 1963): 257.

6 Fuller to Applewhite, July 10, 1973 (see note 2). The prosthetic argument also appears in *No More Second Hand God*, as when Fuller refers to "irreversible physical evolution technologically extrapolated as extra-corporeal simplex or complex of tooled man-process extension and augmentation." Buckminster Fuller, *No More Second Hand God and Other Writings* (Carbondale: Southern Illinois University Press, 1963), 77.

7 McLuhan's text includes passages that resonate particularly strongly with those of Fuller: "Movie, radio, telephone, television, have now reshaped the modes of human sensibility to the point where the merely pictorial ordering of experience, with heavy stress on the visual kinds of enclosure, connection, sequence and control are obsolete [...] as the globe becomes very small by electronic means, the amount which we must know about the globe becomes very much larger. The smaller the globe becomes, the more we must participate, directly, in all its concerns." Marshall McLuhan, "Media Log" (1959), 3, 8. BFP Series 2, Box 105, Folder 8.

8 "Have you encountered the work of Ed. T. Hall? He says he got the idea of our technologies as outerings of sense and function from Buckminster Fuller. I got it from nobody." Marshall McLuhan, *Sheet* (privately circulated newsletter), February 27, 1962, in *Letters of Marshall McLuhan*, 287 (see note 3).

9 "McLuhan has never made any bones about his indebtedness to me as the original source of most of his ideas. The 'Global Village' indeed was my concept. I don't think he has an original idea. Not one. McLuhan says so himself. He's really a very great enthusiast, a marvelous populariser and teacher. He has an irrepressible sense of the histrionic, like no one I've known other than Frank Lloyd Wright. [...] My concept of the 'Mechanical extensions of man' is the basis for his talk of the 'Electrical Extensions' of man. [...] McLuhan has always been the first to say 'Bucky is my master. I am only his disciple.'" Fuller to Applewhite, 10 July 1973 (see note 2). "Regarding McLuhan, I have known him for five years. He acknowledges use of my concept and phrasing of the 'Mechanical' and other 'Extensions of Man' which was first published in the 'predictions' in my preface to the *Nine Chains to the Moon*, Lippincott 1938, and also in my charts in 1938 and republished in my book *The Epic of Industrialization*, written in 1940. I speak about such phenomena as a scientist, McLuhan speaks as a Professor of Literature. He is well read and has good insights [...] [and] he is skilled in verbal dueling. [...] I greatly enjoy his foot and rapier work. I have been present when hostile audiences thought they had him on the run only to discover themselves chasing themselves up dead-end alleys as he himself reappeared far down another highway. I like him, personally, respect him and appreciate the respect and friendliness he shows toward my own work." Buckminster Fuller to John Ragsdale, editor of the *Biophilist*, 7 November 1966, in *Letters of Marshall McLuhan*, 308 (see note 3).

science, language, law, metallurgy, animal genetics, meteorology, biotechnology, aesthetics, physics, history, philosophy, literature, agricultural science, and geography. Each field was seen to have an important contribution to make to architectural discourse. When Doxiadis sent his letter of invitation to McLuhan just seven weeks before the event, for example, he said that he had just read *The Gutenberg Galaxy* of the year before and saw ideas in it that are "essential" to a reconsideration of human settlements.[3] McLuhan had no problem seeing his work in that light. He wrote an unsuccessful fund-raising letter to another Canadian who had been invited to the event, citing the letter of Doxiadis and explaining that he was currently completing a book "which includes matters of immediate concern in housing and town planning." Since the extension of the human nervous system in an electric age "confuses the problems of living space," his own participation in the event "could be of very real importance to the study of changing problems of our national housing."[4]

Once aboard, McLuhan used the event to explore the architectural implications of his work. The boat became an amplifier for his argument that electronics is actually biological, an organic system with particular effects. The evolution of technology is the evolution of the human body. Networks of communication, like any technology, are prosthetic extensions, new body parts that construct a new organism, a new spatial system, a new architecture. This image of prosthetics—which McLuhan had first presented a year earlier in *The Gutenberg Galaxy* and was busy elaborating for *Understanding Media: The Extensions of Man,* which would launch him to superstardom when it came out a year later—was now reframed as an architectural image. McLuhan only waited until the second morning of the boat trip to get up and present his work as a question of urban planning, insisting, in a paradoxical twist, that the latest technologies expanded the body so far that they had shrunk the planet to the size of a village, creating a "tremendous opportunity" for urban planners.[5]

This was all too familiar to Fuller, who had been describing technology as an extension of the brain ever since his first, but not well known, book, *Nine Chains to the Moon* of 1938, and had been insisting that traditional architecture had to give way to a "world wide dwelling services network" modeled on the telephone network. Indeed, Fuller had visualized global electronic networks long before they arrived. Unsurprisingly, he felt that his ideas, including the concept of the global village with which McLuhan would soon become famous, had been taken without acknowledgment. Yet a strong friendship was immediately established. This was greatly assisted by the fact that, as Fuller recalls it, McLuhan was carrying copies of his *Nine Chains to the Moon* (which had just been republished) and *No More Second Hand God* when they first met on the boat, declaring, "I am your disciple. [...] I have joined your conspiracy."[6] Fuller, on the other hand, neglected to say that he had his own annotated copy of McLuhan's mimeographed "Media Log" since 1959.[7] McLuhan, who had denied getting the idea of prosthetic extension from anyone until he met Fuller, later told his friends that Fuller was too much a "linear" thinker.[8] Fuller told his friends that McLuhan never had original ideas, nor claimed to.[9] He simply

remixed available material in an original way. Yet a firm bond was estal
lished, and from then on they exchanged their latest ideas and manuscript
McLuhan wrote immediately after the Delos conference to say what a “gl
rious” thing it was to be with Fuller at the event, making all the differenc
for him, and asked the question he forgot to ask at the time about how t
quantify the relationship between information movement and physica
movement in the contemporary world, repeating his claim that “we ma
be very close, indeed, to a technological extension of consciousness.”[1
Fuller responded that he felt the same way about being together in th
conference but pointed out that consciousness is not simply extended b
electronics since it has always been extended by mathematics such that i
already extends into the invisible nucleus of atoms.[11] He sent a copy of hi
Education Automation and McLuhan sent a copy of his *Gutenberg Galax*
A few weeks later, McLuhan wrote about his idea that the kind of postvis
al space produced by the electric age can be thought as a mosaic.[12] Fulle
enthusiastically responded that McLuhan himself seems to “permeate th
mosaic of the frontiersman’s consciousness” but enclosed a list of his ow
publications so that McLuhan’s work could be “advantaged” by tensegr
ty.[13] Fuller always acted like the teacher in this way but a tight circle o
mutual appreciation was established—as evidenced by complaints whe
there was no response to a manuscript of a book being sent followed b
hasty apologies. In 1967 McLuhan would publish “Bucky,” Fuller’s autob
ographical analysis of his obsessive self-documentation and detailed chart
of his media coverage over the fifty years since 1917, as if to acknowledg
the depth of his influence.[14] They defended each other’s work in a wid
range of contexts, seeking any opportunity to be together and pursuing th
global implications of prosthetics and networks to the limit.

ANIMATE NETS

Doxiadis was ready for such sport. Like Fuller and McLuhan, he alway
thought at the scale of the planet. **fig. 7** To say the least, he was a globa
architect. The design office that he started in Athens in 1951 had alread
completed major buildings, complexes, infrastructures, urban plans, an
regional studies in Greece, Pakistan, India, Ghana, Spain, Denmark, Suda
Libya, Syria, Venezuela, Lebanon, the United States, Australia, Iran, Jo
dan, and Iraq. After just a decade of work, he was able to publish a worl

10 Marshall McLuhan to Buckminster Fuller, 11 August 1963, BFP Series 2, Box 122, Folder 6.

11 Buckminster Fuller to Marshall McLuhan, 23 August 1963, BFP Series 2, Box 122, Folder 6.

12 “Dear Bucky, I enclose a footnote on that kind of space which is an inevitable feature of the Electric Age—namely, the mosaic. The mosaic form explains why we now live in an age of continuous break-throughs and insights. The discontinuous is the natural mode of the tactile. When our senses meet each other in interplay, that is touch. Not the isolated sense. The great mechanical age now receding was one of visual continuity. Its after-image overlayering the new electric world creates the utmost confusion and waste, psychic and social. The enclosed footnote on mosaic may have some relevance here. For years I have been working on a book on the spaces of poetry and the spaces of painting. Warm regards, Marshall.” Marshall McLuhan to Buckminster Fuller, 17 September 1963, BFP Series 2, Box 123, Folder 2.

13 “The Galaxy is superb. [. . .] You seem to permeate the ephemeral mosaic of the frontiersmen’s consciousness. I am enclosing a copy of a book list of books about and by me, together with the publishers. If you are not familiar with my tensegrity structures, I suggest you get either of the books about me in which there are excellent illustrations and explanations. I am not trying to promote my own work but feel that you would be advantaged in your own work by knowledge of the tensegrity.” Buckminster Fuller to Marshall McLuhan, 23 September 1963, BFP Series 2, Box 123, Folder 2.

14 Buckminster Fuller, “Bucky,” in *Explorations*, ed. Marshall McLuhan, insert in *University of Toronto Graduate* 16, no. 1 (December 1967): 66–89.

15 The map appears on the cover of *Ekistics* 12 (July 1961). By 1956 Doxiadis had five hundred colleagues working in six countries and two continents. By 1961 the branches of his office were working on every continent. By 1966 “our responsibilities, commissions and colleagues had increased even more, to the point that growth had to be controlled in order to avoid creating a mammoth organization.” C. A. Doxiadis, “Fifteen Years of Life,” *DA Review: House Organ of Doxiadis Associates, Consultants on Development and Ekistics*, January 1967, 1.

map dotted by all his projects as if by a spreading virus.[15] Indeed, global spread was his obsession. Doxiadis was an expert in growth. His starting point was that cities were expanding out of control, as marked by the Tokyo Taxation Department's decision that it could only keep up with the spread of buildings by using aerial photography. Insisting that the speed and scale of such growth defied traditional analysis, Doxiadis launched the field of Ekistics in the mid-fifties and founded the Athens Technological Institute in 1958 as a research center and architecture school based on the idea of global statistics. The idea was to think at the largest possible scale by domesticating vast amounts of global information. If the data could be controlled, cities could be controlled. Courses in statistical analysis would become indispensable for architectural training. Spatial patterns would follow from detecting patterns in the flow of information. Design would begin with precisely calibrated charts rather than artistic sketches.

For Doxiadis, a settlement is a continually evolving organism, at once biological and technological, a technology with a biology. On the one hand, he kept referring to the city as a body with nerves, arteries, and heart and used the growth and multiplication of organic cells as a model—presenting images from biology textbooks to clarify the behavior of urban form. On the other hand, he represented the evolution of cities with sequences of "electromagnetic maps" and computerized "cartographatrons" showing shifting patterns and hidden force fields through time. **figs. 8 and 9** The combination of biological and technological images creates the impression of a dynamic biotechnological organism, ever widening its scale of operation until it becomes dysfunctional or extinct.

Doxiadis never tired of insisting that the real dimension of cities is not space, but time. What counts is a city's trajectory of development rather than its form. If a city simply grows radially outward from its center, as usually happens, pressure increases on the center until the organism collapses. "Surgery" on its "heart," like feeding new "arteries" as highways into the core, will only speed up its death. Doxiadis's prescription, as worked out in most of his projects since the mid-fifties, is that a city should grow in one direction. The core itself needs to move sideways and expand as the scale of the city increases. Such a city doesn't simply grow; it moves across the landscape. Growth becomes movement.

Settlements become a mobile species, and their movements are further accelerated by the multiple patterns of mobility made available by numerous overlapping networks. Despite designing many fixed buildings, complexes, and neighborhoods, Doxiadis rejected the traditional conception of architecture as a static, self-contained object in favor of nomadic organizations animated by circulation patterns. The internal life of each building is extended by ever-larger-scaled networks, from the pedestrian journey to a neighbor's house to an airline flight to the opposite side of the planet. Doxiadis's basic image of a building is a minimal form, a single thick semicircular line defining a shelter containing a dense internal life that is extended out by the wandering tentacles of different forms of circulation. **fig. 10** Buildings are but "shells" for movement patterns that reach out far beyond them. Whereas buildings house function, networks are

City as Biotechnological Organism on the Move

7 Doxiadis speaking aboard *New Hellas*, 1964

8 Doxiadis, electromagnetic model of 1920 pattern of Typical Urban Renewal Area (TURA), *Ekistics*, January 1962

9 Chicago Transportation Study, cartographatrons of "Desire Lines," 1959, in *Ekistics*, March 1963

10 Doxiadis, diagram of basic shell, inhabited and extended by functions

7

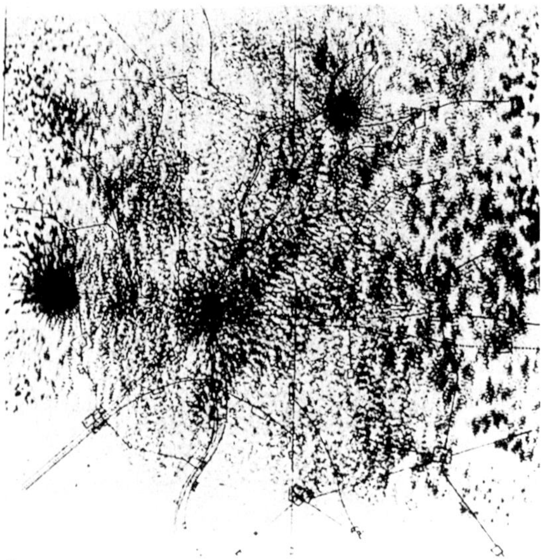

8

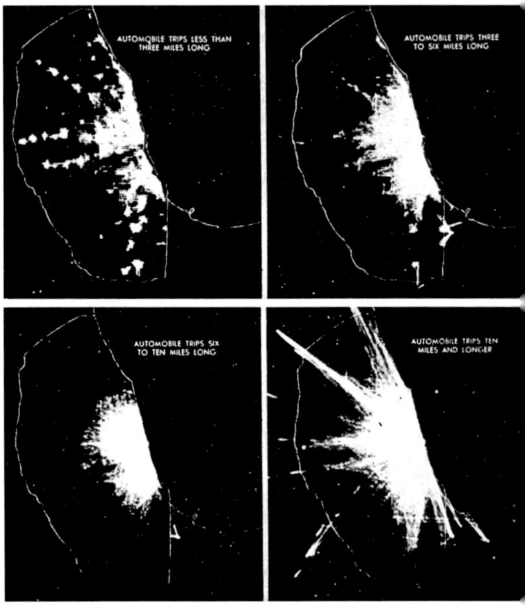

9

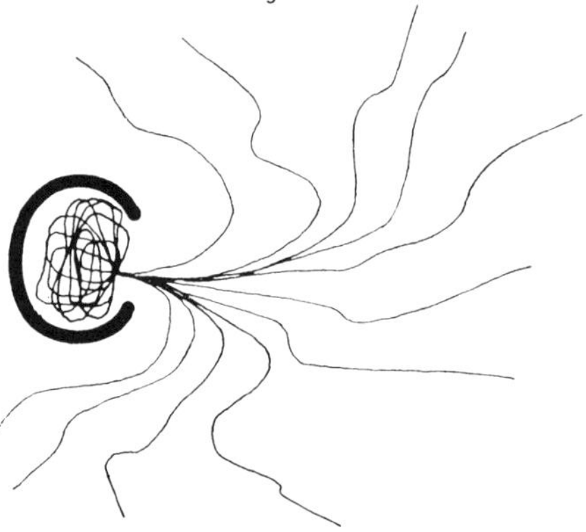

10

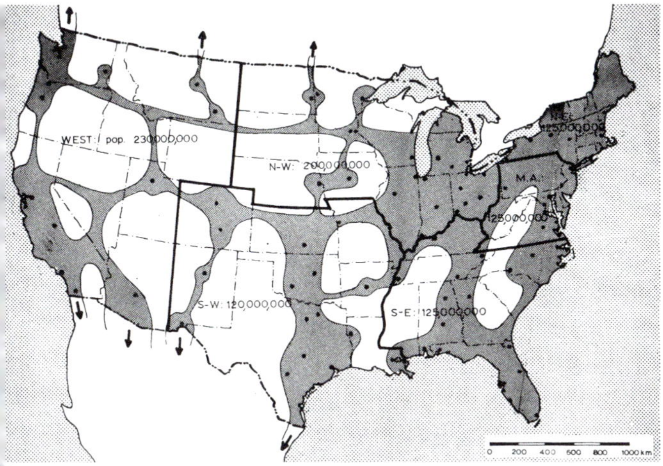

11

11 USA as a single city in Doxiadis, *Ecumenopolis: Toward the Universal City*, Nahros Conference, October 1961

12 Ecumenopolis, world as single city, 1960

13 "Ecumenopolis as the city of life," illustration from *Urban Renewal and the Future of the American City*, 1966

14 Multiscaled triangulated urban network as cover of *Urban Renewal and the Future of the American City*, 1966

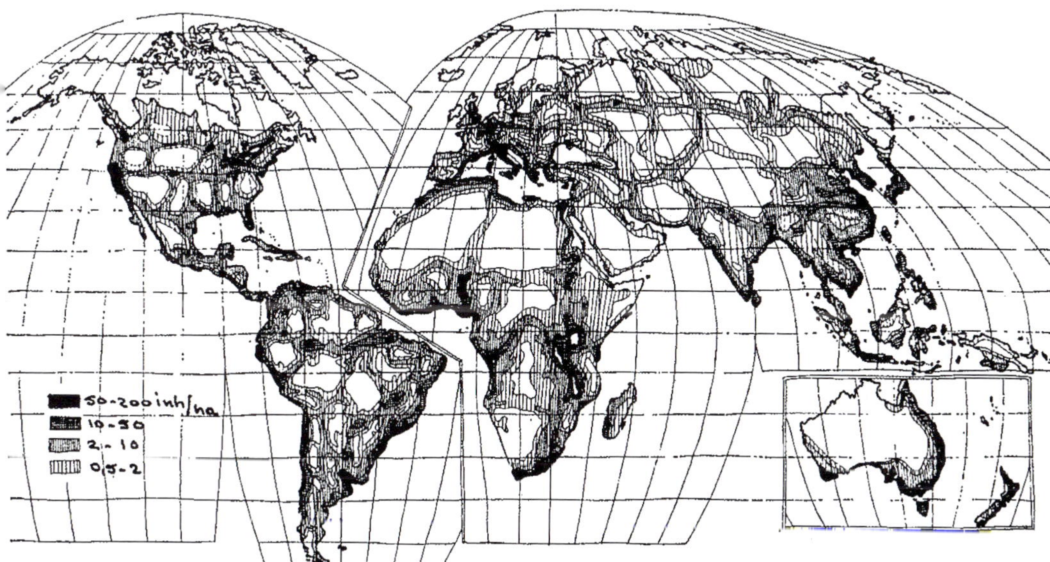

12

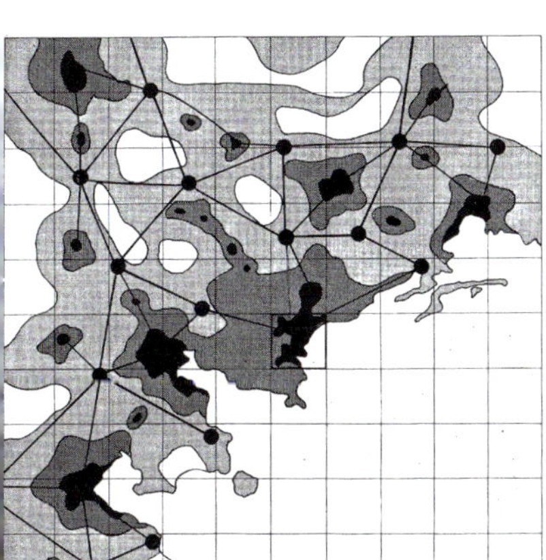

13

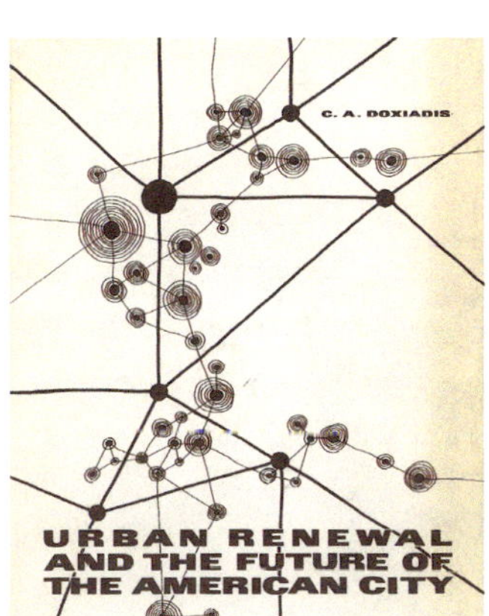

14

pure function, function without shell. If modern architects are serious in their commitment to function, they will have to reduce their fixation on shells and become responsible for networks.

This concern for networks became clearest in the "City of the Future" project that Doxiadis launched in 1960 and kept working on until his death. Starting with an analysis of the United States and first published just a month before the Delos event, it predicts the emergence of a single city covering the whole earth like a lava lamp network, a fluid, biomorphic growth extending itself everywhere. **figs. 11–14** The modern architects' fantasy of free-floating generic forms that could be dispersed anywhere on the planet that had been radicalized by Fuller gives way to a single planetary-scaled dwelling: "a continuous network of centers and lines of communication" in which "all parts of the settlement and all lines of communication will be interwoven into a meaningful organism."[16]

Doxiadis was trying to give form to the global network where Fuller saw form itself as a kind of mirage produced by the internal structure of hidden networks. For Fuller, the nets that structure biological form seen under the microscope—which the City of the Future echoes—are themselves made of even more delicate networks that are in turn made up of suspended nets hovering at the threshold of invisibility. **figs. 15–19** The concept of solidity is "obsolete" in the face of "netting," as he put it in 1961.[17] Substance is but an illusion of the most insubstantial patterns. Every apparent line is but a vibration between overlapping waves. Doxiadis drew networks as two-dimensional patterns while Fuller polemically rejected all fixed lines in the land in favor of omnidirectional connectivity in the air. Yet Fuller remains the key reference for this attempt to visualize the net. When hearing that Fuller was en route to give a lecture in Athens in 1959, Doxiadis had his brother reach out to him in the hope that he would visit the Institute.[18] He asked Fuller to be involved in the City of the Future project in November 1960; and the Dymaxion Airocean Map showing the planet itself as a network had been on every cover of the journal *Ekistics* founded by Doxiadis, from its first issue in October 1957 until mid-1959, when new drawings of nets started to be featured on the cover and only occasionally new variations of Fuller's map were presented. **fig. 20** Fuller's discourse on shelter as a globally networked system of flows, incubated in the late twenties with his idea of the "one-world town," now inspired a new generation of designers to place the planet itself on the drawing board, treating the global ecology as a single building that needed form.

It is not just architectural form that turns into a network and vice versa. Doxiadis draws the discipline of architecture in the same way as he draws the expanded city. To survive the global explosion, architects must be as networked as the spaces they produce. The discipline must take the form of an efficiently webbed biotechnical organism capable of new forms of growth. Architects can only conquer the planet by becoming an animate global net.

16 C. A. Doxiadis, *Ecumenopolis: Towards a Universal Settlement*, Document R-GA 305 (Athens: Athens Technological Institute, June 1963), 116.
17 Buckminster Fuller, "Tensegrity," *Portfolio and Art News Annual*, no. 4 (1961): 122.
18 Kyrkos A. Doxiadis to Buckminster Fuller, 8 July 1959, BFP Series 2, Box 104, Folder 4.

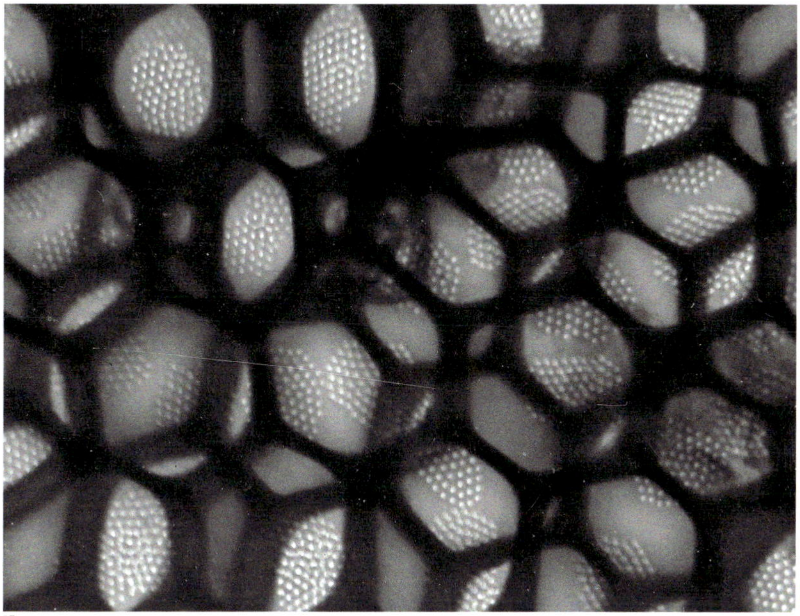

15

The Bio Net

15 1962 electron microscope photograph of diatoms used by RBF as illustration of geodesic structure

16 Biological net from RBF files

17 RBF 1961 drawing showing how even the lines in a porous web are made of discontinuous tensegrity stuctures to demonstrate that “there are no solids in structures”

18 Dr Arthur H. C. von Hochstetter, image of cornea of the human eye used by RBF in 1961 as illustration of tensegrity geodesics “in nature all the way from the atomic nucleus outward”

19 Von Hochstetter, image of “geodesic dome structure” in human testes used by RBF as illustration

20 Dymaxion Map on cover of *Ekistics*, January 1958

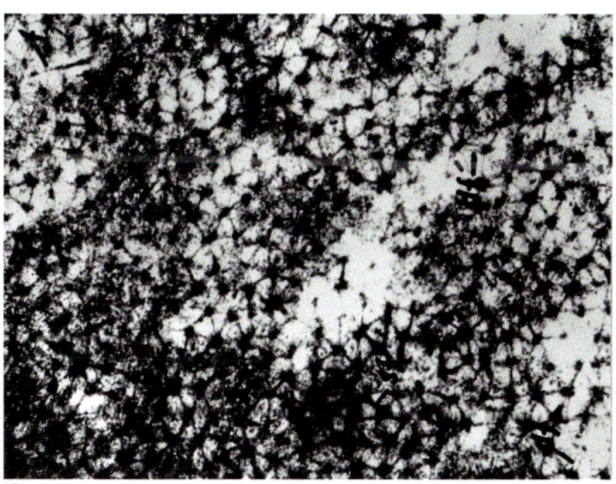

16

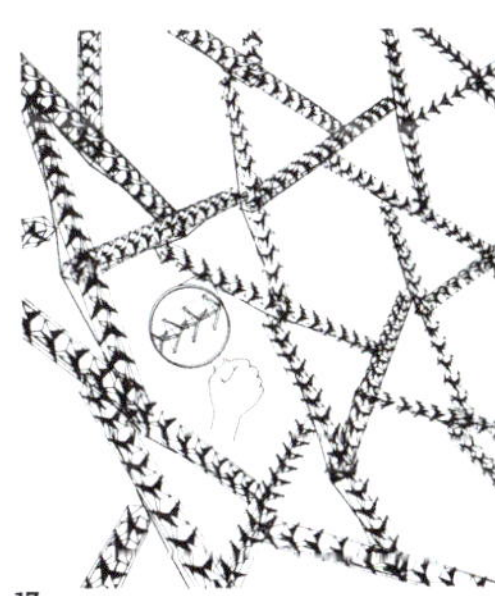

17

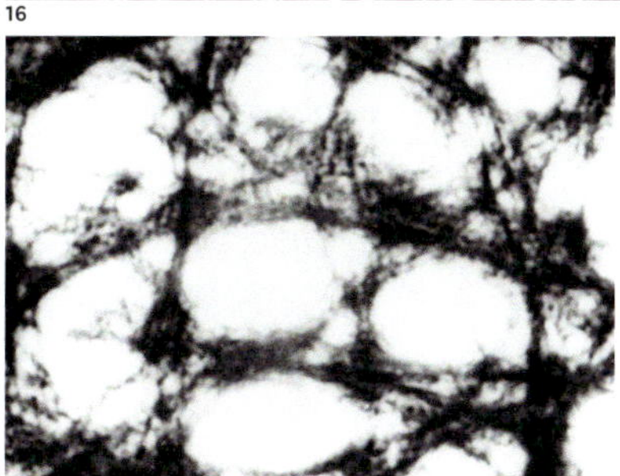

18

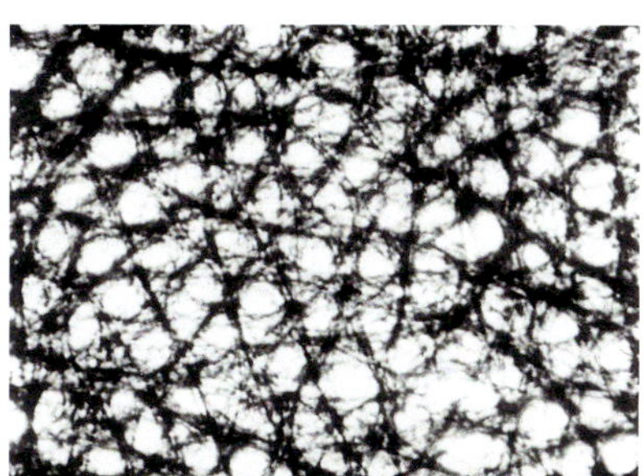

19

20

FLOATING AMPLIFIER

The 1963 boat trip was intended to be such a networking operation. **figs. 21 and 22** Experts from heterogeneous countries and disciplines were linked together in a tight web. Lines of communication were effectively drawn between every participant. Yet this web of global figures took the form of a withdrawal. To engage with the global networks whose key feature is that no point has any more value than any other, the group disconnected from those networks and returned to a very singular point, the ruins of the mythical source of western philosophy in the Greek islands.[19] In withdrawing to archaic origins, they withdrew from the media. All participants were warned before going that there would be no telephone, newspaper, or mail.[20] Once aboard, there were "no formal minutes or records, no stenographers and no tapes," just a set of handwritten notes.[21] The body was used to record the group's analysis of the displacement of the body by new technologies of communication. The only concession was a mimeograph machine that was used to convert typed statements by participants into documents distributed to all the cabins, establishing a local net that only reached as far as the sides of the ship. The implied fantasy is that the boat is a pre- or postdisciplinary space, drifting freely between islands, unaffected by the explosive global growth it so earnestly addresses.

Yet the trip was ultimately a media event. The isolation was staged as such in the very networks supposedly left behind. Edited notes on the discussions, photographs, the boat's itinerary, and biographies of the participants were circulated to the international press and specialist journals in the represented fields. Each participant was sent the same material and encouraged to send further information to journals—which many of them did.[22] The event gathered information, accumulating expert opinion from diverse fields and countries, only to reorganize it and send it back out in a unified form. What was retransmitted around the world was the media image of a premedia event—reinforced by photographs of metropolitan experts in relaxed vacation clothes basking in the sun, at restaurants, ruins, and the water. It is as if the technological expansion of the body could only be faced by returning it to its original state. The images of McLuhan, Mead, and

19 "When the group visited ruins of the ancient cities of Miletus and Priene, in Ionia, they were reminded that they were in the birth place of western philosophy, the place 'Where the first rational myth was born, the myth which gave wings to man's mind and power to his hands to conquer and transform the world.'" "The Delos Symposion," *Ekistics* 16 (October 1963): 205.

20 "For the period of our cruise we shall be to some extent cut off from the outside world. Cables can be received and sent at rates available from the Information Desk, but there are no telephone connections from the boat. We shall not receive newspaper or mail on board, but letters for mailing can be handed in at the Information Desk and will be stamped and sent off at the next convenient port." Delos Symposion Document 9, "General Information, July 1, 1963," 2, Delos Documents, Department of Drawings and Archives, Avery Architectural and Fine Arts Library, Columbia University.

21 C. A. Doxiadis, "Comment on the Delos Symposion," *Ekistics* 16 (October 1963): 204.

22 All participants were sent a copy of the package of information about the meeting that was sent to "the most important national and international technical and scientific journals of all fields represented in the Symposion," along with a list of journals that "we thought might be of special interest to you, just in case you wish to provide them with additional information." Delos Symposion Document 17, Delos Documents, Department of Drawings and Archives, Avery Architectural and Fine Arts Library, Columbia University.

23 "We are citizens of a worldwide city, threatened by its own torrential expansion and [...] at this level our concern and commitment is for man himself." "Delos Declaration," foldout insert, *Ekistics* 16 (October 1963). "The conference eventually decided that all these dynamic changes mean that the city is profoundly involved in the deepest and widest revolution ever to overtake humanity and that unless we adapt human settlements to this change, we shall soon be faced by the gravest risk, short of war, facing the human species." "The Delos Symposion," *DA Newsletter* 3, no. 7 (1963): 15.

24 Buckminster Fuller, cited in "The Delos Symposion," *Ekistics* 16 (October 1963): 205.

25 See the introduction of the Delos Declaration into the *Congressional Record*, for example, along with press clippings on the Delos meetings, in *DA Newsletter* 4, no. 1 (1964): 2–3.

26 *DA Newsletter* 3, no. 7 (1963): 31–33.

27 "When I recall the congress at which we wrote the Charte d'Athens I can only think that Greece has done it again! There must be something in the air to induce a peaceful working together and loosen normally constrained behavior." Sigfried Giedion, quoted in "Ninth Meeting—July 12, 1963. The Declaration of Delos: Statements and Comments," *Ekistics* 16 (October 1963): 254.

Fuller in animated onboard debate are counterposed with those of their rare silence in the face of the ancient landscape and artifacts. **figs. 23 and 24**

This strategic primitivism was exemplified in the closing event, when everyone signed a collective "declaration" in the ancient theater on the island of Delos. The group of globe-trotting intellectuals gathered at sunset in a ruined amphitheater to solemnly endorse a manifesto for a global makeover. **fig. 26** They sat in the first row, a semicircle of closely packed expertise facing a piece of paper that rested at the center of the stage on a rustic altar improvised out of stacked stones. **fig. 25** The sun dropped while they listened to Barbara Ward read out the document and, in a torchlight ceremony, solemnly stepped forward to make a comment and leave their mark.

Unsurprisingly, the Delos Declaration ends by reaffirming Doxiadis's vision of a single global city growing out of control, with the human species portrayed as the victim of the uncontrolled growth of architecture.[23] The "Delians" had withdrawn from this destructive exploding organism to reaffirm their physical, intellectual, and emotional humanity in a symbolic display. Yet the whole point of their radical disconnection from the modern world was to set up a better reconnection, as became clear in Fuller's speech at the beginning of the signing ceremony under the less-than-ancient gaze of a movie camera. **fig. 27** An ancient amplifier was being used for a global broadcast:

> The acoustics of the Greek theatre are phenomenal, and I believe that our voice here, relaying the voice of every man, will be heard around the world and that it will catalyze the efforts to prevent man from eliminating himself from his extraordinary role in the universe.[24]

This fantasy seemed to be realized when each participant became a kind of missionary, spreading the word *Ekistics* around the globe, and the Delos Declaration was reported extensively in newspapers and journals, was cited in discussions on housing at the United Nations, and was entered into the official records of the US Congress—events that were eagerly monitored by the monthly in-house magazine of Doxiadis's design office.[25] Early press coverage and even the press conference in Athens with which the trip had concluded was itself promptly covered with photographs of all the Delians and the rows of journalists making notes. Each participant spoke of their personal experience of the trip. Yet not by chance, it is Fuller who is shown standing and doing the talking.[26]

The model for all this was the fourth meeting of CIAM (Congrès Internationaux d'Architecture Moderne) in 1933, the boat trip from Marseilles to Athens and back, out of which the famous Athens Charter on the future of the city emerged. Sigfried Giedion, the longtime secretary-general of CIAM, was symbolically invited to the Delos event and was asked to give the last speech at the signing ceremony affirming the fundamental "continuity" between the Athens Charter and the Delos Declaration. **fig. 28** He noted that the collegial atmosphere of the two meetings was very similar, insisting that "Greece has done it again!"[27] Ekistics had officially picked up the legacy of CIAM. There would be twelve annual Delos meetings to match the ten CIAM congresses held between 1928 and 1956. But Doxiadis tried to go further than his role model, networking a wide range of disci-

21

22

23

24

Returning to the Cradle

21 Itinerary of *New Hellas* on cover of *DA Newsletter,* July 1963

22 *New Hellas* off island

23 Marshall McLuhan and Margaret Mead on Delos, 1963

24 RBF on Delos, 1963

25 Delians listen to Barbara Ward reading out Delos Declaration in amphitheater at Delos

26 Delians arriving for signing ceremony

27 RBF signing Delos Declaration

25

26

27

plines rather than just architects. Networks had to be taken to the next level.[28] In fact, the starting point of the Delos meetings was the call made at the end of the Athens Charter to improve the condition of transportation networks.

With each Delos meeting, more and more time was devoted to networks, and a collective attitude toward them evolved. In the fourth Delos in 1966, the participants accepted Doxiadis's claim that networks are historically the youngest element of settlements and will therefore change the most radically in the future, while other speakers emphasized that many of the key networks are invisible. By the eighth Delos meeting in 1970, networks had become the official theme, and Doxiadis was arguing that they are the single most important element in settlements: "the foundations of everyday life and the most decisive element for man's well-being."[29] He was even starting to describe buildings as networks. At one point in the morning discussions, he called a house "a network of walls," and at another point he referred to a theater as a "physical network between actor and audience."[30] Other speakers added the idea of social networks to the physical ones, arguing that there had to be an "interface" between them, and Doxiadis agreed that "every nonphysical network requires a physical network for its delivery."[31] The final report of the meeting confirmed that networks "proliferate and interlock, crossing every barrier, physical and political, that has previously divided man. [...] Networks are the key to the making or breaking of cities."[32] Doxiadis also hosted a full month of events in Athens devoted to "Networks and Human Settlements" in association with that year's Delos meeting, with Fuller chairing the flagship four-day seminar immediately after the cruise and delivering the keynote address on "Planetary Planning."

By the tenth Delos in 1972, networks had become the central focus of all urban design, with the final report insisting that their configuration determines the growth patterns of cities. Networks were now the beginning rather than the end point of city form. Everyone now agreed that many of the most decisive networks are invisible and that designers unwisely focus on the dense visible form rather than the diffuse communication patterns that extend that form to constitute the real settlement. Doxiadis argued that cities are simply the product of networks used to minimize effort to maximize contacts, yet typically it is only the shells that are designed. To demonstrate a necessarily wider role for the architect, he redesigned the invisible global airline network to match the latest version of his visible global network on the ground, hanging an immaterial triangulated web over the planet that is linked to the biomorphic physical web on the ground at a series of strategic nodes and would evolve as an integral part of a single global city.[33] **figs. 29–31**

28 Doxiadis was so committed to the idea of the boat that when a meeting of the Delians was held in Washington in May 1968, the so-called Delos 5 1/2, it took place on a barge for an excursion and a picnic lunch. The event was reported in "Delians Stage Special USA Meeting," *DA Review*, July 1968, 15.

29 "Points Made in Discussions," *Ekistics* 30 (October 1970): 261.

30 C. A. Doxiadis, "The Networks We Build and the Networks We Need to Build," *Ekistics* 30 (October 1970): 263; and C. A. Doxiadis, "A Methodological Approach to Networks," *Ekistics* 30 (October 1970): 331.

31 "Points Made in Discussions," *Ekistics* 30 (October 1970): 317.

32 "Report of Delos Eight," *Ekistics* 30 (October 1970): 245.

33 Doxiadis had a long-standing interest in airline systems. In a 1959 project for Pakistan, he had made a detailed study of airline and sea links. *Ekistics* had presented an analysis of global airline connections in July 1966. Again, precedent for this can be found with Le Corbusier, who, in his last book, published a global map showing an airline network linking every continent into one accessible space. "Nations, religions, principalities, powers, going to sleep, waking up, everything is different,

28

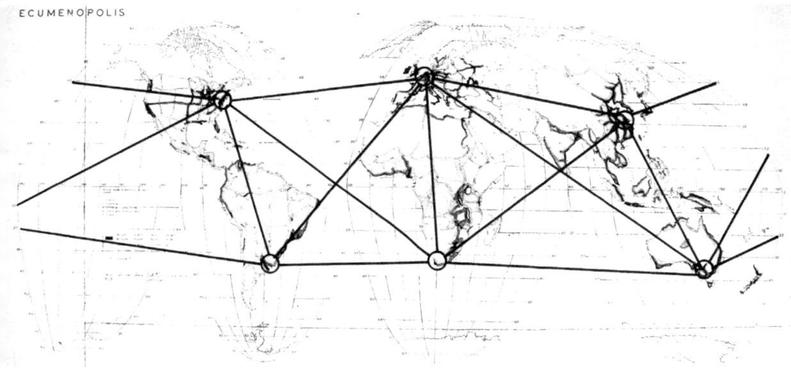

29

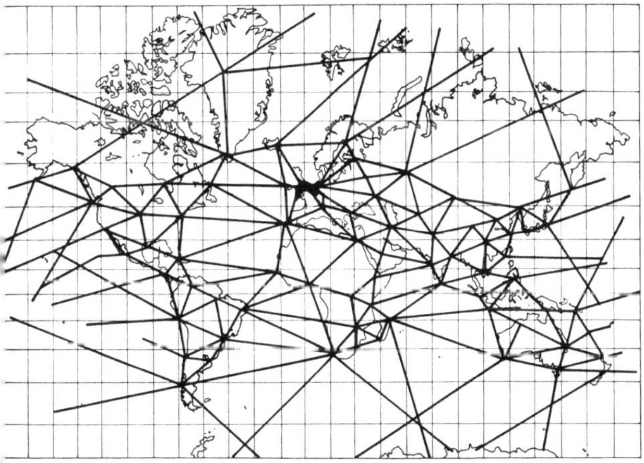
30

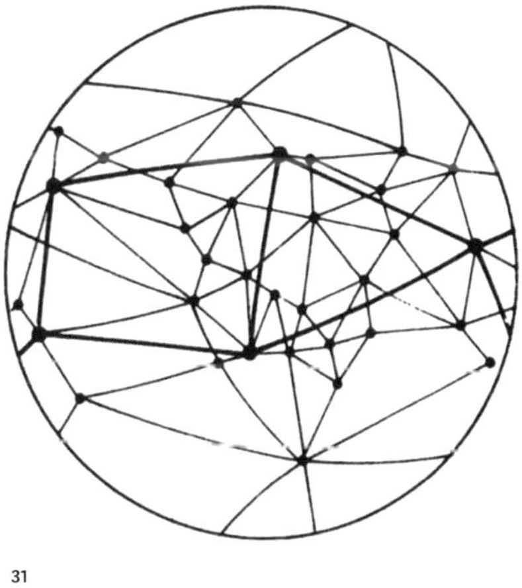
31

32

Drawing Class

28 Sigfried Giedion making speech at Delos Declaration signing, Delos 1, 1963

29 Ecumenopolis network: The biomorphic continental urban web formed by countless triangulated networks is itself suspended within a triangulated transcontinental air net

30 Doxiadis, "global networks in the present," *Ecumenopolis*, 1974

31 Doxiadis, "global networks in the future," *Ecumenopolis*, 1974

32 Doxiadis drawing aboard *New Hellas,* Delos 2, 1964

Such an image of the invisible extension of the physical was always the central goal of the Delos meetings. Instead of sitting in front of finished drawings of projects, as in the CIAM meetings, participants sat around a blackboard, drawing and discussing diagrams of network flows. **fig. 32** No matter what discipline the speakers represented, they all drew and energetically criticized one another's diagrams. Everyone was treated as a kind of architect—or, rather, the whole group tried to act as a single architect. The boat was a collaborative design studio. Following Doxiadis's lead, the Delos events were all about making a certain kind of drawing, trying to visualize the invisible by conjuring up a coherent picture of an unseen order.

FROM SCAN TO PLAN

The major vehicle for disseminating these new kinds of pictures of invisible architecture was *Ekistics*, the journal project that had originated in a different form toward the end of 1955. The latest attempt to come up with a network pattern often appeared on the cover—as a kind of hidden architecture of the month. Each Delos meeting was given a special issue, and the content of other issues was often inspired by discussions at Delos or inspired subsequent discussions. The lines scribbled onto the onboard blackboard in response to the international scene, and repeatedly modified during the morning debates, were quickly sent back out to an international audience.

The special issue on the first meeting begins with a glossy foldout text of the Delos Declaration with all the signatures, followed by detailed notes on the daily debates interspersed with photographs of the morning onboard discussions, afternoon tourism, and evening entertainment—with Fuller seemingly at the heart of everything. Intense discourse about the architectural implications of the latest technologies appears against the background of ancient ruins. There are photographs and short bios of each "Delian" and a collage of newspaper reports of the event. The issue closes with a copy of the original Athens Charter. The result is a carefully constructed image of strategic networking, a particular network trying to draw the very principles of networks.

Ekistics was itself a networking instrument. Indeed, it explicitly exaggerated the networking operations of all magazines. It only published abstracts of already published texts, repackaging and rebroadcasting existing data. The magazine was a scanning device, constantly monitoring information flow in other magazines. Whenever original material appeared, like the annual special issues on the Delos meetings, a special explanation had to be offered, reversing the usual pattern in which journals have to explain the republication of a text. Everything that was picked up in the scan was filtered: abstracted and reframed by editorials and introductions to individual articles. If all magazines are prosthetic extensions of their

changing, moving, flexible. A prodigious new broom has swept through the world order." Le Corbusier, *My Work* (London: Architectural Press, 1960), 152.

34 Le Corbusier, "Description of the CIAM Grid, Bergamo, 1949," appendix to *CIAM 8: The Heart of the City: Towards the Humanisation of Urban Life*, ed. Jaqueline Tyrwhitt, José Luis Sert, and Ernesto Rogers (London: Lund Humphries, 1952), 171–176.

35 C. A. Doxiadis, "The Two-Headed Eagle: From the Past to the Future of Human Settlements," *Ekistics* 33 (May 1972): 406–420.

36 Ibid., 418.

eaders, far-reaching eyes monitoring a distant world for a particular com-nunity, *Ekistics* was a precise and efficient instrument.

This relentless networking logic is most evident in the Ekistic Grid, a lassification system used by the magazine since January 1965. **fig. 33** Every-hing that was republished in the magazine, discussed in conferences, tudied in research projects, taught at the Athens Institute, and even the haracter of students, was codified as a visual pattern within the grid, generic frame through which all planetary activity could be monitored. Once again, this is an extension of modernist ambitions, as it was based on he CIAM Grid that Le Corbusier introduced in 1949.[34] And again it is ised to further intensify the obsession with networks. Within six months of its introduction, "Networks" replaced "Functions" in addition to the our basic elements of settlements ("Nature," "Man," "Society," and Shells") that it monitors. A year later, "Networks" was itself placed into a ıetwork with all the other elements in a new diagram and favorite lecture nodel. **fig. 35** Networks were no longer discrete. Everything was seen to be ıetworked. Even the monitoring grid evolved into a tightly woven net-vork—so tight that by 1971 it was almost unusable. **fig. 34** Likewise, the liagrams of Ekistics itself as a networking of diverse disciplines became lenser and denser. The field had been overwhelmed by network fever.

Seeing the world in terms of networks became indistinguishable from urning the world into a network. It is no surprise, for example, that the Doxiadis transportation plan for the African continent of 1962 so directly esembles the basic network diagram of Ekistics itself and that its more letailed version foreshadows the refinement of the Ekistic Grid with its ever-denser weave of interconnections. **figs. 36 and 37** Design had become a natter of identifying and refining networks as a kind of biological correc-ion. In 1972 Doxiadis presented photographs of a spider's web before and after the animal had been drugged with amphetamines. **figs. 38 and 39** The listorted organization of the doped spider was compared to a map show-ng "the chaos of networks" in the urban Detroit area.[35] **fig. 40** Doxiadis's own design for a neatly geometric system of underground networks of ransportation and utilities for the region tried to negotiate a compromise between the existing arrangement and that of an ideal spider. At this point, ıetwork fever had him firmly in its grip. As with the latest version of the grid, the central role of the architect was no longer just the form of net-vorks but the connections between them: "We must coordinate *all* of our Networks *now*. All networks, from roads to telephones."[36] The architect was seen as a networked animal that networks networks that were them-selves animate. In extending the body, networks would have to extend its organic logic. Doxiadis based design decisions for regional and global sys-tems on the internal operations of the body. The architect would elaborate he human body rather than house it. Designing networks would become a biological necessity.

These associations are classical. The ancient forms of the word *net-work* were applied at once to the work of humans and that of animals—as in fishing nets and spiders' webs. In the eighteenth century, it was com-mon to use the word to describe the inside of the body itself, as in the

NETWORK FEVER

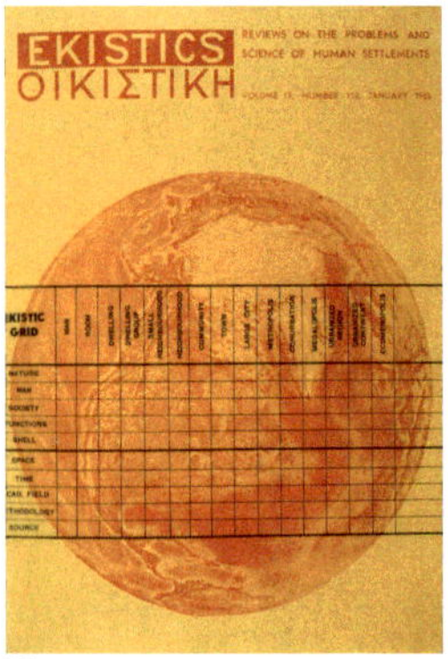

33

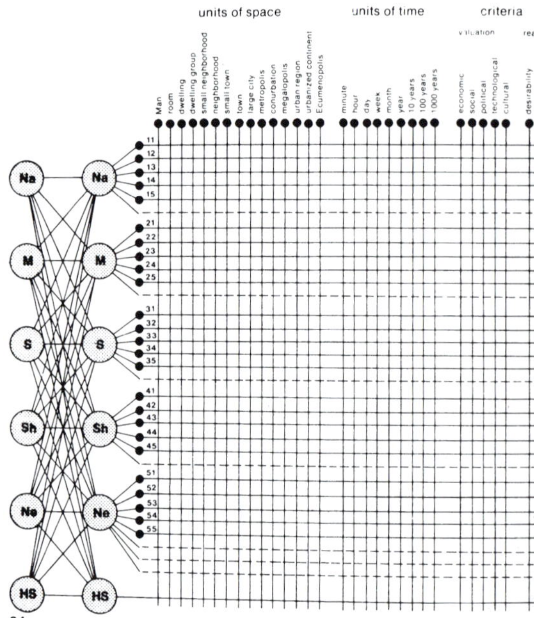

34

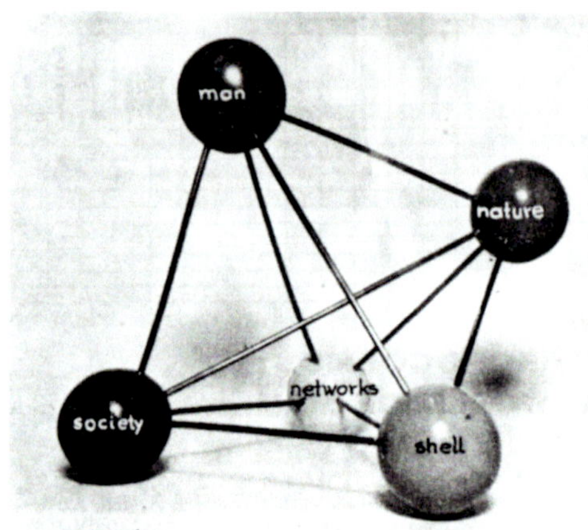

35

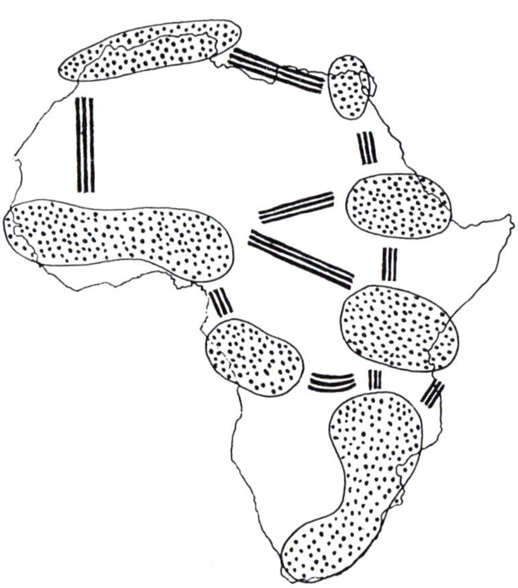

36

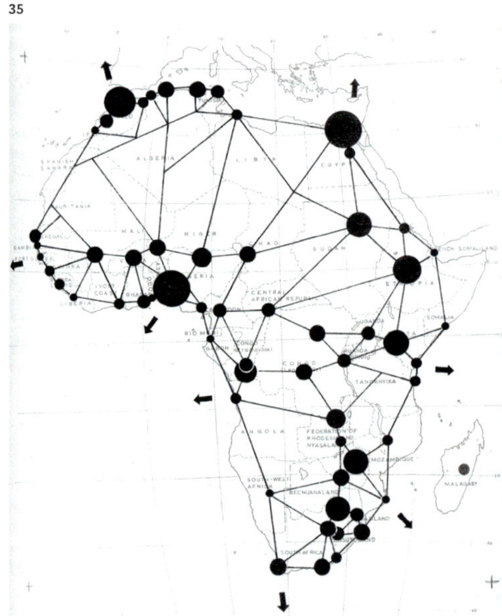

37

8

39

0

Network Pathologies

33 Ekistic Grid on cover of *Ekistics*, January 1965

34 Network of Ekistics elements, 1971

35 Model of networked Ekistics Grid containing "networks," 1966

36 Doxiadis, Regional nodes and transportation links, 1964 abstraction of 1962 drawing

37 Doxiadis, Balanced settlements, in *Toward an African Transport Plan*, 1962

38–39 Spider's web, pre- and post amphetamine, illustration of study by Peter Witt used by Doxiadis as illustration in *The Two-Headed Eagle: From the Past to the Future of Human Settlements*, 1972

40 "The chaos of networks in the Urban Detroit Area, 1971," illustration in *The Two-Headed Eagle: From the Past to the Future of Human Settlements*, 1972

41 Jaqueline Tyrwhitt taking notes aboard *New Hellas* while Edward Mason talks and P. Psomopoulos listens, Delos 5, 1967

41

organization of veins, muscle bundles, etc., and in the nineteenth century it was a standard label for systems of rivers, canals, railways, cable electricity, sewers, etc. Finally, it was applied to organizations of immaterial things like property and groups of people. The word slides seamlessly from biology to technology to society. Any appeal to new networks in the organization of space or society carries some of the original biotechnical association.

Yet it is precisely for this reason that it remains significant that modern architects like Le Corbusier only used the word *network* to describe the old street pattern and the new ones that they proposed. The full biological argument was not used beyond physical form. The key move of the Athens congress of CIAM was precisely to place greater emphasis on the idea of networks. At the first congress in 1928, the key functions of cities were identified as "Dwelling," "Working," and "Recreation." CIAM 4 added "Traffic" (*circuler*—circulation) and gave it a special coordinating relationship to the first three: "The fourth, that of traffic, should have only one objective: to bring the other three into effective communication with one another."[37] Transport networks became an organizing concept. In picking up where CIAM left off, Ekistics simply exponentially increased the role of networks.

The key figure in this escalation of network thinking was the urban planner Jaqueline Tyrwhitt, the editor of *Ekistics* since its first issue and a member of the planning committee of all the Delos meetings. In addition to playing a major role in the selection of the participants, Tyrwhitt was responsible for all organizational details during the events, and she attended every single session, taking the official notes of the discussions and editing them for publication. She typically sat to one side of the lead speaker but rarely spoke. **fig. 41** While all heads were up in animated debate hers was usually down. As secretary-general, she was at the very center of the Delos events yet maintained a low profile, facilitating the interactions of others rather than displaying her remarkable expertise. Despite being the only person who attended all the meetings other than Fuller, she only reluctantly accepted the role of full participant in the tenth Delos almost always adopting the stereotypical role of the ostensibly subordinate woman as secretary. Yet Tyrwhitt had a major effect on Doxiadis. It was not just that she was the one who chose and summarized all the articles in *Ekistics* and produced most of his books. Much of his position actually came through her, along with many of the key organizational strategies he deployed. The ever-public Doxiadis is unthinkable outside the ever-private Tyrwhitt.

37 Le Corbusier, *The Athens Charter*, trans. Anthony Eardley (1943; New York: Grossman, 1973), 98.

38 As in Delos, Tyrwhitt rarely took center stage, but at CIAM 8, at Hoddeston in 1951, again organized by the MARS group (of which she had been the assistant director since 1949), she played a central role in the discussions, put together the proceedings, and edited the resulting book with José Luis Sert and Ernesto Rogers.

39 Tyrwhitt refers to Doxiadis for the first time in a February 1955 article. Jaqueline Tyrwhitt, "The Moving Eye," *Explorations*, no. 4 (February 1955): 115–119.

40 For the first issues, Tyrwhitt was assisted in the selection of material by the architecture librarian at Harvard, a role taken over the following year by the architecture librarian at MIT. The journal was distributed to a private list of people under the title *Tropical Housing and Planning Monthly Bulletin* until October 1957, when the name became *Ekistics: Housing and Planning Abstracts*. The subtitle kept evolving until the January 1975 version, *Ekistics: Problems in Human Settlements*, which has been the title ever since.

In fact, it is Tyrwhitt who provided the key link with CIAM. Giedion was happy to come to Delos because it was Tyrwhitt who invited him. They had first met in 1947 at the sixth CIAM congress, at Bridgewater. Tyrwhitt immediately became an integral part of the CIAM operations, being secretary to the Council of CIAM from 1948 and maintaining a tight circuit of communication between the ringleaders. Giedion, Le Corbusier, José Luis Sert, Walter Gropius, and Tyrwhitt constituted the "committee of five" at the heart of CIAM. Tyrwhitt played the same role at each CIAM congress that she would later play in their Delos descendants, being responsible for organization, communication, notes, and the editing of all the proceedings.[38] She maintained a particularly close working relationship with Giedion, collaborating, corresponding, and translating all the books he published from 1951 onward. For Giedion, coming to the first and third Delos was continuing the project with Tyrwhitt rather than signing on to a new venture with Doxiadis.

Tyrwhitt was a professor in planning at the University of Toronto when Doxiadis first met her in 1954 at a United Nations seminar on housing in Delhi that she was directing. Once again, it was Tyrwhitt making the invitation. And again, the sense of a shared venture was immediate.[39] Shortly afterward, Doxiadis asked if she could help put together a set of relevant readings on third world housing and planning for the use of the branches of his office. She started to do so in 1955, after taking a position at Harvard, and eventually the monthly set of mimeographed abstracts became a full-blown magazine.[40]

The collaboration with Ekistics literally picked up where CIAM left off. Tyrwhitt traveled directly from the final CIAM congress, at Dubrovnik, in August 1956 for the first of her annual summer-long working sessions with Doxiadis. The Athens Technical Institute was founded in 1958, a year before CIAM formally dissolved itself, and in 1960 Doxiadis was announcing all the major moves he had schemed up with Tyrwhitt. She played a key role in the teaching, research, and publication operations at the institute (especially the Athens Center of Ekistics, which was formally established within it in 1963), and she eventually left her position in Harvard in 1969 to take up permanent residence in Greece. Symbolically, she lived in a hillside house designed by her Harvard and CIAM colleague Jerzy Soltan, with a dome by Fuller and an extraordinary garden of her own design that would eventually be the subject of her last, posthumous, book.

If Doxiadis picked up the CIAM mentality, it was Tyrwhitt who affected the form of that pickup and maintained its trajectory. After all, she was really the supreme networking figure. The majority of the key people invited to Delos were from her own circles of London, CIAM, the United Nations, Toronto, Harvard, and MIT, and they shared her particular concerns. She was invaluable to Doxiadis because she had done it all before: launching teaching programs, conferences, proceedings, and books. Their collaboration was extremely fruitful for both because Tyrwhitt was using Doxiadis to continue her long-standing project just as much as he was using her for his.

DIGITAL TRAFFIC

The key move at Delos was to take the CIAM argument in the direction of electronics—starting with McLuhan's announcement on the second morning of the first Delos boat trip that electronics presents new challenges to planners because this latest prosthetic extension of the body defines an entirely new form of space. Tyrwhitt was yet again the link, having been a member of McLuhan's inner circle in Toronto since the end of 1952 (after Giedion had written a letter of recommendation to McLuhan).[41] From 1953 to 1955, Tyrwhitt was one of McLuhan's four colleagues working under a Ford Foundation grant to carry out an interdisciplinary study of the effects of the new media, the key project out of which McLuhan's famous arguments would emerge. It was while she was in the middle of that project and was one of the associate editors of *Explorations*, the group's magazine, that she met Doxiadis. The radical position that McLuhan brought to Delos in 1963, and would not become internationally renowned for until the following year, had been very familiar to Tyrwhitt for a long time. They had been discussing the media's transformation of the world into "one city in space" since the mid-fifties. In December 1960 McLuhan's letter responding to Tyrwhitt's suggestion that he take a position at Harvard spells out the view that the traditional city has been displaced by the electronic extensions of the body that have constructed a "global village" in which traditional conceptions of space have been overturned. This already existing electronic village calls for the construction of a new form of physical world city by planners—"Today with electronics we have discovered that we live in a global village, and the job is to create a global *city*, as center for the village margins"—and McLuhan speculates that this post-Euclidean city will have to be assembled by computer in the same way that airports use computers to coordinate flights.[42]

When making these same points three years later at Delos, McLuhan was supported by Fuller and two former associates of Tyrwhitt, the planners Edmund Bacon and Juliusz Gorynski. They agreed that the "electronic scale" had to be integrated with the human scale and that the latter could actually be maintained within man's "electronic extensions."[43]

41 Giedion recommended Tyrwhitt to McLuhan in a letter thanking him for sending a copy of his first book, *The Mechanical Bride*. Tyrwhitt had arrived in Toronto in July 1951. In 1950 she had become a partner with Wells Coates (one of the original founders of the MARS group in 1933) in London and went to Toronto after a short stint in Yale at the beginning of 1951. She got together with McLuhan for the first time in November 1952.

42 Marshall McLuhan to Jaqueline Tyrwhitt, 23 December 1960, in *Letters of Marshall McLuhan*, 277 (see note 3).

43 "This means that we are today dealing with two widely different dimensions: the eternal human scale — man with his five natural senses — our continuity with the ancient world, and the electronic scale — multi-dimensional integration — our emergence into the new world. Man of the renaissance and technological man no longer directly concern us. The human scale needs to develop the totality of the electronic scale, and the electronic scale the discipline of the human scale. Perhaps the latter can be done by maintaining the proportions of the human scale in man's electronic extensions." Edmund Bacon and Marshall McLuhan, "The Delos Symposion," *Ekistics* 16 (October 1963): 208. For Bacon, the most important thing about the conference was establishing the need for a "new science of human settlement for the purpose of comprehending city and regional growth as a total organic process within the framework of the emerging concepts of the electronic age." Edmund Bacon, cited in "Edmund N. Bacon, USA," *Ekistics* 16 (October 1963): 218.

44 "But beyond his senses, man has his 'electronic extensions.' Do these imply that, in addition to his immediate neighborhood, he can also relate to a wide variety of other centers within a single urban region or on a wider scale?" "Conclusions: Preliminary to a First Draft by Barbara Ward (Lady Jackson), Delos Meeting Document B17," July 11, 1963, Delos Documents, Department of Drawings and Archives, Avery Architectural and Fine Arts Library, Columbia University.

45 The editorial of the August 1959 issue describes the usefulness of analyzing the "mass" of data by punched cards, as shown in the two articles abstracted from recent issues of the *Journal of the Town Planning Institute* and the *Journal of the American Institute of Planners*. The first article describes "a complete handling and mapping of data," and the second, on "Data Processing for City Planning," covers the role of computers, highlighting the cartographatron, an electronic device for displaying "desire lines" on the face of a cathode ray tube as the result of an analysis of more than 700,000 punched cards.

46 The article by Jonathan Barrett, "Will the Computer Change the Practice of Architecture," for example, explores the new kind of shapes that could be modeled digitally and have retained the fascination of designers in recent years. *Ekistics* 19 (April 1965): 247–249.

CIAM thinking had to be retooled for an electronic world. The Delos meetings would turn the CIAM idea of settlements held together by transportation networks into the idea of inhabitable information networks. But it took a while. The final point of the first draft of the Delos Declaration did include a reference to the concept of electronic extensions and its effect on the emergence of urban form.[44] But it did not survive the editing process. It was not until the fourth Delos of 1966 that the whole meeting would accept the basic point of Fuller, McLuhan, and Mead that communication networks have produced a single planetary society—that it was no longer possible to research the city without discussing electronics.

The trajectory from the physical city to the electronic one was even more evident in *Ekistics*, through the strategic selections of Tyrwhitt and her unsigned editorials. Again, the first Delos appears to have acted as a catalyst. Momentum built through the gradual accumulation of individual articles and then special issues on communication. Diverse media were analyzed, including telephone, radio, television, telex, cable, closed circuit, and satellites. Particular attention was paid to their influence on the so-called developing world, where their transformative effect was most pronounced. The journal steadily and increasingly radically explored the displacement of the physical. There was a continuous feedback loop between the journal and the Delos events. On the one hand, the journal presented detailed studies into the questions raised each year at Delos. On the other hand, most of the participants appeared in the journal before being invited to participate. Between the conferences and the journal's monthly scan an extraordinary discourse about the architecture of electronics developed.

In fact, the journal's concern with electronics precedes the first Delos. The computer, for example, had been a theme in the magazine since the late fifties, starting with the editorial of the August 1959 issue that describes the usefulness of computerized analysis of data on punch cards and the graphic representation of that analysis on computer monitors, when introducing two articles on the "science fiction"-type machines that do this.[45] In 1962, a year before Fuller and McHale started using computers for the World Resources Inventory at Carbondale, Doxiadis started using them to develop mathematical models of settlements, and after the first Delos he wanted everything computerized and proudly published photographs of each new computer installed in his office. At the beginning of 1964, the report on the research projects at the Athens Institute said that the main emphasis was now on computer programming, data processing, and methodology. An "Electronic Computer Center" was set up in the office, and the ground floor of the building was actually used as a computer training center once Doxiadis discovered that no one in Athens was qualified to run the machines. The following year, *Ekistics* featured a special issue on "Architecture and the Computer," discussing computer design of buildings, computer conferencing, and so on.[46] The journal itself was soon computerized, with ever more detailed indexes becoming computer printouts, and in 1969 a special issue was needed on "Computers in the Service of Ekistics." By then, three shifts of workers were employed twenty-four hours a day to type in statistical data on cities in a room filled with punch card machines.[47] The more philosophical discussions of the architecture of electronics at Delos were paralleled by their ongoing practical use.

The appeal of the computer is that it offered a new viewing point to survey the explosive rise of ever larger and less visible networks. If the uncontrolled growth of the city had first demanded the surveillance view from the airplane and then the view from outer space, the growth of invisible networks demanded new scanning instruments. The computer was the ideal mechanism to negotiate between the visible and the invisible. The computer is both a means of diagnosis and a symptom, both a mechanism that reveals hidden patterns in an overwhelming conglomeration and one of the forces that dematerializes or transforms the occupation of that physical organization. Ekistics oscillated between using electronics to expose hidden circulation patterns and producing images of hidden electronic patterns.

Basically, Ekistics radicalized the logic of traffic and moved it into the world of electronics. At the fourth Delos trip, it was argued that "modern transport networks extend far beyond the visual horizon."[48] This shift became clear in "From Man's Movements to His Communications," the May 1970 special issue of *Ekistics,* whose foreword speaks of the "more complete move from a mechanical to an electronic environment." At the Delos meeting of that year, it was argued that physical transportation might go away when moving ideas replaces moving bodies. This had become a mantra by the June 1973 special issue on "Networks: Information, Communication and Transportation." The editorial insists that they are inseparable, and the cover conveys McLuhan's basic point by showing the progressive exponential shrinkage of the world to a small point. Electronics is the new form of traffic and therefore the new form of the city.

In the end, this was the key move with which Ekistics transformed the CIAM mentality. Le Corbusier, for example, was acutely aware of the role played by new systems of communication like the telephone and often referred to it.[49] He even had images of the dense weave of the international telephone network in his files in the twenties, but *La ville radieuse* of 1930 only uses the word *network* to refer to the visible traffic patterns of the city.[50] **figs. 42 and 43** When the Athens Charter ends by referring to the inadequacy of the "existing network of urban communications," the issue is likewise only physical traffic. Doxiadis, Tyrwhitt, and their friends set out to multiply the concepts of traffic. Traffic was conceived as information flow. Symptomatically, drawings of cities, continents, disciplines, and computers tended to be the same.

Fuller was again the reference point, having insisted since 1927 that architecture should emulate the operation of communication networks

47 The report on the "Human Community" research project says that the main emphasis in January was on computer programming, data processing, and methodology (IBM punched cards) using IBM 1620 machines. *DA Newsletter* 4, no. 1 (1964): 41. The May 1964 issue published pictures of the new computer and the organization of a new "Electronic Computer Center" in the office. *DA Newsletter* 4, no. 5 (1964): 29. *DA Newsletter* 7, no. 1 (1971) shows all the punched card machines "busy around the clock." The August 1972 issue shows pictures of students with the latest computer system.

48 Diana Rowntree, "The Science of the City," *Ekistics* 22 (October 1966): 243.

49 See Beatriz Colomina, *Privacy and Publicity: Modern Architecture as Mass Media* (Cambridge: MIT Press, 1994).

50 Le Corbusier, *La ville radieuse* [1933], trans. Pamela Knight as *The Radiant City* (New York: Orion Press, 1967). Much of the book is devoted to the coordination of traffic networks handling different speeds.

Traffic Nets

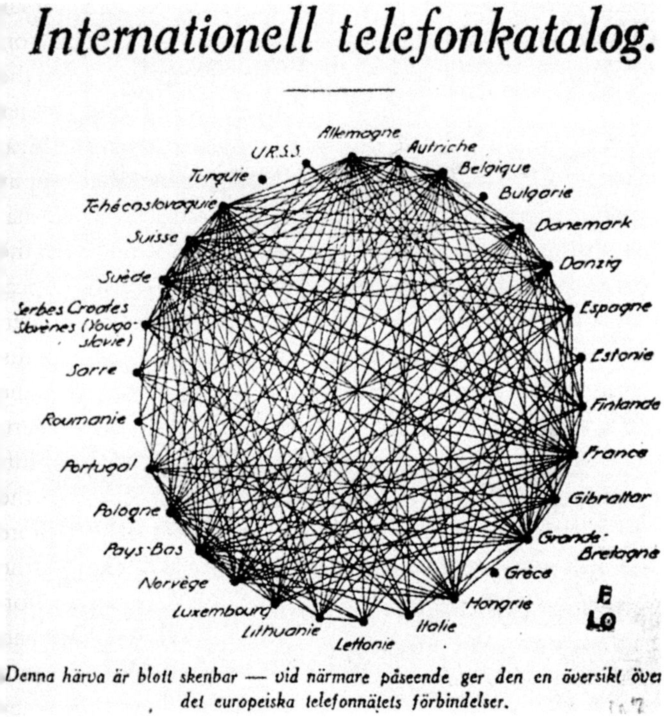

42

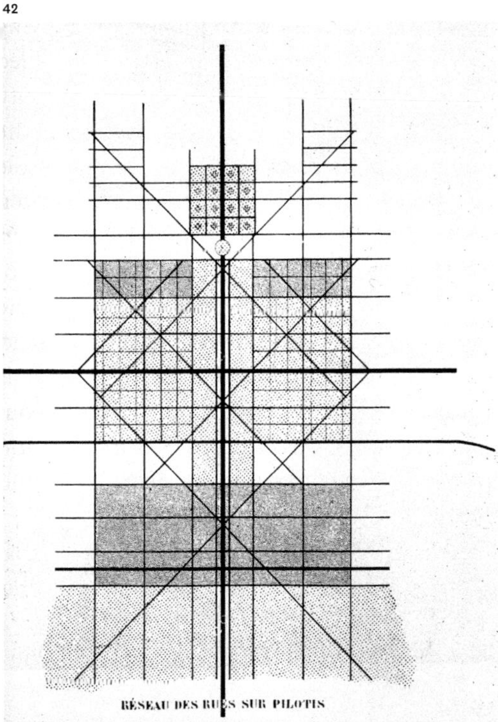

43

42 International telephone network from Le Corbusier's file cabinet collection of material for *L'Esprit nouveau*.

43 Le Corbusier, "network" from *La ville radieuse*, 1933

like the telephone and aspire to the omnidirectional mobility of radio. In 1934 he even wondered in reverse whether the global communications "web" itself would be understood in the future as the real architecture of the early thirties. No longer would shelter need to emulate communication as communication was already shelter:

> Possibly the architecture of today will in time be evident as the air routes, as the great network of transportation, communication, a web which is knitting closely together all the people on the small globe 'World.' [...] The world is now so closely knit in the matter of communication by publishing or wireless that if we assay to a proper contemplation of architecture now in the making it is necessary to take into consideration all the structural expressions upon the surface of the globe, the complete survival mechanism as articulated in the industrial intercoursing.[51]

The focus had moved from individual shelters to the vast industrialized system of connectivity that was increasingly invisible. For Fuller, the visible physical communication nets like highways would inevitably give way to the invisible webs of airline networks which in turn would give way to the unprecedented density of continuous global information traffic. Where Le Corbusier explicitly understood physical communication as an extension of the human organism, Fuller understood the ephemeral traffic of publications and wireless broadcasts as the crucial organic extension. Information flow itself was biological, and its unseen nets were evolving like any other organism.

THE BIOLOGY OF INFORMATION

Aboard *New Hellas*, the new traffic of electronic exchange was seen as biological, once again hyperextending parts of the established discourse of modern architecture rather than abandoning it. A blurring of biology and information occurred throughout the Delos meetings. At the signing of the first Delos Declaration, Conrad Waddington, a renowned animal geneticist who would be a central figure in most of the meetings, said that the type of world city being envisioned by the group would be "a new level of organization of the living material of the universe."[52] This echoed the discussions of the second morning when, in response to McLuhan's first statements about media extensions of the body, he joined with geographer Walter Christaller and psychiatrist Leonard Duhl in inventing urban schemes by comparing the evolution of electronic networks to that of animals:

51 Buckminster Fuller, "Industrially Reproducible Architecture," *Trend: An Illustrated Bi-Monthly of the Arts*, May–June 1934, 121.

52 "The Delos Symposion," *Ekistics* 16 (October 1963): 205. On connections between Waddington and other interdisciplinary communities, see Rheinhold Martin, "Crystal Balls," *Any* 17 (1997): 35–39.

53 "Delos Symposion, Notes from 2nd meeting," Delos Documents, Department of Drawings and Archives, Avery Architectural and Fine Arts Library, Columbia University.

54 Particularly in Delos 3 of 1966, an argument repeated after a discussion of "foodwebs." See C. H. Waddington, "Biology and Human Environment," *Ekistics* 21 (February 1966): 90–94. The spider's web is a model of the resilience of biological systems to change because it is not affected by removing links.

55 "A city is a complex living system. Its anatomy and composition can be studied and analyzed like any other living system. [...] A comprehensive analysis of the interactions within an urban population could be conducted in a manner equivalent to that used by biologists in their studies of living systems were it not for the presence of shields that have been created to fend off messages. This shield is called *privacy*. The small groups clustered inside these screens for communications (homes) are known to exchange messages which the stranger is not granted immediate or complete access." Richard Meier, *A Communication Theory of Urban Growth* (Cambridge: MIT Press, 1962), 1.

56 C.A. Doxiadis, "Ecumenopolis," *Ekistics* 13 (January 1962), 12. Abstracted from an October 30, 1961, lecture in Washington with the same title.

57 The charts are first described in a report on the City of the Future project in *DA Newsletter* 4, no. 3 (1964): 40. The speed drawing first appears in *DA Newsletter* 4, no. 4 (1964): 39–41.

58 C. A. Doxiadis, *Ekistics: An Introduction to the Science of Human Settlements* (New York: Oxford University Press, 1968), 43.

59 Buckminster Fuller, "The Prospects of Humanity: 1965–1985," *Ekistics* 18 (October 1964): 232–242, special issue on Delos 2.

> As animals become more complex they develop increasingly differentiated limbs and organs and a highly efficient communications center. Should we move towards a newly constructed type of organization with highly differentiated centers tied together by a complex communications network, each center having special functions and a special location?[53]

Waddington, whose books Fuller had followed closely since the late forties, read evolution in cybernetic terms. The growth of electronic systems of communication is biological in exactly the same terms that biological growth is itself an evolution of systems of communication. Waddington relentlessly applied this model at most of the Delos meetings, often using spiders' webs as a model system of organization.[54] He was supported by Margaret Mead, who had been a pioneering member of the key group that had established cybernetics after the war. At the second Delos, they got further support in connecting this model to architectural form from Richard Meier, who had published *A Communication Theory of Urban Growth* in 1962, a cybernetic account of the city as a living organism and information system to be analyzed in biological terms.[55] Meier had come to Tyrwhitt's attention when he was writing the book in 1959–1960 at the Joint Center for Urban Studies at MIT and Harvard, of which she was a member. He became one of the leading researchers in the City of the Future project. Already in an October 1961 discussion of the project, Doxiadis said cybernetics and information theory would be necessary,[56] a point repeated at the very end of his 1963 report on the project just before the first Delos, but apart from referring to the city as an "organism" he was not yet talking that much about either biology or information.

In fact, the biological argument rose very slowly in Doxiadis's writing. This is most obvious in the City of the Future project, which gradually became a vast prosthetic. Working closely with Meier, Doxiadis rationalized the new city in 1964 with Fulleresque charts showing the exponential increase in "the average speed of man's displacement since 10,000 BC" and the extension of man's vision through mechanical means."[57] He eventually began to talk of the possibility of developing new organs for the city. A biological organism is capable of improvement. The genetics can be rearranged. A new body can and should be developed. Cities can be helped to reach an ever-higher biological order. Networks, particularly electronic ones, are the means of this upgrade. Doxiadis used computerized traffic control as a model for cities to be higher-order biological individuals than plants, animals, and humans.[58] With each year, he went deeper into the prosthetic logic.

The Delos discussions clearly had an effect. McLuhan's initial image of prosthetic growth was elaborated in more and more detail as the annual boat trips gradually embraced the centrality of electronics. At the second Delos, for example, Fuller reasserted his old line about prosthetic networks in a lengthy argument about the way computers augment the human brain, before rolling around on the floor to make his point about synergy. He concluded that the human's "externalized organics (the world industrial network)" would eventually become as unconscious as the automated operation of internal organs.[59] In immediate agreement was sociologist

Edward T. Hall, who had located architecture as one of the tools within the array of bodily extensions in his 1959 book *The Silent Language* and had been invited to the second Delos after McLuhan suggested it to Tyrwhitt. McLuhan was citing these passages in his latest book and identifying them as the inspiration for his use of the prosthetic argument. But Hall in turn had been inspired by Fuller, having been a close friend of the Fullers ever since he became a college teacher of their daughter Allegra. Margaret Mead was likewise no stranger to the prosthetic argument from her years in the cybernetics debates. This was a very persuasive group, and by the eighth Delos everyone was able to agree that computers were an inevitable "revolution in the use of brain extension systems" displacing the "muscle-power extension systems" of the industrial age.[60] The discussion of prosthetics had become extreme at that point, embracing genetically grown limbs, "Computopia" without human bodies, and so on.

Tyrwhitt's journal relentlessly pursued this more radical view of prosthetics, embracing engineering psychologist J. C. R. Licklider's theory of future "symbiosis" of human and computer and his drawings of the possible interface between the two organisms, with the human network entangled with the electronic.[61] **fig. 44** In this line of argument, it is not so much that the latest technology has constructed a new world for us to inhabit. The global city is the global body. We inhabit our own hyper-extended body. When Ekistics calls for a redesign of networks, it is calling for a redesign of the human body—network, city, and body being the same thing.

This equivalence of prosthetics and architecture is exemplified in a 1969 essay in *Ekistics* by the engineer Koichi Tonuma analyzing contemporary flows of information, with charts of telephone and telex communication within the main island of Japan, to predict the transformation of the island into a single continuous "living space," a vast urban network that looks like a nervous system. **figs. 45 and 46** The invisible electronic lines connecting people become the matrix on which a visible biomorphic form emerges. The necessary correlate of this biological vision of electronics and buildings is a technological vision of the human body, when "our organs are being replaced with artificial tools."[62] It is the confusion of the body and its extensions that explodes a single biotechnical infrastructure across the landscape. Tonuma presents a sequence of drawings showing settlements gathering size and complexity from single cells to complete biological organisms that are similar to those of Doxiadis. In fact, Tonuma spent two years in Athens doing research at the center. Japan played a key

60 D. E. Noble, "So Now We Must Extend Our Brain Power," *Ekistics* 30 (October 1970): 314.

61 This was exemplified in the September 1965 issue, which featured Licklider's article on the "Man-Computer Partnership" and one of his drawings on the cover. J. C. R. Licklider, "Man-Computer Partnership," *Ekistics* 20 (September 1965): 165–169. The article was written when Licklider moved from the Air Force research laboratories to the research center of IBM. Other articles on planning buildings by computer cite his increasingly influential idea of a "symbiosis" between man and computer, and one of them argues that evolution culminates in "computer systems or automata, prostheses which will extend the brain's ability to manipulate symbols just as the bulldozer is a prosthesis for muscles and the microscope, telescope, and laser are for the eye [...] the upgrading of human capacity on a large scale. [...] Men can be upgraded. At the strictly biological level, there is no question that the principles of genetics and selection, used widely by man in the plant and animal world, could be used to enhance desired traits in man." R. W. Gerard, "Intelligence, Information and Education," *Ekistics* 20 (September 1965): 162–164. A similar issue in 1967 begins with John McHale's speculations about the "New Symbiosis," which also cites Licklider and weaves together prosthetics, cybernetics, McLuhan, and Fuller; then a series of other articles explores the roles that computers can play in design and analysis.

62 Koichi Tonuma, "Network City," *Ekistics* 29 (June 1970): 458. This essay was first published in *Journal of High Speed Transportation* 3 (May 1969): 259.

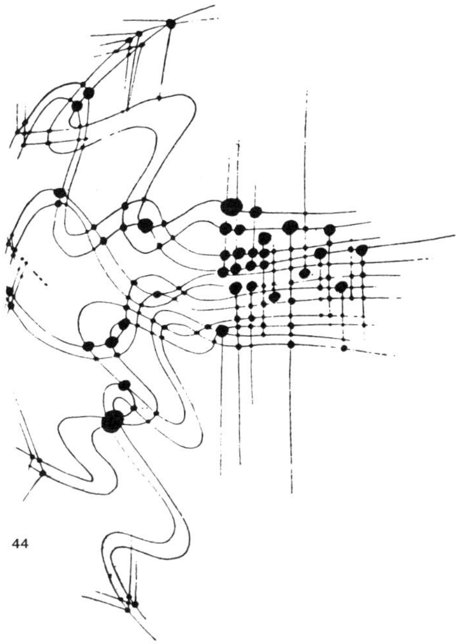

44

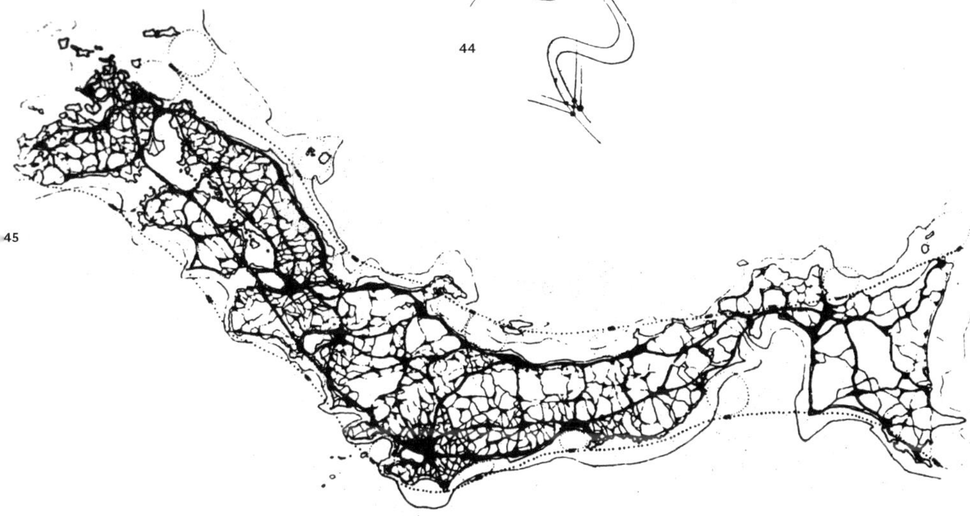

45

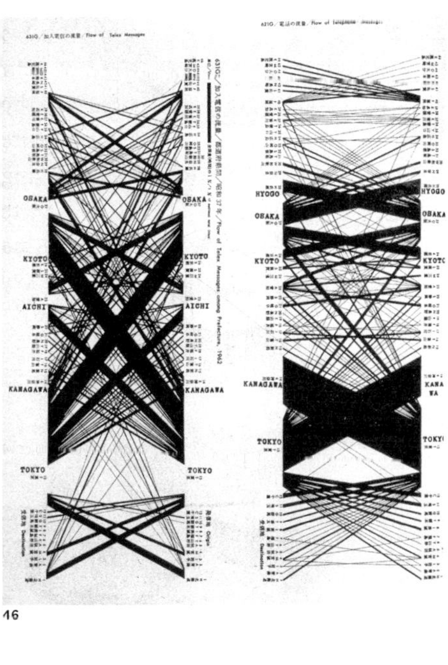

46

The Symbiosis between Brain, Information Machine, and City

44 J. C. R. Licklider, 1965 drawing of "man/computer symbiosis," in *Ekistics*, September 1965

45 Koichi Tonuma, "The Network City—Japan at the Beginning of the 21st Century," *Ekistics*, June 1970

46 Koichi Tonuma, diagram of flow of telex and telephone messages between capital cities in Japan, *Ekistics*, June 1970

role in Ekistics, as a model for contemporary statistical trends and as a site for imagining radical futures, featuring prominently in the City of the Future project from the beginning.

Yet this biotechnical vision is not simply projected onto Japan as a unique experiment of the Athens laboratory. Tonuma's whole argument, even its prosthetic aspect, came from specific architectural proposals made in Japan in the early sixties. All it does is to add particular statistical readouts of information flow and particular drawings of biological cells to an existing scheme that had its own flow readouts and cell drawings. It is crucial to remember that Ekistics was only ever a networking operation, a scanning mechanism coordinating and editing already existing ideas, not just in the sense of design as statistical analysis of given information rather than artistic innovation, but also design as the recirculation of tested strategies. The network fever in Ekistics can be found in the work of numerous architects. Indeed, the fever was endemic to architectural discourse during those years. The specific contribution of Ekistics was simply to relentlessly monitor it and thereby feed it.

NERVE DESIGN

A major accelerant of the fever was Kenzo Tange, the preeminent Japanese architect. As one of the passengers on the fourth Delos boat trip in 1966, for example, he addressed the "tentacles" of the communication network in biological and evolutionary terms. **fig. 47** To inhabit the modern city is to inhabit the information system of an artificial brain:

> Society is evolving into a more advanced state, as plants evolved into animals, and animals into men. We have begun to create a new nervous system in society using the advanced communication technology that will enable the social brain to function more effectively. In large contemporary urban complexes, communications networks twist and interlink into a complex which must be something like the nervous system of the brain. [...] Whirling around in these brains are the people and the information. The citizens are like electrons flowing in an electronic brain.[63]

Tange drew on cybernetics to discuss the influence of all the contemporary systems of communications—arguing, in McLuhanesque fashion, that there had been a second industrial revolution, an information revolution that prosthetically extends the nervous system in the same way that the first one physically extended the body.[64] He predicted that Japan could only maintain its "organic life" by eventually turning into a single colossal city through the linkup of physical, social, and information networks into a single "central nervous system."

63 Kenzo Tange, cited in "Kenzo Tange," *Ekistics* 22 (October 1966): 259.
64 "In the First Industrial Revolution, men learned how to extend the functions of their hands and bodies through the use of tools or machinery. The Second Industrial Revolution, which has begun only recently, is a revolution created by information theory and communications techniques, a revolution in which man is learning to extend the functions of his nervous system." Tange, "Kenzo Tange," *Ekistics* 22 (October 1966): 275.
65 Kenzo Tange, "Tokaido-Megalopolis: The Japanese Archipelago in the Future," in *Kenzo Tange, 1946–1969: Architecture and Urban Design*, ed. Udo Kultermann (Zurich: Artemis, 1970), 150–167.
66 Kenzo Tange, "A Plan for Tokyo, 1960," *Ekistics* 12 (July 1961): 9–19.
67 Kenzo Tange, "A Building and a Project: On the Kurashiki City Hall and a Project at MIT," *Ekistics* 11 (June 1961): 469–472.
68 Sigfried Giedion, "Density and Urbanism," *Ekistics* 20 (October 1965): 208–209.
69 Fumihiko Maki, "Linkage in Collective Form," *Ekistics* 14 (August–September 1962): 100–103. When Maki put together a more formal publication, photographs of Tange's Tokyo Bay and Boston Harbor projects were added as key examples. Fumihiko Maki, *Investigations in Collective Form* (St. Louis: Washington University, 1964).

Tange's spoken statements were actually taken from an article he had published the year before, entitled "Tokaido-Megalopolis: The Japanese Archipelago in the Future," which presented charts of the "evolution" of media use (telegraph, telephone, radio, and computer) and maps of flow in each communication network" of Tokaido (rail, car, mail, and telephone) before drawing the islands as one colossal biomorphic city.[65] **fig. 48** His drawing of the shape of this new organism is similar to those that Doxiadis had been publishing since 1962, but Doxiadis's idea of network form had itself been informed by the earlier work of Tange. The July 1961 *Ekistics* had devoted an unprecedented ten pages to Tange's renowned Tokyo Bay project of 1960, in which a vast floating linear "network of elevated lattices" blurring traffic and building is grafted onto the radial network of the traditional city, and the whole organization is "tied together by the invisible cords of a communication system" (telephone, radio, portable telephone, video telephone). **fig. 49** Alongside images from biology textbooks of the growth of spines, Tange described the project as an "organism" precisely because "communication is the factor that gives organic life to the organization." The paradoxical rationale of the network is that the possibility of infinite extension actually produces density. In an argument that resembles the one McLuhan would present three years later in the first Delos, Tange insisted that the capacity of networks to extend anywhere actually produces the need for concentration: "People say that organization man is alone, but even more alone is the man who is separated from this network. It is in order to connect themselves to this network that people gather in the cities."[66] Tange was an important reference point in taking the discourse about urban networks toward electronics.

Tyrwhitt was very familiar with this discourse since Tange's work had been shown by others at CIAM 8 in 1951, and he had taken part in the 1959 meeting in Otterloo where CIAM dissolved. Her editorial on the Tokyo Bay scheme said that the project was the direct outcome of experimental plans that he developed with MIT students in 1959, which she had seen firsthand and had already published, along with his Boston Harbor project, the scheme based on the growth of plants that is regarded as the first move in the so-called megastructure movement.[67] At the third Delos in 1965, Giedion singled out the Tokyo Bay project when embracing "the youngest generation" for two concepts that handle variable density: "megastructure" and "group form."[68] Tange exemplified the former, while the latter was introduced in the first Metabolist manifesto of 1960 by Fumihiko Maki, the architect who was also the first to publish the term "megastructure," with Tange as the central example, in a little-known 1962 publication that was immediately republished in *Ekistics* because Maki was teaching with Tyrwhitt at Harvard from 1962 to 1965.[69] As a parallel line of research into networks, all the Japanese experiments were closely monitored by *Ekistics* and had their effect on the field's evolving doctrine.

Another parallel trajectory monitored by the journal was that of Team 10, the dissident younger faction of CIAM. Alison Smithson and Peter Smithson, for example, had been designing webbed urban projects since the late fifties, including the extremely influential Hauptstadt Berlin

47

48

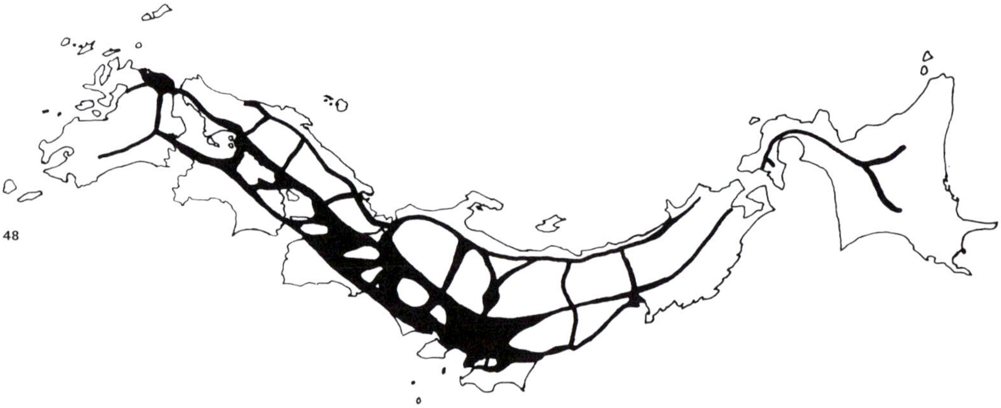

Web Architects

47 RBF and Kenzo Tange aboard *New Hellas*, 1966

48 Kenzo Tange, Japanese archipelago as a single biomorphic city, in “Tokaido-Megalopolis,” 1965

49 Kenzo Tange, A Plan for Tokyo, 1960, in *Kenzo Tange, 1946–1969: Architecture and Urban Design*, 1970

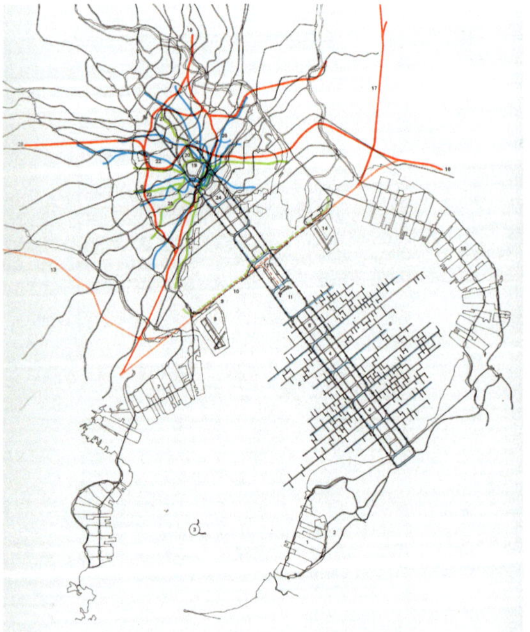

49

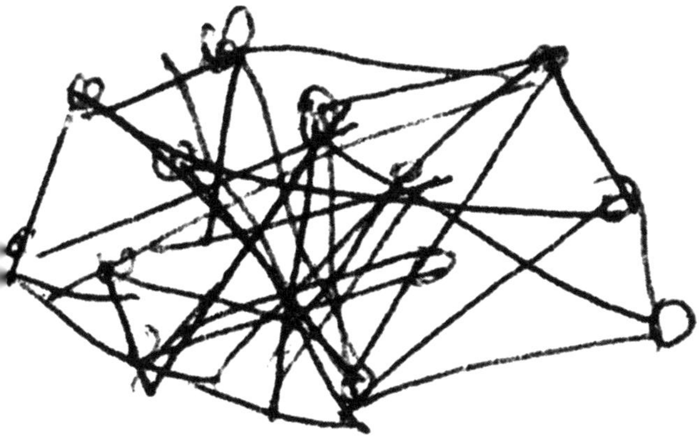

50

50 Peter Smithson, Ideogram of net of human relations, *Architectural Design*, December 1962

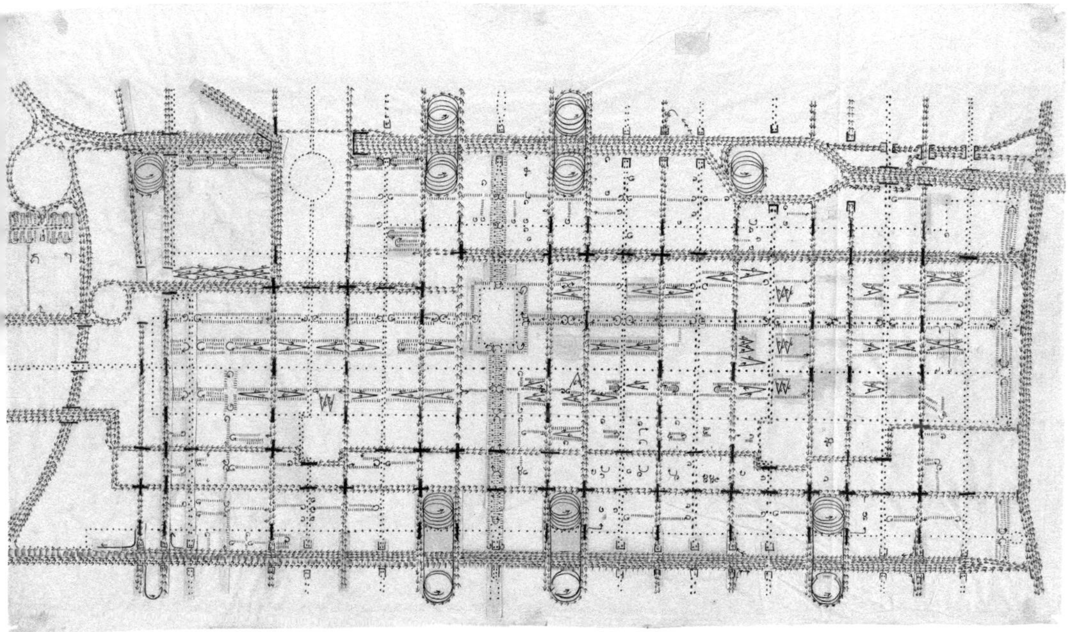

51

51 Louis Kahn and Anne Tyng, Traffic Study project, Philadelphia, plan of proposed traffic-movement pattern, 1952. Ink, graphite, and cut-and-pasted papers on paper, 62.2×108.6 cm. Collection of Museum of Modern Art, New York

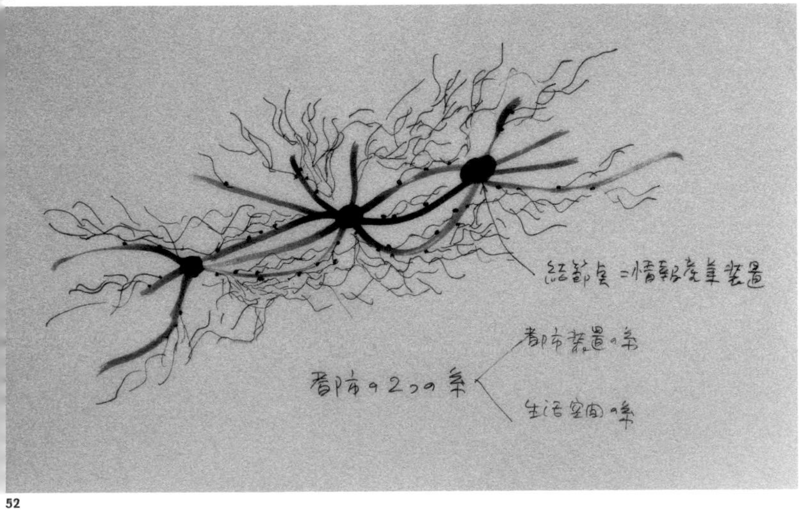

52

52 Kisho Kurokawa, Metamorphosis, 1965. Chinese ink, tracing paper, 25×43.5 cm. Musee National d'Art Moderne, Centre Georges Pompidou, Paris

scheme of 1957.[70] Already at CIAM 9 in 1953 they had been insisting against their elders that "the street and the network of streets has to be seen as the arena in which social relationships were played out" rather than a mode of efficient connection.[71] **fig. 50** Georges Candilis and Shadrach Woods likewise developed huge "mat buildings" as infrastructural weaves of movement patterns and wrote key articles on the principle of "the web" in 1961.[72] Aldo van Eyck saw the role of the architect to provide a "network of crevices." And so on. A different attitude toward the network—both in terms of physical form, social structure, communication system, and analytical concept—was precisely what differentiated the young group from CIAM and led to their separation from it and the subsequent dissolution of the old organization. As Alison Smithson (who seemingly took over Tyrwhitt's role) puts it at the very beginning of her account of the separation, it was decided by the older generation at CIAM 9 that "life falls through the net of the four functions" but "we wanted a more delicate responsive, net."[73] When the group became independent, much of the talk was about networks. The 1962 meeting of Team 10 at Royamount, for example, was dominated by it, as exemplified by Stefan Wewerka's description of cities as "compact bundles of overlaid net-structures."[74] A major influence in this discourse, as it was for the parallel Japanese experiments was Louis Kahn and Anne Tyng's 1953 traffic scheme for Philadelphia which dematerializes the physical form of the city in favor of pure flow like an electrical circuit. **fig. 51** Streaming arrows become more solid than buildings. The image was a key reference point. The new generation of architects was under the spell of its radicalization of CIAM's long-standing commitment to traffic.

But the next step of blending physical network and information flow would only start to become evident in the work of an even younger generation. The bioinformational language that Tange had used since the Tokyo Bay project had actually come from his assistants on the 1960 project: Arata Isozaki, Kisho Kurokawa, and Sadao Watanabe, some of whom were part of the group setting up the Metabolist movement, presenting their founding manifesto with images of organic cell development in May of the same year at the World Design conference in Tokyo, having been

70 Alongside an "ideogram of a net of human relations," Peter Smithson described it as "a constellation with different values of different parts in an immensely complicated web crossing and recrossing. Brubeck! A pattern can emerge." Peter Smithson, in *Team 10 Primer*, ed. Alison Smithson (Cambridge: MIT Press, 1968), 79, caption.

71 Peter Smithson, "Recollection by Peter Smithson, September 20, 1990," in ibid., 60.

72 See Shadrach Woods, "Web," *Le Carrér Bleu*, no. 3 (1962). The article was reprinted in *Ekistics* two years later. The web is "highly flexible," "non-centric," "open-ended," and "can be plugged into at any point and can itself plug in to greater systems at any point." See also Shadrach Woods, "Urban Environment: The Search for System," in *World Architecture*, no. 1, ed. John Donat (London: Studio Vista, 1964), 151–154.

73 Alison Smithson, in *Team 10 Meetings*, ed. Alison Smithson (New York: Rizzoli, 1991), 9.

74 Stefan Wewerka, in ibid., 75.

75 "The capsule is cyborg architecture. Man, machine and space build a new organic body which transcends confrontation. As a human being equipped with a man-made internal organ becomes a new species which is neither machine nor human, so the capsule transcends man and equipment. [...] The capsule is a feedback mechanism in an information-oriented, a 'technetronic,' society." Kisho Kurokawa, "Capsule Declaration," *Space Design* (March 1969), reprinted in Kisho Kurokawa, *Metabolism in Architecture* (London: Studio Vista, 1977), 75–85. On the "Cybernetic Environment," see also Arata Isozaki, "Invisible City," *Tenbou* (November 1967), translated in *Architecture Culture, 1943–1968*, ed. Joan Ockman (New York: Rizzoli, 1993), 403–407.

76 Frequent articles appeared in *Ekistics* from Alison and Peter Smithson, Jaap Bakema, Aldo van Eyck, Georges Candilis and Shadrach Woods, Herman Hertzberger, Fumihiko Maki, Kisho Kurokawa, and others. Tyrwhitt's editorial for the June 1963 issue describes Team 10 as "an intelligent group of thoughtful and highly intelligent architects." In a July 1963 review of a book by Doxiadis, she compares the work of Doxiadis to that of Team 10 and the Japanese architects. Jaqueline Tyrwhitt, "Architecture in Transition, Doxiadis, C. A.: A Review," *Ekistics* 16 (July 1963): 60.

77 Jos Bosman, "CIAM after the War: A Balance of the Modern Movement," *Rassegna* 52 (December 1992): 6–21.

78 Warren Chalk and Ron Herron, "City Interchange — Project," *Living Arts*, no. 2 (June 1963): 73.

affected by Fuller's lectures at the Japan Architects Association in Tokyo in March of 1958 and 1959. The group would write extensively on biology, symbiosis, cyborgs, cybernetics, and prosthetics throughout the sixties.[75] Their projects were drawn as delicate systems of intersecting fibers—architecture as biological circuitry. **fig. 52**

In fact, all these groups were networked together. Tange had shown the first Metabolist projects (Kiyonori Kikutake's 1959 Marine City and Cell City, "a complete network of living facilities," based on a "move-net" in which fixed structures allow building units to "grow and die and grow again") alongside his own megastructure at the September 1959 Otterloo meeting where Team 10 began its independent life and Kahn presented the Philadelphia Plan mobility drawing. The Smithsons included Tange in their Team 10 survey for *Architectural Design* in May 1960; and the conference in Tokyo of the same year, in which the Metabolists launched themselves with Tange speaking as the father figure, was also attended by Kahn and the Smithsons. The younger architects became linked to the evolving Team 10 discourse. Maki was invited to the Team 10 meeting in 1960, and Kurokawa would talk about "nets" at the 1962 and 1966 meetings. A global network of experimental architects devoted to networks was established.

Most of the network organizations dreamed up by these groups were periodically scanned by Tyrwhitt in *Ekistics* as a kindred post-CIAM research.[76] When Team 10 had started its assault on the older generation at the last CIAMs, Tyrwhitt had initially resisted on behalf of the rest of the central committee, but she eventually embraced the idea of handing over to the next generation. When doing so, she circulated a text to Giedion by her close colleague McLuhan on the need for interdisciplinary research to open up unknown horizons through a cubist multiplicity of viewpoints.[77] The impact of electronics represented a shared threshold. The Smithsons, for example, had been in the middle of intense discussions of the new systems of communication in the early fifties with their Independent Group colleagues in London, very much under the influence of McLuhan's first book, *The Mechanical Bride*. Yet electronics was never an overt feature of their projects, nor those of their colleagues. This would be the task of their respectfully rebellious students.

INVISIBLE PICTURES

It was only with the post-1963 work of the young Archigram group that was explicitly inspired by Fuller that information flow became visible as such. Where the Metabolists emphasized the biological side of the biotechnological equation, Archigram emphasized the technological. Architecture became indistinguishable from communication. Warren Chalk and Ron Herron's City Interchange project of 1963 is just a "net" of intersecting forms of traffic, including invisible traffic: "electronic data transmission, traffic control and administration, radio-telephone tower, communication and news service relay station, inter-commercial closed circuit television hookups, public television and telstar rediffusion center."[78] **fig. 55** This principle underlies all the subsequent Archigram work and started to take a particular form, as can be seen in the 1964 projects that *Ekistics* scanned in 1965. What counts in Ron Herron's Walking City, Peter Cook's Plug-in City, and Warren Chalk's Underwater City is movement in a diagonal net. In Walking City, it is the usually overlooked network of diagonal links between the huge mobile animals that makes the system possible. **fig. 54** Plug-in City is likewise a "giant network-structure [...] with diagonals of lifts making up the grid," and in Underwater City, to leave the diagonal structure/movement system is of course to drown. **fig. 53** In each project the diagonal weave becomes the main event. Activity occurs within the net itself.

Even dense, blurry, psychedelic events like the Instant City "traveling metropolis" of 1968 are actually based on a triangulated network plan covering England. Each of its intense explosions of sound, smell, and color occurs on the node of a net or constructs such a node. A series of six drawings showing an Instant City descending on a "sleeping town" concludes with one entitled "Network Takes Over." The apparatus has moved on, but the infiltrated town has become hooked up to all the others by landline and wireless transmitters. Already in 1963, the group raised the possibility that expendable and flexible communication networks would invalidate fixed physical ones,[79] and projects like Peter Cook and David Greene's Ideas Circus, published by *Ekistics* in August 1969, were "offered as a tool for the interim phase until we have a really working all-way information network."[80] When Archigram folded soon afterward, it was not by chance that Peter Cook started the Art Net forum in London and named its journal *Net*—unconsciously echoing McLuhan's 1951 proposal to start a newsletter called *Network*.

In all these projects, the grid gives way to the web. Movement in the spaces defined between intersecting lines gives way to flow within lines. Triangulation rules. Of all of Doxiadis's hundreds of charts, he kept presenting one from 1962 that showed that grids were the most efficient form of network at the smallest scales of rooms and neighborhoods, that hexagons made sense in the local region around a center, and that triangulation is best at the largest scales. This combination of orthogonal grid and triangular net can be seen in all his schemes. But parallel research by other architects had moved triangulation into individual buildings. The 1952–58 project for Tomorrow's Town Hall by Kahn and Tyng, with Tyng having developed its organizing geometric system, was particularly influential in this. Well known since its publication in *Perspecta* in 1953 and *L'architecture d'aujourd'hui* in 1954, the building was conceived as a series of

79 "The foreseeable rapid rate of change in transportation method may eventually make invalid the concept of a rigid mobile communications network as the main urban structure. A whole area of study is open for experiment of expendable systems and more flexible technology in terms of communication networks. [...] Large organizations will control their own visual communications network, allowing for a city center control with satellites dispersed in constant touch with the communication center, no longer dependent on physical communication." text prepared for 1963 *Living City* exhibition, in *Archigram* (London: Studio Vista, 1972), 21.

80 Peter Cook and David Greene, "Metamorphosis," *Ekistics* 28 (August 1969): 104–106.

81 Louis Kahn, "Order in Architecture," *Perspecta* 4 (1957): 64.

82 Sigfried Giedion, *A Decade of New Architecture* (Zurich: Girsberger, 1954), 262. The project was the centerpiece of the special issue on structure of *L'architecture d'aujourd'hui*, no. 55, September 1954.

83 "Archigram Metropolis Issue," *Ekistics* 20 (November 1965): 282. Crompton had already elaborated the idea of the city as a self-regulating biotechnological computer a year earlier: "The city is a living organism—*pulsating*—expanding and contracting, dividing and multiplying. The complete functioning of the city is integrated by its *natural* computer mechanism. This mechanism is at once digital and biological. [...] The overall network is formed from this information and then absorbs it, processes it, and throws out the subsequent stages. [...] The network is modified and amplified and the substance of the city created. [...] The *City Scene* enveloped in a net of inter-relationships, ultimately controlled by the *Natural Computer*." Dennis Crompton, "City Synthesis," *Living Arts* no. 2 (June 1963): 86.

triangulated structural systems operating at different scales. **fig. 56** Appearing from a distance, in Kahn's words, as "a lacey network of metal,"[81] it even stood in the center of a plaza marked with a triangulated networked pattern. Tyng's innovative geometric research evolved in parallel with that of Fuller. They shared a particular fascination with tetrahedrons, repeatedly expressed deep respect for each other's work and were published side by side in special issues of magazines. Another key image was Andre and Jean Polak and Andre Waterkeyn's 1958 Atomium for the Brussels World Fair, which appeared in *Archigram 4* alongside the City Interchange. The Atomium, in which people move up inside the diagonal links to occupy the spherical nodes, has exactly the shape of Doxiadis's drawing of the basic principle of networks. Triangulation is at once identified with the microscale of atoms and the supermacroscale of transplanetary connections.

The application of a physical image of a global network at all scales became polemically clear in the schemes and systems in which there is no difference between building and extended web, notably in a series of projects published at the end of the fifties: Fuller's demonstration of a large Octet Truss at MoMA in 1959; Constant Nieuwenhuys's "wide world web" New Babylon of 1959; and Eckhard Schulze-Fielitz's Space City of 1959. **figs. 57 and 59** Each of these was influenced by Konrad Wachsmann's enormous airline hangar for the US Air Force that was first published in 1954 (and immediately made its way into a section on space frames in Giedion's *A Decade of New Architecture* that was edited by Tyrwhitt in the same year).[82] **fig. 58** Wachsmann had joined Fuller at the Institute of Design in Chicago in 1949 and repeatedly identified his indebtedness to Fuller's experiments. His hangar in turn became a major influence on Japanese architects, as the young architects who would later form the Metabolist group attended his two-month seminar on the project in Japan in 1955 that had been organized by Tange. Yet all these practical schemes by an international community of architects, including Wachsmann's, can be seen as a compromise of the more radical web that Wachsmann had developed in 1953 with students in Chicago. **fig. 60** It envisions a structural system that refuses any difference between the horizontal and vertical strands of the web and the intersections between them. Structural threads are simply twisted together in an endless fabric.

It is symptomatic that information flow is crucial for all these web designers. Wachsmann and Fuller speak of the way communications can activate any point in their systems. Constant and Schulze-Fielitz argue that electronics will change the shape of their spaces, with computers continuously rearranging the forms on the basis of constant feedback from the occupants, an idea that Archigram's Dennis Crompton would take to the extreme with his Computer City project of 1964, in which the city itself is nothing more than a computer, a hardwired "sensitized net" with "local net feedback." **fig. 62** When it was published a year later in the November 1965 *Ekistics*, the short explanatory text asserted: "The activities of an organized society occur within a balanced network of forces which naturally interact to form a continuous chain of change."[83] The mesh of links

53

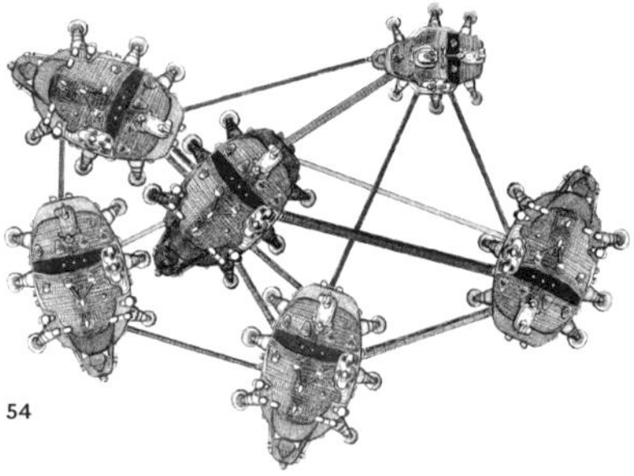

54

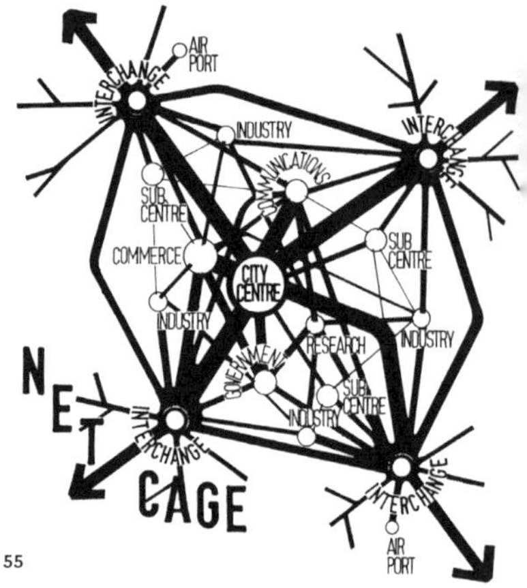

55

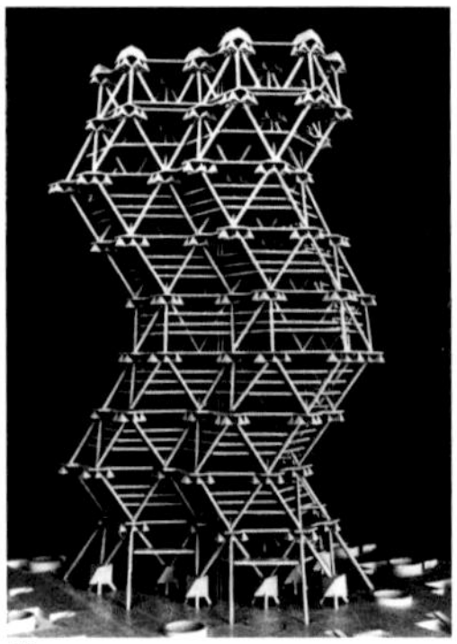

56

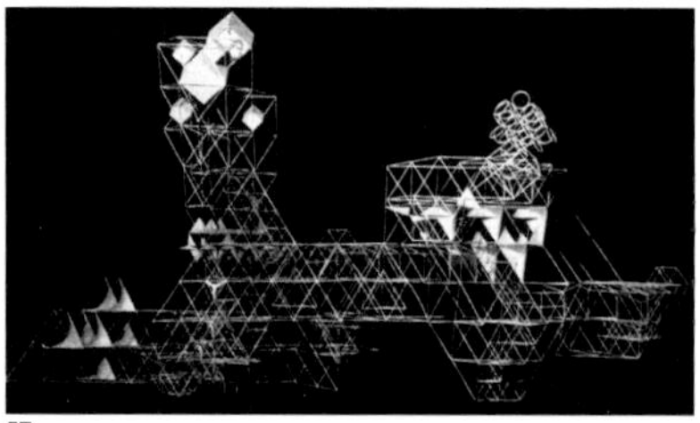

57

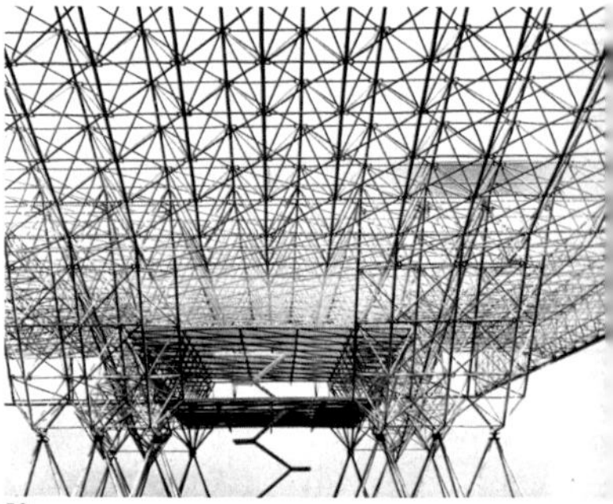

58

59

Visualizing the Communication Net

53 Warren Chalk, Underwater City project, 1964

54 Ron Herron, Walking City, cluster plan of six gathered vehicles, 1964

55 Warren Chalk and Ron Herron, City Interchange, study of a multitransport mode-node zone, 1963

56 Louis Kahn and Anne Tyng, Tomorrow's Town Hall project, 1952–1958, *L'architecture d'aujourd'hui*, June–July 1962

57 Eckhard Schulze-Fielitz, Space City project, 1959, *L'architecture d'aujourd'hui*, June–July 1962

58 Konrad Wachsmann, Airline Hangar project for US Air Force, 1954, in *Wendepunkt im Bauen*, 1959

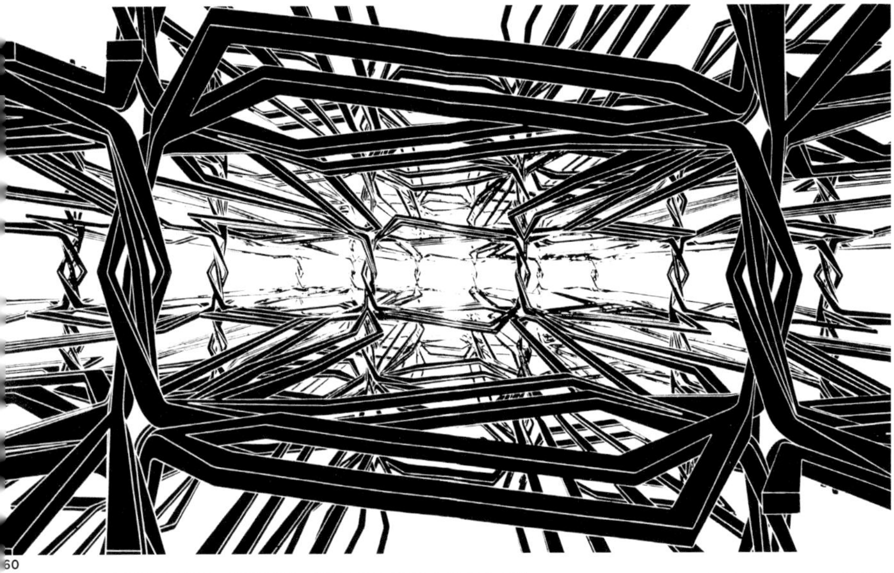

60

61

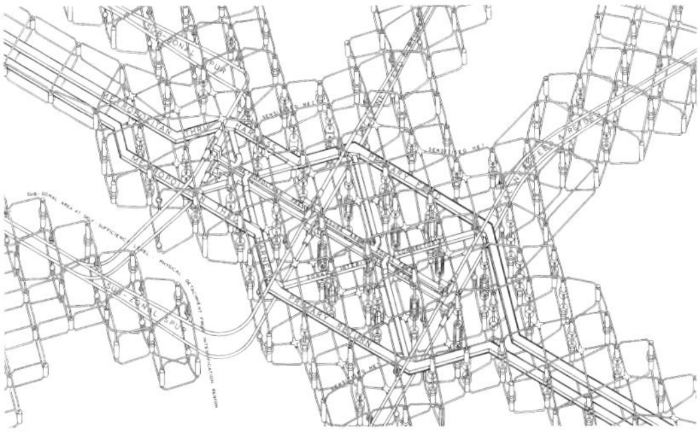

62

63

59 RBF 1959 exhibition in MoMA garden of Tensegrity Mast with Shoji Sadao, Octet Truss with T. C. Howard, and Radome with Bernard Kirschenbaum and William Wainwright

60 Konrad Wachsmann, experimental structural web, 1953, in *Wendepunkt im Bauen*, 1959

61 Frontispiece of *Kenzo Tange, 1946–1969: Architecture and Urban Design*, 1970

62 Dennis Crompton, Computer City, axonometric, 1964

63 Alexander Graham Bell, tetrahedral space frame, 1907, published by Anne Tyng in *Zodiac* 19, 1969

activated or modified by electronics has turned into an endless mesh of self-adjusting information channels.

Indeed, it can be argued that the whole obsession with triangulated space frames in the sixties, and even the concern with building systems as such, was, as it had already been with Fuller since the late twenties, just an attempt to make tangible images of the invisible communication infrastructure whose influence had grown throughout the century—a visible aesthetics for the invisible net. In 1966 Tange, who would so literally echo Fuller in polemically having himself photographed against a dense weave of triangulated scaffolding to open his monograph, said exactly that: "Creating an architecture and a city may be called a process of making the communication network visible in a space."[84] **fig. 61**

It was not by chance, then, that the first triangulated space frame was actually produced in 1902 by the same person who invented the telephone: Alexander Graham Bell, as tetrahedral kites that would be used as antennas to make possible Lee de Forest's first transatlantic radio message in 1906.[85] **fig. 63** Fuller's more famous webbed space frames, hovering as light as they could be, as little in the world as possible, likewise came after his fascination with nonphysical technologies of communication. **fig. 64** Already in the late twenties, Fuller, who would eventually be given Bell's original tetrahedral models by his great-grandchildren, was using the "inter-communicating web" of the telephone as a model for housing and was describing the house as an apparatus for receiving and broadcasting. He always referred to his structural systems as "nets," understood not as systems of physical interconnections but as networks of energy flow information systems—an association between visible and invisible net that would finally become literal in the sphere for Expo 67, intended to be the first computer-controlled structure, with the metal links in the net carrying the wiring for a continuous local adjustment of the opacity of the building's surface.

All the webs that proliferated in the sixties, including Doxiadis's City of the Future, were likewise an attempt to establish a physical image of the invisible space of electronics, even if electronics itself is not discussed. The projects by Tange, the Metabolists, Team 10, Archigram, Constant, and others were practical and even took their character from their engagement with the pragmatics of construction, but they were first and foremost polemical images—and were presented as such. It matters little that virtually nothing from all those experiments was built. Or, to be more precise what was carefully built was a set of images that remain polemical today a commentary on the networks we already inhabit rather than a dream of a future world.

It took decades to forget such experiments so that a new generation could present itself as the first to engage seriously with the architecture of

84 "The other factor is the rapid advancement of organizations in modern civilized society brought about by the modern communication system, informational technology, and the sharp reflection of this phenomenon on spatial organization. In modern civilized society, space is a communication field, and it is becoming more and more organic with the development of the communication system. [...] Creating an architecture and a city may be called a process of making the communication network visible in a space. [...] We can say that the spatial organization is a network of energy and communication." Kenzo Tange, "Function, Structure and Symbol," in *Kenzo Tange*, 240 (see note 65).

85 A picture of Bell's tower is featured in Wachsmann's book and Archigram's collages for the *Living City* exhibition of 1963.

64

64 "Buckminster Fuller explaining principles of Dymaxion building," suspended in Octet Truss, MoMA garden, 1959. Photograph by Yale Joel

electronics. Much of the discourse about computation and communication from the late twentieth century onwards is an echo—but so delayed that it sounds fresh. It is as if the discourse forgets its own history precisely because it is too afraid to leave those earlier positions behind. Supposedly avant-garde visions manifest the discipline's greatest fears.

UNSETTLEMENT

The point here is that McLuhan's influential discourse about networks was exactly paralleled by that of experimental architects during the same years and the architects did not simply follow the communication expert. Rather, both followed an even earlier generation of designers. Indeed, McLuhan's work begins as a kind of rethinking of architecture. McLuhan explicitly based his reading of media on the methodology of Giedion, had corresponded with him since the early forties, and hoped to persuade him to be part of the original Explorations group along with Tyrwhitt in a collaborative investigation of Culture and Communication. It was his close alliance with Giedion and Tyrwhitt that opened up a new way of reading the space of technology, one that leaned heavily on Fuller. The intense international and interdisciplinary discourse about the radical architecture of networks in the sixties and seventies was itself networked by Fuller's polemic. He played a crucial role as a key link between the twenties and the global spread of electronic nets. Not by chance was he the president of the World Society for Ekistics established in 1965 and the only person other than Tyrwhitt to attend all the Delos conferences. His Dymaxion world map was the inevitable original emblem of the *Ekistics* journal and another version of the map symptomatically returned for the cover of the issue on the Delos devoted to "Networks" in 1970. Delos was now positioned at the center of the triangulated map with radiating lines showing where all the participants had come from.[86] It is as if the Ekistics project to network thinking about networks occupied Fuller's world. His vision of a fundamental continuity between visible and invisible architecture had always lurked in the background and slowly took over. McLuhan was a crucial ally in making the same argument from the side of communication. The two hovered over the discourse in the Aegean in the same way that they hovered over all the experimental architects obsessing about networks. **figs. 65 and 66**

Yet Fuller and McLuhan pursued such a radical line that even those deeply infected by network fever could not handle it. Already by the fifth morning of the first Delos, Fuller was saying that the idea of permanent settlements and neighborhoods is obsolete in the contemporary hypermobile age. The very idea of settlement so treasured by Ekistics was challenged in a time characterized by "stirring up rather than settling down."[87] McLuhan was quick to agree and even suggested that the whole framework had to change: "Are we selecting as key problems things that

86 *Ekistics* 30 (October 1970).
87 "The notion of self-contained permanent settlements is obsolete. We live under conditions of mobility which result in continual stirring up rather than settling down. It is indeed doubtful whether the notion of a neighborhood of people who fulfill the internal functions of a village community makes sense for the future." "Notes from the 5th Meeting," Delos Documents, Department of Drawings and Archives, Avery Architectural and Fine Arts Library, Columbia University.

65

66

67

The Electronic Tag Team at Work

65 RBF and Doxiadis talking aboard *New Hellas*, 1964

66 Marshall McLuhan talking aboard *New Hellas*, July 1963

67 A world without lines: One Ocean World Town, in *4D Time Lock*, 1928

are possibly about to disappear with the rise of information levels, such as congestion and confusion?"[88] He had already written about the end of cities in 1954 in a hand-distributed zine that so closely echoes Fuller's polemics of the late twenties:

> The city no longer exists, except as a cultural ghost for tourists. Any highway eatery with its TV set, newspaper, and magazine is as cosmopolitan as New York or Paris. [...] The metropolis is obsolete. Ask the Army. The instantaneous global coverage of radio-TV makes the city form meaningless, functionless.[89]

McLuhan turned the zine into a book in 1969 and changed the middle sentence to the more definitive declaration: "The city is obsolete. Ask the Computer."[90] The new slogan efficiently summarized his long-standing project to demonstrate that the nervous system of the body had already wrapped the planet in a massive extension of human capacity that made the old extensions of houses and cities redundant.

Rather than shape cities in the form of visible networks, Fuller likewise imagined humanity and the whole universe in terms of invisible networks. Form is dissolved by flow. Fuller both mentored the Ekistics group and criticized it. In June 1966 he wrote "the longest letter I have ever written" to Doxiadis outlining his "general strategy." Published in 1969 as "Letter to Doxiadis," it repeats his prosthetic account of architecture as the externalization of the human organism, starting with the body itself as the extension of the brain and the spoken word as the very first industrial tool, and insists that electronics will lead the way.[91] The latest computer techniques will render conventional architecture and planning redundant, substituting static urban planning with "Instant city!" New world networks will foster a hypermobility of bodies and spaces—technologically upgraded and endlessly circulating bodies being the new spaces. Fixed forms will be replaced by rhythms of intermittent occupation by nomadic global citizens living within new airline and information nets. The new biology of technology won't leave the kind of fixed trace that Doxiadis tried to establish since cities themselves are but a passing phase:

> All concepts of urbanization will become obsolete; only the Earth and the Solar System will be his temporary home. The swift shift of humanity from an agricultural to an industrial world economy draws men from the agricultural lands into the city. Urbanization is only temporary as the cities become the launching pads for each human's blast-off into world-shuttling citizenship.[92]

For Fuller, the dispersal of the city is an intensification of collective social life rather than its dissipation. He notes that people are actually more

88 Ibid.
89 Marshall McLuhan, *Counterblast* (hand-distributed zine, 1954; Berlin: Transmediale, 2011), 26.
90 Marshall McLuhan, *Counterblast* (New York: Harcourt, 1969), 12.
91 "In speaking of reforming the environment of man, I include a surgeon's operations on the human body, for the latter is mobile environment of the brain." Buckminster Fuller, "Letter to Doxiadis," *Main Currents in Modern Thought* 25 (March–April 1969): 91. "I define industrialization as the extra-corporeal, organic metabolic regeneration of humanity. Industrialization consists of tools. All the tools are externalizations of originally integral functions of humans. [...] By my definition, the spoken word, which could only be invented by two or more men, was the first industrial tool." Ibid., 92.
92 Ibid., 97.
93 Buckminster Fuller, "Why I Am Interested in Ekistics," *Ekistics* 20 (October 1965): 180–181.
94 Buckminster Fuller in the discussions about energy, *Ekistics* 34 (October 1972): 241. The point was first made in Delos 4 in 1966.
95 "Communication via Humor," *Ekistics* 34 (October 1972): 282–283.
96 Marshall McLuhan to Tom and Dorothy Easterbrook, in *Letters of Marshall McLuhan*, 455; and Marshall McLuhan to Gyorgy Kepes, in ibid., 453 (see note 3). Tom Easterbrook was one of the group of four people, including Tyrwhitt, who carried out the key research with McLuhan from 1953 to 1955.
97 "Marshall McLuhan Executive Seminar," Grand Bahamas Hotel and Country Club, January 7–9, 1970.

"intimate" with those who are remote in space and time, as when writing a letter to someone on the other side of the planet, and inversely have almost no rapport when crammed together in subways and buses. The space of communication is what brings people together, not physical form. Humanity evolves by continuously building on the brain's ability to rearrange increasingly invisible patterns of radiation. Housing, like any other radio broadcast, is going to be "frequency modulated." Form will give way to frequency.

After all, there had always been a fundamental conflict between Fuller's original call in the late twenties for a physical disconnection from infrastructural networks and the Ekistics' obsession with establishing vast physical nets. Fuller shares the commitment to a single world city as his very first project in 1928 was for a "One Ocean World Town Plan," a globally networked shelter system, but everything in his town is mobile and physically disconnected. **fig. 67** Fuller's 4D Towers are transceivers dropped onto the planet by zeppelin, have autonomous service systems of plumbing and electricity, and are only interconnected by invisible air and radio links. It is a world without lines. Fuller rejected physical infrastructure, no matter how flexible, preferring atomized nomadic systems. For him, the capacity to disconnect from a system was as important as the capacity to connect. He was fatally attracted to Ekistics, attending every Delos gathering and publishing articles like "Why I Am Interested in Ekistics,"[93] but ultimately he had to go beyond it.

At the tenth Delos in 1972, Fuller pointed out that the group was not yet ready to deal with the fact that the boat in which they were talking was actually filled with the signals of over a million radio stations.[94] Radio was once again the key. It was radio that had originally drawn Fuller into the question of networks and remained the constant horizon of all his work, which in turn drew so many others toward him, but ultimately its radical ephemerality would leave them behind in the world of apparent substance. At the same meeting, McLuhan also acted as the dissident by presenting James Joyce's *Ulysses* as "the greatest piece of city planning and building in this century" and rock music as "an enormous world-wide network of culture which directly relates to the health of human settlements" since it processes the sounds of the city.[95] He insisted that books and music fossilize buildings. Cities should be designed less for occupancy than for performance, a "global theatre" built out of the hidden electronic networks. Tyrwhitt kept her distance from her old teammate, publishing his intervention in a section entitled "Communication via Humor." The earnest reconfiguration of the global city as a physical image of an invisible order was not to be held up by the thought that physical configurations were already redundant. In letters to friends, McLuhan concluded that the other Delos participants were "earnest men, rather all 19th-century types, still preoccupied with bricks and mortar" and that people already lived electronically in "a new kind of world city far outside the ken of Doxiadis."[96]

Fuller had meanwhile become excited by the idea of strategic unsettlement and had elaborated an even more radical defense of it at an "Emergency Strategy Seminar" in the Bahamas organized by McLuhan.[97] The odd couple was once again in the sun, entertaining each other by taking every argument to the next level. **fig. 68** Ekistics was losing its appeal. At the beginning of the last Delos in 1975, Fuller mourned the death of Doxiadis just two weeks earlier. When the meeting was finished, he went dancing with "young" people in his geodesic dome at Jaqueline Tyrwhitt's house for the last time.[98] A year later, he did attend a United Nations conference on habitat as the representative of Ekistics, but he published his contribution under the title "Accommodating Human Unsettlement," arguing that it is precisely the stability of unseen infrastructural networks that makes global physical instability possible and desirable.[99] The global village supports a hypermobility of people and architecture. Designers are to aim for "formless" systems of unsettlement rather than try to overcome them.

Such thoughts rarely appear in the otherwise faithful but unwitting echo of the sixties that occupies so much contemporary architectural discourse. In the face of destabilizing forces, the figure of the architect offering steadiness is reasserted. Stable forms and technologies are seen to be inspired and enabled by information flows. Data has become the raw material of architecture with a seamless fluidity between analysis, design, detailing, visualization, modeling, prototyping, fabrication, construction, monitoring, and maintenance. Electronic space is being settled rather than unsettled. Radical potentials have become normative industrialized and commercialized conditions. The architect is yet again a figure of order, a security system providing comfort rather than challenge. The architectural species has survived by forgetting a century of extreme discourse about networks. In a kind of Warholian dream, every echo has become an original artwork.

Even the concept of ecology and the intelligent distribution of global resources with which Fuller so polemically and relentlessly assaulted the discipline has become a reassuringly ubiquitous mantra, a sign of self-appointed virtue. His accompanying language of radical prosthetic transformation of body and mind is quietly forgotten or simply unrecognizable in a world in which market-supported mental, physical, technological, and even biological self-reinvention is mandatory from the age of two. The very concept of the radical has been softened by the paradoxically extreme conditions of the everyday.

Yet Fuller's simple 1927 question about architecture's fate in the age of radio remains an urgent one. The point is not simply that his extended attempt to answer it provided so much of the script that is still being unwittingly rehearsed today. Fuller relentlessly dedicated himself to exceeding the discourse. Each label, sentence, poem, lecture, calculation, drawing, model, and book was intended to stretch its audience, to reshape expectation, to change the defaults. It is precisely the sense that this way of thinking still exceeds our grasp that makes the extreme performance that is "Buckminster Fuller" so relevant today and the effects of finally listening to him after such a delay so refreshingly unpredictable.

98 As reported by Koichi Tonuma in *Ekistics* 52 (September–October 1985): 516.

99 Buckminster Fuller, "Accommodating Human Unsettlement," *Town Planning Review* 49 (January 1978): 51–60. Report of Fuller's report to the UN Habitat conference, September 20, 1976.

68 McLuhan and RBF
in the Bahamas, January 1970

CHRONOLOGICAL INDEX

Manuscripts

Interviews

Lectures

NAME INDEX

ll Buckminster Fuller drawings, photographs and manuscripts, unless therwise specified: Buckminster Fuller Papers, Stanford University pecial Collections, Courtesy of The Estate of R. Buckminster Fuller

ront cover, III: Courtesy of the Western Regional Archives, State rchives of North Carolina

ear cover: © F. S. Lincoln archives, Pennsylvania State University

ROADCASTING SHELTER

: Courtesy of History San José, Peham Collection
, 18: Ungers Archiv für Architekturwissenschaft, Köln
1: © F.L.C. / ADAGP, Paris / Artists Rights Society (ARS), New York 2015
2: Drawings and Manuscripts Collection, Avery Architectural and Fine rts Library, Columbia University
8: © Corbis
2: Courtesy of Schenectady Public Library

IPELESS DREAMS

: Courtesy of DPR Construction
3: © AP Photo / WGI
5: Courtesy of Architectural Association Archives
8, 60: © F. S. Lincoln archives, Pennsylvania State University
3, 58: © Archigram
4: © Michael Pilz, Coop Himmelb(l)au
5: © Haus-Rucker-Co, Zamp Kelp
6, 59: © 1965 François Dallegret
7: © Yves Klein / Artists Rights Society (ARS), New York / ADAGP, aris 2015; © Claude Parent, Paris, 2015

HE PLASTIC LINE

: © Archive Hans Hollein
: © Peter Schnetz, Coop Himmelb(l)au
: © Library and Archives of Canada
7, 22, 36: Courtesy of the Western Regional Archives, State Archives of orth Carolina
7: Mark Wigley private collection
9: © Special Collections Research Center, North Carolina State niversity Libraries, College of Design Collection, Architectural Designs UA023.010.032)
3: © The Museum of Modern Art / Licensed by SCALA / Art Resource, NY
4: © Getty Images
0, 81, 83: University of Oregon Libraries, Building Oregon: Architecture f Oregon and the Pacific Northwest Digital Collection, pna_19664, 9665, 19700
05: Architectural Press Archive / RIBA Library Photographs Collection

LANETARY HOMEBOY

: © The Museum of Modern Art / Licensed by SCALA / Art Resource, NY
: Southern Illinois University Carbondale Archives, University News ervice
0, 38: John McHale and Magda Cordell Archives Foundation
9, 20: © Princeton University School of Architecture Archive
9: Monica Pidgeon / RIBA Library Photographs Collection
1: Granger, NY
2: Franklin D. Roosevelt Library and Museum, Hyde Park, Y Files

NETWORK FEVER

1: Courtesy of The Estate of Corinne McLuhan
2, 4, 6, 7, 21, 23, 24, 25, 26, 27, 28, 29, 32, 47, 65, 66: © Constantinos and Emma Doxiadis Foundation
42, 43: © F.L.C. / ADAGP, Paris / Artists Rights Society (ARS), New York 2015
48, 61: © 1970 Verlag für Architektur Artemis, Zürich
49: © Tange Associates
51: © The Museum of Modern Art / Licensed by SCALA / Art Resource, NY
52: © CNAC / MNAM / Dist. RMN-Grand Palais / Art Resource, NY; Kisho Kurokawa Architect & Associates
53: Courtesy of Deutsches Architekturmuseum
54: © Ron Herron, courtesy Ron Herron Archive
55, 62: © Archigram
64: © Yale Joel / *Life* Picture Collection / Getty Images

Although we have tried to indicate copyrights as accurately as possible for the images used in this book, it was not possible to contact all of the copyright holders. Interested parties should contact Lars Müller Publishers.

XI

Richard Buckminster Fuller was born on July 12, 1895, in Milton, Massachusetts. After spending most of his youth in Massachusetts and on Bear Island in Maine, he fell out of Harvard and into the US Navy during World War I. He married Anne Hewlett, the daughter of a prominent New York architect, in 1917 and spent around five years working with his father-in-law on new techniques of housing construction after leaving the navy. From 1927 on he became independent and committed himself to completely rethinking the question of shelter—relentlessly challenging every assumption about structure, function, materials, technology, aesthetics, services, distribution, mobility, communication, collaboration, information, recycling, politics, property, and social norms. He started from first principles to develop a radical philosophy of doing "vastly more with vastly and invisibly less." The constant goal was a much more efficient and equitable distribution of planetary resources to enable the survival and ongoing evolution of the human species. His work paralleled, radicalized, and critiqued the mainstreams of modern architecture and still defies categorization today. He was a nonstop teacher and communicator around the globe in every possible medium—becoming probably the single most exposed designer and design theorist of the twentieth century. He died on July 1, 1983, in Los Angeles at the bedside of his wife, who died thirty-six hours later.

XI RBF photographed by Ray Eames outside the Eames House, Los Angeles, Christmas 1973

I want to express my deep gratitude for the assistance at many archives, especially at the Avery Architectural and Fine Arts Library at Columbia University, the University of Buffalo, the Doxiadis Archives now in the Benaki Museum in Athens, the Marquand Fine Arts Library at Princeton University, the Museum of Modern Art Archives in New York, the Ungers Archiv für Architekturwissenschaft in Cologne, and the Western Regional Archives at the State Archives in Asheville, North Carolina. But above all I want to thank the team of archivists and librarians of the Special Collections at Stanford University for their companionship and professionalism in assisting deep study of the Buckminster Fuller Papers (BFP) and caring so tenderly for the documents.

Earlier versions of parts of this book were published in *ANY* (1997), *Grey Room* (2001), *Volume* (2013), and *Permanent Change: Plastics in Architecture and Engineering* (2014). My thanks to the respective editors. Thanks also to Javier Antón Sancho, the image assistant for the book.

I am very grateful to Allegra Fuller and Jaime Snyder for their insights and encouragement. Lars Müller and his team offered such a wonderful spirit of collaboration and love of bookmaking. The Graduate School of Architecture, Planning, and Preservation of Columbia University was yet again magical in its collegiality and support.

Special thanks to Elise Jaffe and Jeffrey Brown for their kind and generous support of this book.

Most of all, I am grateful to Beatriz for her beauty in all senses, wisdom, and constant innovation.

Mark Wigley

BUCKMINSTER FULLER INC.
ARCHITECTURE IN THE AGE OF RADIO

Design: Integral Lars Müller / Lars Müller and Esther Butterworth
Coordination: Maya Rüegg
Copyediting and proofreading: Keonaona Peterson
Lithography: Ast & Fischer, Wabern, Switzerland
Printing and binding: Kösel, Altusried-Krugzell, Germany
Paper: LuxoArt Samt, 1.05, 135g/m²

Lars Müller Publishers
Zurich, Switzerland
www.lars-mueller-publishers.com

ISBN 978-3-03778-428-0

Printed in Germany